DYNAMIC EDUCATIONAL CHANGE

DYNAMIC EDUCATIONAL CHANGE

Models, Strategies, Tactics, and Management

Gerald Zaltman
David H. Florio
Linda A. Sikorski

THE FREE PRESS
A Division of Macmillan Publishing Co., Inc.
NEW YORK

Collier Macmillan Publishers
LONDON

The Free Press
A Division of Macmillan Publishing Co., Inc.
866 Third Avenue, New York, N.Y. 10022

Collier Macmillan Canada, Ltd.

Library of Congress Catalog Card Number: 76–19645

Printed in the United States of America

printing number
1 2 3 4 5 6 7 8 9 10

Library of Congress Cataloging in Publication Data

Zaltman, Gerald.
    Dynamic educational change.

    Includes bibliographical references and index.
    1. Educational planning--United States.
2. School management and organization--United States.
I. Florio, David, joint author. II. Sikorski, Linda,
joint author. III. Title.
LA217.Z34   370'.973   76-19645   LA
ISBN 0-02-935750-0   217
                                                 .Z34

COPYRIGHT ACKNOWLEDGMENTS

Figure 3-2. Reproduced by special permission from the *Journal of Applied Behavioral Science,* "Educational Reform and Social Change," by Henry M. Levin, p. 308, figure 1, vol. 10, No. 3 © 1975. NTL Institute.

Figure 9-2. From Paul M. Wortman, "Evaluation Research: A Psychological Perspective," *American Psychologist,* Vol. 30, No. 5, May 1975. Copyright 1975 by the American Psychological Association.

Table 2-3. From G. Eicholz and E. M. Rogers, "Resistance to the Adoption of Audio-Visual Aids by Elementary School Teachers," in Matthew B. Miles, Editor, *Innovation in Education.* (New York: Teachers College Press, 1964).

Table 9-1. From *Evaluation in Education: Current Applications,* ed. by W. James Popham. Berkeley: McCutchan Publishing Corporation, 1974. Reprinted by permission of the Publisher.

This book is dedicated to
James S. Coleman (G.Z.)
B. J. Chandler (D.H.F.)
C. L. Hutchins (L.A.S.)
for fostering and encouraging our work
in the field of educational change.

Contents

Foreword xi

Acknowledgments xiii

Preface xv

Part I. The Phenomena and Forces of Change in Education

1. The Nature of Change in Education 3
  The Nature of Change in Education *3*
  The Conduct of Education: Teaching *4*
  Publics and Clients of Schools *7*
  The Influence System: Governance and Control *8*
  Perspectives on Change in Education *13*
  Summary *19*

2. Forces for and Against Change in Education 21
  Forces for Change: Performance Gaps *21*
  Resistance to Change in Education *29*
  Summary *47*

Part II. Models and Strategies of Intentional Change Diffusion

3. Models and Strategies for Educational Change 51
  Models of Change Relevant to Education *51*
  Strategies of Change *71*

Strategy Development in the Self-Renewing School *88*
Summary *89*

4. Tactics for Educational Change: Considerations for the Change
   Planner   91
   Tactics for the Change Planner *92*
   Dimensions for Evaluating Tactics *98*
   Situational Considerations in Evaluating Tactics *108*
   Summary *121*

Part III. Planning and Managing Change: A Normative Guide to Change in Education

5. The Case for Planning   125
   Introduction *125*
   The Planning Model *127*
   Critical Questions in Initiating the Planning Process *130*
   Issues for Planning School Change *131*
   Organizational Decision Making/Action Authority *132*
   The Potential Need for External Change Agents *134*
   Involving Environmental Elements in Decision Making *135*
   A Note on Risk and Temporary Systems *136*
   The Proactive/Interactive Change Model (P/ICM) *139*
   Summary *142*

6. Implementing the Planning Model   144
   Stage One. Stating the Organizational Mission (Goals and
     Objectives) *145*
   Stage Two. Awareness/Diagnosis: Problem Identification *148*
   Stage Three. Objectives: Problem-Solving Purposes *154*
   A Note on Need Assessment *154*
   The Linking Network: In Preparation for Identifying Resources
     and Constraints *155*
   Stage Four. Resources and Constraints *162*
   Stage Five. Alternative Solutions *169*
   Stage Six. Testing/Trial: Demonstration *169*
   Stage Seven. Decision Making: The Adoption or Rejection of
     Alternative Solutions *172*
   Stage Eight. Implementation and Control *174*
   Stage Nine. Evaluation *177*
   Summary *180*

7. Client Need Assessment   182
   Why Assess Clients' Needs? *182*
   Basic Concepts *184*

Basic Procedures *188*
Summary *220*

8. Implementation and Control   221
   Implementation *222*
   Control *230*
   An Educational Organization Information System *245*
   Summary *248*

9. The Evaluation of Educational Change Programs   249
   Fundamental Concepts of Educational Evaluation *253*
   Major Types of Evaluation *260*
   Summary *272*

Part IV. Self-Renewal in Educational Organizations

10. Knowledge Use for Educational Change   277
    What Is Knowledge Use? *278*
    A Survey-Feedback and Problem-Solving Example *280*
    Why Research Is Not Readily Used *288*
    Some Perspectives on Knowledge Use *289*
    Aids and Barriers to Organizational Collaboration *298*
    Fifteen Principles for Effective Knowledge Use *305*
    Summary *310*

11. Basic Principles for Educational Change   311

References   336

Index   351

Foreword

IN RECENT YEARS a great volume of work has appeared on the general topic of human behavior change, including planned change, innovation in organizations, and related matters. These writings have utilized a wide range of theoretic frameworks, have represented a variety of disciplinary viewpoints in the behavioral sciences, and have appeared in diverse sources. As a result, most individuals who might want to utilize this store of accumulated knowledge about change cannot.

The present authors have performed an important function by pulling these materials together into a synthesis that is applied to education. This book is written for the manager and participant in educational change, rather than just for the university scholar. As such, the present volume represents an attempt at research utilization by transforming the products of academic research into a form more useful to the practitioner. This focus on knowledge-into-practice is rare in the social sciences. In fact, there is nothing quite like this book in the field of educational change.

Gerald Zaltman and his colleagues represent a unique set of expertise: A widely-published author of work on change; an educational administrator; a participant in educational R & D. Perhaps no other combination could have written this book. It is theoretic in its framework, on one hand, but also spiced with real-life illustrations from the field of educational change.

The volume begins by showing how schools are different from most other types of complex organizations, and how certain of these distinctive aspects affect change in the school (often retarding it). Much educational change results from "performance gaps" (felt discrepancies between what is, and what ought to be). Other key concepts in this volume are planning change, linking, and client needs. In a closing chapter, 313 useful principles are derived from the previous ten chapters. Special focus is placed on the P/ICM model (a proactive/interactive change model), as a means to facilitate understanding of the stages in the innovation process. In addition, however, a variety of other models and frameworks are brought to bear on the issue of educational change.

So this book is eclectic, encyclopedic, synthetic, and pragmatic. It is a good example of behavior science made useful.

Everett M. Rogers
Institute for Communication Research
Stanford University

Acknowledgments

MANY PEOPLE CONTRIBUTE to a volume such as this. There are first of all countless educators whose successes and failures, frustrations and satisfactions, connected with change have prompted us to write this book. Their experiences and behavior have also served as a source of both illustrations and prescriptions used in this book. These people include both formal and informal change planners as well as those who are the beneficiaries or victims of change efforts.

A second important group of contributors includes those who read parts of the manuscript or listened to our ideas and who provided us with substantial, critical, and constructive advice. We shall list their names in alphabetical order: B. J. Chandler (Northwestern University), Thomas Clemens (National Institute of Education), Richard Coffing (private consultant and author of chapter 7), Samuel Francis (University of Pittsburgh), Zelda F. Gamson (University of Michigan), Larry Hutchins (National Institute of Education), Pol Jacobs (The Faculté Universitaire Catholique de Mons), Laura Klemt (Northwestern University), Robert H. Koff (Roosevelt University), James H. Nelson (Michigan State University), and Everett M. Rogers (Stanford University). We would also like to acknowledge the valuable support provided to two of the authors by the National Institute of Education, School Capacity for Problem-Solving Group.

A third group of contributors consists of those who not only had to help with the technical tasks of preparing this manuscript but also had to cope with its impatient and sometimes fussy authors. These people include Cheryl Bekich (University of Pittsburgh), Edith Bass, Ruth Graf, Rhoda Stockwell (Northwestern University), Kathy Muldoon (University of Pittsburgh), and Doris Smith (Far West Laboratory for Educational Research and Development).

Preface

THE BASIC MOTIVATION FOR WRITING THIS BOOK was the desire to respond constructively to the criticisms we hear so frequently about the difficulty—indeed the futility—of attempting to bring about change in education. We do not think this charge is totally unfounded. Change in education *is* more difficult than in many other sectors of society, but few fields have as much justification for resisting change. The number of ''new'' things thrust upon educators each year is great, and a meaningful response to most of them is impossible.

Resistance among educators is only one reason for the difficulty of creating educational change. Another, very important reason is that the technology for creating change is not well understood or well diffused in education. There are several excellent books on change in education, but nearly all are highly focused on a particular change or a particular context. We found a strong need among educators—teachers, administrators, and various specialists—for a book dealing explicitly with the mechanics of introducing change in a variety of educational settings. We believed that such a book should be equally relevant to professional change agents and to the person who is actively and seriously proposing change for the first time and who may have little anticipation of doing so again in the future. We also felt that the need for a book on change management was strong at all levels of education and in all areas, including curriculum and organizational or administrative change.

Dynamic Educational Change is a response to these felt needs in education. It takes a generic view of change rather than a case study–specific approach. We certainly do not claim it to be a definitive work. For practical reasons, some material has been left uncovered: this book is not intended to be a comprehensive literature review, a restatement of existing material, or a remedy for all problems that may be encountered in educational change. Moreover, research being conducted in and out of education on the technology of creating change will produce new procedures and new principles that may outdate some current ideas and practices about creating change. What this book *does* intend is:

- to provide guidelines for initiating and sustaining change in a broad range of educational settings
- to help build a capacity for self-renewal in educational organizations
- to serve as a primer on the management of educational change for the student of educational administration
- to provide a structure within which much of the literature on educational change can be viewed
- to introduce the reader to the best and most relevant work on change outside the field of education
- to present an eclectic model of change

Personal preferences and biases inevitably find their way into a work such as this. We feel that these should be made explicit at the outset before the reader encounters them in a less obvious form in the text. First, this book has a strong democratic flavor. We argue for the involvement of all affected parties or their representatives in any preplanning, planning, and implementation and evaluation activities. Obviously, this is not always feasible, and we acknowledge that the exercise of enlightened despotism can be beneficial. We also hold the view that conflict—like resistance—is not always bad. It is a phenomenon to be optimized. Another position implicit in this book is that educational systems should be able to initiate change rather than having change imposed on them from the outside or having to respond to external attempts to change. We feel it important for schools to be competent in change skills so that they may counteract those changes perceived as potentially harmful.

Many of the ideas and models are overly rationalistic. We have made them so deliberately to make clear a specific prescriptive point. We do not mean to imply that change is or can always be accomplished in a linear, straightforward way. We feel it important to point this out here because many readers may go directly to part 3 and chapter 11 of part 4 (the "how to" chapters), which are subject to the criticism of being naively rationalistic. Other chapters, particularly 1 and 2, discuss the more realistic factors affecting the context and process of change.

Creating change in education can be a long and lonely task—and frequently an unrewarding one. Critics or opponents of a change will usually not have to look hard or wait long to find a basis for complaint. Errors do occur, and they are often exaggerated by critics. Indeed, collective imaginations are often at their height when it comes to attributing problems to some less than perfectly executed change strategy. We harbor no illusions that our book will drastically change this situation. It is simply intended to help make the change planner's task easier, less lonely, and more successful. We hope, too, that it will help the change planner experience more of the excitement that we have often had in our own efforts to create educational change.

PART 1

The Phenomena and Forces of Change in Education

1

The Nature of Change in Education

CHANGE IN EDUCATION IS SHAPED by the unique nature of educational systems and the organizations involved in those systems. This chapter discusses three factors that affect social change processes in education and help explain the special difficulties of creating change: (1) the nature of the teaching profession, (2) the configuration of the system's constituencies, and (3) the influence system (governance and control). These factors help to explain why educational change has not always followed along lines familiar to students of change in other fields. The chapter goes on to describe various perspectives that have been taken regarding change in education and concludes that different models and strategies are appropriate in different circumstances, necessitating a broad and flexible approach on the part of change planners.

The Nature of Change in Education

Educational institutions are inextricably caught up in the ebb and flow of societal change. The school is contemporary society's most salient educational institution. It is expected to carry the double burden of maintaining traditional values while preparing society's young members to deal with a changing world. Seymour Sarason (1971:7) points to the source of these expectations:

> There are few, if any, social problems for which explanations and solutions do not in some way involve the public school—involvement that may be direct or indirect, relevant or irrelevant, small or large. After all, the argument usually runs, the school is a reflection of our society as well as the principal vehicle by which its young are socialized or prepared for life in adult society.

The motivating forces for institutional change in education can usually be traced to either of two sources: (1) demands for the schools to respond to the socialization needs of society, or (2) use of the schools to solve social problems.

Henry Levin argues that the first is the dominant thrust, since schools cannot outstep the needs and demands of society: "activities and outcomes of education serve and therefore mirror those of the society at large" (1974:306). Attempts to use the schools as primary agents of societal change are thus severely limited. From this point of view, change in school systems comes from shifts or changing needs in the society and not the other way around. Levin's argument, however, does not relegate educational institutions to the role of maintaining their own status quo. Quite the contrary, society is dynamic and its institutions must respond to societal change. There is a need for continual redefinition, renewal, and improvement through directed change.

Regardless of whether the process is initiated within or outside of schools, there is little doubt that schools can be powerful tools of social change. There is a strong relationship between educational institutions and the other forces, institutions, and needs of the larger society in which they exist. For example, the educational system has been successful in its response to the need for a better and more educated populace. In turn, this has helped create shifts in attitudes toward work. As workers have reached higher levels of sophistication, they have become less satisfied with jobs that demand little intellectual exercise. Thus, the relationships between social forces and forces in educational systems are intricate and are often characterized by conflict and contradiction, rather than dominance.

To understand the nature of and need for educational change, it is necessary to explore the conduct of education (teaching), its internal and external constituencies, and its influence system (governance and control) that comprise the context for educational operations.

The Conduct of Education: Teaching

Teachers are charged with implementing the school's education and socialization functions; they are the most significant human factors in the operation of school organizations. The importance of their role is belied by the status of teaching as a profession. Conflicting factors (summarized in list 1-1) act and interact in ways that render teaching less than professional, undereffective, and often poorly regarded.

A unique characteristic of the profession is that although the task of teaching is highly interpersonal in nature, teachers are isolated from professional peers and other adults for most of their working day. This isolation limits interaction among colleagues as well as dependence on mutual support or observation. Some changes have come about through the use of team approaches to teaching; however, for the most part, teachers spend little time sharing perceptions, ideas, and

LIST 1-1. Factors Influencing the Nature of Teaching

---

1. The highly interpersonal nature of the teaching task
2. The isolated classroom (the self-contained unit of a teacher with student group)
3. The limited dependence on peer support or exchange
4. The lack of agreed-upon performance standards or criteria for effective teaching
5. The diverse character of a conscripted student population
6. The demand for flexibility versus the pressures for uniformity of behavior
7. The demand for improved practice without commensurate authority, institutional support, and incentives
8. The diversity among the constituencies that must be served

---

new knowledge with their colleagues. Lunchroom or lounge ''shop talk'' is the limited, yet significant, source of interaction among professional peers.

This isolation has insulated teachers from peer review and specific performance criticism. Any threat to the teaching domain or ''territorial imperative'' meets with strong resistance. In fact, there is an established norm in many urban schools that a teacher's room is his or her own domain, not to be invaded by other adults.

In part because of this insulation from peer interaction and review, the teaching profession lacks agreed-upon criteria or standards of effective teaching. Corwin (1972) has commented that it is the obligation of any profession to ''gain control over its work''—to set its own standards and maintain them. In this sense, teaching has been called a ''semi-profession'' (Lortie 1969). If professional status is reserved for those occupations in which (1) there is a professionally agreed-upon body of knowledge about task performance, (2) entrance to the profession and evaluation of performance are controlled by professional peers, and (3) action decisions are made through interaction among colleagues and autonomous judgment of the professional group, then indeed, teaching does fall short of being truly professional.

This lack of agreed-upon and enforced standards has allowed the continuance of inferior training and weak standards for entry into the field. Historically, the academic and internship requirements for entry have been relatively minimal. Although most states have provided for significant professional input into defining entry standards, most of the standards are legislatively rather than professionally decided. There is reason to believe that, through collective action, teachers are making moves to influence entrance legislation and place more of their members on review and certification panels. However, moves to expand academic and clinical experience are fairly recent.

Thus, relatively untalented and underprepared persons are overrepresented in the teaching profession; and they are the ones who are least likely to support and implement moves to break down protective isolation, reform the profession, and improve teaching effectiveness.

Another factor—a conscripted clientele—reinforces the continuance of uneven, nonconsensual performance standards. Other professions must maintain minimum standards of performance or they will eventually lose their clientele. Along with prisons and mental institutions, public elementary and secondary schools are among the very few social service agencies with a conscripted clientele. Compulsory attendance laws have placed many students in schools against their will.

This factor is a mixed blessing for teachers, for while their clients must select them, they cannot select their clients. The student population is highly diverse, and teachers cannot realistically serve all elements of that group. Thus, even though standards for the profession are ambiguous and generally low, the demands placed on individual teachers may be inordinately high, given the conditions of their work. A diverse student population demands a flexibility of performance, yet the external governance and policy-making structures apply pressure for uniform teacher behavior.

Teachers are left with the perplexing problem of trying to effectively meet the individual needs of a diverse population while operating in a climate and organizational structure that encourage similarity of student treatment and conformity to routine behavior. The external reward structure of school organizations also reinforces a conformity to "accepted behavior." The custodial function of the school often becomes more important to the public than goals such as learning. Teachers' isolated coping atmosphere can also reinforce the routinization of performance. For example, a teacher unable to deal with the diversity of student learning styles may turn to routine make-work assignments in order to keep active minds and bodies busy.

In addition, while demands are high on teachers to improve their practice, teachers presently have little authority to affect or control many of the essential factors that impinge upon their work, such as the length of the school day and year, the nature of the student population, the curriculum and material resources available, the transfer and assignment of students, the use of school facilities, the procedures for student evaluation, the implementation of innovations, and the selection of teaching peers. Furthermore, rather than being supported by their institutional environments, teachers are asked to be effective in spite of them.

Prescribed activities handed down to teachers often take the form of bureaucratic maintenance duties with little application to the primary teaching task. This is attributable partly to the formal bureaucratic organization structure and partly to the lack of agreement on a uniform set of performance criteria. The rules given a teacher to apply in the classroom are directed more at student control than at prescribed teaching performance. Goal displacement over a period of time is common in schools. Teaching and learning often are pushed aside for the more routinely applied and mundane organizational requirements. For example, spontaneous learning exchanges are often interrupted and lost in the rigid time frame of the class period or the demands to supply the school office with attendance sheets or lunch money.

Finally, for the teacher who wants to teach, there are no consistent incentives to improve performance in the classroom. School authorities do not make promotions and recognize ability through the delegation of additional authority; with few exceptions (like the promotion to master teacher or team leader), recognition is expressed by removing the teacher from the classroom, as when an outstanding teacher is made assistant principal.

Just as there are few professional sanctions governing classroom performance, there also are few professional rewards. Sergiovonni (1969), Sarason (1971), and other writers note that *achievement* stands out among the sources of satisfaction for teachers—not the aggregate gain shown on some metric applied to student learning, but rather the satisfaction of the work itself. Often reliant on a spontaneity of interaction, the feeling of achievement derives from the belief that some action or phrasing has led to student learning. With the demands for decorum, custodial care, and organizational maintenance, the control structure and the teaching climate severely limit spontaneous interaction. Often, routine takes command and militates against efforts to reach individual students.

We mentioned earlier that inferior training and entry standards have resulted in a disproportionately high representation of mediocre teachers. Similarly, the standardization of teachers' coping behavior and the socialization of the new teacher to performance routines severly handicap school systems in their attempts to attract and hold intelligent, open, flexible, creative people, and thus there are disproportionately few practitioners with the very qualities needed to reform and improve the profession in ways that would render it attractive to those persons. A negative cycle emerges.

Evident throughout this discussion is the diversity among the constituencies that must be served. The ambiguities and conflicts that influence teaching as a profession are reinforced and maintained by this diversity. It provides a sufficient supply of excuses as well as very real explanations for the uneven performance of teachers.

Publics and Clients of Schools

Just as a diversity among constituencies characterizes the teaching profession, a diversity of publics and clients is characteristic of schools. The change planner must consider the groups who affect and are affected by educational systems. A public is a person or a group of people who have an actual or potential interest and/or impact on an organization (Kotler 1973). A client is a person or group of people intended to be served by that organization. In a very real sense, schools' publics are also their clients, since the educational system serves social purposes important to all members of a society. For the change planners, it is useful to consider for each of these publics/clients the direct power and influence it has over schools and its influence as a client system to be considered in educational operations.

The students are, of course, the primary client group of the schools. Their influence and impact is immediate, internal, and most critical to the operation of the institution. While student influence may not always be direct, the nature of this client group and the interest that others take in its welfare make it the central concern of schools.

Parents also play a primary role in the operational aspects of schools. Related client groups include the future employers of students, the local community residents, and, of course, the taxpayers who support the schools. In addition, there are tax-paying publics of the various governmental units: school district, county and/or township, state, and nation. These publics are represented in the external political bodies that shape educational policy: legislatures, school boards, and so on. The political arena includes state and national executive officials who shape and implement policy. The courts represent governmental units with a substantial and growing interest in and impact on school systems.

The education profession has both internal and external influence on the schools. There are the professional participants in the schooling process: the teachers, the administrators, the counselors, and so forth. There are the system support professionals: superintendents, consultants, evaluators, and business agents. There are the teacher union or association leaders. There are teacher trainers, staff development experts, university professors, scholars, and researchers. Some of these professionals have overlapping memberships both within and without the school system. A teacher may also be a union leader, a professional-society or organization member, an author, and so on. An administrator may also teach in professional preparation programs at a nearby college or university. Interests and motivation for professional action in schools come from a mix of orientations held by organization members. At times these may be congruent and at times they may conflict.

Other employees of schools and school systems also have an influence: janitors and other maintenance personnel, health and safety personnel, diet and food-preparation personnel, and so on. These people can impact the schools in ways beyond their immediate roles. If the school plans an in-service or staff-development program after school or on the weekend, the janitor or engineer may demand compensation for overtime work. If the school must provide breakfast for needy students, the food-service personnel are involved.

The configuration of these various clients and publics are what make the schools unique social systems. Educational change planners need to be aware of these individuals and groups and their various perspectives in viewing the schools. The failure to take them into consideration in planning and implementing institutional change can lead to unforeseen barriers, unexpected demands, and reactive behavior on the part of school professionals.

The Influence System: Governance and Control

Change advocates and planners in school systems must deal with a multilevel bureaucratic control structure that includes a diversity of forces both within and without school districts. This highly complex influence system is characterized by a diverse set of governing bodies, organizational entities, and environmental forces. For example, a school classroom is influenced from within the district by a school administration, intermediate administrative units (in large districts), the central office administration, school boards, local community groups, parents and students, and the representative of the local teacher organization. A school district is influenced by all of the above entities internally and by state government, federal government, local government, regional state governing and taxing bodies, business and professional groups, the courts, and other publics external to the district. The following discussion is divided into two parts: (1) the structure of school districts and (2) the external governance structure. However, it must be noted that there is no sharp distinction between the two regarding influence on educational policy and operation. Overlapping of memberships and relationships between internal and external forces is common.

THE STRUCTURE OF SCHOOL DISTRICTS

It is important to note the limitations of the term *bureaucracy* when used to describe educational structures and authority patterns within such structures. Multilayered school system bureaucracies do exist, especially in large districts; however, there are several factors that make them unworkable as control structures.

Robert Dreeban (1970) points out the distortion of bureaucratic authority patterns as applied to the clients of schools. Students are not bound to the organization through some mutual exchange or contract; compulsory education laws demand their attendance. Thus, no set of bureaucratic rules and regulations can guarantee their involvement or performance. Rules and regulations do exist; but they may have little impact on learning performance by the clients of schools. In fact, most of these rules are concerned with the control of behavior and the maintenance of decorum rather than with learning task performance.

Various additional assumptions of the bureaucratic model are violated in virtually all large urban school systems. Most importantly, the control system of the schools is not highly centralized; rather it is fragmented (Janowitz, 1969). Policy that begins at a school-board or central-district level is then often channeled through a variety of administrative personnel at lower levels, each having a similar but distinctive set of constituencies. The activities of local schools and classrooms are more a result of the pressures and contingencies (often crisis-oriented) at that level than of policy decisions by the boards of education or top-level administration. Schools in large systems are geographically separate from the administrative hierarchy at upper levels. Thus, feedback from the local school to the central office, a critical control mechanism, is often greatly reduced. Under these circumstances, schools cannot be effectively controlled in a classical bureaucratic sense. Adding to this problem is the fact that central office control over the selection of personnel is limited, since certification is often a function of the state (some states delegate this function to large urban districts).

However, despite this weak central control structure, a contradictory and critical feature of school structures is the limited investment of authority in the school professional. James Thompson (1967), Havelock (1971), and other students of organizational behavior agree that "human-centered" organizations function best when there is enough delegation of performance responsibility to accommodate the adaptation of broadly based system goals to local situations. This implies a need for peer interaction and autonomy for teachers in implementing programs, innovations, changes, and organizational goals. Yet little decision-making responsibility is delegated to teachers. An analysis by Coleman (1963) suggests a possible reason. A person or unit is delegated some degree of authority in return for a certain number of obligations. These obligations or responsibilities to perform certain tasks are considered a "return on the investment" of delegated authority. The amount of benefit expected from delegating such authority determines the degree of authority delegated. A criterion that can aid the observer in determining the degree of authority delegated is the time lag between the delegation of authority and the review of performance. The greater the time lag, the greater the amount of authority delegated. It is the predicted rate of return on the investment that is the key to understanding the limited delegation of authority in teachers. How can administrators, boards of education, and legislators predict something for which there are no agreed-upon performance criteria? Teaching is an imprecise and complex task, the competency-based teaching movement notwithstanding. As noted before, no single style or technique is guaranteed to reach all of a variety of students. Evaluation and accountability schemes have revealed the difficulties in attributing student learning success or failure to a teacher or any single source. In short, central authority figures and bodies have few tools for predicting the return on authority investment. In part, this fact may account for the limited authority investment in either the individual teacher or school.

A related constraint on the delegation of authority is the limited education and training given teachers in comparison to members of more autonomous professions, such as law and medicine. This limited training, coupled with the restricted peer support described earlier, leaves teachers unable to deal with demanding tasks in the classroom. Janowitz (1969) comments that urban teachers often react to this energy-draining situation by a "retreat into indifference and detachment." Such retreat is often read by administrators and other observers as "unprofessional" behavior and a lack of commitment to the goals and interests of the organization. One can see a negative performance/authority cycle developing (see figure 1-1).

The lack of performance criteria leads to ineffective performance assessments. Predictions about rate of return are limited by these weak assessments, limited performance expectations (due, in part, to training background), and the observed performance of some frustrated teachers. A normative set of rules is laid down, and attempts at coercion may replace the delegation of authority. Supervision is often directed at the conformity to norms rather than at effective teaching. A codified set of minimal performance requirements becomes the standard rather than the base of performance. External governance groups

FIGURE 1-1.   A Teacher's Negative Authority Cycle
Source: Florio 1973. Used by permission.

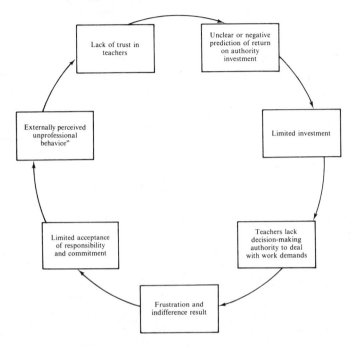

impersonally view teachers and fail to provide needed authority to deal with local problems. Teachers often react to this situation with alienation, apathy, and, in some cases, subversion of the organizational goals. These comments present an extreme picture. With the exception of the heavily burdened urban schools, few schools or school professionals fit the picture completely. However, in varying degrees, the picture provides a useful construction of authority in schools.

ENVIRONMENTAL CONTROL: THE EXTERNAL GOVERNANCE STRUCTURE OF SCHOOLS

The external governance structure of schools is derived from the public-service nature of educational systems, which are supported by means of a three-tiered governance structure: local, state, and federal. Thus, schools are controlled from all three levels. Although the current school finance structure is in a state of flux, it is generally true that the local property tax base, determined by voters who set local tax rates through bond issues and referenda, is the most significant funding source. State funds are an important source as well, and they do not come without certain strings. Most of the federal funds are categorically prescribed and thus have significant influence on local decisions.

Most of the state and federal aid is based on student population of schools. Thus, schooling is further affected by a general decline or growth in population.

Since schools serve a primarily young client group, they are among the first institutions to feel the impact of such demographic changes. As enrollments decline, so does state funding support for school systems. State aid is approaching the 50 percent support level in many states.

A fourth external source of influence on the schools is collective action by teachers. Collective bargaining contracts are acting as new quasi-governments with rules, grievance procedures, constraints on administrative authority, resource allocation decisions, and so on. Collective action by teachers has grown far beyond the local contract-bargaining process. State and national teacher unions and associations are deeply involved in partisan and policy-making political action. Active support of political candidates, sometimes from their own ranks, is among the political tactics of the organized teaching profession. Legislation and policy on the state scene are also influenced by the collective action of teachers through influence over state executives and legislation affecting the fiscal, certification, governance, and other policy matters in the education field.

Governing bodies are not the only environmental forces pressuring schools. Parents and local community leaders are demanding access to the school and, in some cases, the classroom. Attempts to limit such access—which is unworkable because the students are there every day—have built up some animosity to schools and teachers. Limitations on the use of the school facility are also coming under attack. Working parents want greater custodial care of their children. Community organizations and other service agencies want the use of the school for various activities. The summer break, an anachronism from a previous agrarian society, is also under review.

Additionally, taxpayer-publics are showing a rising interest in both the policy and outcomes of educational institutions, partly because of the increasingly limited availability of public funds. Teachers are not the only groups on the public payroll bargaining for a greater share of these funds. Public pressures will be placed on all public service agencies to share and cooperate in order to gain further benefit from limited public resources. Change and innovation that support collaborative resource sharing among individual and institutional units in education will gain in popularity. Community schools that use existing physical structures to house a variety of community services provide a useful example. Federal and state legislation is including provision for support of consortia or network operations among public agencies. In short, interinstitutional linking strategies will be increased.

Despite this extensive external governance and influence network, schools continue to enjoy a protected status among social institutions. Drucker (1973) refers to one of several problems of "public service institutions" when he points to their criteria for success. Unlike "performance-based" or competitive market institutions, schools and other public agencies get their funds from a budget allocation that is not necessarily tied to their operational program. The successful performance of such institutions is evidenced by a larger budget. "The first test of a budget-based institution and the first requirement for its survival is to obtain the budget. And the budget is, by definition, related not to the achievement of any goals, but to the intention of achieving those goals'' (p. 50). Thus, schools and other publicly supported service institutions do not base their survival on the satisfaction of a primary client group. Certainly there is a great deal of pressure to please clients and perform at some minimal accepted standard; and public dissatisfaction can lead to less support of schools. However, standards are nebulous and ill defined, particularly in school systems where the student client group is relatively powerless to make a strong and immediate political impact on the financial support of the institution.

Still, schools are not really under professional control, as noted earlier. Their protected status insulates practitioners, but it does not allow them autonomy or decision-making authority. Being a labor-intensive industry, schooling has little flexibility with regard to the use of fiscal resources. Collective bargaining, a response by teachers to many of the external control factors, has severely limited the local school unit's ability to change budget priorities. Teacher salaries, the most significant element in the school budget, are determined before the operating budget reaches the local school.

The nature of the teaching profession, with all of its ambiguities, is also a major factor in the continuation of the public (lay rather than professional) control of schools. The lack of clear evaluation criteria, the diversity of a conscripted client group, the lack of a highly defined technology, the personal (intrinsic) reward system, ambiguous goals, and the absence of a professional mystique are all significant in influencing the public view of education. Perhaps most significant in perpetuating a distrust of professional control is the *lack of criteria for judgment of effective performance* (Lortie 1969). State and national political bodies have attempted to constrain the autonomy of local governmental bodies. The states have the plenary power to control aspects of the school systems within their borders, and the federal government has placed restrictions on the provision of funds for categorical projects, programs, and target groups. In some urban school districts, city governments have a direct link to their school districts through the power to approve budgets and/or appoint school boards. It should also be noted that the courts have had a strong influence on decision making about schools in various governmental bodies.

Thus, the teaching task, which should be maximally flexible, is ultimately controlled by a distant lay governing structure and other environmental forces. The ability of the local school to work effectively with its environment is important in its effective performance. This is consistent with research findings reported by Baldridge (1974), who confirms that schools with viable linking mechanisms to their environments adopt more innovations.

Perspectives on Change in Education

The expectations one has for the performance of school systems depend largely on the perspective from which one views them. The taxpayer concerned with what he is "buying" or the school administrator concerned with progress reporting will be concerned with fiscal accountability and reform; the parent may demand curriculum relevance or custodial competence; the lawmaker will consider seriously any discrepancies between performance and legal requirements. The educational change planner should be familiar with the variety of perspectives that can be taken.

J. Alan Thomas (1971) distinguishes three "production functions" or relationships between inputs and outputs in school systems. These form the basis for the three perspectives: the *administrator's,* the *psychologist's,* and the *economist's.* They are distinguished by their views on the outputs of the schools. For the administrator, the output is the educational program with its various "units of specific service." For the psychologist, the output is the change in student behavior or "value added or . . .increments in achievement, however achievement is defined" (p. 13). For the economist, outputs are the "additional earnings which result from an increment of schooling" (p. 22). To these three, there can be added an additional perspective, that of the *educational policy maker.* The outputs for the policy maker can be viewed as the abilities of those student clients of schools to participate productively in the larger society. These four perspectives are shown in table 1-1. The change planner should be familiar with all of them. The success of a change program may be judged quite differently, depending on which perspective is taken.

Another way in which observers of educational change differ is in their vantage point. Some observers consider that most change in educational institutions has been imposed from outside (Stiles and Robinson 1973). Literature on the failure of educational change efforts, however, points out the limited scope of

TABLE 1-1. Functional Perspectives of Schools.

PERSPECTIVE	INPUT	OUTPUT
Administrator's	Human resources, material resources (space, people, materials, equipment, etc.)	The educational program of the school (units of specific service)
Psychologist's	The units of school service, time on task, qualities of human service agents, student background and abilities, program quality, etc.	Changes in human behavior: value added to student as shown in student achievement (broadly defined)
Economist's	Increments of schooling	Additional earnings (individual and aggregate societal)
Policy maker's	The configuration of elements or subunits within the educational system of a society	The ability of individuals to productively participate in the society

the "outside-in" perspective with regard to educational change (Havelock et al. 1971). Regardless of where innovations and change efforts are initiated, implementation must take place inside the educational organization. Forced or pressured change often does not last. The "adoption" of a particular innovation may have little impact when the implementation process distorts the intent and scope of the innovation. Similarly, an inside perspective on organizational change often neglects external forces, resources, and barriers that can make or break a change effort. In short, educational change planners must see the importance of both internal and external sources plus that of the interface between them. The legitimate need to see the organization as a whole, with various subsystems and system/environment exchanges, should not prevent the planner from recognizing the need to allow the individuals affected by change to participate in change decisions.

Educational decision-making concepts are currently undergoing comparison, experimentation, and debate. The "comprehensive/prescriptive" and the "incremental/remedial" paradigms of educational decision making (Schmidtlein 1974) stand as prototypes at the two ends of a decision-making continuum. This continuum ranges from the tightly planned and controlled systems analysis and control decision-making concept to the loose, individualized laissez-faire concept. This bifurcated view of decision processes in education is useful for the planner of educational change. Much of the recent literature and study of organizational change places a great deal of emphasis on the *planning* of the intended change process. Systems analysis is a tool for viewing the "whole" organization, and systems thinking is designed to demonstrate the interlocking relationships of subunits within organizations and between organizations and their environments. This is the "comprehensive" nature of the modern planning mode of decision making. Often, along with this comprehensive and organizational (as opposed to individual) view comes a more prescriptive mode.

The incremental/remedial (I/R) concept of change is much more of an individual-based mode. Schmidtlein (1974:5) points out that the "roots of the I/R paradigm lead back to the classical liberal formulation of the Marketplace. Lindbloom's (1959) concept of management by "muddling through" exemplifies a reflection on the difficulties of administration in human-centered public service organizations like schools. The notions of "academic freedom" and "professional autonomy" support the individual orientation of the incremental/remedial decision mode. An educational manager attempting to impose the planning processes of a comprehensive/prescriptive mode will meet with strong resistance from participants of an organization with a normative base closer to a traditional academic perspective on change.

Katz and Kahn (1966:390–91) claim that the major error in dealing with organizational change is the confusion between individual and organizational change, a distinction "between behavior determined largely by structured roles within a system and behavior determined more directly by personality needs and values." The perspectives on social change outlined above indicate the need for strategies that address both the technical and social subsystems of organizations and the relationships of those subsystems to each other and the organizational environment. Analysis of the target organization's current decision mode is an essential preliminary step in building a change strategy. The change planner must not only be aware of his or her own perspective and bias, but must also have a clear view of the normative decision-making mode in the target organization and its environment. This includes an assessment of the authority structure, organizational climate, and environmental characteristics. Part 3 of this book provides a broadly based planning model that takes into consideration both the organizational and individual perspectives for change. The neglect of either may make the planned-change process both difficult and ineffective. These analyses must be targeted on the unit or system most affected by the change effort (e.g., the individual school, the school district, a university, an academic unit within a university, or some other unit).

The manager of educational change can keep his perspective flexible if he views the specific organizational context from five analytical viewpoints: (1) the organizational climate, (2) the nature of the organization's environment, (3) the relationship between system and environment, (4) the characteristics of the individuals involved in the change process and/or affected by it, and (5) the nature (type and attributes) of the intended change(s). The background provided by this chapter and the admonition to broadly base a change perspective are highlighted by these analytical areas.

The *organizational climate* is the atmosphere within the target system. The following factors, which are detailed in later chapters, provide a useful overview of the elements in an organizational climate:

1. *cosmopolitan* or *local orientation* of organization members
2. the *sources of satisfaction* and *motivation orientation* in members' work
3. the *authority structure* of the organizations (Who makes decisions? Who is affected by decisions? Who participates in decision processes? etc.)
4. the *innovativeness* of the school and the internal *support for organizational change*
5. the *administrative mode and style* (formal/informal, open/closed, authoritarian/participative, etc.)
6. the *centralized or decentralized decision-making* structure
7. *conflict management* or coping styles
8. *communications patterns* (flow, barriers, inhibitors, stimulants, etc.)
9. *atmosphere of trust*
10. the willingness of members to participate in *self-diagnosis and renewal*

The *organizational environment* can be viewed as a multilayered atmosphere surrounding the target institution. There is the immediate community surrounding the educational institution; there are regional economic, political, and social forces; there is the state educational, governmental, and socioeconomic environment; and there are the national considerations of government, politics, economics, knowledge, and so forth. The local community and municipality often have the most direct impact on the school institution as an element of the educational system; however, the state, regional, national, and even the international environmental levels also have impact. Change planners in schools will need to consider the following variables, among others, in analyzing the impact of the environment:

1. the *socioeconomic* status of the community
2. the *demographic character* of the institution's location (urban, suburban, town, rural, etc.)
3. the strength and *impact of professional organizations and unions*
4. *the attitudes of the clients and publics toward the institution and change*
5. *the support for educational activities in the community and support for change and renewal*
6. the influence, history of support or criticism, and accuracy of the *media* when reporting on educational activities
7. the *resources available* from various layers within the environment (knowledge, financial, human, material, etc.)

The *relationship between the system and environment* provides one basis for the planning needs in chapter 5; however, the system-environment interface variables given below provide an introduction for the change planner in schools:

1. the open/closed relationship of the school and community
2. the overlapping membership between the school and various segments and layers of the environment (e.g., teacher and union member, administrator and community organization member, school professional and professional association member)
3. community involvement in school activities and decisions
4. the reactive/initiative stance of the school in relation to pressure for change.

The *individual characteristics* of the members involved in and affected by change in the organization are also critical for the agent or planner of change. Diagnosis of the aggregate membership may leave the planner ignorant of some of the critical personal characteristics of individual organization members. Some important individual characteristics in school organizations are:

1. *innovativeness*
2. *teaching style* (subject matter–oriented, process-oriented, etc.)
3. *teaching environment* (isolated classroom, team teaching, etc.)
4. the degree of *interaction* with and/or *isolation* from professional peers
5. *cosmopolitan/local orientation* (overlapping membership, participation in external affairs, etc.)
6. *source of satisfaction* from work (from the instrumental rewards of money, leisure time, etc., or from the rewards of the work itself)

7. the nature of *motivation* to work
8. willingness to take risks (*risk capital*)
9. the individual *authority to act and participate* in decisions affecting the member
10. the open or closed *interpersonal relationships* among members
11. *awareness of current developments* and "state of the art" in the profession
12. general *feelings of efficacy* (ability to participate in and control the personal environment of the members)
13. the *sources of information* regarding the institution, profession, community, etc.

The *nature and attributes of the intended change* and/or innovation cannot always be assessed until the organization has begun to identify problems, a need for change, available resources, and alternative solutions; however, it is essential for the change planner to know the potential type of change and the impact that various attributes of change or innovation might have on the organization and its members. The examples of attributes that follow can apply to the types of change common in educational institutions: policy, curricular, and structural. Pincus (1974: 117) describes innovations by their impact on school operations:

1. "increasing the level of resource use only ('more of the same' . . .)"; e.g.: more classrooms, smaller class size
2. "changing the resource mix" e.g., increased use of teacher aids, use of equipment versus people
3. "changing the instructional processes or methods without significantly changing the resource level or mix"; e.g., a new curriculum in a subject area such as math, social studies, reading
4. "affecting administrative management, without significant effects on organizational power structures"; e.g., new management information and data collection systems, different evaluation processes
5. "changing either the organizational structure of the schools or their relation to external authority"; e.g., team teaching, community control of schools

The Pincus typology or the more simple policy/structural/curricular breakdown is useful in viewing the impact of change; however, the innovations have various attributes that members may find to be important considerations when making adoption and implementation decisions. Zaltman and Lin (1971) have developed the following list of attributes of innovations:

1. *costs* (financial, psychological, and social, forgone opportunities or expenditure of resources needed to adopt and implement)
2. *efficiency* (Is it worth the effort given the cost and potential benefit?)
3. *communicability* (Can it be spread to other parts of the organization? What is the ease of explanation?)

4. *clarity of results* (ease or difficulty in assessing the effects)
5. *compatibility* (with past practice)
6. *pervasiveness* (degree of effect on the organization)
7. *divisibility* (ability to try it out on a limited basis within the organization)
8. *complexity* (difficulty in understanding, implementing, and operating)
9. *perceived relative advantage* (over alternative courses of action)
10. *demonstrability* (how it works and how it benefits)
11. *structural radicalness* (degree to which it changes the structural elements of the organization, e.g., communication, authority, reward system
12. *terminality and reversibility* (the points in time or cycle when adoption and operation are most appropriate, and the ability to return to the status quo after initiation)
13. *degree of commitment* (financial, human, and other resources needed)
14. *impact on interpersonal relationships*
15. *publicness versus privateness* (availability to all members)
16. *size of the decision-making body*
17. *number of gatekeepers* (channels through which information concerning the change or innovation must travel to reach a target audience)
18. *adaptability* (susceptibility of the innovation to modification both for the context of the target organization and as the innovation meets new contingencies when in operation)
19. *ego involvement* (the impact of the change on the normative structure of the organizational membership)

The five analytical viewpoints provide the agent or planner of change with a sound basis for organizational/environmental diagnosis. The diagnosis of the organization calls for a broadly based data pool that can draw upon (1) the various perspectives of organizational members, external publics, clients, and other environmental forces; (2) the different analytical viewpoints regarding the context and climate of the organization; (3) characteristics of groups both in the organization and its environment; and (4) the analysis of the resources available for solving problems and carrying out the organizational mission.

Summary

This chapter has outlined the background and perspectives specific to educational organizations. The complex pattern of governance, influence, control, and operation of educational institutions provides for some unique attributes. Different perspectives often bring different expectations. The various individual members of educational institutions have different ambitions and professional aspirations, and each views the organization from an individual base. The structure of school systems is often in conflict with the individual and professional goals of the participating members and clients. Power groups in the community, among teachers, and among various interested publics vie for influence in directing the educational organizations. These factors and others provide the background and perspective from which the educational change planner must plan, build strategies, interact with organizational members and environmental forces, diagnose situations and identify problems, review the resources available, and so forth. The problem of educational change is complex. The neglect of the elements of a target institution and their configuration is the basic flaw in many change perspectives. Though it may be impossible to know all of the various contingencies and forces, internal and external, of an organization, the variables and categories provided here should aid the change planner in identifying many that have been previously neglected in educational change efforts.

2

Forces for and Against Change in Education

CHANGE IN EDUCATION IS SHAPED by a number of forces, some of which facilitate and some of which deflect or impede the process. It is important for the change planner to be aware of these forces. Knowing what forces tend to precipitate change enables him to manipulate them where possible or to adapt his efforts so as to make creative use of them. Similarly, the change planner needs to be sensitive to various sources of resistance to change and to have contingency plans for any particular sources of resistance that may arise.

"Performance gaps," or felt discrepancies between what is and what ought to be, provide the major force for change in education. Such gaps develop through a variety of conditions, both internal and external to the system. Similarly, resistance to change derives from cultural, social, and psychological forces, within and outside of the school system itself.

Forces for Change: Performance Gaps

Certain forces in education act to create or intensify performance gaps, or discrepancies between what an individual or group is doing and what decision makers believe an individual or group ought to be doing (Downs 1966:191). A performance gap stimulates a search for alternative actions that would better satisfy needs—that is, that would lessen or close the gap between actual and desired performance (assuming that needs or desired performance are not altered). When the search leads to an acceptable alternative course of action and that action is implemented, change is said to have occurred.

The concept of performance gaps is important for the planning of change. The educator–change planner may create or capitalize on a performance gap in order to initiate processes to resolve it. The change planner must then provide direction or a means for closing the performance gap, particularly if he was instrumental in establishing the gap in the first place.

Basically, performance gaps can be closed in two ways. One way is to bring performance up to the level of expectation or level of demand. The other way is to lower expectations or to lower the desired level of performance so that it is in accord with actual performance. While the latter approach is frequently a necessary or appropriate action, only the first can be considered to involve change. For example, performance standards may be raised when system members become aware of a new technology such as computer-assisted instruction (CAI). The consequent gap can be closed by moving toward the use of CAI to improve instruction, or it can be closed by convincing those involved that their performance without CAI is adequate. The first resolution will require system change.

In resolving performance gaps, the change planner can consider a number of ways to upgrade performance. The above example suggests the introduction of new technologies as one way. Applications of knowledge to practice may also stimulate teacher, student, and administrator performance. For example, research findings show that it is important for students to feel that they exercise some control over factors affecting them, and these findings are leading to innovative ways of bringing "late bloomers" into blossom earlier. Marketing techniques for screening, developing, and disseminating new products are apparently being applied successfully to research and development activities and dissemination activities in educational R&D.

Performance can also be upgraded by introducing new personnel who are particularly well qualified to perform a special function such as career guidance or remedial reading. New personnel, in addition to contributing their special expertise, often create a pump-priming effect. A school district in the state of Florida is experimenting with a visiting-teacher program in which at least one experienced teacher is present in each school building on a one-year visiting basis only. The intent of this program, particularly in the elementary schools, is to provide tenured and other long-time teachers with a source of new ideas and alternative perspectives for viewing problems unique to that school district. This approach is very similar in philosophy to visiting-foreign-student programs.

The locus of a perceived performance gap is very important. Performance gaps may be perceived by either outsiders or insiders, or by both. If the gap is perceived only by outsiders, then the outside change planner must establish this perception within the target group. If only insiders perceive a gap, they face the task of convincing an outside agency to provide assistance. Similar considerations pertain within school systems. Teachers, principals, curriculum consultants, and others may disagree strenuously about whether or not a gap exists. Even with consensus, considerable disagreement may exist as to what appropriate remedial action is necessary for closing the gap. Performance gaps may exist simultaneously within and without the system (Belasco 1973).

Zaltman, Duncan, and Holbek (1973), in their review and synthesis of the literature, describe several ways a performance gap can occur. These are discussed below.

UNREALISTIC EXPECTATIONS

A major cause of performance gaps is the unrealistic expectation of what a particular product, service, or concept will yield. Excessive claims about the effectiveness of a new pedagogical device or a teacher-training program may create expectations beyond the true capability of the innovation. Disappointment after the adoption and implementation of such a change establishes the basis for future pressure not to change.

If an innovation that produces dissatisfaction is one that cannot be easily discontinued, then an appropriate strategy would be to adjust expectation downward. This can be done by showing that the initial expectation resulted from claims which the object or activity in question could not possibly satisfy or, perhaps, that uncontrollable circumstances are restricting the ability of the object or activity to realize its full potential in satisfying needs. Another way to decrease expectation would be to demonstrate that other users of the object or activity are experiencing even poorer results. For example, in one change project involving survey feedback, individual principals became less dissatisfied with current methods for maintaining an adequate inventory of supplies when they learned that other principals in their district were also experiencing difficulties. And teachers became less critical of their principal's handling of materials and supplies when they learned that teachers in other schools were having problems similar to their own.

Unrealistically high expectations may yield to rational argument or explanation. For instance, in a district in the metropolitan area of Chicago, a speech therapist was hired on a permanent basis for the first time in 1973 and was greeted enthusiastically by faculty and parents in the district. However, there was some misconception or misinformation, especially among parents, about the type of problems the therapist was trained to handle and the level of difficulty the student had to experience to qualify for special treatment. Thus, many parents who anticipated treatment of their children were disappointed to learn that their children did not qualify. Extensive explanation was necessary before these parents withdrew their demands for personnel change.

Sometimes, unrealistically high expectations cannot be adjusted downward, at least not very readily. It then becomes necessary to adjust performance upward through change. One small publisher was excessive in its claim about the merits of a high school social studies text, although the author protested that the book was not developed to meet all the needs the publisher said it did. Teachers were able to determine this easily for themselves from examination copies, and many complained to the publisher. At first the publisher considered dampening its promotional efforts. Finally, however, it decided to improve the performance of the book instead. The author was asked to prepare a student study guide and a more detailed teacher guide, and with these additions the book did approximate the claims made for it.

An educational research and development lab reports that in the past two years it had to make substantial changes in two teacher kits because of unusually high expectations concerning their effectiveness. The high expectations were discovered in a survey of kit users and nonusers. The survey was prompted by low teacher acceptance during the first eight months that the kits were available. Unfortunately, the survey did not attempt to measure the reasons for the unusually high expectations (or at least the research report did not mention any reasons). The lab decided to redesign the two products to improve their performances rather than attempt a campaign to lower teacher expectations.

UPWARD ADJUSTMENT OF EXPECTATIONS

Another pressure for change can result when members of a school system adjust their expectations upward. Thus, an existing object or practice whose performance is constant may become a source of dissatisfaction because expectations change. The object or practice is perceived as performing below newly established standards, and pressure to replace it is applied.

Here it is useful to distinguish between, say, an object whose use could be improved and an object that must be replaced if an improvement in performance is desired. Advocates of change frequently employ a strategy whereby they raise expectations about what can be accomplished in a given unit by contrasting the achievements attained by use of the advocated change with those attained by the current method of conducting that unit. A Boston-based firm promoted certain curriculum innovations in this manner and met with considerable success. The firm's promotional brochure presented the results of an experiment in which elementary school students using the firm's foreign-language learning package attained greater achievement levels than comparable students following an alternative approach over the same period of time. Copies of the study were available on request. A follow-up market survey indicated that 67 percent of all teachers or department chairmen who requested a copy of the study actually adopted the package, compared with 31 percent who requested additional information without specifying the nature of the information desired, and 4 percent who did not request additional information.

Society (or, in Levin's terms, the polity) may also adjust its expectations upward. This was clearly the case concerning science curriculums immediately after the launching of Sputnik. Similarly, the changing composition of communities may alter expectations. A study by a private firm under contract with a school district in a Boston suburb found that one cause of dissatisfaction with the school program in the community at large was that the socioeconomic structure of the community had changed considerably during the twelve years preceding the study. At one time it had been common for a substantial number of students to go on to college, and the program of the school district had emphasized college preparation. Over the years, however, people of different backgrounds moved into the community, resulting in changes in the mix of aspirations among the student body. This created dissatisfaction among many parents, who complained that the school was not supplying competent and thorough vocational training.

NEW PERSONNEL

The addition of new faculty and staff who have different and perhaps higher expectations can lead to a general increase in the level of expectations (Corwin 1972). The higher expectations of these new people may cause them to experience a performance gap. Additionally, by communicating to their colleagues that better alternative solutions to a problem are available and have been used successfully elsewhere, they can instill in the existing staff a dissatisfaction with current practices. This is known as the missionary effect. Visiting professorships are used in part by host institutions to engender a pump-priming effect among the existing faculty.

NEW TREATMENTS FOR EXISTING PERSONNEL

Another source of change results from in-service training, institute days, and other programs to improve the skills and knowledge base of present teachers and administrators. The importance of contacts and interaction with outside or external influences has long been noted as a force for change in education (Carlson 1965; Pincus 1974) and in other contexts (Rogers and Shoemaker 1971; Zaltman, Duncan, and Holbek 1973). An external orientation, often referred to as cosmopolitanism, increases the likelihood that members of any one system will encounter new ideas. Attending conferences has been found to influence the behavior of attenders after they return to their own school situations. The degree to which this influence occurs and the duration of the change-oriented effect is debated (Nelson 1970).The fact that external stimulation for change may not have a lasting effect led one now defunct laboratory school in North Carolina to require that at least two teachers from any one school participate in any of its training programs (concerning the motivation of underachievers). It was felt that the two or more teachers would reinforce each other and thereby maintain their change-oriented enthusiasm longer, thus increasing the possibility that change would become rooted in their school.

In another setting, an experimental program using survey feedback and collective problem-solving techniques demonstrated clearly that the training of teachers and administrators in techniques for problem solving and instituting change could be very effective. A key ingredient of the effectiveness was that at least two persons in any problem-solving group in the school district received the necessary training.

KNOWLEDGE AND TECHNOLOGICAL CHANGE

The development of new technologies is a major impetus for change. Cynics have labeled this the law of the hammer: Give a child a hammer and he'll find something to pound on. The presence of a new technology such as computer-assisted instruction undoubtedly raises performance evaluation criteria or expectations, along with a corresponding pressure to apply the technology to the problem at hand.

Changes in knowledge also lead to change. Stiles and Robinson (1973: 264–65) observe:

> As knowledge is verified and refined, it leads to modifications in both curricula and instruction. A recent example is the expansion of knowledge about the space sciences. It presses for inclusion in science programs at all levels of the school system. New knowledge about how children learn to read or respond to particular kinds of reinforcement can alter teaching procedures. Similarly, knowledge about the cultural characteristics of different types of students can shape goal priorities and educational services as well as invalidate the results of culturally biased intelligence and achievement tests.

There are numerous instances in which advances in knowledge have brought about new technologies to use the new knowledge. For instance, knowledge about the simultaneous effects of competition and cooperation upon student motivation led in part to the development of all-man simulation games. Simulation games involve both competition and cooperation. In similar fashion, knowledge gained about group problem solving and collective decision making based on survey feedback has produced new social-process technologies (as opposed to physical technologies) that are of substantial benefit in undertaking organizational change in school systems (Cooke et al. 1974).

Unfortunately far more knowledge is generated than is ever converted into practice for curriculum or organizational structure innovation. This is due to what might be labeled a research-use gap. For a large variety of reasons, much of the knowledge generated through research is seldom translated into its practical implications and hence is never systematically developed in the form of usable innovations for either the teacher or educational administrator.

CHANGES IN POWER RELATIONSHIPS

Performance gaps can develop when power relationships change. The development of a strong teachers' union may increase the power of the faculty vis-à-vis the administration. The union may have different criteria for assessing the adequacy of existing procedures for disciplinary action, granting of monetary awards, assignment of administrative tasks, and so forth. These new criteria established in the school system by the union may not be satisfied by existing practices and hence a performance gap develops.

REFERENCE GROUP

Perceptions of improved status or accomplishment by a reference group can also lead to performance gaps. For example, seeing another school or teacher being rewarded more for a given act can lead teachers and administrators to perceive a gap between what they are receiving for rewards and what they should be receiving. In the absence of knowledge that some comparable group was being rewarded more for the same level of performance, no gap would be perceived. One superintendent from a school system in western Massachusetts felt that he and his staff had been adequately, though informally, rewarded for innovative efforts—until he learned of a comparable school district in another part of the state that was offering, on an experimental basis, direct monetary rewards to teachers and administrators for successful innovative efforts. Having become dissatisfied with the informal reward system, the superintendent proposed a detailed system of incentives for innovations to his school board.

SOCIAL VALUE OF OUTPUT

General shifts in prevailing public values and attitudes toward what is being taught in schools may also create performance gaps. The discrepancy between what is and what the public feels ought to be can act as a powerful force for change in education. As mentioned earlier, the launching of Sputnik stimulated among many educators a dissatisfaction with science education in precollege schooling. This led to many science curriculum innovations and an increase in science training programs for educators. Many schools of business are changing their programs (and names) to meet the demands of such professions as health and education, which have recognized the relevance of management training for their own problems. Increased concern with ecology and limited natural resources in society in general has led to the inclusion of environmental education programs in school curriculums. Similarly, concern with minorities and women has led many universities to offer special courses focusing on those groups. And alarm expressed by health officials about the increase in veneral disease may have contributed to the inclusion of sex education in high school curriculums.

CLIENT GROUPS

Demands made by students, parents, and public authorities may be sources of pressure for change. Johnson et al. (1973) report that in several cities demands made by black groups effectively lessened pressure on black children to conform to standard English language requirements and instead allowed greater use of ghetto grammar. Similarly, in many universities, black studies were successfully initiated only after substantial pressure from black and white students.

EXTERNAL FORCES

Many external forces may operate to produce change in education, among them the civil rights movement, changes in economic conditions, political and governmental activities, and the actions of private foundations. In fact, educational institutions may seldom change without external influence. Stiles and Robinson (1973: 258) paint the following picture:

> When considering the roles of educational professionals in advancing change, a distinction needs to be made between *initiation,* the function of conceiving and introducing new practices, and *implementation,* a process of enacting changes that others have instigated. By this type of comparison, it is a myth that educational administrators, supervisors, teachers, and professors are leaders for change, despite the fact that they are always involved when changes occur. What school and college personnel do is implement or carry out changes imposed by outside forces. In some cases, educators are sufficiently sensitive to emerging external mandates for change and so skillful in adapting to them they they, like good politicians, actually take credit for new developments. Riding the ground-swells of change, however, involves a kind of brinkmanship that few educators are willing to risk. To move ahead of public opnion is to lose the game, which may mean loss of employment. Chances of failure are so great that most education professionals choose to react to and implement, rather than to lead, change.

Shifting demographic patterns are an important source of change. For example, a community outside Chicago, like many other communities, is experiencing for the first time a drop in the absolute number of elementary school students and has forecast a pronounced continued trend in this direction for at least several years. Faced with the prospect of empty elementary schools, the community is actively studying various social innovations that it could adopt to take up the slack in facilities and personnel.

Changes in the source of fiscal resources constitute a powerful force for change. As federal funding for such programs as training for the handicapped, adult education, vocational training, school-lunch and research programs increases, emphasis in activities will tend to shift in the direction of available funds. Greater federal concern with research use as a criterion for funding has stimulated many researchers to increase greatly the practical relevance of their work and to demonstrate its potential use in advance.

PERSONAL FRUSTRATION

Sikes et al. (1974) identify a set of forces they label personal frustration. These have some similarities to forces already discussed but still warrant separate attention here. One consideration is the "I get lost in the system" syndrome. Dissatisfaction because of a lack of influence or power, coupled with a feeling of not being cared about by the school, may lead to demands for change. (Such dissatisfaction may also lead to apathy and be a source of resistance as well. It is not yet clear what set of factors will cause a dissatisfied teacher or administrator to actively demand change instead of becoming apathetic.)

Underuse of capabilities may create a performance gap. Students in colleges and universities have complained that they cannot use their abilities to serve their own goals or even institutional objectives. Typical comments are: "My activities are irrelevant to me and to the institution." "I have unused resources." "I am more capable than I am allowed to be." "I am not learning what I want to learn" (Sikes et al. 1974:30). The felt need to close this gap can thus be a source of pressure for new opportunities to apply unused abilities.

OTHER FACTORS

In his literature review, Corwin (1972) concludes that organizational change in education may be facilitated by having young, flexible, supportive, and competent boundary personnel or gatekeepers. These people permit information to flow into the school system, which can raise expectations, for instance. Another important facilitator of change is the availability of funds to lessen the financial burden of organizational change. This permits members of the organization to consider a broader range of innovations as solutions to a problem. Security from social risks of change such as loss of status encourages a staff to be more venturesome and willing to experiment.

The desire for a favorable self-image may lead to the voluntary adoption of change if the change can promote the school as being:

"Up-to-date"—introducing modern physical plant, new curricula, not requiring changes in bureaucratic organization or staff rules, reduction of class size, use of teacher notes, team teaching.

"Efficient"—adoption of electronic data processing, new budgeting and accounting systems, portable classrooms.

"Professional"—adoption of curricula that are espoused by the educational leadership, hiring well-trained teachers, subsidizing in-service training and workshops, consulting with faculty of leading schools of education.

"Responsive"—establishing formalized links to parents, using blue-ribbon advisory committees to submit reports on policy issues, establishing counseling and guidance functions, establishing special programs for handicapped, gifted, slow learners, etc., providing vocational programs that respond to needs of local industry, offering a variety of adult extension courses. [Pincus 1974: 111]

Resistance to Change in Education

Educators are often criticized for being among the most conservative professional groups in the face of change. What is usually overlooked is that educators have more reason to resist change than other professionals. Few groups have as many innovations or pseudo-innovations presented to them with as little hard evidence about their effectiveness as do educators.

Resistance is, in fact, a healthy phenomenon. When the advocated change is harmful, resistance is a positive force. In such instances, threatened individuals or groups may want to actively promote or diffuse resistance to thwart acceptance. Even if resistance cannot be adequately diffused, it may at least cause the advocates of change to be careful in introducing the change or to modify it in a way that would be more consistent with the interests of the resisters.

For educational change planners, recognizing and dealing with opposition "is not a matter of choice, preference, or personal aesthetics. The chances of achieving intended outcomes become near zero when the sources of opposition are not faced, if only because it is tantamount to denial or avoidance of the reality of existing social forces and relationships in the particular setting'' (Sarason 1971: 59).

Moreover, change planners can use resistance to their benefit. By resisting change, a teacher, an administrator, or some educational group is providing data about itself. The data may reflect resources and constraints affecting the individual or group, may provide insight into its attitudes, values, and norms, and may inform about its relationship to other social systems. Data on all of these topics can help guide the change planner in his selection of strategies.

It is important to distinguish between resistance whose premise is that a proposed change is the wrong solution to an acknowledged problem and resistance whose premise is that the proposed change is irrelevant because there is no corresponding problem. It is an empirical question as to which premise is more common and which is more difficult to confront, although on an a priori basis it would seem that resistance arising from the lack of a perceived need for change is harder to overcome. It might be noted here that public educational institutions are in a unique position with regard to ignoring forces for change. They enjoy the "protected status" of a public agency with a conscripted client and are less subject to the immediate pressures of the marketplace.

We shall define resistance here as any conduct that serves to maintain the status quo in the face of pressure to alter the status quo (Zaltman and Duncan 1977). Resistance is not simply the lack of acceptance or the reverse of acceptance. For one thing, the process of learning, which is sometimes involved in acceptance, is not the same as the process of forgetting, which is sometimes involved in resistance. Also, the process of unlearning or "unfreezing" involves dynamics not associated with learning. However, in many cases the same factor can be involved in both acceptance and resistance. For example, when an innovation is compatible with a particular norm (the relevant factor), it may be adopted by one person as a symbol of defiance and rejected by another for fear of social disapproval. Similarly, the uniqueness of an innovation may be a source of attraction for innovators and a source of resistance for more conservative people (Zaltman and Pinson 1974).

Lippitt (1974) presents four categories of dimensions relevant to both facilitating and hindering change in education. First are peer and authority relations involving the dimensions of communication, competition for recognition, openness to ideas, peer support, principal involvement, teacher participation, and provisions for continuing education. Second are personal attitudes involving such dimensions as openess to innovation, openness to outside assistance, dogmatism, group participativeness, optimism, and risk taking. A third area concerns the characteristics of the practice, which includes such dimensions as relevance to needs, commitment, behavioral change, and attitude and value congruity. Finally, there are physical and temporal arrangements involving availability of time, clerical assistance, and opportunities for interpersonal interaction. All of these dimensions and examples of how they can function as facilitating and hindering forces are summarized in table 2-1.

Barriers to change in any one setting can be numerous (cf. Carpenter-Huffman et al. 1974: 8ff., 148ff., 165ff.). For example, Telfer (1966: 131–35), speaking just of curriculum change, merely scratches the surface in identifying the following barriers: lack of time, lack of effective means of communication, lack of agreement about what is to be done, lack of money to do the necessary tasks, staff turnover, poor teacher preparation, lack of teacher interest and cooperation, lack of top-level administrative support, and teacher apathy. Notice that these barriers include those arising from the social system as well as those produced by individuals.

In the following sections, we shall look separately at general cultural barriers, social and organizational barriers, and psychological barriers, and then at barriers arising from the nature of the innovation itself. Although discussed separately for ease of presentation, these sources of resistance are interrelated. The relative importance of the different sources may vary greatly from situation to situation and from innovation to innovation within any given situation.

CULTURAL BARRIERS

One major barrier to change stems from cultural values and beliefs. A good treatment of this barrier can be found in Seymour Sarason's *The Culture of the School and the Problem of Change* (1971). Earlier writers—Weber (1956), for example—described the lack of a work ethic, the absence of desire for upward mobility, and other factors as major barriers to economic development before the rise of capitalism in Europe. Rostow (1960) notes the absence of entrepreneurship and willingness to accept innovations as sources of resistance to economic change. Hagen (1962) describes as cultural barriers to change the lack of development in early childhood of key social values such as achievement and autonomy. Similarly, McClelland (1961) notes the absence of the central social value he calls achievement motivation, which is an inner drive to compete or do well relative to some standard of excellence. Strongly related to the absence of cultural values and attitudes such as thrift and achievement motivation is a trust in traditional ways of doing things.

TABLE 2-1. Forces Relevant to the Facilitation and Hindrance of Innovation and Diffusion of Teaching Practices

FACILITATING FORCES	HINDERING FORCES

1. Peer and Authority Relations

A. Sharing sessions or staff bulletins become a matter of school routine	A. Little communication among teachers
B. Public recognition given to innovators and adopters; innovation-diffusion seen as a cooperative task	B. Competition for prestige among teachers
C. Sharing ideas is expected and rewarded; norms support asking for and giving help; regular talent search for new ideas	C. Norms enforce privatism
D. Area team liaison supports new ideas	D. Colleagues reject ideas
E. Principal or superintendent supports innovation-diffusion activity	E. Principal not interested in new ideas
F. Principal helps create a staff atmosphere of sharing and experimentation	F. School climate doesn't support experimentation
G. Staff meetings used as two-way informing and educating sessions	G. Principal doesn't know what's going on
H. Teachers influence the sharing process	H. Teacher ideas don't matter
I. In-service training program gives skills needed to innovate and adapt	I. No continuing education program for staff

2. Personal Attitudes

A. Seeking new ways	A. Resistance to change
B. Seeking peer and consultant help	B. Fear of evaluation and rejection or failure
C. Always open to adapting and modifying practices	C. Dogmatism about already knowing about new practices
D. Public rewards for professional growth	D. Professional growth not important
E. See groups as endemic and relevant for academic learning	E. Negative feelings about group work
F. Understand connection between mental health and academic learning	F. Mental health is "extra"
G. Optimism	G. Pessimism
H. Test ideas slowly	H. Afraid to experiment
I. Suiting and changing practice to fit one's own style and class	I. Resistance to imitating others

TABLE 2-1. *(Continued)*

Facilitating Forces	Hindering Forces

3. Characteristics of the Practice

Facilitating Forces	Hindering Forces
A. Relevant to universal student problems	A. Does not meet the needs of a class
B. Can be done a little at a time	B. Requires a lot of energy
C. Consultant and peer help available; needed skills are clearly outlined	C. Requires new skills
D. Clearly aids student growth	D. Requires change in teacher values
E. A behavioral change with no new gimmicks	E. Requires new facilities
F. Built in evaluation to see progress	F. Won't work
G. Innovation has tried a new twist	G. Not new
H. Student-, not subject-oriented	H. Not for my grade level or subject
I. No social practice can be duplicated exactly	I. Effectiveness reduced if practice gains general use

4. Physical and Temporal Arrangements

Facilitating Forces	Hindering Forces
A. Staff meetings used for professional growth; substitutes hired to free teacher(s) to visit other classrooms; lunchtime used for discussions; students sent home for an afternoon so teachers can all meet together	A. No time to get together
B. Extra clerical help provided	B. Too many clerical duties to have time to share ideas
C. Staff meetings for everyone to get together occasionally; grade level or departmental meetings	C. Classrooms are isolated
D. Meetings held in classrooms	D. No rooms to meet in

Source: Lippit 1974.

Control beliefs are another source of resistance that is deeply embedded in culture (Foster 1962). In many societies, individuals believe that whatever happens is fate and that the individual must adjust to it; he is powerless to change the direction of his life or influence events. This feeling is fatalism defined as "the degree to which an individual perceives a lack of ability to control his future" (Rogers 1969: 273). Niehoff and Anderson (1966) have suggested that control beliefs are perhaps a post hoc rationalization about behavior and thus not a variable that directly impedes social change in education. However, considerable research using the Rotter Internal/External Test suggests that fatalism is indeed an important influence on many different groups in the United States. This test measures the degree to which a person feels he has control over things that affect his behavior. One study (Zaltman 1974) found a positive relationship between low degrees of felt control and innovativeness in education—that is, the lower the feelings of control, the less innovative a person is.

Cultural ethnocentrism is a barrier to change in two ways. First, the change planner who comes from a different culture than that of his client or target group may view his own culture as superior to the one with which he is working. University-based consultants and researchers have been blamed for representing their cultural milieu (the university) as being superior to the public elementary and secondary schools with which they work. Communication of such feelings of superiority, however indirect or unintentional, produces resistance to the planner and thus to the advocated change or innovation. In addition, the client may see his own culture as superior to others, at least in certain respects, and hence may passively resist borrowing or adopting artifacts from other cultures (Sarason 1971). Often underlying this problem is the failure to involve the client system in the change development and planning processes. The change advocate simply says, in effect, "Here it is, use it." Even when clients have helped to formulate a change, they may be reluctant to adopt it if they were not adequately involved in defining the problem to which the change is addressed. Different cultural perspectives held by change planners and clients may cause different expectations of what a commonly agreed-upon change should achieve.

SOCIAL BARRIERS TO CHANGE

There are a number of social barriers to change in education (Carpenter-Huffman et al., 1974). An important barrier may be due to *group solidarity*. Solidarity involves the issue of interdependence. "Readiness for change on one part of a system may be negated by the unwillingness or inability of other interdependent parts to change. A change sequence which would be strong enough to modify a subpart if it existed in isolation may have no effect on the system as a whole, and consequently it may fail to have any real effect on any part of the system" (Lippitt et al. 1958:77). This is also what Watson (1973) refers to as systemic coherence. Coherence or interdependence may be a strong force for resistance if the subsystem that is the object of change satisfies important needs or functions in many other parts of the social system. In addition, the behavior of one group may be governed by what another group expects of it. Resistance would occur if the influence of the reference group were strong and its expectations of the target group would be violated by adopting an advocated change. The more a reference group is threatened by a possible change, the more active it will be in expressing its opposition to the target or client group.

Rejection of outsiders is another source of resistance to change that is caused in part by a high degree of in-group identification (Watson 1973:128). As Watson concludes: "A major problem in introducing social change is to secure enough local initiative and participation so the enterprise will not be vulnerable as a foreign importation" (p. 129). One way of overcoming this problem is to create a change whose second-order consequence is the intended change. Because the advocated change is a second-order consequence, it is less likely to be associated with an external change agent.

A second type of social barrier derives from *conformity to norms*. Norms provide stability and behavioral guidelines that define what individuals can expect from one another. They are essential for the conduct of any social system. Consequently, any change that is incompatible with existing norms will tend to be resisted by most members of the social system. The critical question for a change planner to ask is "Why do people participate in this norm?" Knowing the answer to this question may enable the planner to modify his change to meet the need satisfied by the norm.

A third source of resistance may be due to *conflict and factionalism* within an organization or society. Any change adopted or espoused by one faction in the conflict may be automatically rejected by other factions. The change or innovation suffers guilt by association. Conflict may occur between two anxieties which Frey (1969) refers to as conservative anxiety ("Let's be careful about losing what we've got") and radical anxiety ("Let's be careful and clear out all this stuff and have a fresh breeze blow through"). Radical anxiety holders, when they communicate their anxieties effectively, reinforce the anxieties of the conservative and vice versa. When the conservative anxiety holders are more numerous or more powerful, the existing order may become still more deeply entrenched. A good example of this is when an aggressive senior administrator assumes new responsibility. One new dean in a southern university attempted to revitalize all at once the entire teaching program and the general research atmosphere of his division. His choice of tactics involved a broad assault on the several problems he perceived. His actions were so threatening that early supporters joined in informal opposition to the dean and effectively neutralized his actions. As one faculty member put it, "He was throwing the baby out with the bath water."

Conflict can also be a positive force for change when used creatively, in which case the absence of conflict may be a barrier to change. Conflict causes the contending parties to be more thoughtful in expressing their respective views, resulting in more carefully constructed positions about change. In particular, evidence from studies in a variety of contexts indicates that when advocates of a position are challenged by opponents, they are more likely to take into account the possible dysfunctional consequences of their position and to develop remedial contingency plans for those consequences. Thus, if the advocates succeed in implementing their proposed change, the school system will be better protected against dysfunctional consequences. When conflicting changes are being advocated by two groups, skillful conflict management by administrators can also lead to a third (compromise) solution that is better for the school system than either of the two original proposals (Sarason 1971).

A fourth social barrier has to do with *group insight*. Lippitt et al. (1958:181) suggest that one of the major barriers to change in small groups is "the members' imperfect awareness of their own interpersonal processes and their lack of a frame of reference in which to judge their performance and their possibilities for improvement." The absence of such feedback may be rooted in resistance to the conduct of evaluation research and/or the reluctance to use the findings of evaluation research (Eaton 1962). Concern with this general problem has led to various kinds of organizational development techniques for educational systems, such as the survey feedback–collective decision making–problem solving technique (Cooke et al. 1974) and sensitivity training techniques.

ORGANIZATIONAL BARRIERS

A special class of social barriers includes those rooted in the hierarchy and social structure of the school organization. Several investigations (Zaltman, Duncan, and Holbek 1973) have observed that certain structural characteristics of organizations facilitate the initiation of change or innovation but operate to restrict the implementation of change. For example, a highly complex organization—that is, one having many different roles—may often initiate change more readily than a comparatively less complex organization. The large number of different roles appears to increase the likelihood that an organization will encounter an innovation. Decentralization of authority helps initiate change because individuals have authority to explore innovations initially. However, an innovation affecting several persons may be difficult to implement if the number of affected persons is large and there is little centralized authority for making decisions. Consequently, to facilitate both the initiation and implementation of change, a "differentiated" organizational structure is necessary. Thus, the organization would be complex and decentralized in the initiation phase of change and less complex and more centralized in the implementation stage.

A successful application of this theory was achieved by a large high school in a large New York state city. This school established a change team consisting of a number of different roles including students, parents, noneducator professionals without children in school, various teachers, various administrators, and even some secretarial staff. Limited financial resources were provided which allowed the team to purchase or order sample innovations. This team with its highly varied personnel examined more innovations in its first four months of operation than, according to the school principal, had been considered formally in that school during the preceding five and a half years. The decision to implement any changes, however, was formally in the hands of only two members of the change team plus the school principal. According to a survey of teachers and administrators conducted eighteen months after the change team was in operation, more innovations were implemented, with great success, than had ever been implemented during the entire preceding four years.

Organizational rigidity is another source of resistance. An excellent paper by Hawley (1974) identifies a number of symptoms and consequences of organizational rigidity. For example, where key decision making is restricted to the superintendent's office, teachers have little latitude to innovate with curriculum or tests, the use of facilities, and student evaluation procedures. Highly standardized and routinized methods for dealing with students, parents, and other nonschool adults are another symptom of resistance to change. Examples of such standardization and routinization are restrictions on student movement, pre-scheduled and limited periods of instruction, and ability grouping. Each of these examples and the many others not cited has its own generally sound rationale. However, in aggregate they produce a substantial side effect, which is to restrict innovativeness. Teachers are not delegated authority to experiment; they have restricted horizontal communication, little professional interaction, and, at most, a small role in developing policies on matters that affect them.

A study by Gross et al. (1971) concerning the introduction of the so-called catalytic role model for motivating lower-class students and raising their academic performance demonstrates how certain innovations can be incompatible with organizational arrangements. The study found that rigid scheduling of school time, age grading, and subject-oriented report cards were incompatible with the catalytic role model innovation, and the failure to make significant alterations in these arrangements greatly hampered the experiment.

Organizational rigidity in public schools is rooted in several causes. One is the difficulty of measuring the effectiveness of schools as producers of educated citizens. Because of this difficulty, administrations often turn their attention to things that can be measured more easily, such as the teacher's conformity to rules or norms. Thus, emphasis is placed on degree of compliance, which is inversely related to experimentation and change.

Outside of education, an organization's clients will shift patronage when service deteriorates because of problems such as those stemming from excessive organizational rigidity. This serves as feedback to the organization, which presumably will adapt and become less rigid in response. However, a school organization has a conscriptive clientele and so is under less pressure to remedy the effects of rigidity. Similarly, since "public schools face virtually no interorganizational competition, they have no self-interests in determining what other school systems are doing" (Hawley 1974:15).

Inadequate communication within school systems is yet another source of resistance to change. Effective upward communication is an important ingredient of proper management control. In educational systems, proper upward communication is made difficult by the fact that teachers experience their problems in self-contained classrooms and thus have little opportunity to show senior administration personnel many of the problems that require innovative or at least alternative solutions. This problem is made difficult for teacher-principal and principal-superintendent relationships, in which the second person of each pair plays the sometimes contradictory dual roles of supervisor and colleague. It is difficult to be both boss and friend. Sarason (1971:120) describes this very well:

> The principal views going into the classroom for purposes of evaluation and change as an act that will be viewed by the teacher as a hostile intrusion. The presence of the principal in a classroom, particularly if it is in the context of a problem in that classroom, is experienced by the teacher with anxiety and/or hostility. . . . From the standpoint of the principal there is little that he feels he can do about what goes on in a classroom. . . . As a result, the principal tolerates situations that by his values or standards are "wrong". Because this toleration is frequently accompanied by feelings of guilt and inadequacy, it frequently has an additional consequence: the tendency to deny that these situations exist in the school.

A lack of communication among schools within the same district may also produce, or at least support, rigidity. This problem has been cited by many persons involved in organizational change in school systems. When schools share with each other their stories of success or failure, the likelihood that a particular school will succeed in its change attempts is enhanced. Unfortunately, mechanisms to facilitate such sharing are often absent, especially at the teacher level. This situation may make life easier for the superintendent, however. Lack of district-wide communication among schools makes it difficult for personnel at the school building level to see their problems as extending beyond their own building, and thus schools are less likely to make collective demands for changes at the district level.

An element of communication networks with the potential to block change is the gatekeeper. A gatekeeper is a person who has sufficient control over a channel of communication so as to be able to control what information flows through the channel to the rest of the social system. Gatekeepers are particularly important or influential in school systems, where the criteria for allowing new elements into the system are unclear or vague, thus requiring greater judgmental activity (Nagi 1974:47–58). "When the services of an organization are controversial, gatekeeping decisions (in that organization) will be influenced less by organizational norms and more by the orientations of individual decision makers" (p. 53). Gatekeepers in such organizations are relatively more influential in the adoption or rejection process. The incompatibility of an advocated change with the personal characteristics of the gatekeeper is very likely to produce a barrier to the introduction of change in that social system.

Many other aspects of the school organization may cause resistance or create barriers. When the decision-making authority is not clearly defined, it is difficult for the change planner to secure the adoption of an innovation. When an organization is relatively new, it may be reluctant to make a decision or take action with regard to external affairs until internal organizational problems associated with start-up activities are overcome. The initiation of change is made difficult when an organization or situation is highly formalized (Zaltman, Duncan, and Holbek 1973). The introduction of change can be made very difficult for the change planner unfamiliar with the informal power structure. The greater the discrepancy between formal power structure and informal structure, the greater the resistance (probably passive) the unaware planner will face.

The absence of a pervasive and sustaining philosophy of change in a social system can result in the lack of any systematic support for encouraging and reinforcing the desire and willingness to change. In general, the lack of social system rewards for innovative performance is an inhibitor of subsequent innovative behavior.

Rogers (1973*b*:75–87) suggests a number of propositions concerning social structure and change. These propositions will not be presented here, but their relevance to resistance should be noted. First, power elites will tend to prevent or oppose innovations that threaten to restructure the social system. They will attempt to do this initially by preventing the basic idea of an innovation or change from entering the social system. Censorship and control of the mass media are among the most obvious examples of this. Second, leaders will attempt to alter in a way favorable to them the nature of an advocated change and the nature and distribution of the consequences of the change. These attempts to alter the change and its consequences may not be consistent with the change planner's intentions and hence represent a form of resistance. Third, change initiated at the grassroots level (bottom-up change) is likely to encounter resistance by power elites. "The power structure of a system is a force toward the success of top-down change, whereas it works against bottom-up change." Other things being equal, the change planner should either initiate change by working through or with power elites or make certain that the change is not a threat to the power elites.

PSYCHOLOGICAL BARRIERS TO CHANGE

Of the many possible psychological barriers, perception is perhaps the most important. *Selective perception and retention* may prevent a person from seeing that the status quo is inadequate (Watson 1973:121). For various reasons a person may not "see" problems requiring significant change for remedial purposes, or may not "see" solutions even if a problem is recognized. Moreover, when data suggesting problems and indicating solutions are thrust upon someone, they may become distorted or even forgotten.

One important cause of resistance to change arises when a change planner and target system agree upon a problem but do not share common perceptions about its nature and causes and hence have different perceptions of how to remedy the problem. Early in their school life, black ghetto children have been found to experience considerable conflict resulting from two different linguistic demands. On the one hand, there is the language spoken by family and friends and, on the other hand, the language expected by the teacher. Some black groups have insisted that ghetto English be accepted in schools, whereas many teachers insist on teaching standard English (Johnson et al. 1973). Both groups perceive the problem in the same way, but they have very different perceptions of the appropriate solution.

Lack of clarity about the innovation itself is often an obstacle to change. One study (Gross et al. 1971) concerning the implementation of the catalytic role model identified ambiguity about the advocated change as a major barrier to its successful implementation. The catalytic role model is a proposed solution to the problem of motivating lower-class children and raising their academic achievement. Interestingly, not only were the teachers largely unclear about the innovation at the time it was announced, and again later just prior to its implementation, but they were not significantly clearer about it at the evaluation stage after its implementation.

Lack of clarity about the behaviors required by a change or innovation may be a source of resistance at the trial or adoption stage (Gross et al. 1971). The change planner may have made inadequate efforts to communicate the nature of the change clearly. He may have assumed, unjustifiably, that the nature of a role would become clear once the teacher was placed in it. Incomplete or inadequate information may initially result in adoption but because of unexpected negative experiences may become a barrier to further change.

There may also be different perceptions of what behaviors are expected of a given role. If the change planner engages in an activity that the client or target system feels is inappropriate, they may show indifference or hostility to all actions he undertakes. This may happen when someone perceived to be in an advisory role becomes actively involved in change or when, without invitation a change planner expands his activity to include another sector of life in a client system (Niehoff 1966).

Another source of resistance to change may occur when assistance is provided free. There has long been noted an association between price and quality where price has a causal impact on perceived quality (Zaltman and Burger, 1975). Foster (1962) provides examples in which something given free may be perceived as valueless.

Insecurity is another important source of resistance. Uncertainty and anxiety about one's ability to perform, the expectations of superiors, evaluation procedures, and so forth, may also discourage change, particularly among elementary school teachers. Teachers will not respond to a problem with innovative solutions, but rather will withdraw from the problem, or transfer it to parents, social workers, school specialists, or other parties. Insecurity is a partial consequence of low status. Perhaps low teacher status produces low self-esteem, which in turn creates insecurity in the face of opportunities to experiment.

McKeachie (1973) has observed similar phenomena among college professors resisting the introduction of teaching-evaluation plans. Such plans may be viewed as potentially damaging to professional reputations, particularly if the evaluations are made public. A professor may feel insecure if his own (favorable) self-image as a teacher is discrepant with the results of the evaluation—although he may also try to close such a gap by denying the accuracy or fairness of the evaluation system. The potential for negative evaluation may lead to insecurity about promotion, salary, and other rewards provided by the administration and colleagues. In general, it appears that insecurity about evaluations of teaching performance—and hence resistance to them—will be greater when teachers have little say in the decision to establish an evaluation program and no involvement in developing the evaluation system, and when the program is perceived as a basis for punishment.

Another source of resistance has been termed *homeostasis*. Watson (1973) observes that although organisms are not naturally complacent, they do seek a comfortable level of arousal and stimulation and try to maintain that state. Many programs of social change involve a level of arousal and stimulation well above what is comfortable to the individual. In such instances, there is a natural tendency to avoid or resist that change effort. Many factors may account for homeostasis. Lippitt et al. (1958:180–81) suggest the reluctance to admit having weaknesses, the awkwardness and fear of failure associated with doing something new, bad experiences with past change efforts, and concern about the possible loss of present satisfaction.

Conformity and commitment may become psychological barriers to change. Conformity is a major force working against change (Kiesler and Kiesler 1970; Homans 1974). Similarly, commitment is a powerful force working against change (Kiesler 1970). Financial and social psychological investment in programs and practices help root people in the status quo, and special efforts, often in the form of incentives, must be used to create alternative investments in the advocated change.

Professional training and the associated professional socialization process and its attendant pressures for conformity and commitment can contribute to resistance to change.

INNOVATION ATTRIBUTES

It is important to consider sources of resistance rooted in the innovation or change being advocated. The innovation may be inherently weak in some capacity, or certain of its attributes may be improperly presented or perhaps inadequately developed.

Innovation attributes most frequently causing resistance are differentially important at different decision stages. The *communicability* of an innovation— the ease with which its pertinent information can be disseminated—is especially important at the awareness stage. For example, a major barrier to the diffusion of simulation games was the difficulty of adequately conveying in written form the basic idea of what an all-man simulation game was and how it worked in a classroom setting. Communication via workshops was quite effective but only reached a minute number of potential adopters.

The number of gatekeepers required to bring a change to the potential adopter's attention is also relevant at the awareness stage. Commerical salesmen for education products apparently give priority to those innovations that are compatible with decentralized decision making. As one salesman put it, ''When the innovation and school district are such that authorization is necessary by the school superintendent or an associate superintendent and then again by the school principal before I can talk with teachers, I simply forget about that product for that school district'' (quoted in Zaltman 1974).

Perceived relative advantage is especially important at the interest or motivation stage. If the possibility of some major advantage resulting from change is not evident, teachers, students, and administrators will lack incentive to continue to consider voluntarily the adoption of change. The difficulty of demonstrating clear advantages, such as significant increments in student achievement through a proposed curriculum innovation, may cause a loss of interest (Turnbull et al. 1974). This is a particularly important source of resistance in education, where changes in student, teacher, or administrator performance are difficult to measure. The ''Technology for Children'' program, a K-6 child-centered program that couples career education activities with traditional academic subjects, has been very slow in diffusing, and one reason given is the difficulty of developing accurate instruments for measuring its impact. Thus, difficulties in measurement make it hard to provide the evidence needed to persuade a teacher to make the effort involved in considering a change. As Lucius Gary, Viscount Falkland, once said, ''If it is not necessary to change, then it is necessary not to change.''

At the comprehension stage, the *complexity* of the innovation becomes important. An innovation may be complex in its *operation* or may have a complex *underlying theory*. For example, considerable resistance was encountered by a change team attempting to introduce into school districts a survey feedback– collective decision making–problem solving organizational development program. The approach was based on a number of theories including a set of complex propositions asserting that the collective decision-making approach being advocated did *not* reduce principal and superintendent power. While this theory proved well founded, its complexity, coupled with its surface contradiction with common sense, created much initial resistance among school authorities. Difficulties in understanding how to use a kit designed to instruct teachers and administrators in problem analysis and strategy selection proved to be a barrier to the widespread use of an otherwise very effective professional development aid for educators (Turnbull et al. 1974).

The *radicalness* of an innovation may be a likely source of resistance at the comprehension stage. An easily implemented change that involves very basic social science principles or theory but that represents a major departure from current practice may not be understood. Barnett (1953) was among the first social-change scholars to observe this phenomenon. *Demonstrability* is important at the comprehension stage as well as at the attitude and trial stages. The more radical and complex an innovation, the more desirable that it be easily demonstrated. It is especially important for demonstrations to be active, rather than passive ''show and tell'' affairs.

Several attributes are meaningful at the attitude-formation stage. The source or *point of origin* of an innovation can bestow an image on the innovation that determines how it is received. "The institutional prestige of a developer or disseminator may impress purchasers. Those involved in Minicourse dissemination say that the Far West Laboratory's name has added to the product's appeal" (Turnbull et al. 1974:8). (However, "the fact that a product originates with a research and development agency does not automatically increase user demand.") Similarly, an innovation or change originating from or otherwise associated with a poorly regarded agent or agency may face considerable resistance.

Also important at the attitude stage is the *compatibility* of the innovation with the social and technical environment. An organizational change involving a sharp increase in the role of teachers in administrative decisions or of students in curriculum development may be incompatible with the social values of administrators or teachers, respectively. Similarly, a simulation game involving consumer economics that does not blend in well with the general social studies unit may be viewed unfavorably.

The legitimation stage occurs when an individual or group becomes convinced that the basic idea a change or innovation represents is appropriate. This does not necessarily mean that a particular change under consideration is worth adopting, but simply that it does not violate basic norms and values. The point of origin of the innovation is again an important factor. A suggested curriculum change or organizational structure change initiated by the superintendent may achieve greater legitimacy more quickly than the same change suggested first by a colleague in another school district. Again, the compatibility of the innovation with the cultural and technical setting of the school system will be a factor determining whether and to what extent resistance will occur. The *size of the decision-making body* involved in approving a change also appears to have an influence on the perceived appropriateness of an educational change (Kasulis 1975). Apparently, the larger the decision group involved, the more appropriate nongroup members will consider the change to be.

At the trial stage, several factors become potential barriers to change. An educational change that is not easily reversible is especially likely to meet with resistance. For example, the voucher scheme for the selection of schools by parents, if adopted and found unsatisfactory, would be difficult to discontinue for a return to the earlier system. This irreversibility appears to be one of the major causes of reluctance to switch to a voucher system. Similarly, programs requiring large sums of money or other resources that cannot be recovered if the change is discontinued are likely to meet with resistance. The opportunity cost is very high. Changes that are not divisible—that is, that cannot be tried on a small scale within a school building or within just a few schools in a school system—are also likely to encounter resistance at the trial stage.

During the evaluation stage, such related factors as risk and uncertainty, the scientific status of the advocated change, susceptibility of the innovation to modification, the efficiency of the change, and the estimated influence of the adoption on subsequent opportunities for change (gateway capacity) are important. The pervasiveness of the innovation will also be important: the greater the need for change among the existing elements of the school system in order to accommodate the advocated change, the more reluctant that system will be to judge the change desirable. Related to pervasiveness is the *impact* the change has on *interpersonal relations*. This is very important both for curriculum innovations and organizational structure innovations (Cooke et al. 1974).

The financial *costs* of initial and continued or sustained implementation are important considerations during the adoption and resolution stages. If operating costs, whether financial or nonfinancial (e.g., teacher release time), are high, discontinuance is likely. The high initial costs of innovations or changes whose implementation requires the hiring of outside consultants may be rejected at the adoption or resolution stages despite a favorable evaluation (Turnbull et al. 1974; Rogers and Shoemaker 1971).

OTHER DISCUSSIONS OF RESISTANCE

Other investigators have elaborated further upon the various sources of resistance or have looked at them from somewhat different perspectives. Sikorski and Hutchins (1974) present a model in which *unavailability of resources or other preconditions* for implementing change are the sources of concern.

Personality factors of individuals in the system are believed by many to be important. Rogers and Shoemaker (1971:187–88) in their review of the literature suggest as barriers such factors as low empathetic ability, high dogmatism, inability to deal with abstractions, fatalism, and low achievement motivation. Lack of conceptual and inquiring skills may limit motivation and the ability to reexamine, evaluate, and alter behavior (D. W. Johnson 1969:143–53). Barnett (1953) sees the lack of creativity as a barrier to innovation, and Grinstaff (1969) suggests the inability to tolerate ambiguity as a source of resistance to change.

Willingness to take risks is a particularly important personal trait as well as a social-system trait. For example, the professional educator is likely to be a follower rather than a leader of change, and hence much change in education comes from outside the field. As Carter and Silberman (1965) observe, "most [educational] changes are originated for the schools rather than by them."

Sikes et al. (1974) note that barriers may be produced by competing forces in the change setting. Efforts by threatened parties to "inoculate" adopters against the advocated change in advance of its presentation have been known to work well in commerical situations, community development programs, and political promotional campaigns. Alternatively, there may be a better substitute for the advocated change. This substitute could be the present practice or product or one being sponsored by a competing agency.

Personal incompatibility between the change advocate and the client may cause the client to reject the advocated change (Homans 1974; Heider 1958). Using a model developed by Robertson (1971), Zaltman and Stiff (1973) analyze resistance resulting from change-advocate behavior and then from client behavior as it can manifest itself at the different decision-making stages. Table 2-2 displays causes of resistance from this perspective.

Sikes et al. (1974:38–45) mention the following sources of resistance: (1) difficulty of demonstrating value of change, (2) difficult role of the change agent, (3) parochialism, (4) ambiguous role of administrators, (5) lack of change-oriented concepts and skills, (6) change-oriented people not in mainstream, (7) discouraging policies and practices, and (8) difficulty of maintaining volunteer efforts.

Eichholz and Rogers (1964) have identified additional sources or causes of resistance: rejection through ignorance or through default (knowledge of an innovation but no interest in it), erroneous logic (rational but unfounded reasons), and unsuccessful experience with the change. They provide a useful framework for the identification of various forms of rejection. This is presented in table 2-3.

Havelock and Havelock (1973:153) have identified a number of barriers to change encountered by school district superintendents in very successful, self-reported change efforts. These eighteen barriers are presented in list 2-1 in order of importance.

TABLE 2-2. Potential Causes of Incomplete Acceptance Processes

ACCEPTANCE PROCESS STAGE	CHANGE-AGENT CAUSES OF INCOMPLETE ACCEPTANCE PROCESSES	ADOPTER CAUSES OF INCOMPLETE ACCEPTANCE PROCESSES
Problem Perception	Failure to comprehend relevant situation	Perceptual defense Satisfaction with status quo
Awareness	Poorly used or too little communication	Selective exposure Selective perception
Comprehension	Communication difficult to understand	Faulty organization of information
Attitude	Communication not persuasive	Complacency Suspended judgment
Legitimation	Poor source effect of communications	Bending to social pressure against adoption
Trial	Behavioral response not specified in communications	Evaluating alternative or status quo as equally good
Adoption	Failure to adapt innovation to meet needs	Replacing with another innovation
Dissonance	Innovation attributes incorrectly communicated	Expectations greater than reality

TABLE 2-3. A Framework for the Identification of Forms of Rejection

Form of Rejection	Cause of Rejection	State of Subject	Anticipated Rejection Responses
1. Ignorance	Lack of dissemination	Uninformed	"The information is not easily available."
2. Suspended judgment	Data not logically compelling	Doubtful	"I want to wait and see how good it is before I try."
3. Situational	Data not materially compelling	1. Comparing	"Other things are equally good."
		2. Defensive	"The school regulations will not permit it."
		3. Deprived	"It costs too much to use in time and/or money."
4. Personal	Data not psycho-logically compelling	1. Anxious	"I don't know if I can operate the equipment."
		2. Guilty	"I know I should use them, but I don't have time."
		3. Alienated (or estranged)	"These gadgets will never replace a teacher." ("If we use these gadgets, they might replace us.")
5. Experimental	Present or past trials	Convinced	"I tried them once and they aren't any good."

Source: Eicholz and Rogers 1964. Used by permission.

46

List 2-1.   Barriers to the Showcase Innovation Process

1.   Confusion among staff about the purpose of the innovation
2.   Unwillingness of teachers and school personnel to change or listen to new ideas
3.   Shortage of funds allocated for the innovation
4.   Staff's lack of precise information about the innovation
5.   Frustration and difficulty encountered by teachers and/or relevant staff in trying to adopt
6.   Lack of communication among the staff
7.   Inadequacy of school plant, facilities, equipment or supplies
8.   Shortage of qualified personnel
9.   Feeling by teachers and staff that the innovation would have little benefit for them
10.   Rigidity of school system structure and bureaucracy
11.   Lack of communication between staff and students
12.   Lack of coordination and teamwork within the school system
13.   Disorganization of the planning and implementation efforts
14.   Lack of adequate contacts with outside resource groups (e.g., universities, consultants, labs, etc.)
15.   Absence of a concerted campaign to put the new ideas across
16.   Frustration and difficulty encountered by the students during the adoption process
17.   Lack of contact with other school systems who had considered the same innovation
18.   Unwillingness of resource groups to help us revise or adapt

SOURCE: Havelock and Havelock 1973:153

Summary

This chapter presented various forces for and against change, so that the change planner may be aware of these forces and be able to manage them as much as possible. "Performance gaps" were identified as the major force for change in education. Several elements were discussed that could create, identify, or intensify performance gaps. These elements included unrealistic or changed expectations, new personnel or new treatment of existing personnel, technological change, power changes, perceived change in a reference group, and several other factors. The change planner can make use of the performance gap by providing a means for closing the gap. Many sources of resistance to change were considered. General cultural barriers and cultural ethnocentrism, social and organizational barriers, organizational rigidity, psychological barriers, and the nature of the innovation, may all cause resistance to change. Various other perspectives on resistance include personality factors of organization members, competing forces against the change, and personal incompatibility between the change advocate and the client. Several tables list many barriers or sources of resistance. One must remember, however, that resistance to change is a necessary and healthy phenomenon. It can provide useful information about organization resources, constraints, attitudes, values, norms, and external relationshps, which can help the change planner in selecting strategies.

Part II

Models and Strategies of Intentional Change Diffusion

3

Models and Strategies for Educational Change

NUMEROUS THEORIES HAVE BEEN OFFERED describing or recommending processes for change in individuals, organizations, or systems. Such theories provide the change planner with a structure for conceptualizing the change process and the background necessary for developing change strategies. This chapter has two main parts: (1) a discussion of models of change appropriate to education and (2) a discussion of strategies for implementing change.

Models of Change Relevant to Education

As noted in chapter 1, there are a number of different perspectives from which planners and managers of change view individuals and organizations. Single models of change are generally limited by one perspective, and it is therefore useful to be familiar with a variety of models, to see their value as well as their limitations. This kind of background makes evident the need for a synthesis model of change in educational organizations. Chapters 5 and 6 represent the authors' model, one which addresses organizational change, individual change (for organizational members), and system change. System change includes the organization, its subunits, its environment, and its control structure. A failure to attend to any of these elements and their relationships has been the downfall of many efforts to bring about purposeful change in education.

The bias of much of the research and commentary on change has been the overemphasis on the individual adopter of changes or innovations (Zaltman and Duncan 1977; Katz and Kahn 1966). An erroneous assumption made by many

51

change theorists and change planners is that change in an organization can be effected by changing the individuals within it. This error highlights the need to address organizational variables that not only affect the individual adopter, but that also have a strong impact on the group's change behavior. In a similar kind of error, system or organizational models of change often neglect the critical human variables. The obvious need is for a model that deals with both the organization and the individual. Getzels, Lipham, and Campbell (1968) present a general model of the major dimensions of behavior in a social system (see figure 3-1). It should be noted that even this model has its limitations. Although its authors have addressed in various writings the human interactions among the individuals within organizations, these not shown in the figure. The model does point out the interplay between the individual and organizational dimensions; but the informal interaction among individuals within systems and between a system and its environment must also be considered.

Using this behavioral model, Getzels and his associates refer to three leadership styles in social systems. The *nomothetic* style emphasizes the institution, role, and role-expectation directiveness for organizational members. This corresponds to McGregor's (1960) Theory X style of leadership and Blake and Mouton's (1964) 9 × 1 Managerial Grid position, both of which emphasize the needs of the organization over the needs of the individual members. The *ideographic* style emphasizes the individual, personality, and need dispositions of organizational members over the organizational needs. This corresponds to McGregor's Theory Y and Blake and Mouton's 1 × 9 leadership orientations, which assume a primary focus on individual members and that organizations will perform better with "satisfied" personnel. The *transactional* leadership style is

FIGURE 3-1.   General Model of the Major Dimensions of Behavior in a Social System
Source: Getzels, Lipham, and Campbell 1968:105. Used by permission.

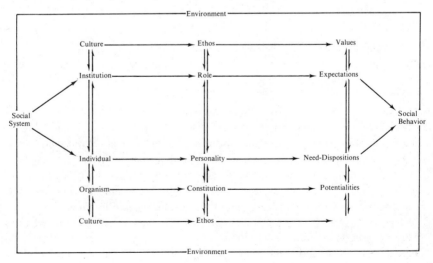

oriented to the interaction of organization and member needs. Commitment comes from interdependence based on a common ownership in the organization mission, and relationships reflect trust and respect. The leader uses various tactics in context-specific situations as the need to work with individuals and organizations becomes apparent. This corresponds to Blake and Mouton's 9 × 9 leadership orientation.

An "individualistic bias" toward the individual adopter neglects these important interactions between individual and organizational needs. In addition, it includes a bias toward the "single technical invention" (innovation). This concentration on the invention, dissemination, diffusion, and adoption of single products stems from the basic research and development model of change. The research-development-dissemination-adoption (RDDA) model is based on the assumption that the adopter is passive and that most educational change comes from outside schools.

> With that perspective, the research and development community may be tempted to huckster particular products, and, in the urgency to sell, they may overlook the need to build problem-solving capacity into the organizations they are serving. Researchers, developers, administrators, and educators have seldom created an innovative environment where alternatives could be considered and options explored. [Baldridge and Deal 1975:6]

There is a need for educational planners to have a problem orientation rather than a product orientation. Donald Campbell (1972:189) advocates a policy "shift from the advocacy of a specific reform to the advocacy of the seriousness of the problem, and hence to the *advocacy of persistence in alternative reform efforts*" (emphasis added). With this in mind, the scholars, advocates, planners, and managers of educational change should concentrate their efforts on the organization as target of change and the process as a problem identification and solution model.

INTERNAL VERSUS EXTERNAL CHANGE MODELS

Several authors view change theories as falling into two categories distinguished by the origin of change (Coleman 1973; Zaltman, Duncan, and Holbek 1973). These categories include theories that conceptualize change as (1) originating within organizations or individuals or (2) beginning with changes in the social conditions or the environment. Theories in the first category assume either explicitly or implicitly that changes within individuals or organizations will be followed by changes in their environment. Theories in the second category assume that changes in the broader social conditions affecting individuals are prerequisites for enduring individual or organizational change.

This distinction is particularly germane to the issue of educational change. It has been widely acknowledged that most changes in education are externally generated (Stiles and Robinson 1973; Coleman 1973; Levin 1974; Carlson

1965). Levin argues that efforts to reform educational institutions must correspond to changes in society. The use of educational institutions as units of change affecting society at large are destined, he says, to failure. Others disagree with this position (cf. Giles, Gatlin, and Cataldo 1974). It is somewhat fruitless to attempt to distinguish between the chicken and egg of social and institutional change. We are a society of groups, organizations, and interlocking systems. To argue that one system is always or nearly always relegated to a reactive status in relationships with others and with the broader social system is to neglect the reciprocal nature of social change among institutions. Systems thinking highlights the interaction among subsystems. When one element within a broader social system changes or shifts positions, all others are affected. For example, changes in the demographic nature of a community from wealthy to less affluent, young families to elderly people, black to white, and so on, all affect schools. Likewise, efforts to desegregate schools in metropolitan areas have affected the housing patterns of those areas. Many of these effects have been unintended, and it cannot be determined exactly which set of changes led to changes in other systems (Kirby, Harris, and Crain 1973).

Further discussion of change models categorizes them as environmental (external) change models, organizational (internal) change models, models covering both internal and external change, and individual-oriented models.

ENVIRONMENTAL MODELS OF EDUCATIONAL CHANGE

Levin's Polity Model   Levin (1974) argues that educational change reflects changes in the organized society or "polity." He concludes that educational institutions cannot move ahead of the polity in attempts to affect the social, economic, or political system's "major tenets."

Levin's basic conceptual framework is presented in figure 3-2. The arrows represent flows of decision outcomes, resources, and so forth from one cell to another. Notice that the polity directly influences (1) the goals set by educational systems and the financial resources available to achieve those goals; (2) the selection of nonfinancial educational resources such as personnel; (3) the process whereby resources are mobilized and coordinated to achieve goals; and (4) the social, economic, and political results of educational processes. The social, political, and economic outcomes in turn feed back and reinforce the polity that brought them about. Not only does the polity directly impact each of these aspects of the educational process, but, since the aspects have a serial relationship to one another, the polity exercises an indirect influence as well.

The Levin model has several implications for those who aspire to create change in education. First, any attempted change should be developed and presented in a way that appears consistent with the values and goals of the larger society. Second, major educational changes should be introduced when major changes are occuring in the larger society. In this circumstance, the status quo of

FIGURE 3-2.   The Educational Sector
Source: Levin 1974:308. Used by permission.

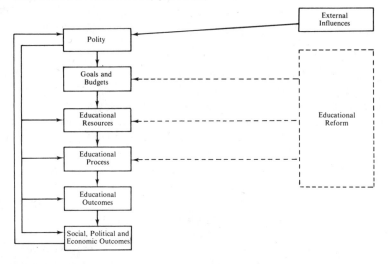

the polity is less effective as a force retarding change. Third, the change planner must try to identify the particular sources of influence in the polity at large which are most important to the education reform being attempted. For example, in attempting to seek a larger budget for the school district to strengthen vocational training, the superintendent must be sensitive to the relative importance of other municipal services that might have to be curtailed or not expanded in order to allocate more funds for schooling. Community interests and regional employment needs must be assessed as well. In short, a move to change the product goals of schools must reflect a need within the polity.

Stiles and Robinson's Political Process Model   Stiles and Robinson (1973) suggest a political process model of educational change that reflects the present mode of external forces for internal change. The five basic steps in the model are as follows:

Step 1. *Development:* marshaling of forces having unmet needs and articulating complaints and proposals

Step 2. *Diffusion:* Dissemination of the complaints and remedial proposals through public protest and criticism

Step 3. *Legitimation:* recognition of the need for change among policy makers and resource allocators at the local level or, depending upon resistance at the local level, recognition of the need for change among legislators or courts

Step 4. *Adoption:* acceptance by professional educators of their responsibility for carrying out the change

Step 5. *Adaptation:* Actual implementation of change with or without modification

For example, problems of drug abuse among youth come to the attention of parents and other community leaders (development). Hearings are demanded to explore the various problems and locations of drug use (diffusion). Hearings are held by both local governmental officials and legislators representing the community in state and/or national government (legitimation). Laws are passed mandating drug education programs in schools (legitimation). School district boards of education and administrators adopt a policy regarding drug education in the schools (adoption), and programs are initiated in the local schools (adaptation). Note that educators are often placed in a reactive position late in the process. Although they may participate in hearings, they often wait for external demands such as legislative or court mandates before taking action.

A major implication of the political process model for the change planner is the importance of connecting a desired change with an unmet need of one or more vocal interest groups or stimulating the growth of an interest group centering on the desired change. Creative use of interest groups can greatly speed up the development, diffusion, and legitimation phases. The educational change planner can play an important role in these phases as a disseminator of information. This suggests another implication of the political process model. Each phase may require different kinds of information, and the change planner as disseminator should be aware of such requirements. For example, in the development phase, information about the nature and severity of a problem should be stressed; while at the diffusion stage, information about particular solutions or remedial proposals should be emphasized.

ORGANIZATIONAL CHANGE MODELS

Many models or theories of change are concerned primarily with group processes and phenomena of change. Most such models focus on formal organizations but also take into account informal processes operating within the formal structure of the group. While they often acknowledge the importance of environmental factors, for the most part they do not treat these factors very adequately. However, organizational and environmental models should be viewed as complementary rather than mutually exclusive.

The Zaltman, Duncan, and Holbek Model   The Zaltman, Duncan, and Holbek (1973) model considers the effects of the internal environment of an organization on the change process. This model posits two basic change stages, initiation and implementation, with each subsuming several substages:

Initiation
1. Knowledge–awareness
2. Attitude formation
3. Decision

Implementation
1. Initial implementation
2. Continued–sustained implementation

During the initiation stage, potential adopters must first learn of the existence of the innovation. This knowledge or awareness may result from a conscious search for an innovation to meet a need, or the need to innovate may result from the awareness of the innovation's existence. In the second stage, members of the organization form attitudes toward the innovation. Factors influencing the formation of positive or negative attitudes include openness to the innovation and perceived potential for the innovation. The first of these involves organizational members' willingness to consider the innovation, as well as their perceptions concerning its possibilities for making a favorable contribution. The second involves their perceptions of their ability to use the innovation successfully, as well as their commitment to the goal of making it work.

The decision substage consists of the processing of all available information concerning the innovation. Effective channels of communication are therefore essential. If the decision makers have developed favorable attitudes toward the innovation, they are likely to feel favorably disposed toward an implementation decision.

During the first implementation substage, initial implementation, the organization may use the innovation on a trial basis. If organization members view the trial as a success, the innovation is likely to be retained on a permanent basis (continued-sustained implementation).

The authors of this model recognize, however, that the innovation process will not always follow this exact pattern. The process will vary according to the nature of the organization and the particular innovation in question. In fact, the process is probably not linear, with a clear-cut beginning and end, but rather circular. Each new decision or outcome is likely to affect one or more of the previous outcomes or stages. Five organizational characteristics may affect the two stages: complexity, formalization, centralization, interpersonal relations, and dealing with conflict.

Complexity refers to the "number of occupational specialties, their professionalism and differentiated task structure" (Zaltman et al. 1973:159–60) within an organization. Although schools contain relatively few occupational specialists who play a signifcant role in the actual process of education (primarily teachers and administrators), the school remains as a complex organization, in part because of the isolation of teachers in relatively autonomous classrooms and the diversity of the conscripted clientele. This complexity facilitates the initiation phase. Teachers work with a reasonable amount of independence, and they have considerable opportunity to discover areas in need of innovation. However, because of a diversity in perspectives among faculty members, arriving at a common decision regarding what or how to innovate is likely to be difficult. Thus, a high degree of complexity facilitates initiation but interferes with the implementation of an innovation.

Formalization refers to the relative emphasis that an organization places on following specific guidelines, rules, and procedures in the execution of job functions. Within certain broad constraints, teachers are free to determine how their individual classrooms operate. However, when performance gaps that affect other levels of the school environment are identified, initiation and implementation of innovations are inhibited. Schmuck and Schmuck (1974b) identify four levels that must be considered and must work together if a significant change in the organization is to occur: (1) the individual, (2) the learning group, (3) the school organization, and (4) the school environment. Each facet has its own norms, expectations, and operating procedures. Thus, overall, schools are highly formal. This characteristic makes initiation of innovations difficult, since each subunit may perceive problems and solutions differently. The paradox of formal organization in school units and informal control of classroom operations makes sustained implementation difficult.

Centralization refers to the locus of decision-making power within an organization. A highly centralized organization is one in which authority and decision making are concentrated heavily at the top of the organizational hierarchy. According to this definition, schools tend to be rather highly centralized. As discussed previously, decisions to innovate tend to originate at the top or even from sources external to the school. This characteristic lends itself to awareness/decision more than initiation and implementation of change programs. Ideas may be generated farther down the hierarchy but fail to achieve recognition because of inadequate upward communication channels. Even when recognized, they may easily be voted down. This highlights the need to include the informal organization in decision stages.

Close *interpersonal relations* among organizational members facilitate both stages of the innovation process. Group cohesiveness as well as open and honest communication among group members can help in dealing with problems. It has been noted (e.g., Stiles and Robinson 1973) that communication among educational personnel is often sporadic and superficial. The change planner working in the schools must usually take steps to improve the relationships among group members.

Finally, the *ability to deal with conflict* may influence the innovation process. Conflict inevitably arises during both the initiation and implementation phases. During the former, conflicts generally revolve around deciding which innovation to accept. During the latter, they are generally concerned with choosing processes for implementation. Recognition of the existence of conflict and an open discussion and resolution of disputed issues will facilitate the innovation process. Interpersonal relationships play an important role in the resolution of conflict. In schools, as in other kinds of organizations, a broader base of decision making provides greater opportunity for recognition and discussion of conflicting attitudes and opinions.

Table 3-1 summarizes the effects of these five organizational variables on each stage of the innovation process. A plus sign indicates a facilitating effect on

TABLE 3-1. The Effects of Five Organizational Variables on the Innovation Process

		INITIATION	IMPLEMENTATION
Complexity	High	+	−
	Low	−	+
Formalization	High	−	+
	Low	+	−
Centralization	High	−	+
	Low	+	−
Interpersonal Relations	High	+	+
	Low	−	−
Dealing with Conflict	High	+	+
	Low	−	−

the process, and a minus sign an inhibiting effect. For example, high complexity facilitates initiation but inhibits implementation.

Thus, an important implication of the Zaltman, Duncan, and Holbek model is that organizational characteristics which facilitate introduction of innovations may make implementation difficult, and characteristics favoring easy implementation may make initiation difficult. The change planner may wish to consider special organization designs for coping with this dilemma. For example, when an organization is highly centralized, the initiation of change is more difficult than its implementation. To overcome this situation, some schools have created special change teams at the teacher level to identify and evaluate innovations and recommend decisions to adopt or not adopt particular innovations. Similarly, since the lack of a formal mechanism can make implementation of change relatively difficult, many schools the authors have worked with have developed and successfully used special, very clear-cut procedures for this purpose.

A second important implication of this model lies in its distinction between initiation and implementation. Many changes are initiated but not implemented fully or at all. Curriculum innovations may be purchased only to gather dust in a storeroom. Lack of teacher commitment may produce only passive compliance with change and thus the potential benefits of the change may not be realized. Similarly, administrators may agree to a special change program but not allocate the financial and other resources necessary for it to succeed. It becomes essential, then, for the change planner to be certain that follow-through mechanisms exist. Some schools have experimented with implementation committees whose primary task is to monitor and, in a few instances, assist in the initial implementation of change. A follow-through approach that has experienced success is one that requires the users of an innovation or change to report periodically on various aspects of its use, such as volume of use, degree of success, and sources of problems.

The Survey Feedback–Problem Solving–Collective Decision Model   The survey feedback–problem solving–collective decision model (SF-PS-CD) represents a problem solving perspective for organizational change (Coughlan et al. 1972). This strategy was developed to serve as an organizational development approach to planned change, focusing on group processes and problems rather than individual growth. Its seven phases, depicted in figure 3-3, are evaluation, stimulation, internal diffusion, legitimation, adoption, implementation, and routinization. In an educational application of the model, a randomized experiment compared an SF-PS-CD grouping with three control groups, involving forty-eight elementary schools in all (Coughlan et al. 1972). The various stages of the study were conducted to demonstrate the effectiveness of this type of intervention for improving teachers' attitudes toward their work environment and favorably altering their perceptions of their schools' collective decision making. This study is a useful illustration of the early phases of the model.

Evaluation pertains to the identification of problems as perceived by members of the organization. In the study under consideration, a group of teachers anonymously completed a standardized questionnaire reflecting attitudes toward their respective schools. Results of the survey were tabulated by an external agent and presented to the teachers for "evaluation." The group was charged with the responsibility of achieving consensus about the nature of problems and clarifying change goals.

The generation of an array of solutions for the problems that have been identified is the function of phase two, stimulation. Five two-hour problem-solving meetings were scheduled for the teachers to accomplish this end. The meetings were conducted by specially trained teachers who had been nominated for the role by their peers. After careful consideration of all of the alternatives, the group decided which course of action to pursue.

Internal diffusion refers to the communication of suggested changes to other members of the organization who might be affected by them. The function of this phase is to provide for modification of solutions based on feedback from other members of the organization, to increase input into the decision-making process, and to improve communication among organizational members. The need for

FIGURE 3-3.   The Collective Innovation Decision Process
Source: Coughlan, Cooke, and Safer 1972:21.

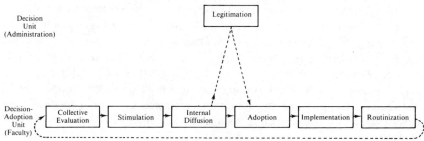

internal-diffusion activities was minimal in the Coughlan et al. study, since all teachers within each participating school were members of the original decision-making group.

During the *legitimation* phase, the proposed action plan is presented to traditional authority figures within the organization for approval, rejection, or modification. Although some decisions do not require legitimation, the proposals generated in the study required approval by members of the school district office.

The *adoption* phase entails the acceptance of the final change proposal by members of the group. The final proposal reflects any changes required by the previous phase as well as a plan for implementation.

During the *implementation* phase, the final proposal is translated into practice. To increase the likelihood of successful implementation, individual responsibilities, schedules, and deadlines are carefully delineated. *Routinization* refers to the successful and lasting integration of the new program within the organizational structure. It depends upon the degree to which participants are involved in collective evaluation of the implemented change. Thus, the process is cyclical, with events assessed for further data gathering and feedback.

AUTHORITATIVE/PARTICIPATIVE MODELS

These are descriptive models, depicting the approach to change in terms of the extent to which decisions are made by authority figures. In authoritative approaches, decisions regarding the nature and process of change are made entirely by individuals holding positions of power. In education, the authority figures demanding change may come from within the organization (e.g., principals, deans) or from outside (e.g., school boards, legislators). Education is unique in that pressures for change are more often externally generated. In either case, however, persons who will implement and/or be affected by the innovation often have a negligible input in the various stages of decision making. To the extent that this input is increased, the approach can be described as participative. An example of a participative approach would be one in which teacher input into the decisions at hand is sought. In such a case, teachers would play an active role in generating a variety of proposals and then choosing from among them the course to be followed. Although change is effected more slowly when a participative approach is employed, there is generally less resistance to change as well as a greater probability that change will be sustained.

Authority Versus Collective Innovative Decision Rogers and Shoemaker (1971) discuss the "authority innovative decision" as an authoritative approach to educational change. They stress the importance of the superior-subordinate contact. Three stages of decision making are separated from an implementation phase. *Knowledge* of the need for change, *persuasion* regarding intended changes, and *decisions* regarding acceptance or rejection of changes are handled by authority figures prior to implementation. The implementation phase includes *communication* of the decision to adoption units within the organization and *action* by the adopting unit to implement or reject the change. While consultation may occur, authority innovative decisions are made for and not by the adopting unit.

Rogers and Shoemaker's "collective innovative decision" is a more participative approach. The stages of this approach are:

Step 1. *Stimulation:* the subprocess "at which someone becomes aware that a need exists for a certain innovation within a social system" (p. 277).

Step 2. *Initiation:* the subprocess "by which the new idea receives increased attention by members of the social system and is further adapted to the needs of the system" (p. 278).

Step 3. *Legitimation:* the subprocess at which the new idea "is approved or sanctioned by those who informally represent the social system in its norms and values and in the social power they possess" (p. 280).

Step 4. *Decision:* the subprocess of establishing consensus to accept or reject the new idea.

Step 5. *Action:* the subprocess of putting the new idea into effect or of preventing the new idea from being put into effect.

There are a number of ways the change planner may implement the collective decision model. For example, he may wish to assume the role of stimulator and initiator. Or he may help facilitate the performance of these roles by providing information, creating opportunities for stimulators and initiators to interact with others, identifying legitimators, and helping initiators to gain access to legitimators. The change planner can also facilitate the decision and action phases of this model. For example, a superintendent may make school time available for decision-making sessions or provide financial resources or special consultants to aid in the implementation of the change. If the planner is someone other than the superintendent, then he should try to secure resource commitment from the superintendent to enhance the likelihood that change will be carried out successfully.

Collaborative Versus Noncollaborative Approaches.   Bennis (1966*b*) employs a somewhat more involved classification scheme that attempts to categorize unplanned as well as planned change. His typology of change processes identifies eight relatively discrete types of change, which he categorizes as either collaborative or noncollaborative.

1. *Planned change* When decisions are derived mutually and deliberately with an equal balance of power between change agent and client system, planned change* is the outcome. Specific strategies for bringing about planned change include the systems analysis model (Bushnell and Rappaport 1971) and the SF-PS-CD model (Coughlan et al. 1972).

2. *Indoctrination* When goals and decisions are both mutual and deliberate but a larger share of the power rests with the initiator of change, the change

*It should be noted that the authors of this book use the term *planned change* for a broader class of change phenomena, not limited to the collaborative approach as defined by Bennis.

phenomenon would be classified as indoctrination. For example, all school personnel may agree that a new reading program is needed; however, the reading consultant may have access to information about new programs and thus be able to shape the decision regarding the specific programs adopted.

3. *Coercive change* When objectives are determined deliberately but without significant collaboration, the process is termed coercive change. Here, teachers would play an insignificant role in decision making. The Stiles and Robinson political process model is an example of a coercive strategy.

4. *Technocratic change* Here change is realized through the collection and analysis of data. Technocratic change is both deliberate and one-sided, although there is no clear-cut relationship between change planner and client system. It occurs when a problem has been defined entirely in terms of insufficient knowledge in some area. Suppose, for example, that a school district is planning to build some additions to existing facilities. They do not know, however, what their needs will be. They hire a demographer to gather data from which to project the population of school-age children in their community over the next twenty years. When the data are available, the school district can then plan the expansion program. The objective, which was to fill the knowledge gap, was determined entirely by the client system (the school district). Therefore, on the goal-setting dimension, technocratic change fits well as a noncollaborative approach. The other dimension, the ratio of power between change agent and client system, seems to be irrelevant to this type of change process. At this point, Bennis's typology begins to break down.

5. *Interactional change* When change is unintentional and a relatively equal power distribution exists, interactional change can be said to have occurred. The commitment to change when this phenomenon occurs is most often unconscious. A teacher may be influenced to adopt a less punitive classroom discipline policy through informal interactions with other teachers. This may occur without any conscious effort by the other teachers to bring about such a change. Collaboration, however, implies intent on the part of all parties involved. There are problems, therefore, in categorizing any nondeliberate change process as collaborative.

6. *Socialization change* This occurs through the interaction of two individuals who are not "equals." Examples of socialization change that occur in educational settings are found in relationships between administrators and teachers and between teachers and students. In addition, novice teachers learn a great deal about the operations of their school through social interactions with more experienced teachers.

7. *Emulative change* When subordinates admire and model the behaviors of their superiors, emulative change has occurred.

8. *Natural change* The category of natural change is meant to account for any spontaneous occurrences that cannot be classified by any of the other seven species of change.

It is likely that change planners in education engage in several of the species of change identified by Bennis, although they may not be aware of the style they employ in any given situation. Thus, a benefit of the Bennis scheme is that it can help sensitize planners to their own patterns of behavior. The planner should try to identify the mode he is using and ask whether it is appropriate for a given set of circumstances. For instance, when time constraints are severe and an immediate decision is necessary, indoctrination or coercive change may be the only alternative. On the other hand, when a problem needs clarification and an immediate decision is not essential, then a technocratic approach stressing data collection and analysis may be desirable.

INDIVIDUAL-ORIENTED MODELS

Many models of change focus on the individual decision maker or adopter. These models describe the cognitive processes that persons undergo, whether their decisions are made in a group or organizational context or in relative isolation. Although the models are oriented to the individual, several elements are parallel to those of organizational change models. For example, nearly all of the individual models have an awareness/perception stage in which the individual becomes cognizant of a need for change or innovation. Similar processes are needed in intentional organizational change. Some paradigms of individual-oriented change models are presented in figure 3-4.

These models range from the early rural sociology model of adoption of new farm practices (Rogers 1962) to the more recent Zaltman and Brooker (1971) and Rogers and Shoemaker (1971) models, which recognize the rejection process as equally important in individual innovation decisions.

The models presented in figure 3-4 have many similarities. The initial stimulus for change in individuals comes from some *awareness, perception,* or *problem recognition* by the individual. This is the discovery or awareness that there is a gap between real and desired circumstances and therefore a need for some change or innovation designed to close that gap. Although stated in different ways, the awareness of a need for change is the *sine qua non* of the individual models.

A *knowledge* or *information* stage involves various change possibilities and their attributes. As Rogers and Shoemaker point out, this knowledge can come from a deliberate exploration by the individual, by accident, or from some external source seeking to influence the individual. *Persuasion and/or interest* are closely tied to the knowledge element. Initial information may contain persuasive messages concerning the innovation. If enough interest is generated, an individual seeks more information. In any event, further understanding and knowledge are necessary, or the consideration of a particular innovation may be dropped. Robertson (1971) calls this further understanding *comprehension.* Comprehension includes the perception of the individual regarding the "fit" between the problem gap and the use of the innovation to fill that gap.

The persuasion, comprehension, and further understanding of the innovation

FIGURE 3-4.   Summary of Individual-Oriented Models of the Innovation Process

Source: Zaltman, Duncan, and Holbek 1973:61. Used by permission.

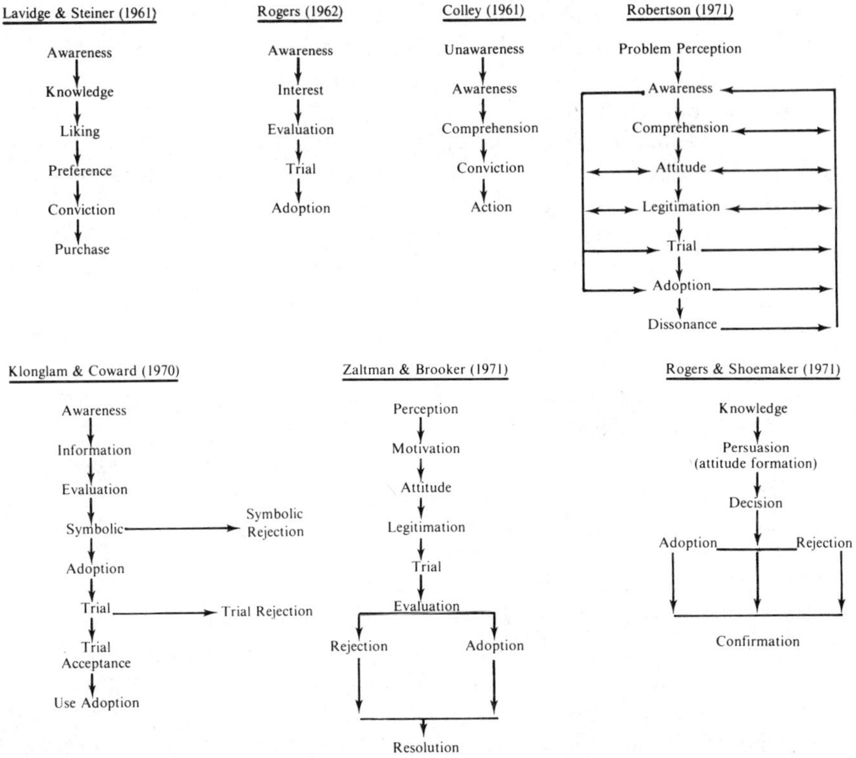

initiate the *attitude formation* processes. Attitude formation is sometimes referred to as mental evaluation or as liking (or disliking). The process involves a mental check on the innovation with regard to its relative advantage over other alternatives in solving problems, its compatibility with the individual's values and mode of operation, its degree of complexity with regard to use, its potential for trial on a small scale without full commitment, and its ability to demonstrate usefulness in problem solving.

Attitude formation leads to some form of *legitimation*. Legitimation is the support gained through the review processes in attitude formation. This element in the individual adoption process is called preference, symbolic adoption, conviction, or some other description alluding to the fact that the individual is persuaded that he or she should at least try, if not firmly adopt, the innovation or change.

Some of the models include a *trial stage* in the individual adoption process. This may consist of some form of mental trail or scenario developed by the individual in predicting the consequences of adoption. Where actual trials occur, they are usually designed as the final test before a decision to adopt is made. A form of *evaluation* is used following either mental or actual trial of the innovation or change.

Following trial or legitimation, an *adoption/rejection decision* is made. This decision stage is sometimes called action, resolution, or confirmation. At this stage, the innovation or change is either adopted or rejected; however, rejection may not be total. A phase not included in the above models is an *adaptation* phase in which inadequate or rejected innovations may be modified. Rejection may also be temporary and the innovation tried again under different circumstances or at a different time.

A problem with these models is that little thought is given to the implementation of the decision. Many of them describe a purchasing or selection action. The initial and/or sustained use of the innovation is neglected. Trial phases may help individuals see the value of implementation and continued use; however, they often reveal little about the implications of innovations in new circumstances.

Another problem lies in the presentation of individual change stages as linear. In fact, the various elements may occur simultaneously or in a different order from that presented in the above models, and they are generally cyclical. For example, once an innovation is adopted and implemented, it may bring about awareness of new problems or need for change and thus move the individual into a new cycle.

The individual change/innovation models have implications regarding the kinds of efforts and strategies required to mediate different change stages. In the initial awareness stage, efforts to gain individual adoption of change or innovation need to include some stimulus to encourage the perception by the change target that there is a need to change. Knowledge of the actual or potential availability of a solution to a problem must be made available. It then becomes necessary to stimulate interest in the advocated change or set of alternative innovations and to facilitate the individual's efforts to acquire further information. The planner or advocate of change must make sure that the innovation is mentally tested against the realities of the individual's environment and arrange for a trial in order for legitimation and adoption-decision stages to be used effectively. Finally, the change planner/advocate can reinforce the adoption decision (if made) by supporting the implementation of the innovation by the individual.

OTHER MODELS OF CHANGE

Not all models fall conveniently into the categories presented thus far. Several others are presented here and compared to some of the models already discussed.

Research, Development, and Diffusion Models Models characterizing the research, development, and diffusion (RD&D) perspective describe change processes from an earlier point in the evolutionary process of an innovation.

They emphasize the perspective of the "orginator" or "developer" of an innovation.

A good illustration is the original Clark and Guba (1967) version of the RD&D model designed specifically as a vehicle to aid in "bridging the gap between theory and practice" in education. The four sequential phases described to achieve this are research, development, diffusion, and adoption. Evaluation is seen as an integral part of each phase.

The function of *research* in this model is to secure knowledge, irrespective of whether or not it is eventually incorporated into the innovation. The research effort is judged in terms of quality or validity of the research and not in terms of its immediate applicability.

The *development* phase consists of two activities: invention and design. The first involves generating solutions for the problem at hand and selecting from among them the course to be pursued. Research findings, experience, and intuition may be drawn upon during this activity. Evaluative criteria are face validity, feasibility, and the perceived importance of the innovation solution.

In the design process, the innovation is refined and prepared for implementation in the field. Evaluation of this process is geared to determining whether the product performs as anticipated and estimating its generalizability across a variety of settings.

The remaining phases, diffusion and adoption, follow much the same pattern as the classic rural sociology five-stage model of individual adoption processes (Rogers 1962). The two components of the *diffusion* process are dissemination and demonstration. "Dissemination" corresponds to "awareness" in the sense that each is an introduction to the innovation. A similar relationship exists between "demonstration" and the rural sciologists' conceptualization of the "interest" stage. In either scheme, the potential client is provided with more detailed information about the innovation so that he may mentally evaluate its propriety for use or problem solving.

The final stage of the model, *adoption,* comprises three components: trial, installation, and institutionalization. The classic early model views this as a two-stage process of trial and adoption.

The term *trial* is used both by Clark and Guba and by the early rural sociologists in referring to the process of ascertaining the feasibility and utility of the invention for the client's setting. This may take the form of a small-scale, temporary adoption of the invention or may simply involve further logical rational analysis. Adaptability, feasibility, and performance in the client's situation are the criteria by which the innovation may be judged during this phase.

If the client is pleased with the trial outcomes, *installation* may follow. During this phase, the invention is refined and adapted to meet the particular characteristics of the adopting institution. A successful installation is one that accomplishes these ends in an efficient manner.

The RDDA process comes to its conclusion when the invention is successfully assimilated or *institutionalized* within the adopting system. An invention ceases to be an innovation when it becomes an integral part of the system. The success of the institutionalization phase can be judged by the degree to which members of the adopting institution value, support, and continue to use the invention.

The programed instruction movement in the United States evolved through what is essentially a research and development process. During the 1940s and 1950s, a great deal of basic research was conducted to clarify the principles and theory of animal learning through operant conditioning. During those years, B. F. Skinner and his associates could only speculate about the impact of their work on educational practice. When enough evidence had been accumulated, generalizations of these principles to humans were attempted. At least five more years of applied research and development were involved before the technology of programed instruction was sufficiently advanced for widespread diffusion of the innovation. It is probably accurate to say that the innovation has been sucessfully assimilated within the American educational scene. Programed texts are fairly widely used for a variety of purposes at all educational levels, although the magnitude of the impact is less than some would have predicted. Furthermore, numerous instructional strategies have evolved that are founded in behavioral theory and share many characteristics of programed instruction, such as mastery learning (Bloom 1968) and the personalized system of instruction (Keller 1968).

Figure 3-5 depicts the research and development process. The four columns correspond to the phases of the model; column I to the research phase, column II to the development phase, and so forth. Diffusion, however, is inadequately shown in the model and would come between columns II and III.

RDDA models are neither authoritative nor participative (Rogers and Shoemaker 1971), at least until diffusion activities begin. The distinguishing characteristic of authoritative and participative change processes is the locus of distribution of decision-making power within the organization where change will be effected. Since research and development activities take place independently of potential client systems, the two models view the change process from different perspectives. The authoritative-participative scheme considers change from the perspective of the adopting system, while the RDDA model views it from the point of view of the developers. (There are some exceptions to this division of R&D activities and diffusion/adoption activities. Educational institutions have, at times, participated in both field research and development pilot testing activities. Participation by potential users has helped shape the development of innovations to meet existing conditions more adequately.)

When diffusion activities are begun, one might then be interested in the interpersonal relationships among members of potential adopting institutions. At this point, an RDDA effort may be classified as either authoritative or participative with respect to the "receivers" of the innovation. To make such a classification, however, requires a departure from the emphasis of RDDA theoreticians.

Bennis (1966b) would classify RD&D models as technocratic change phenomena—one of the examples of noncollaborative approaches to change. They are noncollaborative because the goal-setting phase of the development

FIGURE 3-5.   RDDA Process
Source: Stiles and Robinson 1973:275. Used by permission.

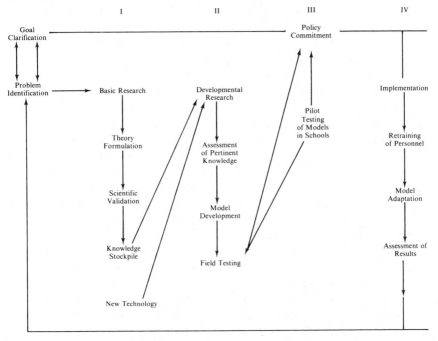

process does not involve potential consumers of the innovation. Once again, the relationship between change agent and client system does not begin until the diffusion stage.

The Lippitt, Watson, and Westley Problem-Solving Model   Some models describe problem-solving processes in which an external change planner works closely with members of the client system throughout the stages of change. In a model offered by Lippitt, Watson, and Westley (1958), planned change is seen as a seven-phase process. This is an expansion of the three stages of change described by Kurt Lewin (1952): unfreezing, moving, and freezing. The Lippitt et al. model is intended to encompass formal and informal groups as well as isolated individuals as targets of change. The seven phases are as follows:

1. Development of a need for change
2. Establishment of a change relationship
3. Clarification or diagnosis of the client system's problems
4. Examination of alternative routes and goals; establishment of goals and intentions of action
5. Transformation of intentions into actual change efforts
6. Generalization and stabilization of change
7. Termination of the relationship

Phase one, the *development of a need for change,* consists of three steps. An *awareness* of the specific problem that is creating a nonoptimally functioning system is the necessary first step. Once general awareness of the problem has been achieved, a *desire* for change must develop among members of the system. This desire is founded in a belief that improvements are possible. The final step is the act of *seeking* outside assistance. This model assumes that necessary resources are not available within the system in question.

The second phase, the *establishment of a change relationship,* is perhaps the most crucial in any change effort. Communication channels must be opened and a mutual feeling of trust and understanding must be developed between change planner and client system for the change process to evolve smoothly.

Three miniphases are subsumed within phase three, the *diagnosis of the client system's problem.* In logical sequence, these are (1) *data gathering,* (2) *data analysis,* and (3) *reinterpretation of the client's problem* in light of this newly available information. This phase may be fraught with difficulty. For example, the problem may emerge as being more complex than originally anticipated and/or the client may take issue with a particular diagnosis. An atmosphere of cooperation and compromise is essential for dealing with such difficulties and differences of opinion.

Ideas generated by phase three are transformed into *action plans* during the fourth phase. A variety of *alternatives are conceived* and, from among those, the *plan to be followed is selected.* Motivational problems may arise here, particularly at the decision-making point. One means of assuaging these anxieties is for the change planner to encourage a trial run of the innovation before full-scale adoption. It is inferred from the model that if results of the trial are unsatisfactory, the change team may reconsider the problem (return to phase three) and/or reexamine alternative goals and action plans (return to phase four) before proceeding in a linear fashion through the remaining stages.

During phase five, the *transformation of intentions into actual change efforts,* the innovation is fully adopted within the institution or by the individual. At this point, the success of the innovation in alleviating the original problem may be evaluated. Data are necessary to make such a judgment, and it is vital that they be communicated clearly to the client so that decisions to continue or discontinue the innovation are well founded.

Successful change necessitates a stable period of use by the target system. This is the first function of phase six, the *generalization and stabilization* phase. This is likely to occur naturally if the innovation is perceived as meeting the needs of the various levels within the system. Generalization to other parts of the system will usually follow a successful stabilization.

Although the relationship between change planner and client system may conclude at any number of earlier points in the process, Lippitt et al. see a continuation of the relationship as being highly desirable at least until there is a successful institutionalization of the innovation. Problems associated with phase seven, *termination of the relationship,* are usually connected to the dependency of the client on the change planner. Two solutions are offered to ease the transition: (1) the change planner may remain available on a consulting basis or (2) individuals within the system may be trained to assume change-planning roles. The first of these, while perhaps desirable under some circumstances, only perpetuates the dependency problem. The goal of self-renewing systems is best aided by the second solution. Change planners should aid organization members in gaining the requisite skills to systematically solve their own problems—both those that are related and those that are unrelated to the newly adopted innovation.

Strategies of Change

Models of change describe or perhaps prescribe in a formal way the general process of change. When the planner begins to outline an approach for actually executing change, his mode becomes strategic. The notion of deliberate and conscious change implies that, at some point in the process, some means or strategy is selected or created for effecting change. The strategy may be developed along the lines of a particular change model or according to the planner's intuition. Either way, the building and application of change strategies is a highly visible and central management activity, and the one that most educational practitioners associate with the term *change planning*.

One reason for having a clear command of the process of diagnosing and prescribing change is so that optional strategies for achieving it can be devised. Once a school knows where it wants to go, there are many possible routes for getting there; but not all of them would be considered acceptable to those involved, so it is important to evaluate them adequately. For example, a school system that wants to improve reading scores is faced with several alternatives: it can mandate the use of a specific program; it can offer new incentives for teachers or students; or it can adopt a new organizational arrangement for individualizing instruction. The mandate may have high initial impact but may be so threatening to traditional teachers that over time they will sabotage it. The offer of incentives may also be initially effective but may break down when particular incentives lose their potency over time. The new organizational arrangement may have high potential impact but may fail initially when the need to clearly communicate the potential impact to teacher-users is overlooked.

While most educators would readily accept the usefulness in being able to make an analysis of alternative routes to change, they do not always want to invest heavily in time and resources to develop and apply change strategies. As a result, educational change is typically unsystematic and disruptive. As Deal and Baldridge (1974) put it, "Most educational change management is based largely on intuition and 'seat of the pants' strategy." Generally, strategies have been selected and developed without sufficient attention to the factors that influence their success. The educational change planner often fails to foresee possible complications of the approach he develops or selects. Many educational products are useful but too costly, effective but not amenable to in-school use, or attractive but technically difficult for the teacher to use. Educational change planners often aim for immediate change when a more effective strategy would implement a series of small-scale changes over time. As noted before, there is usually too much dependence on changing individuals and not enough concern with the fact that the setting for educational innovation is social and organizational in nature, involving formal and informal relationships in an organizational structure with goals, rewards, and decision-making substructures.

A review of some actual strategies for change in education reveals not only how often the process is uncoordinated and poorly planned, but how this fact works against school autonomy and self-renewal. For example, an important form of change planning has involved economic incentives for change. Schools that would otherwise *not* implement a particular policy often do so because of financial opportunities. This is one area in which schools voluntarily relinquish their treasured autonomy, one area in which external forces most clearly intrude (Peterson 1974). Title III of the Elementary and Secondary Education Act provides an example of how change can be shaped this way. Evaluations of Title III have reported that projects may be discontinued because the school district was unable to absorb the costs of the project after the withdrawal of federal funds, giving rise to the question of whether districts ever really needed or intended to continue those projects (Denham 1971; Widmer 1975; Berman and McLaughlin 1974).

Economic incentives of this type are frequently provided by state and federal government agencies, and those agencies may dictate priorities or program procedures. The Right to Read Program, which has provided technical assistance for using one of five model programs, and ESEA Title VII (Bilingual Program) and Title VI (Handicapped) are examples of programs that have prescribed the nature of the change to be taken.

Another form that planned educational change may take involves political legal strategies for change in schools. Here, there is direct intervention by external forces. California's Stull Bill put many schools into a reactive mode, forcing them to reform teacher evaluation procedures quickly. Because few schools are in a position to provide the kind of planning, training, and evaluation needed to make this law really effective, schools have had to rely heavily on outsiders for this.

Even product-development approaches to planned change, in which schools are free to choose to use educational innovations, have historically had an external locus of control. Innovative educational products have usually been developed separately from the ultimate consumers of those products (Turnbull et al. 1974). Knowledge production has occurred independently of the practitioner's requirements, and the knowledge produced has frequently existed in forms he could not use. Even where product forms have been made usable, the perspectives of developers and potential users have been different. "Instead of innovations being viewed as part of a universe of means, schools are viewed as part of a universe of adopters'' (Fullan and Eastabrook 1973).

Where change planning has taken the form of providing practitioners with new or different competencies, there has been too little regard for the locus of control; the forms of training are frequently threatening, disruptive, and costly. Among a sample of Chicago schools asked to respond to the program "Man: A Course of Study" (MACOS), one frequent objection to its training requirements had to do not with the substance of the training but with the *time* required. In schools where the program had been adopted, teachers had usually taken the training on their own time during the summer (Sikorski and Hutchins 1974).

These examples make clear how schools find themselves in a subordinate and reactive relationship with their environment. McCune (1974) points out that political rather than educational factors increase in importance when professional planning skills are missing. *If schools are to become viable self-renewing institutions, decision makers in schools must achieve a better understanding and acceptance of the strategies and tactics that can be and are being used to promote change.* The next sections present and describe the array of strategies available to educational change planners.

TYPES OF CHANGE STRATEGIES

A change strategy is an approach taken to mediate appropriate change behavior by relevant actors. A review of the change literature produces three basic types: power, manipulative, and rational approaches.

In a sense, the distinction is artifical, since educational change depends on certain fundamental processes and always involves rewards and/or punishments, communication, and some configuring of the environment. However, specific approaches differ in the nature of motivating forces and specific activities emphasized. Power strategies are based on the offer or application of basic rewards and punishments; manipulative strategies involve a deliberate arranging of messages and/or aspects of the environment; and rational strategies involve transmitting high-fidelity messages that justify change.

Of the three kinds of approaches, *power strategies* are perhaps easiest to apply. These strategies are based on control of rewards and punishments, deprivation and restrictions, which are meaningful to individuals or groups who are important actors in the change process. Their satisfaction, comfort, prestige, mobility, and so forth are made contingent on appropriate change behavior.

The exercise of power may involve positive rewards for change behavior or negative outcomes for inappropriate behavior or apathy. The influencing agent may derive his power from control over funding, from legal sanctions—even from status considerations.* He has some control over something wanted or needed—either because he can give it, withhold it, or can take it away.

---

*It is interesting to note that the process may also be reciprocal. Smith and Sandler (1974) recently presented cases that show status being derived from power. In these cases, teachers confer highest status to colleagues who are seen as having social power or influence over others.

The notable aspect of power strategies is that the reason for compliance or motivation for change does not lie in the nature of the change itself or even in anything meaningfully related to it; rather, it is related to the change object and change process on a contingency basis. The activities emphasized in a power strategy include communication about the relevant rewards and punishments and about the specific behavior on which they depend.

Some power tactics used in education include passing bills or laws to force change; withholding funding; having change directions come from legitimate leaders; providing material rewards; and offering prestige or satisfaction.

The success of a power strategy rests on the extent to which the sources of power are really valued or important or compelling. The individual or group involved must be sufficiently motivated, and ultimately the strategy depends on the willingness of individuals to carry out the specified behavior. Even legal sanctions are ineffective if the target is more willing to be jailed or fined than he is to carry out the behavior. Hierarchy tactics won't work if the threat of losing one's job is inconsequential. Similarly, if rewards for change behavior are not sufficiently compelling, a power strategy based on them will be ineffective.

Manipulative strategies are based on some measure of control over features of the change environment. They involve manipulating some aspect of the change environment so that the target comes to see the situation differently—that is, as favorable or more favorable to the change effort. He is persuaded that the change is a good course of action and/or change-related behavior is made more appropriate. Often, the change planner tries to effectively structure a "biased message" urging change (Zaltman 1972). However, we include here facilitative approaches, whereby other aspects of the environment may be manipulated so that the desirability or ease of change is more strongly indicated.

Unlike power strategies, manipulative strategies use motivators that are meaningfully tied to the change itself. Thus, where monetary rewards are contingent on change, this is a power tactic; where funding is provided to help implement change (e.g., Title III), this is a manipulative tactic. It follows that manipulative tactics are more generally supportive of change—in effect, they serve a double-barreled purpose. They are useful for mediating change-related behavior, and they are compatible with and supportive of it as well.

Activities to implement manipulative strategies are concerned with rearranging, biasing, adding to, or subtracting from the environment. The change planner's influence depends on his own skills in doing this rather than on his control over rewards and punishments.

Examples of tactics to implement manipulative strategies include product development (making available materials that can be used for change), persuasive communications (advertising, promotion), and training (to impart skills necessary for or facilitative of change). In product development, the intent is to add something to the environment that makes it more compatible with a particular change. For example, to get teachers to begin using more effective questioning skills, provide them with a minicourse that teaches those skills. Persuasive communications involve presenting messages that are biased toward change because of their content (e.g., emotional versus rational appeal, one- versus two-sided message, arguments emphasized) or because of their structure (e.g., order of presentation, use of distraction, testimonial, establishment of pleasant associations). Training, again, is carried out with the intent of adding to or subtracting from the change environment— in this case, by establishing new skills and attitudes and perhaps extinguishing old behaviors. An important manipulative approach is represented by organizational development (OD) as a strategy for social change. Here the approach is to change social norms and values, to create a "culture that institutionalizes the use of various social technologies to regulate change." (Hornstein et al. 1971.)

The success of a manipulative strategy rests on the strategist's knowledge of the target system as well as on his skill in manipulating the environment to favor change.

Rational or reason strategies form a third group. These are based on the nature of the change itself—the extent to which it appears to the user that change is in his own best interest. The strategist provides justification for change.

Like manipulative strategies, rational strategies depend on getting the user to accept change for itself rather than for some other reason (as with power strategies). Rational strategies could be considered a subclass of manipulative strategies in that they involve selecting and structuring messages to promote change. They are distinguished here because the motivating force behind "rational change" is more closely tied to the change itself—that is, the motivating force *is* the change. The target perceives that change is in his own best interests.

Rational strategies emphasize activities that involve communication about the nature of the change and why it is justified. It is important that messages have high fidelity and that they are attended to by important change actors. Thus, the activities stressed are those relevant to providing evidence to support change and transmitting high-fidelity messages about that evidence.

Tactics used to mediate change through appeals to reason include education (preservice and in-service training), knowledge production and information dissemination, demonstrations, and field agents (to fit change to needs). If education is used to implement a rational strategy, the approach is to present evidence for change in a classroom or training context—in graduate school or workshops or seminars, for example, where data and arguments for change are provided. Much change in education occurs in this way; as in other fields, young or recent graduates are frequently most receptive to change (Havelock et al. 1971). Part of the dissemination program for the innovative Human Sciences Program for grades six through nine is "to provide preservice teachers experiences with the philosophy and rationale, and the content and pedagogy for teaching emerging adolescents, utilizing the Human Sciences Program as an example..." (Eckenrod 1975).

Knowledge building and dissemination of information about new findings are two parts of a complex process that has received much support as a rational tactic for educational change. Here the belief is that legitimate needs are being addressed and, if communication channels are adequate, practitioners will themselves initiate changes.

Obviously, rational strategies depend for their success on the quality of the change itself: if target needs are addressed and relevant incentives made salient, if competing forces are not stronger, and if evidence to this effect is communicated, a strategy based on reason will be successful. Further, since attitudes and beliefs favorable to change are internalized, later change stages are favored. Since the motivating force is the change itself, there can be no removal of that force, as is possible with power and manipulative strategies.

Other Classifications   Classifications by other investigators have sometimes included more or fewer types, or have given the types somewhat different emphases, but they tend to follow along the same lines—in effect, those of Kelman's (1961) three processes of social influence: compliance, identification, and internalization. Change behavior of individuals or groups is mediated by application of rewards or punishments, by associating the change with another influencing agent, or by communicating the value of the change itself. Thus, Kester and Hull (1973) distinguish among coercive, persuasive, and informative educational change strategies. Coercive strategies are based on threats or application of rewards and punishments. In education, schools may be "coerced" into integrating classrooms through a threat of reprisals for noncompliance. Persuasive strategies are based on attractive associations or manipulations involving the change and something else. School integration is also promoted through attempts at attitude change and through developing a more conducive, encouraging, and constructive context for integration. (The General Assistance Centers funded under Title IV of the Civil Rights Act are meant to provide support services such as consultants and workshops to assist school districts as they desegregate.) Informative strategies are based on providing facts about change. Many educational researchers felt that disposing of the separate-but-equal fallacy would be convincing enough to mediate voluntary school integration or at least acceptance of mandated integration.

A 1967 breakdown presented by Guba develops several approaches for each kind of basic strategy. He proposes a typology based on the appeals made to the potential changer. A value strategy uses appeal to values as they relate to the substance of the change. A rational strategy involves presenting evidence and logical argument in favor of change. A didactic strategy involves imparting the skills and knowledge needed to change. A psychological strategy manipulates the potential changer's needs for acceptance and involvement. An economic strategy is based on control of resources and compensation. A political strategy involves influence through conflict and compromise. And an authority strategy involves influencing subordinates.

The authority and economic strategies are examples of change based on the consideration of punishments or rewards. In schools, teachers usually go along with district adoptions, since they perceive that the district office has authority over them. Moreover, they frequently acquire continued schooling solely for the gain in salary that this can represent for them.

Value strategies and rational strategies assume that change will occur when evidence of its value is presented. In education, this has been how some changes have come about—the widespread adoption of new math, for example, or the general acceptance of the philosophy of individualized instruction (although adoption and sustained implementation of a program of individualized instruction usually requires extensive training, reorganization, and other facilitative tactics as well).

Didactic strategies also follow this line, but with an emphasis on the learning or relearning that must occur. For example, teachers may accept the philosophy of individualized instruction but may not be able to implement it without formal training. A didactic strategy would make some provision for formal training.

Psychological and political strategies suggest manipulation. Resistant parents may come to accept busing if they can be convinced not only that it is necessary for equal opportunity but also that it will bring benefits to their own children that did not exist before. Principals may adopt new practices to compromise with other schools in the district; teachers may teach particular content because they are provided with ready-made, useful materials. The strategist relies on appeals rather than commands, and the appeals are based on what he knows about the values and motivation of those who are to participate in change.

The usefulness of Guba's typology lies in its suggestiveness with regard to the relevant motivations for educational change: the potential changer may be motivated by the value of the change itself, or by secondary characteristics of the change (e.g., how easy it is to implement), or by the contingency relationship between the change and other rewards or punishments.

Another typology (Chin 1967) distinguishes among empirical-rational, normative-reeducative, and power strategies. In a further development of this typology, Chin and Benne (1969) outline the assumptions relevant to each category. Empirical-rational strategies rely on (1) the ability of the agent to demonstrate that change itself is desirable and (2) the assumption that people are guided by reason and will follow their rational self-interest, that is, will do what is desirable. Rational people adopt changes that they see as effective and desirable. An important example of a reliance on the assumptions basic to empirical-rational strategies is that of supporting educational research and knowledge building. The belief is that good ideas will be used to improve education.

In the second type of strategy, change occurs with changes in normative orientations to the environment. Normative-reeducative strategists assume that people are motivated by basic needs and that change is centered in a social as opposed to an individual environment. "Changes in patterns of action or practice are, therefore, changes, not alone in the rational informational equipment of men, but at the personal level, in habits and values as well and, at the sociocultural level, changes are alterations in normative structures and in institutionalized roles and relationships, as well as in cognitive and perceptual orientations'' (p. 43).

An example of a normative-reeducative strategy is to improve, by training or by supplying materials, the target's capability of implementing the change in question. When the people and/or the environment are thus altered, the change will occur. The OD approach described earlier is an example of this. Research for Better Schools, Inc., employs strategies based on this kind of assumption, namely, that ''significant educational improvement will result from improving the competencies of . . .personnel'' (Scanlon 1973).

Power-coercive strategies involve the use of political, economic, and moral sanctions. ''The influence process is basically that of compliance of those with less power to the plans, directions, and leadership of those with greater power'' (Chin and Benne, 1969: p. 34). There are many examples in education of this strategy. Teacher strikes depend on political and moral support; legislation for racial or financial balancing depends on political and economic support; implementation of district adoptions depends on economic support.

Jones (1969) describes six strategy types, including three basic strategies described earlier by Niaz (1963) and three made by pairing the basic strategies. In the Jones typology, a coercive strategy mediates compliance through pressure or force that relates directly to the satisfactions, comforts, and mobility of the change. As with the Chin and Benne power-coercive strategy, there is no need to relate incentives to change goals, except on a contingency basis. A normative strategy involves getting actors to change by convincing them of the benefits of change. Here the motivation to change rests directly in the change itself. This is akin to the Chin and Benne rational strategy and Guba's value and rational strategies. A utilitarian strategy involves the manipulating of material rewards to shape behavior. This is the more positive version of a coercive strategy, in which change is motivated by outside factors, but in this case the factors are remunerative rather than coercive. Six strategy variations evolve, depending on whether and how two of the three general approaches are combined. For example, a coercive-utilitarian strategy would apply pressure by manipulating rewards, as when teachers implement programs mandated by the district in order to achieve favor from authority figures.

Zaltman (1972) uses four categories: (1) power strategies, which involve the use or threat of force; (2) persuasive strategies, which like the normative and utilitarian strategies described above involve the manipulation of messages, rewards, or symbols to urge acceptance of change; (3) reeducative strategies, which involve the communication of facts about change; (4) and facilitative strategies, which involve increasing the ease with which the change can be implemented.

In this analysis, persuasive strategies involve ''bias in the structuring and presentation of a message'' (p. 86). They differ from reeducative strategies, which are more like the empirical-rational strategies described by Chin and Benne, and from facilitative strategies, which are used with targets already predisposed to change but in need of more receptivity or supportiveness in the environment.

In education, persuasive strategies may be used for a variety of change problems. Voters may pass bond issues if they associate a yes vote with a particular favored political candidate; many times teachers adopt new practices because of slick promotion using a bandwagon appeal; a district may adopt a new organizational arrangement because influential decision makers are persuaded that it will ultimately give them more autonomy or influence. Reeducative strategies may also use promotional tactics, but the emphasis here is on communication of facts: educators change old ideas and develop new ones either because of logical arguments or because of some data base supporting change. Reeducative strategies include the rational strategies so far described, plus training or sensitivity-group approaches. Examples of facilitative strategies include provision of materials or funding for implementing change and organizational development for a more supportive change climate.

Obviously, the four types of strategies can be mutually reinforcing rather than exclusive. For example, persuasive tactics may be used to initiate a reeducative strategy that in turn promotes a more supportive climate for change. Or power tactics may be preceded by persuasive tactics to give the threat of force increased salience. Or a facilitative strategy may be followed up by a reeducative strategy so that whatever has been done to ease change implementation is brought to the awareness of the target group. As an example, the product-development strategy so strongly supported for educational reform in the late 1960s has required subsequent promotional efforts in order to bring the fruits of development to the attention of potential users.

Other investigators use similar distinctions and descriptions. Sieber (1968) differentiates among strategies that demand different extents of motivation from participants. "Rational man" strategies are most demanding, "powerless participant" strategies are least demanding, and "cooperation" strategies are somewhere in between. If the changer is depended on to be rational, he is expected to take the initiative in responding to change directives or information. Or, if powerless, he may be totally manipulated, responding as he has to, regardless of how he feels. Most change efforts are somewhere in between, in which case the target takes some but not all of the initiative and responsibility for change. In such a case, facilitative tactics are highly appropriate, but the target also changes because of new knowledge, new attitudes, or pressure. The Research for Better Schools approach referred to earlier is mostly facilitative (in that it improves competency), but it also relies on a data network to provide information to motivate change.

Walton (1965) divides strategies for social change into a power category and an attitude category, noting that the former involves force while the latter is based on favorable interpersonal influences. Again, the distinction is between strategies that involve involuntary adoption of change and those that involve voluntary change.

All of the classifications we have reviewed can be represented as power, manipulative, or rational approaches, as shown in table 3-2.

Types of Change Tactics   Other classifications are offered, but they emerge as typologies more relevant to the specific *tactics* chosen to implement broad strategies. Thus, Rosenau (1974) distinguishes among personal, interpersonal, and impersonal change tactics. Each kind of tactic can be used in implementing power, persuasive, or rational strategies. For example, both a rational and a power strategy may involve an impersonal tactic such as informing the target system by direct mail of a new practice; the difference would be in the force for compliance with the practice rather than with the tactic used. With the power strategy, the message would include information about sanctions; with the rational strategy, it would provide evidence or justification for change.

Warwick and Kelman's (1973) "strategies" for overcoming resistance are actually specific activities that may be used in any of the broad strategy types. For example, they mention removing social supports for existing behavior patterns, a tactic that can occur as part of a coercive strategy, or through persuasion or communication of fact. Miles's (1964) typology is based on two dimensions of tactics: locus of change initiation (within or without) and use of existing versus new structures. Guba (1967) delineates basic tactic variations: show/tell/help/ involve/train/intervene. Katz and Kahn (1966) offer six categories of techniques for change: information, counseling and therapy, peer group influence, sensitivity training, group therapy, feedback and group discussion, and systemic change.

A Benzen and Tye (1972) five-part classification actually consists of one category—political strategies—that describes approaches based on several of the strategy types, and four categories—personnel, systems planning, alternative schools, and mass communication—that describe tactics for implementing strategies. Political "strategies" involve power over rewards and punishments to motivate change, and conflict to catalyze change. The Benzen and Tye political strategy can take on the dominant features of Guba's economic, political, and authority strategies, Chin and Benne's normative-reeducative and power-coercive strategies, and Jones's coercive and utilitarian strategies, in that there is the assumption that a changer will not automatically see that change is in his own best interests. The difference is that the Benzen and Tye category emphasizes the processes involved in tying together change behavior and relevant incentives.

The second category, personnel strategies, really refers to a class of tactics particularly useful for implementing a normative strategy—that is, tactics of imparting skills and knowledge necessary for or facilitative of change. The remaining categories of systems planning, alternative schooling, and mass communication also describe more specific tactics for achieving change. Systems planning is essentially a rational tactic, while alternative schooling and mass

TABLE 3.2. A Typology of Change Strategies

	POWER	MANIPULATIVE	RATIONAL
Strategy Type:	(threat/application of rewards and punishments)	(rearranging features of environment)	(communicating the justification for change)
Examples:	Guba's economic, political, and authority strategies	Guba's didactic and psychological strategies	Guba's value and rational strategies
	Chin & Benne's power-coercive	Chin & Benne's normative	Chin & Benne's empirical-rational
	Niaz/Jones's coercive-utilitarian	Niaz/Jones's utilitarian	Niaz/Jones's normative
	Sieber's "powerless participant"	Sieber's "cooperation"	Sieber's "rational man"
	Walton's power	Walton's attitude	
	Zaltman's power	Zaltman's persuasive & facilitative	Zaltman's reeducative
	Kester & Hull's coercive	Kester & Hull's persuasive	Kester & Hull's informative
Examples of Tactics:	Legal sanctions (e.g., court-ordered busing)	Advertising	In-service training
	Withholding funds	Product development	Publicity
	Rewards (e.g., university credit)	Stress induction	Action research
	Hierarchy (e.g., district mandates)	Testimonial	Goal setting

communication are more usually normative-reeducative tactics. The point of the Benzen and Tye classification is not to be comprehensive but to focus on strategies that are internally controlled, effective, and rational. As they put it, "All of the change strategies which have been widely accepted [in the past] for working with schools proceed from the same fundamental definition of the task to be accomplished: some identified body of knowledge must be transmitted from an outside source to the schools in such a form that the schools will use it (p. 87)." A more contemporary approach places the emphasis on the school itself and calls for strategies in which change is initiated and controlled from within.

Presenting these schemes illustrates the relationship of tactics to strategy. That is, in general, particular tactics might be employed to implement any of the broad strategies; and in fact it is likely that in studying different strategies we can observe the same tactics being used. Certain tactics may be more useful for one of the broad strategy types, but essentially they are the "tools" the strategist has available regardless of the broad approach he decides to use.

CONSIDERATIONS FOR STRATEGY DEVELOPMENT

The three types of approaches to change or change strategies differ in a number of requirements that have important implications for the strategist. Four of these are discussed here.

Knowledge of the User System   All three strategy types require some knowledge of the target system, but in general, manipulative strategies require more sensitivity regarding its motivations, values, needs, and resources. A rational strategy requires that the planner be able to identify target groups whose needs are met by the innovation. A power strategy requires some feeling for basic desires, fears, or needs that may motivate target groups—but this is likely to be knowledge that is general enough to apply to any group.

Power and rational strategies share the "strength" that they may often be externally imposed without heavy investment in learning about the target system. Even internally initiated change may require more knowledge than it is feasible to get if a manipulative strategy is used. The knowledge required for successful structuring of the environment is usually subtle and detailed. Thus, if important knowledge about the target system is difficult to acquire (as it often is when change is being externally imposed), a manipulative strategy could easily fail. A weakness of manipulative strategies from the planner's point of view is that successful implementation is dependent on spending considerable time and having sufficient sensitivity to be maximally familiar with the system.

In education, the product-development approach to reform and change has suffered from this basic weakness. Developers learned the hard way that meaningful involvement of potential users, buyers, and facilitators is crucial to successful product design (Turnbull et al. 1974). Those who have developed products have often overlooked important facts about potential users, such as the adequacy and nature of their financial resources, the fears and status considerations that motivate them, and their abilities and concerns. Additionally, persuasive messages are sometimes sent to the wrong decision makers; educational products are made too expensive for schools to adopt; and training is offered at inappropriate times.

Power strategies and rational strategies are often less costly than manipulative strategies because less needs to be learned about the target system. Activating a hierarchy of authority (a power approach) requires less specific knowledge than involving all levels in a decision (a manipulative approach); issuing mandates is more straightforward than targeting persuasive communications; and applying or withholding basic rewards such as money or prestige is a simpler matter than establishing meaningful associations between complex innovations and user needs and goals.

Commitment to Change   All change strategies require some commitment on the part of relevant individual actors and groups. The basis for this commitment is different in each of the three types of strategies.

In the case of power strategies, the changer is committed to change because there is some other goal attached to it. His primary commitment is to that other goal. Manipulative strategies mediate some commitment to the change itself, but this is based on the fact that the desired behavior has what Warwick and Kelman (1973) refer to as "prepotency," or unique relevance in the situation. The change itself is favored because other, related goals are favored. Rational strategies mediate commitment to the change itself. There is evidence that the change is in the best interests of the changer, regardless of related goals.

Thus, many schools comply with integration guidelines not because of a general commitment to integrated schooling, but because of a commitment to continued federal support and to peaceful conduct of daily activities. This duality of motivations is characteristic of what is going on to make a power strategy work. It also is one potential source of unintended consequences. When the issue is sufficiently important to the persons involved, those who find themselves complying may feel guilt, anger, and frustration. They have been placed in a dilemma, the resolution of which can reflect on their own integrity. Some of education's most bitter episodes have resulted from placing persons in such a dilemma. Busing is a prime example. Instead of merely keeping their own children home, resisters have sometimes gone further to support their own position by overturning buses or picketing to force others to take the same position. Much bitterness derives from an inability to reconcile one's behavior with the more worthy goal—that of improved schooling—as opposed to a personal, more basic goal—that of isolating one's own children.

Where change occurs because the environment has been made more conducive to change, such goal conflict is less likely. Persons involved are given a more dignified choice—they may comply because of considerations that are somewhat separate from the substance of the change itself, but the considerations are related and compatible with change. The push for computer-assisted instruction has given educators many outside reasons to adopt the practice—increased status and increased funding, for example. However, these can be achieved through behavior that is acceptable and, in fact, freely chosen.

With a rational strategy, there should be no conflict of commitments. Change is adopted because it is something to which a commitment is attached. When change occurs this way, as with the slow but ultimately widespread adoption of the philosophy of individualization, the process has been strongly, often unequivocally, supported—such that it becomes the way of things and not really debatable.

The basis for commitment has implications for the success of a change strategy. Where the individual is seeking other rewards (as with a power strategy), his change-related behavior will last only as long as those rewards remain important and unattained. If he is avoiding punishment, his change behavior depends on vigilance on the part of the influencing agent. Thus, the change-related behavior will be unstable.

Where there is commitment to the change itself, change behavior is self-motivating and can be expected to be more stable. "It becomes relatively independent of the original source and . . . tends to be more idiosyncratic, more flexible, and more complex" (Kelman and Warwick 1973).

If the commitment depends on the fact that the agent has somehow manipulated the change environment so that a specific change is favored, it is more fickle than commitment mediated by a rational strategy, but the threat to change behavior comes from some (presumably) superior competitor.

When commitment is tied directly to the change itself, the participant has made a choice and is thus subject to dissonance if other factors in the environment are inconsistent with it. This can be expected to result in his taking the initiative himself to somehow justify that choice and restructure other aspects of the environment to pull them in line. If a particular course of action has been chosen at least in part because it appears best in a given situation, as with a manipulative strategy, probably it is easier for the changer to abandon that course than when it has been chosen because of its unique value, as with a rational strategy. In short, where actors change because they choose to, they will attend to information supportive of the change (Festinger 1957). For example, a Chicago school building staff readily adopted Individually Guided Education when they were moved to a new building designed for nongraded instruction; but they also quickly adapted or abandoned parts of that program when new forms of instruction suitable to the building were made available. In contrast, many other IGE schools in the same area have implemented the arrangement much more faithfully, apparently screening out or rejecting messages about new instructional forms adopted by the first school. In the first case, decision makers were committed to anything that fit well into the new environment, while in the other schools, the commitment was to the program itself. It follows that the first school was more open to information "against" IGE but "for" the new environment.

In sum, the more closely the commitment to change is based on the change itself, the more self-sustaining will be the resultant change behavior.

Motivation for Change   The individual actors in change must perceive that their behavior leads to some kind of satisfaction, or to avoidance of punishment. It has already been noted that the three types of strategies will differ in the basis for compliance or acceptance of change. With power strategies, the motivators involved have no meaningful relationship to the change itself; with manipulative strategies, motivators are meaningfully related; and with rational strategies, the substance of the change itself is the motivator. .

The investment represented by particular rewards and punishments is multiplied if motivators are tied to change in a meaningful way. Thus, providing educators with skills that are relevant to individualizing instruction promotes the possibility that individualizing will occur. Moreover, use of the skills is supportive of communication and selective perception favorable to continued change. This is not so likely to be the case where the same use of skills is carried out to achieve, for example, monetary reward or university credit (unrelated motivators).

Thus, where a power strategy may frequently be easiest and cheapest to apply, in the long run it may not be as cost-effective as a manipulative or rational strategy where actual application of rewards or withholding of punishment are in themselves supportive of change.

The strength of manipulative strategies is this tying of motivators to change itself. For example, the Defense Civil Preparedness Agency has had little problem seeing that public schools have some kind of civil defense plan, since many schools have a state or district mandate for this (a power strategy). However, when the agency distributed highly attractive manuals for preparedness instruction, schools began developing imaginative, effective in-school programs for going beyond basic civil defense plans to achieve interest in and learning of relevant concepts, rationale, and so forth (Altman and Sikorski 1975). Where the mandate resulted in the minimum possible response, the distribution of manuals encouraged self-renewing internally generated programs.

Appropriate Settings   It should by now be clear that any of the three approaches can be applied in various settings, but they do have some characteristic strengths and weaknesses.

Power strategies that involve force or pressure—that are based on threat or application of negative sanctions—are used when it is felt, either by outsiders or by insiders, that it will be difficult or impossible to have participants agree on the form change should take. Many believe, for example, that schools will never be persuaded to implement continuous and effective systems of accountability. California's Stull Bill is a move to reform teacher evaluation procedures regardless of how teachers themselves feel. Legal sanctions have been applied to force parents to send children to school and to cooperate with integration plans. Within school systems, change in schools is frequently mandated by the district office.

External or internal change planners and managers may use the tactic of withholding rewards if it is felt that schools won't change simply because change is seen as inherently valuable. Government funding may be withheld when schools fail to meet standards for integration, for example.

Positive rewards for particular behaviors are widely used in education. States have allocated federal money according to the number of "disadvantaged" students schools can muster; teachers are offered credit or honoraria for participating in workshops and seminars; "innovative" principals and administrators are invited to speak at national meetings and conferences.

When the power strategist has control over factors that are sufficiently motivating, he can achieve dramatic results even with severe time and resource constraints. In fact, situations where change must occur rapidly and/or where resources available to the change agent are limited constitute one of two kinds of settings in which a power strategy is strongly indicated (Niaz 1963; Jones 1969; Zaltman 1973). The second is the situation in which the incentives systems and values of the target group are so opposed to the change that the strategist decides it is more cost-effective to change behavior first, and hope that attitude changes will follow (Niaz 1963; Warwick and Kelman 1973).

The weakness of power strategies lies in the tenuous link between incentives for changing and the change itself. If the participant already relates his behavior only to the source of power, he will abandon it if that source is removed. However, where there is no problem in establishing and maintaining vigilance, commitment to the change itself may be unnecessary and in fact too costly and time-consuming to obtain.

Rational strategies are most appropriate where a performance gap is clear and failure to change is due mainly to a lack of knowledge about alternatives. Such settings are perhaps more rare than would at first be believed. "New knowledge and technology, however pertinent they may be to educational operations, can produce change only if put to work. As contrasted to other fields, education is slow to adopt new discoveries to modify practice" (Stiles and Robinson, 1973).

Educational research has always been regarded as an important way to improve educational practice; it is only in the past decade that researchers have come to grips with the problem that informing practitioners about alternatives is rarely enough to produce change.

Rational strategies will work best in settings in which target-system goals are well defined and generally accepted by different factions. Communication channels must be open and the relationship between change and target-system goals must be clear and communicable. In addition, the means to implement change must be clear and must be feasible.

Sometimes, such settings exist so that, at the right time and the right place, changes are agreed upon and easily implemented by some user system. A good example is the setting for the adoption and use of the current civil defense manuals referred to earlier. In each state studied, materials relevant to local disasters were immediately incorporated into the curriculum. In Mississippi, for example, where severe natural disasters are fairly commonplace, extensive programs have been implemented. Here is a case in which there is widespread agreement regarding a problem that is clearly addressed by the new materials. So long as potential users were made aware of their availability, the materials were used extensively and successfully, and schools were changed as a result (Altman and Sikorski 1975).

However, educational change is almost always far more complex than this. Baldridge (1974:9) points out that most educational innovations of the sixties "have not been of such a specific technical nature that they can be easily understood and readily articulated into the framework of the ongoing educational enterprise." In addition, as mentioned earlier, consensus and clear-cut goals do not usually exist; even where they do, appropriate linkages for tying available means to desired ends do not always exist.

Clarity of goals, a realistic assessment of present conditions, and a feeling for the discrepancy between them do not characterize most educational institutions (Miles 1965; Sieber 1968; Gideonse 1974; Crandall 1974). In short, the appropriate setting for a purely rational strategy is rare.

Probably the most generally appropriate strategies in education are those that we are calling manipulative. In most situations, there will be strong forces both for and against change. There has been some tendency to focus on one or the other exclusively. Thus, power strategists frequently concentrate on overcoming resistance, while rational strategists try to mobilize certain forces for change. The early proponents of educational research as a stimulus for effective change are now considered to have erred by overlooking resistances. On the other hand, Defense Civil Preparedness Agency officials are now learning that there are powerful forces for voluntary change that they have overlooked in their dependence on mandated change. The strategies we are terming manipulative must take into account the various forces for change, if they are to capitalize on them, and the forces against change, if they are to dissolve or mitigate them. In most educational settings, meaningful change will be complex and difficult and ultimately will depend on cooperation from many levels within the system. Many resistances that seem irrational are actually quite legitimate, given the nature of the system. Stiles and Robinson (1973) point out that it is usually more rewarding for educational practitioners to wait for change to be initiated by some other force before adopting it. "Only when the changes espoused are successful...does the heretic have a chance of surviving professionally." (p. 260).

In addition, resistance may be due to having been burned too often. Many products have not been what was promised. There are internal as well as external reasons for this. In the rush to adopt innovative-appearing products without incurring real risks, educators have often failed to give adequate consideration to their substance. As Sieber (1973) puts it, "this would seem to be the case in education, where faddish jargon and shortlived innovations are frequently encountered (p. 4).'' In the middle and late sixties, audiovisual media were widely adopted, at great expense but frequently with dubious outcomes, more because of the visibility and impact of the innovation itself rather than from a clear conception of what could be done with instructional media. Pierce (1974) points out that this kind of adoption, without knowledge of why an idea may succeed or fail, is inevitably dangerous and helps to account for the ''credibility gap'' between the schools and the public.

Power strategies may be effective, but in education, where professionalism is so fragile, they are very likely to be resented. And considering the complexity of most educational change, they do not provide for the participation and cooperation required to implement continued changes. Sabotage and subversion are important forms of resistance to power strategies.

Manipulative strategies recognize that changers won't automatically accept change as being in their own best interest but also that they will accept change when the environment is conducive. Manipulative strategies aim at structuring and restructuring the environment to achieve this—to capitalize on forces for change and to deal effectively with forces against it.

Strategy Development in the Self-Renewing School

Schools have typically been in a reactive relationship with the environment as regards change and reform. For a number of reasons discussed earlier, educational practitioners have found this to be professionally more comfortable. One of the most important reasons has been the structure of rewards for conservative behavior and high cost for failure. Stiles and Robinson (1973:262) describe ''a system of tenure that protects incompetence but not the leader for change; a loose conception of academic freedom that allows no challenge to the teacher; and a subtle system for indoctrination of new members to accept and defend the status quo.''

Part of the contention here is that, rather than avoid failure by avoiding change, school decision makers should reduce the possibilities for failure by incorporating into their schools systematic and effective change-management procedures. In effect, this would act not to change incentive systems to favor risk, but rather to reduce risk, and an important ingredient for success would be the capability of creating effective and appropriate change strategies.

It is important for the educational change planner to be aware of the alternatives to what has been done in the past to create change, and to be able to judge conditions and contexts for the successful uses of alternative strategies. Development of this ability is a necessary part of building a capacity for renewal within schools.

It is particularly appropriate that change strategies be developed from within, since the success of a strategy usually depends in great measure on a knowledge of the relevant resources, constraints, motivations, and resistances of the target system. Watson (1974:148) points out that "the practitioner who occupies a powerful position in the educational system may be the person with the greatest potential for becoming a change agent."

Since the strategy-development process must be a creative part of planning, there should be a minimum of antagonism or conflict among planners. Again, this argues for an internally generated process, minimizing a natural resistance to intervention from outside.

A recent paper (Far West Laboratory 1974) on the factors related to building change capabilities in schools makes the point that "practitioners in education are professionals. . . . Change in education cannot be dictated but can emerge only through self-determined change in practitioner behavior." Further, "part of the knowledge and skills needed to plan and implement change is . . . uniquely possessed by practitioners in the field." Change must come from within; the effectiveness of change will depend on internal planners' knowledge and skills relevant to change management and strategy development.

However, self-renewing organizations are not parochial institutions that must rely solely on internal energy, ideas, and resources for development. Rather, they are outward-reaching systems, dynamically interacting with their environments. There are environmental resources available to educational organizations, and, as pointed out in this chapter, many organizations are actively working to bring those resources to educational organizations. Building a self-renewing capacity involves knowing when outside resources are necessary and when those resources are inappropriate or in violation of the purposes of the organization.

The next chapter describes change tactics traditionally used by external change planners. They are presented so that internal planners as well can develop some understanding of and skill in their application.

Summary

Models of social-change processes are categorized as environmental, organizational, authoritative/participative, and individual-oriented. The first category includes models which consider that organizational change results from changes in external social conditions. These include Levin's polity model and Stiles and Robinson's political process model.

Organizational change models are primarily concerned with group processes and phenomena of change. The Zaltman, Duncan, and Holbek model considers the effects of the internal environment of the organization on the stages of the change process. The survey feedback–problem solving–collective decision model is an internal problem-solving perspective for change in organizations.

Authoritative/participative models emphasize the locus of authority. Rogers and Shoemaker describe the authority innovative decision and the collective innovative decision, the latter implying decision making at all levels of the adopting unit. Bennis offers a range of change types from totally collaborative to totally noncollaborative.

Individual-oriented models focus on the cognitive process of individual decision makers as they move from awareness to adoption/rejection or adaptation of change.

Other models that do not fall conveniently into one of the four categories are research, development, and diffusion models and the Lippitt, Watson, and Westley problem solving model. A review of the variety of models presented makes evident the need for a synthesis model, one that addresses the various levels involved in change and that accounts for both externally and internally initiated change processes.

Models of change describe or perhaps prescribe in a formal way the general process of change. When the planner begins to outline an approach for actually executing change, his mode becomes strategic. A strategy, the approach taken to mediate appropriate change behavior by relevant actors, can be categorized as a power strategy, a manipulative strategy, or a rational strategy. The types differ mainly in the motivation or basis for change. Power strategies are based on the strategist's control over basic rewards and punishments. Manipulative strategies are based on the strategist's control over features of the environment that can be arranged or rearranged to favor change. Rational strategies depend for their success on the change target's perceiving that the change per se is in his own best interests.

The strategies differ in several important ways. For instance, manipulative strategies, more than the other two, require knowledge of the target system. Power strategies involve the least commitment to the substance of change, while rational strategies require the most. Power strategies are most useful for quick and dramatic results, rational strategies for situations in which goals and needs are clear, and manipulative strategies for complex situations with conflicting forces for and against change.

Strategy selection involves judging which approach or combination of approaches will be best, given the situational opportunities and constraints.

4

Tactics for Educational Change: Considerations for the Change Planner

IN THE PRECEDING CHAPTER, it was pointed out that the change planner or planning team will probably rely on an approach that uses more than one of the three basic types of strategies, and that the use of each type would be likely to have certain outcomes, depending on the situation in which it was applied.

Regardless of his overall strategy or combination of strategies, the change planner will have to devise or select specific tactics for achieving his goals. That is, he will select and carry out actions that involve change-related information, change targets, and change environments. For example, he may decide to purchase a new math program, or send brochures to teachers advocating a particular practice, or offer a training session to teach individualizing skills, or offer financial incentives for change. These are all examples of change tactics, each of which could be used for implementing one of the three broad strategy types.

The selection or evaluation of tactics to introduce and implement specific changes in education has generally been a casual process. Usually, educational change planners do not know as much as they would like about what innovations or types of innovations disseminated in what manner to what kinds of schools result in educational renewal and reform. A defendable cost-effective framework has not been developed for making decisions about the use of tactics such as demonstrations and information campaigns. Change planners need more information on how to design and modify educational products to maximize their usefulness, and on how to distinguish among potential users for effective targeting and training decisions (Sikorski and Hutchins 1974).

Effective change planning requires more systematic evaluation of available tactics for introducing change or innovations. The various tactics differ in characteristics that have particular implications for their cost-effectiveness, and there are important trade-offs that must be considered when choosing which ones to employ. Additionally, since planners within schools and districts are often the subject of these tactics employed from outside, it is important for them to understand their operations and intent.

This chapter reviews the array of tactics that can be selected to introduce and implement change. It indicates the characteristics or dimensions that can be used to evaluate tactics. A final section presents conclusions regarding their usefulness in particular change situations.

Tactics for the Change Planner

What specific tactics are available for introducing and implementing change? The list is long and varied. To familiarize potential users with new educational technology, the change planner may use workshops, demonstrations, or other information tactics. To obtain commitment, he may assign change roles in school systems to carry out decision making to solve problems. To ensure that change will take a particular direction, he may offer consultation as problem-solving help and specific forms of installation support. To motivate potential changers, he may use direct mail or other print material.

Essentially, there are five kinds of tactics that can be used, singly or in combination. *Information/linkage* tactics stimulate, motivate, or fuel the change effort by providing pertinent information. *Product-development* tactics involve developing or modifying products, the use of which is consistent with a particular change effort. *User-involvement* tactics are aimed at having the potential user commit himself to change through his own behavior and involvement. *Training/installation/support* tactics provide assistance and skills necessary to or facilitative of change. *Legal* tactics set up regulations or arrangements that have the force of law and thereby mandate change.

Many specific tactics could be classified under more than one of the five categories. For example, classes for preschool teacher training are here considered as training tactics; however, preschool classes may also serve to involve trainees in particular reform movements (user involvement) or to mandate change behavior through work assignments (legal) or to provide change-relevant information (information). The divisions here reflect the authors' best judgment regarding the *usual* application of specific tactics. In the case of preschool classes, usually the intent is to develop skills that new teachers will apply when they infiltrate the school system.

INFORMATION/LINKAGE TACTICS

One of the major stumbling blocks to educational renewal and reform is that practitioners and school systems do not have the level of information necessary for motivating or guiding change. Most educational practitioners do not have access to information for maintaining the school as a self-renewing organization.

Usually, the practitioner complains that information is physically inaccessible: "some types of information do not seem to get into print at all and, if they do, they are not easily located or retrieved. . .[and/or are] in unsuitable formats, too lengthy, or not presented in easily understood language" (Hood 1974). In short, the information is poorly targeted.

Chorness et al. (1968*a*) report that educators lack time to find and sort information for themselves, and they therefore use informal, interpersonal sources most often. More recent work continues to confirm this (Hood 1975). This reliance on interpersonal sources is inimical to the rather lonely condition of the education profession, and it is not surprising if practitioners are unable to maintain a knowledge level appropriate for continuous self-renewal. At the individual level, most teachers perform their roles in isolation from other adults; and administrators, although they have more interaction with each other, tend not to have many contacts outside a limited sphere of associates (Smith and Sandler 1974; Stiles and Robinson 1973). Just as practitioners are often isolated within schools, schools and districts are also isolated, if not so much from influence and pressure groups, then from resource systems (Stiles and Robinson 1973).

Much reported research confirms that external contact and openness of an adopting system play an important role in change (Klingenberg 1966; Temkin 1974; Hawkins 1968; Crandall 1972). It seems logical that isolation should work against innovation. Certainly this has been found to be true at the individual level, where innovation adoption tends to follow friendship patterns (Carlson 1965; Eibler 1965; Hughes 1965) and professional meetings and interactions are found to be used more by more innovative individuals (Carlson 1965; Hage and Dewar 1971). On the organizational level, Baldridge (1974) reports research findings confirming that organizations with viable linking mechanisms to their environments adopt more innovations.

Information/linkage tactics are generally considered as sources of information necessary for and/or facilitative of change. However, since they may frequently be combined to set up relationships and channels for breaking down isolation, the term *linkage* is included to emphasize the salience of this function. A linkage system refers to some arrangement of information sources that connects them to the potential user to provide him with guidelines or motivation to change. This is usually a complex arrangement that combines several information tactics, such as field agents, information systems, action research, and workshops.

Among the most important tactics for conveying information are direct mail, advertising, articles/reports/books, demonstrations, salespeople, field agents, telephone use, meetings, action research, confrontation, workshops, information systems, packaging, and training manuals.

Direct mail as defined here involves writing to all or the most important of those who will be involved in change and encouraging them to take a particular action to further the change effort. Direct mail may be relatively selective or undifferentiated. The latter case is obviously more wasteful but perhaps more feasible, since few really meaningful mailing lists exist for educational messages, and those that do exist may be expensive to acquire.

Advertising is defined here as the use of mass media to channel persuasive messages in favor of a particular action. Educational journals and publications may be used, or ads may be placed in the print media, radio, and television. More rare is the use of films to carry a message relevant to change.

Articles, reports, books, and other products of the professional literature are important ways of providing information. The published and nonpublished professional literature differ in their implications for change. For example, information in the published professional literature is likely to be less radical.

Demonstrations take three forms. User-site demonstrations involve the actual implementation of a particular change on a trial basis by a school or district. Demonstration centers are set up to provide demonstrations upon demand. Demonstrations at conferences are traveling displays designed to provide a demonstration at one or more professional conferences.

Salespeople visit potential users to "sell" them on a particular course of action. Field agents represent the same form of tactic, but they generally do not advocate one course of action; their function is more one of technical assistance. Also, they are less likely to offer their services unsolicited.

The telephone may be used as a "hotline" to provide information on demand or for campaigns to persuade receivers to take a particular action.

Meetings, as defined here, are conferences where practitioners gather to exhange ideas or resolve problems.

Action research refers to the tactic of presenting the receiver with results of research on himself or his organization which demonstrate the need for change.

Similarly, confrontations are interactions where the target system receives information pointing out a previously avoided performance gap.

Workshops are meetings between two or more people that are organized primarily to inform and motivate by allowing trainees to observe processes and procedures and to interact with knowledgeable persons.

Information systems are set up to make information about new developments in education available to practitioners. Those systems that work through a field agent are classified as field-agent tactics; the term *information systems* as used here refers to retrieval systems such as ERIC that are available to practitioners as they need to use them.

Packaging is the tactic whereby results of educational research or new educational techniques are changed in form so that they are more appealing and accessible for use. This is usually a product-development technique; however, when it is used simply to improve the cogency of information, it is considered an information tactic.

Training manuals are included among information rather than training tactics, since they have more in common with other information tactics (e.g., published literature, packaging) than with tactics described in a later section as training tactics (e.g., classes).

PRODUCT-DEVELOPMENT TACTICS

Like the commerical marketer, the educational change planner frequently uses a tangible product or definable procedure as the vehicle for change. The rationale is that to use the product or procedure is to implement a specific change.

There are two general product-development tactics: (1) developing a new product or procedure and (2) modifying an existing product or procedure. Variations are different means of making products available.

Studies of educational developments show that the process has usually been systematic but shortsighted. Potential users of products are not consulted early enough or in sufficiently realistic contexts, and resulting product decisions are often wrong (Turnbull et al. 1974). Nevertheless, this is an important means for educational change. Results of educational research are rarely in forms educational practitioners can use; the product-development approach is intended to remedy this problem and thereby promote the use of this knowledge.

The change tactics available in this category include providing all or part of a product at different levels of expense for the user and providing low-cost or free samples.

USER-INVOLVEMENT TACTICS

Innovation is facilitated by the meaningful and early involvement of those who will implement change, and it is seriously hampered when participants are not involved. This point has been well documented in the literature on educational change (see, for example, Fullan and Eastabrook 1973; Widmer 1975; Turnbull et al. 1974; Miller 1974; Lin et al. 1966; Schmuck et al. 1971; Pierce 1974; Blanzy 1974). Studies of R&D products and programs with *high* impact have shown continuous, open communication with user representatives *throughout* the development effort (Turnbull et al. 1974) and the obtaining of early commitment from actual users (Widmer 1975). If the key participants are not meaningfully involved, they may fail to implement change effectively, in certain cases even acting to sabotage it (Hall and Rutherford 1975).

It is not enough to simply consult with or ask the approval of those who will implement change; rather, they must be actively involved in shaping change, there must be real resolution of conflicts and differences, and there needs to be meaningful collaboration among key actors. Studies of school decision making and problem solving (Coney et al. 1968; Chorness et al. 1968a; Mosher 1969;

Carlisle et al. 1971); other research (Miles 1974; Havelock 1974; Miller 1974; McCune 1974); reviews of literature (Chorness et al. 1968b; York 1968,); case studies of the diffusion process (Turnbull et al. 1974); and field tests of practitioner-targeted information packages and systems (Sikorski 1971; Hutchins et al. 1970) indicate that significant educational planning and decision making in schools must be a collaborative effort. This is an important finding, since schools do not typically exhibit "collaborative norms." In recognition of this, organizational development theorists are concerned with creating climates that promote collaboration by maximizing participation and institutionalizing planning capabilities at all levels of school systems (Schmuck and Miles 1971; Schmuck et al. 1972).

User-involvement tactics are actions intended to obtain commitment from those who must implement change by having them participate in the decision-making and trial activities that precede change. One tactic is to require that key actors in change approve the change decision. For example, the developers of the Multiunit school in Wisconsin hold conferences with representatives of all groups who will be affected by adoption of that innovation, to ensure that they will contribute to the initial decision.

A second tactic is to involve potential users in field-testing an educational innovation. This is like a user-site demonstration except that *both* developers and users obtain needed information, and the user-involvement tactic involves the user with the product before it is finished.

A third tactic is to train potential users not only to implement a specific change, but to train others to implement it, so that trainees become trainers. Also, there is the tactic of endorsements, or obtaining early commitments from opinion leaders within a system, so that their leadership ensures fuller participation from others in the system.

Finally, there is the institutionalization of change roles in school systems. A number of investigators make the case that the educational establishment does not now favor risk or innovation, and change participation frequently must be at the expense of spending time accomplishing more accepted goals (see, for example, Stiles & Robinson 1973; Knight and Gorth 1975; Carlson 1965; Baldridge 1974). Thus, change may be promoted where there are incentives and authority patterns relevant to the conduct of change roles.

TRAINING/INSTALLATION/SUPPORT TACTICS

Even at the level of the individual, factors related to innovativeness usually have to do with a person's activity and ability levels and with characteristics such as level of education and job satisfaction (Knight and Gorth 1975). At the organizational level, findings suggest that maturity and experience with innovations are important (Baldridge 1974; Deal 1975; Denham 1971; Widmer 1975). Thus, as noted earlier, typical approaches to the problem of implementation of curriculum stress training (e.g., Tempkin 1974). A set of case studies of change

(Turnbull et al. 1974) provides empirical evidence that training is important; it is stressed that adequate incentives for both trainers and trainees are vitally necessary.

Tempkin and Brown (1974:22) summarize the implication of research in this area as follows:

> R&D delivery strategies aimed at bringing research findings, knowledge and products to the schools have less potential for change than those strategies that emphasize strengthening the capabilities of school districts to actively be responsible for their own improvement.

Training/installation/support tactics include those aimed at facilitating change by ensuring that personnel have the necessary skills, by helping with the installation process, and by monitoring change. In this category, we discuss ten tactics: subsidizing change; helping the system to generate finances; providing training via preservice classes; providing in-service classes on the use of an innovative product or procedure; providing preservice and in-service classes for improved planning skills; providing problem-solving help (consultation); providing a feedback system for monitoring; setting up temporary systems; and network building.

When the stumbling block to change is lack of funds, it may be useful to provide the necessary funding or to assist the school system in generating funding. In fact, this has been found to be effective in getting innovations adopted (Turnbull et al. 1974).

Most complex curriculum innovations involve some training in use of the materials. Where the concern is with developing general change capabilities, training for improved planning skills may be provided. Problems arise in the process of implementing change, and users need a source of help with these problems. Thus, a tactic is to provide free or at a minimal charge consultation and problem-solving help.

Providing a feedback system for monitoring progress is one means of quality control. This allows the change planner to act on information about implementation and, in a meaningful way, guide installation and implementation of innovations.

A temporary system is a nonpermanent arrangement that is a model of what the actual change process will involve.

Network building is a concept from the work of Havelock (1969) that refers to the use of existing relationships of users with each other and with resource systems to provide a medium for diffusion.

LEGAL TACTICS

Change can be mandated, or it can be facilitated by regulations that favor it. This category of tactics includes legal or quasi-legal sanctions for behavior. The simplest legal tactic is that of invoking authority to command change behavior. A second legal tactic is the setting up of a law or regulation requiring the implementation of a specific change. A third related tactic common in education is to get particular materials on the "approved list" of curriculum materials for a state or district.

There is at least one caution in the use of legal tactics such as the first and second: where authority patterns and organizational sanctions are activated to command change behavior, change may not be sustained over time or may be somehow sabotaged by participants (Zaltman 1972; Hall and Rutherford 1975). Where participants are acting not from a commitment to the curriculum innovation but rather to achieve some other reward or to avoid some negative outcome, change behavior will last only so long as the other outcome remains salient; in addition, it may require vigilance over time. In general, then, the motivation for change should include at least some commitment to the change; again, the importance of early and meaningful involvement of users is underscored.

Dimensions for Evaluating Tactics

Considered in a general way, each of these tactics can be characterized on a number of dimensions, such as noise, activity level, and ease of use. Such dimensions relate to the impact or usefulness of the tactic in various kinds of change situations. For example, a "low-activity" or passive information tactic in which interaction must be initiated by the target (e.g., information systems) is likely to be more useful in a change situation where the change stage mediated is evaluation or implementation rather than an early stage such as awareness, since generally the target of a tactic to achieve awareness will not be as likely to initiate the process. As another example, a tactic that is expensive to employ will not be as appropriate when it must be used repeatedly—as with the many different members of a divided audience—as it would in circumstances where one application could reach all or most of the intended target.

If the change planner is to ably evaluate and select from the available array of tactics he must have a clear understanding of the various dimensions he can use to differentiate among them. The dimensions that characterize each tactic determine its usefulness for the different goals, target systems, and change situations that might be encountered.

Table 4-1 rates the various tactics described in earlier pages on sixteen dimensions that have significance for promoting change. Not all dimensions in the table apply meaningfully to each tactic, and many of the tactics can represent more than one value on a dimension. Thus, the analysis is necessarily general; obviously, specific examples or variations of each tactic may be characterized differently. The change planner should be aware of how his unique array of tactics can be rated and what this implies.

The remainder of this section elaborates each dimension and its implications for change goals, situational contexts, unit of adoption, target, and so forth.

STABILITY

Stability refers to the extent to which the tactic, once implemented, is likely to operate in the manner predicted—that is, in the manner intended for it. For example, product development is a fairly stable method for achieving change. Its form and operation are predictable. A less stable tactic is the use of salesmen, since the "pitch" may vary from situation to situation.

Roughly speaking, stability is low if application of the tactic may take a wide variety of forms; medium if the tactic is generally dependable but could take unexpected forms; and high if there is little chance of its taking unexpected forms. Stable messages tend to have high fidelity.

Stability is important where the change planner has less tolerance for risk, where the relevant actors are likely to be hostile or resistant, where there will be only one opportunity to reach the target, or where the unit of change is a divided group in which different members make individual decisions, later coming together for some agreement. Unstable tactics may fail if these kinds of conditions exist.

However, in many change situations, there is the need to retain maximum flexibility and to avoid commitments to specific arguments or messages. In these situations, stable tactics may prove to be dysfunctional, or at least not cost-effective.

For example, stability would be important for a school system wanting to rapidly improve achievement scores in a situation where those who will implement new programs are disorganized and perhaps hostile. In this kind of situation, the system may choose to present clear guidelines for action, without risking misunderstanding or failure. Tactics such as mandating change or adopting a developed curriculum alternative may be selected to ensure rapid, relatively predictable results. In another situation, the system may feel the need for improving scores, but decision makers may not be convinced that any existing solution is exactly right; the interest here would be in shaping change, in moving slowly and developing consensus. Thus, action research, consultation, use of field agents, or other low-stability tactics may be employed to inform, involve, or train participants.

PERSONAL CONTACT

Tactics differ in the extent of in-person contact they involve. In a tactic considered to be "high-personal," one or more persons, *in person,* can be seen to be involved in implementing that tactic. For example, use of a salesperson is a high-personal tactic for conveying information. Obtaining commitment from leadership also involves personal contact, but in general this would be somewhat less "high" on this dimension, since the influence of the leader may be indirect

TABLE 4-1. Dimension of Tactics

Tactics	Stability	Personal Contact	Feedback/Interaction	Activity	Action Implications	Noise
Information/Linkage						
use of direct mail	H	L	L	H	M	L
use of advertising (mass media)	H	L	L	M	M	M
use of articles/reports/books	H	L	L	L-M	L	H
use of demonstrations	M	M	M	M	M-H	M
use of salespeople	L	H	H	H	H	L-M
use of field agents	L	H	H	L-H	L-M	M-H
use of telephone	M	M	M-H	L-H	L-M	L-M
meetings	L	M-H	M-H	L-H	L-M	M-H
action research	M	L	L-M	M	M-H	M-H
confrontation	L	M-H	M-H	M	M-H	L-M
workshops	L-M	M-H	M-H	M	M	M
information systems	H	L	M	L	L	H
packaging	H	L	L	H	H	L
training manuals	H	L	L	M	H	L
Product Development						
provide all of product free	H	L	L	H	H	L
provide part of product free	H	L	L	H	H	L
sell product	H	L	L	M	H	L
sell part of the product	H	L	L	M	H	L
rent all of the product	H	L	L-M	M	H	L
rent part of the product	H	L	L-M	M	H	L
provide samples	H	L	L	H	H	L
User Involvement						
involve in approval	L	M-H	M-H	M	M-H	M-H
involve in field testing	L	M-H	M-H	M	M-H	M
trainees-become-trainers	M	M-H	M-H	M	M-H	L-M
endorsements (leadership)	L-M	M-H	L-M	H	L-M	M
institutionalize change roles	M	M	M	M	M	M
Legal						
invoke authority	M-H	L-M	L	H	H	L
set up law or regulation	H	L	L	H	H	L
approved list	H	L	L	H	M-H	L-M
Training/Installation/Support						
subsidizing change	H	L	L	H	H	L
helping find $	M-H	L-M	M	M	H	L
preservice classes	M	M-H	M-H	M	L-M	H
in-service classes	M-H	M-H	M-H	M	M-H	M
preservice planning	L-M	M-H	M-H	M	L	H
in-service planning	L-M	M-H	M-H	M	L	H
consultation	L	H	H	M	M-H	M
providing feedback (monitoring) system	M	L-M	M	M	M-H	L-M
temporary system	M	M	M	M	M-H	M
network building	M	M	M	M	M	M

L = Low, M = Medium, H = High

Repeatability	Potential Coverage	Follow-up	Immediacy	Time Required: Target	Ease of Use	User Convenience	Cost to Sender (Financial, Material)	Cost to Target (Financial, Material)	Imagery
M	M-H	L-M	H	L	M-H	H	M-H	L	L
H	H	L-M	H	L	M	H	H	L	L-M
H	H	L	M-H	M	M	M	H	L	L
M	M	M	L	M-H	L	L-M	M	M-H	H
L	L-M	H	H	L	M	H	H	L	H
L	L-M	M-H	H	M	M	M-H	H	M	H
L	L	M	H	L	H	H	H	L	L
L	M	M	M-H	M	:	M	M	M	M-H
L	H	M	M	L-M	L	M	M	M	L
L	L-M	H	M-H	M	M	M	M	M	L
L	L-M	M-H	M	M	L	M	M	M	M
H	H	L	L-M	M	H	M	H	M	L-M
H	M-H	M	H	L	H	H	H	M	M
H	M-H	M	M	M	H	M	M	M	M
H	L-M	M	L	L	L	H	H	L	M
H	L-M	M	L	L	L	H	H	L	M
H	M	M	L	L	L	H	L-H	M-H	M
H	M	M	L	L	L	H	L-H	M	M
H	M	M	L	L	L	M-H	L-H	M	M
H	M	M	L	L	L	M-H	L-H	M	M
H	M	H	L	L	L	H	L-H	L	M
L	L-M	H	L-M	M	L	L	M-H	L	M-H
L	M	H	L-M	M-H	L	L	M-H	M	H
M	M-H	M	L-M	H	L	L	L-M	M-H	H
H	M-H	L-M	M	M	M	H	L	L	L
L/H	M	M-H	M	H	M	L	L-M	M-H	L
H	H	H	H	—	H	H	L	L-H	L
H	H	M-H	M	—	M	H	L	L-H	L
H	H	L	L	L	M	H	L	L	L
L	M	H	H	M	H	M	H	L	L
L	M	M-H	M-H	M-H	M	L-M	M	L-H	L
L-M	M	L	L-M	H	L	L	M	L	M-H
L	M	H	M	H	L	L	M	H	M-H
L-M	M	M	L	H	L	L	M	L	L-M
L	M	M	M	H	L	L	M	H	M
L	L-M	M-H	M-H	H	M	M		L/H	M
L	M	M-H	M	M-H	L	M	H	L	L
L	L-M	M-H	M	H	L	L	H	M	H
M-H	M-H	M-H	L/H	M-H	L/H	L-M	H	M	M

or at a distance. On the other extreme are low-personal tactics such as direct mail and advertising to convey information. In between (medium-personal tactics) are those that involve in-person contacts along with nonpersonal media (e.g., training), and those that involve audiovisual, visual, or auditory images of people (e.g., A-V advertising).

There is no clear basis for assigning a value for tactics on this dimension; and it is more appropriately used to characterize information tactics than the other categories of tactics. However, gross distinctions can be made, and there is some usefulness in describing tactics on this dimension.

In general, the more personal a message is, the more the receiver attends to it and is influenced by it. Educators in particular prefer a "warm terminal" for retrieving or receiving information. However, the same phenomenon that makes personal tactics have high impact may backfire if the person is unappealing. Thus, there is increased risk of failure for in-person tactics. Since these tactics are often also relatively unstable, the use or reuse of a high-personal tactic may take an unexpected form. Also, increasing the extent of personal contact will usually increase cost to the sender, through not necessarily to the receiver or target.

High-personal tactics may not be as readily reusable as low-personal tactics and therefore may be less appropriate where the change planner wants to repeat the effort many times. For example, having teacher-trainers visit school systems may have high impact for a small number of systems, but if many systems must be reached, a low-personal information tactic such as training manuals would probably have to be used.

Personal contact is important when the change stage mediated is very early (e.g., awareness/interest) or very late (e.g., decision); when there is a certain tolerance for risk; if the change object is new or threatening; if the change planner is trying for high early impact and if the unit of change is the individual. Rogers and Shoemaker (1971) point out that commercial change planners are important at a trial-adoption stage—mainly because personal interaction contributes to persuasiveness at this stage. However, the "personal touch" may also mediate initial awareness, if it involves an attractive source. Threatening changes may appear less so if the target can identify with some other person involved; similarly, individuals may feel more compelled by the appeal of another person.

FEEDBACK/INTERACTION

This dimension refers to the extent of interaction possible between the receiver or target of change efforts and the initiator or source of change efforts. On one extreme (high interaction) is the one-to-one interaction of two people in which the amount and content of interaction are virtually unlimited; usually, salespeople or field agents hope for this extent of interaction. On the other extreme (low interaction) is a tactic that allows for no response from the receiver, as with a taped telephone message. In between (medium interaction) are tactics in which the amount of interaction is limited by time or distance, or the content of interaction is limited, or the interaction lacks immediacy, as when it occurs via mail.

In general, increased allowance for interaction improves learning and allows the strategist to judge whether his tactic has the desired effect. Thus, it is important if there is concern that a message may not get across, either because it is highly complex or because it may be ignored or misinterpreted. However, tactics allowing interaction are usually more expensive to employ; there is increased instability, and thus more risk, with high-interaction messages, since the nature of interaction cannot be completely slated in advance.

Rosenau (1974) classifies tactics as impersonal, personal, and interpersonal to indicate the extent of personal contact and interaction/feedback. He notes that tactics with high personal contact and interaction are appropriate for complex, risky, and expensive innovations; impersonal tactics are more appropriate for simple and inexpensive innovations.

ACTIVITY

Tactics can be characterized according to their level of activity, which is inversely related to the initiative required of the target individual or system to be reached by the change tactic. At one extreme are high-activity tactics such as visiting salespeople and unsolicited direct mail to convey information. At the other extreme are low-activity tactics such as demonstration centers, where intended receivers must themselves initiate communication. In between are arrangements in which it is sometimes one way, sometimes another or in which initiative is required on both ends, or in which the user must elect to be reached even though the sender provides most of the initiative (e.g., advertising).

Obviously, high-activity tactics are less assured of impact; if users must initiate the interaction, they will be more meaningfully involved. However, low-activity tactics may not mediate attention—users must be already motivated to attend to them. Thus, high-activity tactics are more useful for mediating the early change stages, awareness and interest. With low-activity tactics, there is more assurance of receipt and fidelity. Lower-activity tactics may be seen as somewhat more "professional" by educators.

ACTION IMPLICATIONS

One of the four P's in the marketing lexicon is the "place" variable—does the tactic used leave the target with some definite option to act in accordance with the change strategist's intent?

The action-implications dimension is related to this place variable. It refers to the extent to which a tactic, by its nature, implies a specific course of action for the target. For example, product-development tactics and some training tactics, by their nature, generally prescribe a more definite course of action then user-involvement tactics or some information tactics.

Tactics should have more definite action implications when the change effort is more an advocacy of a specific change than an attempt to develop renewal capabilities in a school. If the change planner wants to mediate a specific change, he should choose a tactic that has more potential for structuring the target's subsequent actions.

It is likely that when the favored change has competition, when there is less tolerance for risk, when there is a desire to have quality control, the change planner should consider a tactic with more potential for structuring action. Or, when dealing with a target system that has an informal and/or complex organizational structure, it can be useful to use tactics with more definite action implications, since organizational complexity relates negatively to efficient implementation of change.

However, such tactics may alienate the target of change, particularly in educational settings where practitioners resist restrictions or channeling of their behavior. There is some evidence that these tactics should be avoided with low-authoritarian individuals or groups, or in situations where there will be less opportunity for quality control and thus more need to rely on the motivation of the target subject for sustained change.

NOISE/REDUNDANCY

Tactics differ in their directness. Some information tactics, for example, require that receivers sift through much irrelevant content to receive a specific message. "Noise" refers to this waste-effort; to the extent that a tactic has a specific immediate result, it is less noisy. Action research is likely to be a noisier tactic than training; training is generally noisier than product development.

In general, noisier tactics are more expensive and demanding for both the change manager and the receiver. Noise probably increases risk and may delay results. However, better learning is possible where there is increased redundancy and/or when more of the choices involved in responding are left up to the target. Thus, complex change efforts can be furthered by noisy tactics. Also, efforts aimed at developing a capacity for self-renewal will be noisier in most cases, because messages involved are less direct. In situations of product advocacy, effectiveness is generally better with less noise; but in renewal efforts, noise should enhance effectiveness.

REPEATABILITY

Some of the tactics described here can be used only once, with repeated uses involving effort or cost equal to that involved in the first use. Others can be repeated with minimized additional expenditure of resources or effort for the change planner and the target system. For example, the initial effort to develop information for the published literature represents the bulk of effort required, even though the planner may want to use the article or book repeatedly.

In general, the use of a durable medium to convey information allows for more repeatability, and this is important where financial resources are limited, where the message involved will remain the same, where the target of change includes groups or persons who cannot be reached at the same time, where the effort is actually of a "trial balloon" nature to sense the readiness for change, or where the primary target is not the ultimate target (i.e., later efforts must reach other groups).

EASE OF USE

A tactic rated high on ease of use is one that requires no unusual skills or level of effort to employ. Examples are the use of the telephone to convey information, the simple subsidizing of change, and the invoking of authority. Tactics rated low on ease of use include things like workshops and demonstrations, which require skills; product-development tactics, which require unusual degrees of skill and effort; involvement of users in approval; using temporary systems; and classes, which require a great deal of effort.

In general, the change planner will want to choose tactics that are easy to use. However, ease of use is more important in some situations than in others. If the initiator of change is not highly motivated, tactics that are difficult to use should be avoided. Ease of use will be a consideration when the change planner expects to repeat a tactic or when cooperation from others is necessary. If the change planner feels confident of success, he may choose an easier tactic. If he has a number of goals or tasks rather than just one, he might deliberately choose easy tactics to help maintain his level of effort over all the tasks.

USER CONVENIENCE

This dimension refers to the ease of use for the target of the tactic. A tactic rated high on user convenience does not require for its effectiveness an unusual level of skill or effort on the part of receivers. For example, direct mail and advertising require no particular skills or effort to receive and process. Tactics rated low on user convenience require skill or effort by receivers. Workshops and most training tactics are low in user convenience; receivers must participate fully and skillfully if these are to be effectively employed.

Unlike the dimension of ease of use, this dimension is not automatically considered desirable. One way to mediate commitment to a change is to have target-system members invest some effort in implementing it. Thus, if the change planner has not generated commitment in some other way, he may do so by deliberately choosing a tactic with low user convenience. However, such tactics can discourage the initial decision to participate, so they should not be chosen before participation has been ensured.

POTENTIAL COVERAGE

A related dimension is potential coverage. Different tactics may be used for differing extents of outreach. There may be concern with reaching a mass audience or just one or a few individuals. On the "high" extreme are tactics that allow virtually unlimited coverage with a single effort; on the low extreme are tactics that reach one or a few persons. In between are medium-coverage tactics, which can reach a limited number of people—perhaps all the members of a school system or people attending a professional conference.

Included as an aspect of this dimension is the "multiplier" or ripple potential a tactic may have. In general, if a tactic initially reaches a small group but the liklihood of their influencing a larger group is high, the tactic has higher potential coverage than if it did not have this ripple effect. Thus, training of trainers as a tactic is considered to have higher potential coverage than in-service training because it includes this multiplier consideration.

The importance of potential coverage is obvious. If a large group is to be reached, high potential coverage is an advantage.

FOLLOW-UP

With some tactics, the change planner knows whether his message has gotten across or whether he has achieved his desired impact. With others, he may have no indication of this. By their nature, the tactics described differ in this regard.

Tactics with high follow-up, such as preservice classes, involve some evaluation to determine impact, plus the opportunity to do something to improve impact, if necessary. This evaluation aspect may be indirect, as when laws are passed to which noncompliance will be evident but compliance not noted. Low follow-up tactics are those in which the initiator of the tactic cannot determine the effects of his action. An example is the publishing of articles or books intended to promote change; in general, this allows relatively little opportunity to determine impact. In between are those tactics in which there is fairly good information available regarding impact, but less opportunity to act if desired results have not been achieved (e.g., having an educational innovation placed on the "approved list" for a district or state), and tactics in which results can be fairly easily known, if the change planner is interested (e.g., helping users find funding for change).

Follow-up is important when the effort is one of a series to be carried out. For example, where the planner is concerned with providing a climate for change so that he may later promote a specific change effort, he should be concerned with follow-up. If he is intending to repeat the change effort, he should be concerned with follow-up. When the problem or solution is complex and there is some question regarding the utility of change efforts, there should be concern with follow-up.

IMMEDIACY

How much time elapses from the initiation of the tactic and the beginning of its impact on the target system? The dimension of immediacy refers to the time it takes to achieve effect, other things being equal.

A tactic rated high on this dimension is one that can operate rapidly to mediate change. Examples are information tactics such as direct mail and advertising. Low-immediacy tactics, such as network building or training for improved planning, are those that generally require an extended time period for effect.

TIME REQUIRED FOR TARGET

Related to immediacy is the time required for the target system to be involved in the implementation of the tactic. Time is one of the most important of the resources of a school system. Generally, target systems will resist becoming involved with efforts that require much of their time. However, the time they do give generally tends to strengthen their involvement and commitment. In advocacy situations, it is usually better to select tactics with lower target-time requirements; in renewal situations, increased time spent should work to improve the result.

COST TO SENDER (FINANCIAL/MATERIAL)

This is very roughly estimated for the various tactics. In general, increased costs threaten the change effort, since funding for educational change is usually shortsighted and sometimes extremely inadequate.

COST TO RECEIVER (FINANCIAL/MATERIAL)

The financial and material resources of a system provide a concrete limit to what that system can do. Some tactics require less and therefore do not strain the limit. However, it is usually a sound assumption that the value perceived by receivers is increased by the expenditure they make.

IMAGERY

This refers to the isomorphism possible for messages conveyed when a particular tactic is used.

Tactics that present information in an abstract form are rated low in imagery. Examples are use of the telephone or the print media. Those that allow the receiver to manipulate and otherwise ''use'' an innovative product or procedure—such as user-site demonstrations—are high-imagery tactics. In between are tactics that provide partial or simulated experience, such as workshops or providing part of a product free.

Educators usually need some hands-on experience with innovations before they will make a final commitment. Thus, high-imagery tactics are needed to mediate the final change stages. When change goals involve renewal rather than advocacy, however, low-imagery tactics may be more useful, to avoid structuring user perceptions and to maintain flexibility and openness.

Situational Considerations in Evaluating Tactics

Evaluation of tactics for promoting change involves analyzing them according to the characteristics just described, and then analyzing the nature of the change situation as well. Thus, once the change planner has characterized tactics according to the sixteen dimensions, he will want to come to conclusions regarding their appropriateness to his particular situation.

As indicated earlier, some ways to characterize a situation include the following:

●*What are the goals of the change planner*? What decision stage is to be reached? Is the intent one of advocacy or one involving the building of a renewal capability? Is it necessary to "beat out" competition? Can he tolerate risk of failure? Does he want to maintain quality control?

● *What are the goals of the change target*? Is the target system desirous of really substantive change or is the intent one of simple compliance, immediate effect, "showcase" change, or some other more superficial action?

●*What is the nature of the change situation*? What is the scope of change? How complex are the problem and the solution? What risks are involved? What is the nature of the change object? How rapidly must the change occur? How many opportunities for change will there be? What incentives are available to manipulate?

● *What is the nature of the target system*? Who are the relevant actors? What organizational/authority structure exists? What skills, knowledge, and resources are available? What is the willingness to risk? What attitudes, values, and commitments characterize the system? What is the size and locale of the system; what is its stage of change; what incentives are operating? Is the unit of change the individual or the group? Are members separated or massed?

There are many examples that illustrate how the above considerations affect the success with which the various tactics might be employed. For example, the resources available for initiating and sustaining educational change must be adequate for the tactic chosen. Application of a feedback or data-based tactic may require two-way communication, and channels for this must exist; product development requires much time and, in addition, must reflect contemporary thinking; advertising may require extensive financial and skill resources.

As regards the stage in the adoption process to be mediated, Rosenau (1974) notes that tactics involving impersonal communication are more cost-effective for creating awareness; those involving interpersonal or personal communication may be favored for generating change.

The characteristics of the innovation in question have much to do with the success of specific change tactics. An example from education is discussed by Turnbull et al. (1974), who point out that "one of the main factors in the success of [an educational] product has been its form. . . . In general, when materials are deemphasized and when the product or program differs markedly from traditional practices, teacher training becomes an essential element. . . ."

The risk involved in adoption should be considered in the choice of tactics. As a general rule, in education, practitioners are not rewarded for successful risk taking to the same degree that they are punished for failure. If a change effort has highly uncertain outcomes, tactics aimed at converting individuals rather than groups are unlikely to be successful.

The locus of initiation of change is important to consider. Tactics that could work well for internally or collaboratively initiated change may fail when change is externally imposed. One problem in the acceptance of organizational arrangements for improved instruction has been that the in-school cooperation necessary for the effective implementation of such total programs does not develop when the decision to use the program comes from outside, even when "outside" refers to the district office rather than the school.

A related consideration is the relationship of the school with the environment. If that relationship is interactive, with the school having an internal self-renewing mechanism to handle new inputs, then simple awareness tactics, such as providing information about new developments, may be sufficient to initiate change. However, if the school depends on outside forces for reform or renewal, information alone is not likely to generate activity.

The nature of the "competition" should affect the choice of tactics. When the competition is traditional practice, superficial tactics are unlikely to disentrench it; when other forms of innovations are competing, it may be necessary to allow for two-way communication.

Many other examples could be offered; the point is that the evaluation of tactics cannot be complete until situational considerations are included.

The final section of this chapter presents further illustrations of the kinds of conclusions about the tactics in table 4-1 that can be drawn by considering them in light of the change situation. Before proceeding to this exercise, however, we shall elaborate one situational aspect—the goals of the change planner—that is crucial in the selection of tactics.

The goals of the change planner, whether he is an internal or external agent, are perhaps the most important consideration for the selection of tactics. Different tactics are differentially useful for mediating different change stages; some are more useful for product advocacy than for developing renewal capability, and vice versa; certain contingencies (e.g., tolerance of risk) suggest avoidance of particular tactics and/or the highly appropriate use of others.

Perhaps most important, the change planner must consider what he really wants to do, in strictly operational terms. Whom does he want to have behave in what way? The field of social marketing provides a useful framework for this kind of operationalizing of his goals.

When the change planner is at the stage of selecting tactics, he is doing just what the definition of social marketing specifies, that is, "the design, implementation, and control of programs calculated to influence the acceptability of social ideas and involving considerations of product planning, pricing, communication, distribution, and marketing research . . . [and] the deliberate use of marketing skills to help translate social action efforts into more effectively designed and communicated programs that elicit desired audience response'' (Kotler and Zaltman 1971:5).

This process can be facilitated by considering which of the nine marketing strategies presented in list 4-1 is implied for each change goal. For example, if the goal is to improve math scores, is it to be achieved by increasing the numbers of students benefiting from a good program (strategy 2), or by developing an alternative to existing programs for the current population of students (strategy 3), or by offering a variety of programs to be certain all needs are served (strategy 6 or 7)?

List 4-1 illustrates how each of the nine basic strategies may apply to an educational change goal. As should be apparent, if the change planner can determine which of these he is actually doing, this will have implications for which tactics he should use.

LIST 4-1.   Marketing Strategies Expressed in Terms of Educational Questions

1. *Market Penetration:* To improve the company's position with its present products in its current markets.
    Marketing Question: What should be done to gain further acceptance of existing products?
    Social Marketing (Education) Questions: e.g., What should be done to get more teachers in the school to participate in ongoing group problem-solving sessions? How can more teachers in the district be stimulated to use existing innovative curriculum materials?
2. *Market Development:* To find new classes of customers that can use the company's present products.
    Marketing Question: What new users are there for the present product line?
    Social Marketing (Education) Questions: e.g., Can simulation games designed for use by high school students be used in adult education courses as well? Should mail brochures about an R&D lab's products be sent to parents as well as to teachers and administrators?
3. *Reformulation Strategies:* Improve present products to increase sales to current customers.
    Marketing Question: What product changes are suggested?
    Social Marketing (Education) Questions: e.g., How might concepts such as team teaching or the ungraded classroom be adapted to function better and thus be used more effectively in schools (districts)? How might existing educational innovations be changed to prompt more intensive use of them by present users?
4. *Market Extension Strategies:* Reach new classes of customers by modifying present products.
    Marketing Question: What changes in goods and service are necessary to reach non-users?
    Social Marketing (Education) Questions: e.g., Would the incorporation of regional workshops as part of an innovation package make it more attractive to geographically isolated schools? Should different versions (e.g., simplified versus complex, lengthy versus brief) be developed for different types of students? teachers? communities?

LIST 4-1. *(Continued)*

5. *Replacement Strategy:* Replace current products with improved products.
   Marketing Question: What should replace present products?
   Social Marketing (Education) Questions: e.g., Should a new text be adopted in lieu of the textbook currently in use? Should a laboratory be working on educational innovation to replace already accepted and used materials and practices? Should a specially designated change team be used to replace current decision-making processes for the acquisition of educational products and services?

6. *Marketing Segmentation/Product Differentiation Strategy:* Attract new customers by expanding the assortment of existing product lines.
   Marketing Question: Should products be supplemented to appeal to different groups of buyers and/or users?
   Social Marketing (Education) Questions: e.g., Would additional students be attracted by offering more courses within a major or more majors within a university or by the institution of evening programs? Should an R&D lab develop versions of its educational products for the mentally handicapped? Should a school district expand its organizational structure to include a research-utilization program in order to attract and keep innovative staff?

7. *Product-Line Extension Strategy:* Add more products based on the same technology.
   Marketing Question: Should additional goods and service be made available to current consumers?
   Social Marketing (Education) Questions: e.g., Should the university offer additional and more specialized electives? Should an additional text be assigned as required reading? Should an R&D lab undertake additional curriculum improvement projects based on the same basic research guiding past product devcelopment? Should the next teachers hired have the same skills as those presently in the department or be different in some significant way?

8. *Concentric Diversification Strategy:* Attract new customers by adding products that have synergistic effects with the present line.
   Marketing Question: Are there new products suggested by research that will attract consumers who will also start buying existing items in the product line?
   Social Marketing (Education) Questions: e.g., Can teachers or administrators presently using products from one lab or commercial publishing house be encouraged to try other products and services offered by the lab or publisher? Can teachers or administrators who have had one successful experience in innovating be more easily encouraged to attempt more innovative activity?

9. *Forward/Backward Integration Strategy:* Improve efficiency by directing efforts to activities prior to, or following, current efforts.
   Marketing Question: What opportunities exist for vertical expansion of the company's activities?
   Social Marketing (Education) Questions: e.g., Should the school board and other decision makers establish a municipal junior college within the district? Should kindergarten and nursery school be required? Should a non-profit lab undertake commercial dissemination of its products and services?

INFORMATION/LINKAGE TACTICS

The various tactics in table 4-1 have characteristic strengths and drawbacks for particular kinds of change goals, target systems, and change situations. That is, the nature of the change situation affects the probable success of the tactics that might be chosen to introduce or implement change. This section illustrates for each tactic some conclusions that can be drawn regarding its appropriateness in different situations.

Direct Mail   Direct mail is relatively high in stability, activity, potential coverage, immediacy, and user convenience. It is a good tactic in situations where the audience is large and divided, and not inclined to be seeking the information. There is good assurance that the message intended is the message received, but less assurance that the message will be received. Direct mail can be used quickly and thus it should be considered where timing is a factor—for example, in advocacy situations where competition is great. It may be used for market-penetration or market-development goals, to increase the numbers of receivers involved. It may also be appropriate for informing receivers about something that is new but familiar, that is, for reformulation, replacement, or product-line extension goals.

Direct mail is usually low in personal contact and interaction, in noise, in imagery, and in time required and cost for the target. Thus, it is better for simple messages, where the content has some cogency and where the change stage mediated is an early one—awareness and/or interest. It should not be expected to mediate commitment or learning or involvement. In this sense, it is a low-impact tactic (Rosenau 1974); however, it is also relatively cheap and easy to use.

Use of Advertising (Mass Media)   As indicated in table 4-1, this tactic has stability, high potential coverage, high repeatability, high user convenience, high immediacy, and high cost to sender. There is low personal contact, low feedback/interaction, low follow-up, low time/cost to target.

Thus, we expect the tactic to be good in situations where there is a low tolerance for risk because of infidelity/misunderstandings; where the target group is large and divided; but where the message itself has expected congency since the tactic is less persuasive. There is high cost, but mass media persuasion can be cost-effective for large groups and/or repeated messages and for earlier change stages rather than later ones. There is potential for immediate impact, but the sender must expend some skill and effort to develop the message.

Havelock et al. (1971) point out that mass media dissemination is usually most effective for reaching opinion leaders (mass media–oriented), creating awareness, conveying simple ideas, and disseminating in crisis situations.

Rosenau (1974) evaluates mass media as having relatively low "cost per impression" and high "relative coverage"; having relatively high user convenience but low impact and low feedback; and being most suited for awareness and arousal but not suited to conveying information about complex innovations. Thus, it may be useful for information about existing, familiar objects—for market-penetration, reformulation, or product-line extension goals—but not appropriate for radically moving receivers—such as market-development goals.

Use of Articles/Reports/Books   This tactic is similar to the use of mass media in that it ensures relatively high fidelity and there is potential for high coverage, repeatability, and immediacy. But in general this tactic is less persuasive. There is little follow-up, lower activity, lower action implications, higher noise, more time required for receiver, and less user convenience.

Therefore, the tactic is good for a mass audience and/or a divided audience when the message has its own cogency. It may be better received than advertising because of slightly lower activity. However, noise level and time and effort and resources required of receiver, combined with low action implications, may lead to lessened attention. Usually, use of the professional literature is more appropriate for somewhat more complex messages; those users who do attend are likely to be more motivated and change-oriented. The tactic should be avoided if the goal is market penetration, or market extension, where passive receivers are assumed.

Rosenau generally agrees that "printed matter" (the professional literature) has similar coverage and cost, impact, and feedback compared to mass media messages, and that it may have somewhat higher user convenience. This is due to his broader definition of mass media to include the public noneducational media.

Use of Demonstrations   In general, this tactic may have relatively high action implications and time required of target; relatively low ease of use and user convenience; and relatively high imagery and cost to the target system.

Demonstrations are usually fairly expensive and difficult for both target and sender, and they are unlikely to be useful for immediate impact. However, they can convey complex information and by their nature can lend cogency to the message. Therefore, demonstrations are good if resistance is expected and good at later change stages. They should be effective for concentric-diversification or forward/backward integration goals, where users are self-motivated but need something to evaluate.

Rosenau (1974) rates demonstrations as generally costly but with good relative impact and feedback; he notes that they are good for complex, high-risk innovations. Havelock et al. (1971) report that a demonstration of an innovation can be "quite powerful for adoption."

Use of Salespeople   This tactic has low stability, low potential coverage, low noise, low repeatability, low time required of target, low cost to target, high personal contact, high feedback/interaction, high action implications, high follow-up, high immediacy, high user convenience, high cost to sender, and high imagery.

Salespeople are costly to the initiator and should not be used where the audience is very large and/or a series of repeated messages to different portions of the audience is required. However, it is a potentially impactful tactic that can lend cogency to a message and that requires little effort/resources from the target system. There is good opportunity for the imagery, interaction, and follow-up necessary for conveying complex information and for mediating a firm and perhaps quick decision. A danger is that the target system may not see this kind of source as professional (because of high activity), particularly given the low level of effort required to use it. This tactic is more appropriate for advocacy as opposed to renewal efforts. Thus, it is good for getting more practitioners to take a particular action (market penetration, market development) but probably not for mediating further action with an already motivated target system.

Use of Field Agents   As can be seen in table 4-1, this tactic has essentially the same characteristics as the use of salespeople except that more is required (higher cost, lower convenience) of the target system, and generally the field agent is less likely to prescribe a definite course of action (lower action implications). Thus, this tactic is better for renewal efforts than for advocacy efforts, and may have a more professional image.

Rosenau (1974) compares commercial and noncommerical agents (i.e., sales people and field agents) somewhat similarly—that is, both are costly, but both have high feedback and good impact. He sees the commercial agent as having more relative impact (because he is more likely to offer a definite course of action); he sees both as having high user convenience. Field agents can present new practices (market development and extension) effectively, but a more important use may be helping clients integrate new practices with old (concentric diversification; forward/backward integration).

Use of Telephone   The characteristic strength of this tactic comes from its combined immediacy and ease of use and user convenience. If the change manager is working with time constraints, or if the receiver needs quick information, the telephone provides a quick means. But it is relatively costly, with relatively low potential coverage, and lacks the noise, contact, and imagery necessary for complex messages. Thus, it is best for simple awareness information.

Use of Meetings   This tactic is most appropriate for either very early or very late decision stages. The initiator can fairly well assess his success, and there is opportunity to dress up or lend cogency to messages involved. But this tactic is difficult to use and has limited potential coverage unless some ripple effect can be activated.

Action Research   Havelock et al. (1971) note that this tactic has intrinsic value, since it provides the school system with "an increasing knowledge of scientific methods of diagnosis and evaluation" as well as self-evaluation data to guide change. This tactic should be well received by the target system and probably is one to choose in complacent or traditional systems, since it has a good deal of credibility. But there is a price for this. Information is more abstract (low imagery, low contact, relatively low feedback/interaction), and potential coverage and repeatability are low. The implication is that if the tactic is employed, results should be good, particularly in renewal situations, but it is not as easily employed as other information tactics, such as use of field agents or conveying information via training manuals or the mass media. Action research is appropriate at all change stages, but for different reasons. At early stages, it is part of the diagnosis effort; at later stages, it is used to guide change efforts.

Action research is convincing for new ideas (market development, extension, replacement).

Confrontation This refers generally to providing information that forces the target system to face previously avoided performance gaps. This is an unpredictable tactic (low stability), but it can have definite action implications and quick effect. It may be less effective when complex changes are contemplated, since by its nature it must present a target system with unfamiliar, perhaps unpleasant information quickly enough to prevent a marshaling of defense. However, it may be useful for mediating awareness and interest, and if the initiator's goal is to develop a renewal capability rather than to advocate a specific change, he may find that this kind of tactic can pave the way for applying other tactics to mediate later change stages. The initiator should expect a good chance of failure and should not use this tactic if he cannot afford failure. Thus, it should not be used if there will be only one opportunity for effect, or only one system to be changed. It should be considered a probability tactic, with a probability of both "hits" and "misses."

Workshops Information may be conveyed to a captive workshop audience. Obviously, it must be somehow relevant to the workshop content. This is rated relatively low in stability because the initiator cannot be very certain of how his message will be interpreted—whether it will transfer from the workshop situation to a real situation. There can be good effect, owing to personal contact and interaction.

Information Systems To convey information through information systems, a sender depends on the initiative of the receiver. This is a low-activity tactic, with low personal contact and usually low action implications. It is cheap, with high repeatability and potential coverage, and it is easy to use and has good fidelity. But information systems are not good for advocacy messages, since the tactic is passive and has low immediacy and low action implications; it does not lend cogency to a message. It is a tactic that is well suited when a receptive, self-motivated audience is expected. For the user, it is not very convenient, and most information systems are noisy, but they are also capable of extensive coverage.

Packaging This is appropriate for situations in which change should take a particular form and occur efficiently. It is usually an advocacy tactic, involving making an innovation more attractive so that it will be used. It is inappropriate for complex changes or for changes where use may give way to disillusionment—

again, it is not for effecting substantial broad change but rather for mediating use of a small-scale, rewarding program or practice. It is good for quick, directed effect. Packaging may be crucial to get an existing target system to increase some practice (market penetration).

Training Manuals   This is a high-stability information tactic, with high action implications, low noise, and high ease of use. Thus, it is good for efficiently conveying specific information aimed at a particular form of change. It is low in personal contact and feedback/interaction, and thus lacks cogency and usefulness for complex or risky information. It can be inexpensive because of its relatively good repeatability and potential coverage. It is good for later change stages, where interest already exists and the receiver simply needs information to "get on with it." It is good in advocacy situations, where there is interest in change following along definite lines. It is good for use with large, physically separated target groups and where resources of users are sufficient to support the change in question.

PRODUCT-DEVELOPMENT TACTICS

In general, product-development tactics are a good approach in situations where the change is fairly limited in scope, is not overly complex, and has a form and nature that are generally acceptable and agreed on by the various parties involved. In these situations, their stability, action implications, and user convenience allow for change to take place relatively easily and in a defined manner, with predictable effects and relatively little deviation. Thus, product-development tactics are good for advocacy situations or where the intent is to set up circumstances that pave the way for more complex and controversial renewal efforts (for example, a product may be used to train internal change planners). Other situations in which product development may be good are those where change must occur, regardless of resistances, and the need is to make it as painless and easy as possible while retaining some minimum level of effect; or where the goal of the target system is to achieve a particular effect as conveniently as possible.

But product-development tactics used alone are not good for complex or controversial changes. They are low in personal contact, noise, and feedback, and in general do not allow for optimum flexibility.

Also, there is high cost involved for the initiator. In some instances this is returned through cost to users, but generally, if the initiator is using product development for a desired change rather than to make a profit, he will not make many of the compromises involved in getting a return on his own investment (e.g., lowering quality or increasing its price).

This tactic for change also has generally low immediacy (development takes time) and low ease of use (development is difficult).

Seven variations are listed in table 4-1. They differ mainly in who absorbs the cost. Thus, if the goal of the change planner is to get some target system to change, he will likely choose to reduce that system's cost. However, if he wants some return—in the form of either a profit or continued high motivation for users to use that and other products—he is wise to require some investment from the target system.

USER-INVOLVEMENT TACTICS

Involve in Approval/Involve in Field Testing   The user-involvement tactics of involving potential users in approval of the change and involving them in field testing have many of the same characteristics. Both are low in stability and thus should not be used in situations where the outcome of the tactic must take a particular form to be useful. For example, if change must occur, regardless of whether users approve, or if a negative evaluation of potential users cannot be turned to constructive advantage, the change planner may not want to take on the risk of using either of these tactics. However, if user input can serve a truly useful purpose, both tactics are valuable ways to get it. Both are relatively expensive (low repeatability, low to medium potential coverage, low in ease of use), and they are demanding of potential users (low user convenience, high time requirement). However, they are good for complex messages and can enhance cogency (relatively high contact, feedback, follow-up). Of the two, field testing is slightly more demanding of the user but also higher in imagery.

User involvement of this sort is risky if there exists a change object that probably won't be altered (e.g., market penetration or development), but it is highly appropriate for reformulation and replacement goals.

Trainees-Become-Trainers   This tactic has a multiplier effect and thus is higher in potential coverage than a simple training tactic. It maintains relatively high contact and interaction along with action implications and imagery and is thus useful for complex messages. It is most cost-effective at a later change stage, after initial interest is achieved.

Endorsements   Havelock (1970) points out that opinion leadership to promote change should be used with caution, since there are many variables that determine its effectiveness. That is, it is relatively low in stability. By its nature, the tactic of endorsements is usually inexpensive to use and can lend cogency to the suggested change.

Institutionalize Change Roles   This tactic is low in repeatability over educational systems, but if the need is for repeatability over time, it is relatively high. It is demanding of the target of change, but the payoff may be great, if the institutionalized role is properly applied. Thus, it is a good tactic for renewal but a poor tactic for advocacy.

LEGAL TACTICS

The three legal tactics described here have most characteristics in common. All three are good for effecting change in a specified form (high stability, high action implications) and over a large group (high repeatability, high potential coverage) with high user convenience. They are poor for complex changes, and they may easily arouse resistance and even hostility, since they lack cogency (low personal contact and interaction, low imagery) and may be viewed as unprofessional (high activity, high action implications). Thus, their best use is for less significant changes or noncontroversial changes or for changes that are not dependent on cooperation from various corners. Ironically, the opposite of these are the situations in which they are usually used (e.g., for integration and busing).

The tactic of getting some innovation on an approved list is lower in action implications, follow-up, and immediacy relative to the other two. Thus, it may engender less hostility, but it also may have less impact.

These tactics are more appropriate for advocacy situations and, in the case of the first and second, for changes that might arouse excessive initial resistance but would be accepted easily once passed, or for changes that could be accepted immediately. They are inappropriate for complex, debatable efforts, or for renewal-type efforts.

TRAINING/INSTALLATION TACTICS

Subsidizing Change   This tactic is stable and predictable, usually having high action implications, follow-up, immediacy, and ease of use. Thus, by its nature, it is efficient. However, it is—obviously—costly, and not a good tactic where the initiator is interested in getting a complex message across or a complicated change implemented. It is good in advocacy situations and in situations where change should occur rapidly. If it is to be used in a renewal situation, or with a complex change, it should be used in combination with a training tactic.

Helping Users Find Financial Resources for Change   This tactic is similar to subsidizing change except that it usually involves more interaction of the initiator with system representatives and it implies less control over them. It requires more of that target system. Thus, if change is initiated internally, this is the tactic that is applicable. This tactic is useful for market-development goals.

Preservice Classes   Sometimes change comes about because skills and attitudes of new system members influence their operations and spread through the system. This is the logic behind instilling particular skills and attitudes in a preservice audience—that is, its potential coverage comes solely from a hoped-for multiplier effect. Thus, it is more appropriate for renewal efforts than for advocacy efforts. Effects are relatively uncertain; follow-up is low; action implications, immediacy, and ease of use are relatively low. For the initiator of the tactic, the potential payoff is that if it works, it should work very well, having potentially high cogency and imagery.

In-service Classes   This tactic is different in that there is more possibility of monitoring the effects and more opportunity to structure their nature. Usually it is more direct and therefore more efficient (less noisy) training, with better odds for relatively fast change. In-service classes other than those described as "planning" classes are better for advocacy situations, for teaching limited skills for immediate application to effect a particular change. Developers of educational innovations are learning that in-service training is vital in later change stages for effective use of complex products.

Preservice Classes: Planning   The teaching of generalized planning and change competencies is now a fairly common feature of educational administration majors in university departments. The notion is that new teachers with such skills can impact on the school systems they join. The tactic can be applied in several ways. For internally initiated change, the internal planner can look for these skills in teacher selection and hiring. The external planner can develop packages or campaigns to further this kind of training in universities; the product advocate may try to have his product used in an illustrative way.

However, the tactic is obviously not useful for mediating specific changes, for high-risk situations or for rapid change. It is expensive and has a low rate of return. However, over time it should be a cogent and highly effective means of developing renewal capabilities in schools.

In-service Classes: Planning   The aim here is similar to that of preservice training, but there is more control over outcomes and more assurance of impact—and of more rapid impact. Thus, in certain situations, such as an advocacy situation where training in planning skills appears needed, in-service training is better than preservice training. This disadvantage is that more resources for the target system are required.

Consultation   Havelock (1970) sees consultation as a tactic to help a system "work through its own problems and define its own needs, primarily through the use of reflection and authentic feedback." It is a low-stability, high-contact, high-interaction tactic primarily for use in situations where maximum flexibility is desired—where the change is complex, perhaps controversial, and will depend on effective, cooperative implementation by members of a school system. As might be expected, it is expensive in time for both the initiator and the target system, and is financially costly to someone—although the bearer of the expense may be either. It can have relatively high immediacy, action implications, and follow-up, and for these reasons may be good in an advocacy situation. However, a target system may not be willing to be involved in consultation if it perceives that the consultant has an ax to grind. Thus, it is generally better for renewal efforts and for efforts where any form of outcome can serve some constructive purpose.

It is a better technique if the decision-making group is small and/or cohesive; it is better for middle and later change stages, since target systems at the earliest stages are less likely to cooperate fully.

Providing a Feedback (Monitoring) System   There are many ways to implement this kind of tactic, but essentially it involves performing the service of collecting and presenting data about the performance of the school system in some manner. If this is done externally, "the client system is then able to generate an accurate self-diagnosis and specific remedial actions. . ." (Havelock 1970). This tactic is useful at early change stages for making users aware of performance gaps, and at later change stages for monitoring and revising the change effort for better effect. It is not a tactic that lends cogency to information conveyed, so at early change stages it may meet with resistance.

There are usually fairly clear action implications. The tactic is relatively expensive and not easy or convenient for either the initiator or the target. Again, this implies that it should be used only if fair to good receptivity on the part of the target system is expected.

Temporary System   In general, this refers to any nonpermanent arrangement through which the school system can experience part or all of the change. It is useful for early change stages—that is, for introducing change—but only if the target system is receptive to the idea of change and therefore willing to cooperate with a temporary system. It is useful where the benefits of the arrangement are not obvious, as when change is going to be complex; or where change will be expensive or is otherwise tied into high risk. It is expensive and difficult to use, but highly effective.

Network Building   Havelock (1970) points out that a network has great multiplier potential and can provide a speedy, effective medium for innumerable related innovations. Thus, this tactic is rated both low and high on immediacy and ease of use, since building a network takes time but working through an existing network is very efficient. However, building and maintaining a network can involve fairly high financial cost.

Since network building is slow and not particularly easy, the change planner may feel it is more useful for renewal situations than for advocacy situations. However, use of an existing network is an excellent tactic in advocacy situations.

In a similar manner, mediation of early change stages may be effectively done through a network but probably should not be the reason for network building.

Networks allow for optimal quality control and for supporting complex, substantive changes. If the target system is large and diffuse, network building is a good tactic. If change must occur rapidly, network building is a poor tactic but use of a network is a good tactic.

Summary

The change planner needs to devise or select specific tactics for achieving his goals. Although it has usually been a rather informal, hit-or-miss process, the evaluation of change tactics can and should be systematic. Chapter 4 discusses five kinds of tactics and sixteen dimensions that can be used to describe or characterize them. The chapter offers guidelines for analyzing the change situation and notes that tactics with different characteristics will be differentially effective for different change situations.

The five kinds of tactics presented are information/linkage tactics, product-development tactics, user-involvement tactics, legal tactics, and training/installation tactics. The sixteen dimensions used to characterize them include stability, personal contact, feedback/interaction, activity, action implications, noise/redundancy, repeatability, ease of use, user convenience, potential coverage, follow-up, immediacy, time required for target, cost to sender, cost to receiver, and imagery. Aspects of the change situation that should be considered in the selection of tactics include goals of the change planner, goals of the change target, the nature of the setting, and the nature of the target system.

PART III

Planning and Managing Change: A Normative Guide to Change in Education

5

The Case for Planning

Introduction

PLANNING FOR INTENTIONAL CHANGE is the *sine qua non* of successful adoption, implementation, and institutionalization of educational change. *Planning is viewed here as the systematic preparation and decision making for action.* It should not be a one-instance, temporary activity, but a continuous process involving *diagnosis, monitoring, data collection and analysis, evaluation, feedback, agenda building, need assessment, review and screening of resources and alternative innovations, strategy building,* and *decision making.* Several premises pertinent to change planning are presented below. This chapter is intended to aid the planner in preparing the school organization for a continual process of planning and renewal. At various points in the chapter, we identify premises that are the bases for the ideas presented.

CHANGE

Premise 5-1. Change is a consequence of viable open social systems.

Educational institutions are dominated by human subsystems. Such social systems are subject to continual changes (Schon 1971), and their viability rests on their ability to cope with both environmental and internal forces for change. The nature of the forces for and against change in these public institutions often leads to random and chaotic change. Educational managers, in the absence of preparation for dealing with these forces, are ill-prepared to lead their institutions through a quagmire of competing and interacting pressures on educational institutions.

RELATIONSHIPS WITH ENVIRONMENTAL ELEMENTS

Premise 5-2. Systems change as a result of three kinds of relationships with their environment: reactive, proactive, and interactive.

A fourth relationship between system and environment, termed *inactive* or *frozen,* is indicative of a system losing its viability. Inactive relationships are characterized by the lack of flow of energy and resources between a system and its environment. Inaction between a system and its environment reveals a system cut off from its lifeblood of resources and thus incapable of growing and developing. The ability of a system to grow and develop is the essential element of viability.

Dynamic relationships with environmental elements and forces allow the system to remain operative and functional. The three kinds of relationships are as follows:

1. Reactive relationships, in which the system continually responds to external forces (e.g., social, political, economic, cultural)
2. Proactive relationships, in which the system takes the lead in initiating changes and development through innovation and actively seeking needed external resources, energy, and knowledge
3. Interactive relationships, in which growth, development, and change come about in a system through the dynamic interchange on a collaborative or synergistic basis between system and environment

Schools, as open social systems, are often characterized as having reactive relationships with environmental entities. Planned, deliberate organizational change is unlikely to happen in such organizations.

THE NEED FOR INTERACTION

Premise 5-3. Systematic, intentional change for social organizations is dependent on proactive and interactive relations with the environment.

Reactive educational system/environment relations can force social organizations into a subordinate role with regard to external forces. This can produce a situation where a principal, superintendent, dean, and others engage primarily in crisis decision making. Changes produced under a crisis decision-making mode are seldom well planned, implemented, or integrated with other prior decisions and the organizational mission.

Proactive and interactive relations allow the organization to have some control over the forces for change whether they stem from inside or outside the school system. The institution is able to decrease the random nature of change by preparing itself for dealing with these forces or, in fact, helping seek out and develop environmental energies. For example, the school system that actively works with parent groups can find them to be a valuable ally when working with other forces in the surrounding political community. How does such a system prepare for these relationships? This is the critical question for the management of educational change. This chapter and the next provide some of the tools available for such preparation.

THE NEED FOR SYSTEMATIC PLANNING

Premise 5-4. The ability of social systems to shape and direct their activities is dependent on their involvement in systematic planning for intentional change and innovation.

Before social organizations can take part in an active interchange with their environments, they must know the direction they wish to take and be able to plan systematically to get there.

THE ESSENTIAL ELEMENTS IN THE PLANNING PROCESS

The activities necessary to bring about a productive relationship between educational systems and their environments are the *essential elements of the planning process*. To plan for organizational change, it is necessary to:

1. identify the organizational mission by stating the goals and objectives explicitly
2. identify problems
3. assess needs
4. identify resources and constraints
5. structure alternative courses of action in light of available resources, existing or forthcoming constraints, and barriers both within the system and in the environment
6. build alternative strategies for problem solving
7. build alternative strategies for resource use
8. build alternative strategies for testing alternatives
9. build alternative strategies for making decisions
10. build alternative strategies for evaluating changes or innovations in the light of goals and objectives

These elements are elaborated below.

The Planning Model

Organizational planning for change presupposes a proactive/interactive process for innovation or change. The following model (figure 5-1) describes an internally initiated change process involving several stages in which the educational system and environment interact purposively. Although the model seems to imply a linear progression of stages, situational factors will bring about vari-

FIGURE 5-1. A Simplified Proactive/Interactive Planning and Change Process

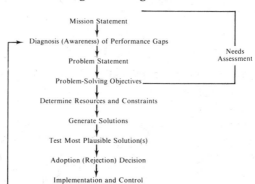

ous alterations in any given series of actions leading to change. For example, the system may begin the process at different stages, stages may be omitted, or the order of stages might be changed. A more fully developed model clarifying these points will come later in this and the next chapter.

This model is descriptive of a rational change strategy—specifically of the rational-empirical strategy for organizational change (Chin and Benne 1969). The systems analysis model of organizational change implies a rational, systematic planning and changing process. The model shown in figure 5-1, taken alone, would seem to fit that description with little regard for informal (interpersonal) structure, normative barriers, and the cultural environment of educational institutions. In this sense the model is unrealistic or naive.

On the surface, planning is a rational process involving the elements shown in the figure. The organization should identify its mission through a series of goal statements. There would be a diagnosis of performance gaps between the ideal (goal striving) and real (actual state) organization.

The diagnosis will lead to an awareness of a need for change that necessitates a problem statement and a set of objectives needed for solving the problem or closing the performance gap. The motivation here is the need for lowering the dissonance between expected and actual actions or outcomes. The rational implication is that the people agree on the organizational mission and thus are able to build a consensus around a common problem identification.

Following the generation of objectives needed for problem solving, the planners move to identify resources available for organization use. They must also begin to identify the limitations of resources in the form of constraints. This stage of the process is where the planners systematically become aware of the forces for and against change in the organization and its environment.

Before going further, it is useful to call attention to the *Need Assessment* process in the planning model. As defined here, need assessment is broadly based and is a critical element in moving the planning model from a purely rational systems analysis model to a more realistic model. In educational institutions, with their multiple client structure, there is great potential for diversity in expectations for the institution. Additionally, the labor-intensive nature of educational institutions heightens the potential for diversity. Thus, we cannot say that agreement on a mission statement is a given. There is a need for specific activity in the planning process to assess the needs of the various people in the system and affecting the system from outside. A later chapter will detail some of the processes involved in need assessment; however, it is important to note that the planning model's use of systems analysis is but one step toward dealing with cultural, personal, and other environmental variables that limit a purely rational planning process in social systems.

In part, the identification of resources, constraints, aids, and barriers to the planning process itself will highlight the need for dealing with the informal, yet critical, factors in the planning process. It is difficult to diagram the critical processes needed in this area; however, these issues and techniques are discussed in the following chapter on implementing the planning model.

Moving through the simplified model, the planning team goes on to generate alternative solutions in the light of the resources and constraints. They test or try on a pilot basis the most attractive alternatives and make decisions based on data from these trials or tests. Once decisions are made, the planners aid the organization in the adoption, implementation, control, and evaluation of the change or innovation.

This simple description is less than adequate to describe either the planning process advocated here or the elements in planning essential to ensure that adoption decisions are, in fact, implemented by the organization. Educational institutions, like institutions in many other social systems, are subject to gaps between the ''verbal'' or outward adoption of a change or innovation and its actual implementation. Chapter 6, ''Implementing the Planning Model,'' deals with various issues surrounding planning in educational organizations. However, it is important to deal with some of these issues here.

THE LOCUS OF PLANNING

Among the most critical issues facing the change planner is the decision concerning the locus of planning. Educational systems are broad and elaborate, with a diversity of personnel, interested publics, and client groups. Educational systems are multilayered, with a diversity of subsystems, and this raises a critical decision prior to planning. What specific institution within a broader educational system is the primary planning unit?

Premise 5-5. If intentional change is to occur in educational systems, planning must occur within the unit most closely associated with the client group.

In most cases, this is the school. This is not to say that other units may not also benefit from planned change; however, the unique nature of school systems places the focus on the school as the basic unit of the intended change. Other units within the system (e.g., central district offices, area or district administrative units, research and development units) may, however, play significant roles in aiding the planning process in the school unit. The role played by each unit will be determined by its resource capability as seen by the primary planning unit.

THE LINKING PROCESS

This brings us to the linking elements in the planning model. Linking refers to the interactive processes in the Proactive/Interactive Change Model (P/ICM). If the school is the primary planning unit in the change process, there is a necessity throughout the planning process to link the planning team with other units in a school system as well as with forces and entities in the external environment. In this sense, the other units of the school system become part of the environment of the planning process and are essential forces to be dealt with.

Critical Questions in Initiating the Planning Process

Early chapters have noted the unique properties of school systems. People involved in initiating a planning process need to be aware of certain preliminary preparations for planning in school systems. These preliminary factors, including the decision as to the target of change, are identified in list 5-1 in the form of critical questions to be asked prior to initiating the planning process.

Of course, not all of these questions must or can be answered prior to

LIST 5-1.   Critical Questions for Planning

---

1. What is the unit of change?
2. Who are the relevant actors in the unit of change?
3. Who is to be involved in the planning/decision-making process?
4. What is the current authority/decision-making structure in the unit of change?
5. What will be the decision-making authority of the planning group members?
6. What are the diagnostic and problem-solving skills (knowledge/experience) held by those involved in the planning process?
7. What are the educational/training needs of members of the planning group?
8. What are the organizational variables that have potential for change?
9. What is the current nature of the system/environment relationship?
10. What human resources from the environment should be included in the planning process?
11. What is the current willingness to take risks among change unit members?

---

initiating change; however, they should be considered. The questions, given as a guide to preparation for planning, are designed to identify the unit of change and the significant people involved in that change; to assess problem-solving and diagnostic skills; to surface the current authority structure; and to determine the "readiness to change" of the actors in the change process.

THE NEED TO INVOLVE CRITICAL PEOPLE

As noted earlier, there is often a gap between the adoption of an innovation by a group or planning team within educational institutions and the successful implementation of innovation or change within the target unit. This brings us to several issues dealing with the involvement of critical people in the planning and decision-making processes.

Premise 5-6. The degree of acceptance, satisfaction, commitment, and follow-up action with regard to planning decisions is positively related to the degree of involvement that members of the system feel they have in the decision-making process.

Premise 5-7. Constructive participation and involvement cannot occur unless system members (1) believe their participation will lead to action and (2) are able to perform tasks in the planning process.

Premises 5-6 and 5-7 highlight the need to both structure the educational organization for collaborative decision making and develop the decision-making skills of the planning group. These premises stem from work in the areas of organizational development (OD) and planned change (Rogers and Shoemaker 1971; Zaltman, Duncan, and Holbek 1973; Miles 1964; Schmuck and Miles 1971; Bennis, Benne, and Chin 1969; Schein and Bennis 1965; Lippitt, Watson, and Westley 1958; and others).

Issues for Planning School Change

Blumberg, May, and Perry (1974:224) have reported on the difficulties of implementing a participatory decision-making process in an urban school:

1. Teachers became frustrated with themselves because they found they were relatively inept in group problem-solving and decision-making skills.
2. Teachers became unsure and insecure about the limits of their power. They did not know whether to trust the principal.
3. The stability that accompanies a traditional principal-teacher relationship was greatly reduced.

The first three questions in list 5-1 concern the establishment of a collaborative process prior to planning. These questions serve to identify (1) the unit of change, (2) the relevant people in the unit, and (3) the people to be involved in the planning process. Following up on premise 5-6, persons initiating the planning process must be able to identify not only the people to be involved in the planning process, but also those needed for decision making and follow-up action. As noted in earlier chapters, a great many innovations are seemingly "adopted" in educational institutions; however, many of these are not implemented because of a failure to coopt relevant people in the planning process. If action is to follow planning decisions, then those people involved in follow-up activities or their representatives should be part of the planning process. This brings up several specific issues of special relevance to school systems:

1. Is the school the unit of planning and change? If so, who are the relevant actors?
2. Are students, as system clients, to be included in the planning process?
3. Who is to be in the planning group?
4. Are parents to be involved?
5. In addition to teachers and administrators, who are the other staff members in the planning process?
6. Are there other human resources in the community needed in the planning process? And, perhaps most important,
7. What are the potential costs (in terms of successful change) of excluding any of the relevant actors in the planning process?

Many OD theorists would argue for involving all professional staff (Schmuck, Runkel, and Langmeyer 1969). Others would involve parents, students, and community groups as well (Schmuck 1974; Blumberg et al. 1974). However, these participation decisions must be made relative to the situation and past experience of the institution. Initial planning efforts may begin with little or no representation from client (parent and student) and community groups. Later in the planning process, representatives from these groups may prove beneficial in avoiding problems.

The way in which the above issues in educational institutions are dealt with will depend, in part, on the answers to questions 4, 5, 6, and 7 in list 5-1. These refer to the current change unit decision-making/authority structure, decision-making/action authority of planning group members, diagnostic and problem-solving skills currently held by those involved in the planning process, and the educational/training needs of the planning group.

Not all of these issues will be dealt with before initiating a planning process under the P/ICM. In fact, several of these issues may surface in the diagnosis and awareness stages of problem identification.

Organizational Decision Making/Action Authority

Identification of the current involvement and authority structure of the organization and of that designed for the planning group is essential for the preparation stages of planning. In deciding who will be involved in planning, it is important to know what the past experience and abilities of the relevant people are concerning group decision-making activities, interaction with colleagues, and authority to act. As mentioned in part 1 of this book and highlighted by the problems noted by Blumberg et al. (1974), teachers have a tradition and subculture reinforcing isolation from peers and autonomous classroom activities. If, in educational institutions, the authority structure has followed a classic bureaucratic pattern, several issues must be considered both in the preparation and in the initiation of the planning process. These issues include trust, involvement, risk, and stability. A unilateral decision by those initiating the planning process to change decision-making patterns from authoritative (top-down) to collaborative may be unrealistic in the light of a particular organization's history. A belief that participation leads to action, premise 5-7 (a), will not come about by simply bringing people together in groups. In short, the preparation for planning may require a training and learning session involving members of the planning group in order to sharpen skills, bring hidden concerns and anxieties to the surface, and develop a trust in the planning process. This trust comes only from the belief that planning decisions will lead to action.

Given premise 5-6—that acceptance and commitment are positively related to involvement—the P/ICM is designed to be a collaborative model. Collaboration is dependent on the belief that participants in the planning process have the authority to act on their decisions. With this in mind, the spectrogram in figure

FIGURE 5-2.   An Organizational Decision Making/Action Authority Spectrum*

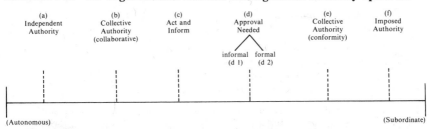

*The spectrum is limited to the human subsystem of an organization and does not include authoritative forces in the environment. It is used for descriptive purposes and is not intended to diminish the need for awareness of external authority.
(a)   Independent Authority = ability of individual members to act without constraint from superiors or peer pressure
(b)   Collective Authority (collaborative) = ability of members to act upon decisions made through collective interaction
(c)   Act and Inform = members' actions (individual or collectively decided) must be followed by a report to a superior
(d)   Approval Needed:
    (d_1)   informal = members must discuss decisions and perceive agreement with a superior prior to action
    (d_2)   formal = members must get decision approval from a superior prior to action
(e)   Collective Authority (conformity) = members' actions are conditioned upon compliance with accepted practice
(f)   Imposed Authority = members' actions follow directives from a superior

5-2 will be a helpful tool in assessing both current authority patterns and those designated for the planning group.

It is not necessary that "collective authority (collaborative)" be well established prior to initiating the P/ICM; however, provision must be made in the planning process to strengthen the collaborative authority pattern through planning actions. This may bring about additional need for training and skill development. The limited history of participatory collaborative decision making in an organization may bring about another barrier to motivating people to take part in the planning process. As noted in earlier chapters, negative personal feelings of *efficacy* and ability in planning tasks may prevent people from becoming actively involved. If collaborative decision-making skills are missing or somewhat rusty from lack of use, it will be useful to ask if planners would like additional training either before or during the planning process. It may be more useful to use actual organizational problems in such training activities. In this way, training can be a periodic tool to aid the diagnostic and decision-making elements of the planning process. As an ongoing element in the planning process, training can help build a collaborative, collective-authority atmosphere in the organization.

The Potential Need for External Change Agents

Educational organizations may need to break traditional authority patterns and develop unused abilities through external agents. Lack of collaborative authority and decision-making skills can block early progress in the planning process. Actively seeking external training resources is a proactive provision made by the planning initiators. OD experts and change agents working with the planning initiators can aid in group process skills necessary for collaborative decision making. Administrators or internal change agents may see the need for changing authority patterns and developing problem-solving skills; however, their current roles and performance expectations may block their effectiveness in developing the collaborative process. A disinterested third party can be used as an intervention early in the planning process to aid the shift in authority patterns and build the feelings of efficacy among planning group members. The planning initiator(s) should indicate the current or potential blocks to collaborative planning, such as lack of trust, restricted communication flow, lack of openness, and unwillingness to take risk. Appropriate education/training action can be taken by the external planner to surface barriers and to develop skills without threatening the persons involved.

More will be said about intervention strategies later; however, in the planning preparation activities, change planners in education should be aware of the resources available through these external agents. The linking process for the planning team should be open-ended, with periodic forays into the environment for the purposes of tapping new resources and connecting with potential knowledge sources. Chapter 6 will develop the concept of a linking network as a valuable tool in the planning process.

Question 8 of list 5-1 deals with the variables with potential for change in the organization. Although it is important not to get bogged down in the preparation for planning, the planning team may want to have an inventory of potential elements in the organization or between organization and environment that may change as a result of planning. Much of this will come about during the diagnosis and the resources/constraints assessment stages of planning. Several categories of variables in organizations may be useful as indicators of potential barriers to planning and changing: (1) individual personality and leadership styles of managers, (2) power and authority configurations, (3) role expectations for faculty and staff, (4) technology (methods of performing primary tasks), (5) system/environment relationships, (6) goals or outcomes, (7) methods of individual and organizational renewal, (8) acquisition and allocation of fiscal resources.

The authority/power questions for the preparation of planning are very important considerations. The collaborative authority pattern of the planning group may directly challenge the current power structure in the educational system. Sensitivity to this can alert planners to team-building needs and the need to prepare for conflict as power shifts or is perceived to be shifting away from current power holders. If participants in the planning process have a tradition of subordinate action (e.g., needing approval, following imposed directives, or conforming to collective patterns of action), efforts may be needed to interrupt the traditional mode of behavior. Structural changes in the organization will, in the P/ICM, follow the generation of solutions and the trial stage; however, the organization of the planning group itself may provide at least a temporary structural change. Preparation should be made for facilitating the creation of new structures and working with individual discomfort involved in the instability of the planning process. If these preparatory steps are not taken, changes in task, technology, and people are very unlikely to flow from the planning and implementation processes.

Involving Environmental Elements in Decision Making

Premise 5-8. The decision-making process should involve not only members of the educational system concerned, but also, members of that system's environment who have potential for facilitating or blocking the change effort.

Although not all environmental members with this potential can be identified prior to the initiation of the P/ICM, preparation should be made for entry at the different stages of the process. This will not only bring about a need for making space at the meeting table, but will also necessitate provision for legitimizing new members into the process.

Preparation for planning must include an awareness of the current system/

environment relationship and the identification of potential human resources that can be used in the planning process (questions 9 and 10 in list 5-1). Again, it must be emphasized that this awareness process will be incomplete. The P/ICM is designed to identify environment forces and resources; however, some preliminary decisions should be made with regard to including members of the environment in the process. Are community members and parents currently participating in decisions that affect various aspects of the school? Are valuable knowledge and skill resources available in the community? What is the current link between the school and other educational and knowledge-production institutions? Is there a need to develop collaborative decision-making skills among potential participants from the community?

Planning initiators may choose not to include all potential members of the change process in the initial stages of planning. It is, however, important to be aware of who the resource people are and how they may fit into the planning and implementation stages of change efforts. It is also important to note the potential costs to both planning and change if critical environmental human forces are excluded from the planning process.

A Note on Risk and Temporary Systems

RISK AND THE INITIATION OF CHANGE

Risk is perhaps the most critical variable in the initiation of organizational change (question 11). Retention of the status quo is not always risk-free in open social systems; however, it is often perceived to be less threatening than entering into new and uncharted waters of educational change. The sources of risk most salient to potential innovators are the unintended, unanticipated, and dysfunctional consequences of the change action. This leads to two additional premises.

Premise 5-9. The degree to which educational organizations are willing to take risks is positively related to the successful initiation of change.

Premise 5-10. The willingness of organizational members to take risks is inversely related to the perceived negative consequences for the individual (s) involved in the initiation of a change.

These premises are supported by the literature in OD, planned change, organizational behavior, and knowledge production and use (KP&U) (Havelock et al 1971; Havelock and Havelock 1973; J. D. Thompson 1967; March and Simon 1958; Schon 1967; Argyris 1965; Watson 1966; Schmuck et al. 1972; Schmuck and Miles 1971; and others).

It is not the purpose here to discuss all of the various aspects of risk and their consequences for change. Awareness of potential risk in both the planning for and implementation of change is essential for the preparation for planning stages of the change process. What is needed for the planning process are preparatory strategies for minimizing the perception of risk in the planning process; increasing the ability of planning-team members to live with risk; and decreasing the degree to which negative consequences of change efforts fall on the backs of individual members of the organization.

Premise 5-11. The degree to which individuals believe the consequences of the innovation or change will be attributed to them alone is inversely related to their willingness to take risks.

The more innovative an individual is, the more likely it is that he or she will be alone in initiating innovations. This is emphasized in school systems, in which teachers are relatively isolated in performing their responsibilities. Although this isolation allows certain actions to be hidden from peers, superiors, and others, significant change cannot be hidden for very long, especially from student clients. This process of isolated change is well known to teachers and is tied to a reluctance to initiate change. The innovator is often perceived as a threat by others in the school or office who are more closely tied to the traditional way of doing things. Thus, the innovator may become further isolated from peer interaction and support.

What kinds of steps can be taken to reduce risk or increase willingness to take risks in educational organizations? One way to reduce the risk of a given innovation or change strategy is the "testing/trial" stage of the P/ICM. Here the planning process allows for a small-scale, experimental, or short-term pilot use of the innovation. However, this does little to reduce the threat of participation in the planning process itself when the broad scope of the organization is involved.

TEMPORARY SYSTEMS

The use of temporary systems is a strategy for reducing risk, sharing responsibility for consequences of change, introducing the systematic planning and implementation process of organizational development and change, initiating system/environment linkage, sharing resources and opening communications without status and role barriers, and facilitating short-term planning around a specific problem or concern. Traditional temporary systems include training courses, seminars, conferences, and conventions. More recent temporary systems include laboratory training, survey feedback and problem solving, action research, and task force or team problem solving.

The critical difference between temporary and more permanent systems is the time element. Temporary systems have a starting point, a collaborative decision-making and action stage, and an ending or closure point. Miles (1964) describes these features as input characteristics, process characteristics, and output characteristics, respectively.

Input characteristics include time limits, goal/objective definition, boundary definition and maintenance, and size limitations. Process characteristics include new role definitions, formation of communications patterns, new norms and group sentiments, goal redefinition, socialization, redefinition of authority structures and power sources, group-determined operating procedures, and lower status barriers. Output characteristics include changes resulting from group planning and decision making, attitude changes on the part of the members, knowledge and behavior shifts, new and reformed interpersonal relations, action decisions, and strategies for linking and integration into the larger system.

The use of the temporary system as a demonstration for the P/ICM in educational organizations allows members to plan and develop change strategies in an environment free from the normative constraints of the organization. Members participate as coequals and are released from many of the day-to-day constraints of their organizational tasks.

Temporary-system tasks are assigned through the process of the group interaction. Goals are set, reviewed, and redefined with an eye to flexibility. Authority and power decisions are temporary and shift on the basis of group decision and need. Process activities are designed for collaborative interaction and decision making. Cohesiveness is the team-building goal of the temporary system. Action decisions are supported by the team members. In short, the temporary system allows planning and implementation to occur without the traditional bureaucratic authority and communications barriers of the larger and more complex organization. In fact, some students of organizational development and change forecast the use of temporary-system planning and decision making as the dominant mode for future organization problem solving (Bennis and Slater 1968).

The initiators of the planning process in school systems can use the temporary system for the P/ICM. This will allow participants to share risk and responsibility for action decisions and adoption of innovations. Successful demonstration of the use of P/ICM in the temporary system will increase the credibility of planning processes.

The reduction of risk, the lowering of traditional status barriers to resource use and communication flow, and the shared planning and responsibility for actions allow the temporary system to bring organizational members into the planning and decision-making process without the awesome consequences (as perceived by the neophyte) of bringing the entire organization into the planning process.

Derr and Demb (1974) discuss the willingness of change agents and OD trainers to initiate OD activities on a small scale in educational organizations in order to provide a less threatening entry process. Another valuable use of temporary systems will come in the development of linking systems with environmental human and organizational resources (Florio 1973a; Havelock and Havelock 1973; Miles 1964). The linking system is designed to encourage the organization members to increase their "cosmopoliteness" or the degree to which the orientation of members is external to the social system. Initiating a temporary planning system as an introduction device for the P/ICM will also demonstrate the benefits of temporary linking systems needed for the "development of reciprocal and collaborative relations with a variety of resource systems (cosmopoliteness)'' (Havelock and Havelock 1973:31) during the linking stages of the P/ICM. Once the value of the planning model has been demonstrated in the temporary system, it will usually be easier to involve the larger organization in planning and implementing change efforts.

Additionally, the temporary system allows the breaking of the traditional isolation of teachers and administrators in practice institutions (schools). The "organizationally nonintegrative" teaching role (Blumberg and Schmuck 1972) needs to be broken for the successful application of the P/ICM. The temporary system is a useful tool in breaking through these isolation barriers.

The Proactive/Interactive Change Model (P/ICM)

THE PLANNING MODEL AND THE NEED FOR LINKING

Many strategies of change in educational organizations start with the "entry process" for the external change agent, consultant, and so forth. This is particularly true with the organizational development and intervention theorists (e.g., Argyris 1970; Derr 1972; Blake and Mouton 1964, 1974; Miles 1964; Schmuck and Miles 1971; Bennis, Benne, and Chin 1969). Many of their strategies were developed in laboratory training and noneducational organizations and were transferred to the education or school setting. It is not the intent here to suggest that intervention from external agents is unnecessary in the change process in school systems; however, the elaborated Proactive/Interactive Change Model presented below is based on the assumption that change can be initiated through internal forces and that educational systems can be self-renewing. The model and planning tools presented in this chapter are intended as guidelines for all change planners but with special concern for the internal planner—for example, the manager, administrator, or teacher within school systems. Note that *organizational* planning presupposes an internally initiated change process, as opposed to having outsiders plan *for* the organization.

Other chapters have reviewed various models of change. Unlike those models, the P/ICM is not meant to describe how change occurs in school systems. Rather, the model is given to provide a conceptual planning framework for internally initiated change processes. To the extent that it is used, it may well describe change in an organization. Its use here, however, is primarily prescriptive rather than descriptive. Being prescriptive, it takes on a more rational perspective. This is intentional, although it would be naive to assume that it would operate in the absence of so-called political factors.

There is necessary interaction between system and environment in open social systems. A self-renewing social system is one that is better able to plan for and select the time, process, and nature of that interaction with its environment than those organizations not engaged in a systematic change process. The school, as an open social system, is in constant contact with its environment and must build structures to accommodate that contact if it is to be constructive. The school, in planning for social change through a systematic process, places constraints on the random nature of system/environment interaction. In this manner, the manager, planner, or change agent actively seeks constructive contact with environmental forces and resources.

Figure 5-3 is a visual elaboration of the proactive/interactive change process.

THE NEED FOR DIVERSITY AND FLEXIBILITY

The model presented in figure 5-3 indicates the dynamic state of the change process when internally initiated, yet with significant interplay between system and environment. Throughout the various activities in the planning process, the model provides considerable *flexibility*. The flexibility is shown in the broken feedback lines leading from later planning stages to earlier activities as the team or planning group sees fit. The broken lines in the model indicate a potential need to work back up the planning process in order to expand a diagnosis, increase awareness of resources and/or constraints, generate additional alternatives, try or test different or revised innovations, or make additional need assessments. Although the P/ICM indicates a linear progression, indicative of a rational systems analysis problem-solving process, the synthesis of organizational development activities with the more rational approach may point out the need to skip a stage or start at different points in the process. In short, self-renewing institutions generally view planning and diagnosis through need assessments and evaluation as a continual process in the organization. As such, the planning group may pick up the planning effort for change at the stage most sensible for the organization.

The "turnkey phase" in the P/ICM represents the need for transition in the planning and decision-making efforts. The previous comments on temporary systems and the planning team have indicated that the earlier stages of planning (e.g., awareness through resources/constraints) may be carried out by a group representing various role sets in the organization. The turnkey phase of the planning process is an attempt to involve other critical people in the latter stages of planning and decision making with regard to specific changes or innovations. Beginning with the generation of alternative solutions or in the testing/trial (demonstration) stage of planning, the planning group should begin to involve others in the review and demonstration of potential innovations or changes. The movement from a decision to adopt to a commitment to change calls for a much greater depth of involvement in the system. This is specifically designed to close the gaps between adoption and implementation. The turnkey phase and other integration steps between the temporary and larger system are elaborated in chapter 6.

THE LINKING SYSTEM AND NETWORK

The term *linking* is used here to refer to the various formal and informal relationships between the planning group and various elements and organizations

FIGURE   5-3.   The   Proactive/Interactive Change Model[1]

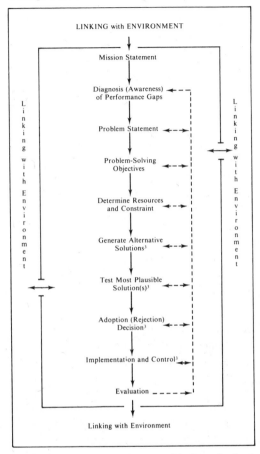

1. Dotted lines represent potential direct feedback and recycling from any one stage to any other stage.
2. Need assessment is a particularly relevant input for this stage.
3. Turnkey phases.

in the environment. As the planners move through the various stages of the P/ICM, there will be occasional need for activating relationships with individuals, information sources, and other resources in the environment of the organization. As the planning team gets closer to taking some action, forces of resistance in external groups may arise. The need for proactive and interactive planning and changing in educational systems has been developed earlier. The P/ICM includes the potential for linking with these forces at various stages in the planning and changing process. The need assessment effort must include systematic association with various publics and client groups in the environment. Although this is

FIGURE 5-4. A Simplified Linking Network Model

true for social system planning in general, its importance is heightened for publicly supported social agencies such as schools, health care centers, and various social service organizations.

The model shows a solid line leading from linking to the *resources/ constraints* stage of planning. A more informal linking system will exist throughout the P/ICM process, as shown in figure 5-4. A linking network will be a valuable tool for the development of an inventory of resources and constraints: aids, barriers, external innovations, resistance, and other forces for and against change both within and without the organization. The linking network is more fully developed in chapter 6; however, figure 5-4 is a simplified linking model that describes the relationship between the planning group, potential resource systems in the environment, and the change-targeted social system.

The planning team has formal ties with both system types. Resource and user system memberships may overlap or come together in the planning process. Of course, individuals from either resource-producing systems or resource-user systems may have dual membership or, in fact, may shift membership. The planning team may include members from both organizations and thus strengthen the linkages among the ongoing organizations.

The latter stages of the P/ICM (implementation, control, and evaluation) will be covered in later chapters. It is important to mention here that all stages of the planning process should be open for feedback to the organizational members and, specifically, the planning group. In this manner, the flow of data is a constant stimulus for the planning group or organizational leaders to take appropriate problem-solving efforts. The evaluation stage is mentioned last in the P/ICM; however, it is also the first step in the regeneration of a self-renewing organizational process. Feedback from the evaluation provides data for diagnosing additional organizational problems in the continuous planning and changing process of viable open social systems.

Summary

This chapter introduced the planning process and provided a model for planning and changing in educational systems. The model is designed to bring about self-renewal, and does this by having the system initiate planning and proactively seek relationships and interplay with environmental elements. Through interaction with the environment, the system is able to diagnose its current condition and begin to systematically plan for movement and change needed to correct any ailments.

A simplified planning model for proactive/interactive changing was presented for educational organizations, with an emphasis on those institutions closest to the primary client group of parents and students, that is, the schools. The case was made for involving a broadly based representative group in the planning process, and some critical questions that need attention prior to initiating a planning effort were considered. Involvement is not enough to guarantee active participation. Therefore, a case was made for analysis of current power and authority relationships within the organization and with primary client groups. This points out the potential need for external change agents to aid the organizational members in developing capacity to plan and change productively.

The use of a representative group for planning can alleviate the potential risks in planning and innovating. Temporary systems allow for broad-based representation, shared risk, and time away from the day-to-day role expectations for organizational participants.

The Proactive/Interactive Change Model was presented, indicating a need for flexibility, transition from temporary to full systems, and feedback at various stages in the planning and changing process. A linking process to increase the awareness of the interaction between system and environment was discussed. A more formal linking network was advocated for the identification of forces for and against both planning and change. The following chapter develops the planning stages of the P/ICM in an effort to provide a conceptual basis for various stages with specific suggested procedures for implementing the planning process.

6

Implementing the Planning Model

THE PROACTIVE/INTERACTIVE CHANGE MODEL is a suggested planning and changing process for viable open social systems. It is an effort to increase the capacity of education to marshall the various forces affecting internally initiated change. Rather than continually reacting to environmental forces, the educational institution can direct and shape the course of system and environmental relationships. While no planning process will allow for the system to control all such forces and relationships, systematic planning for problem solving can greatly enhance self-renewal capabilities.

The previous chapter introduced a model and discussed the need for planning. Here we shall conduct a "guided tour" through the planning process. For describing the planning and changing processes advocated, key words are *open, flexible, thoughtful,* and *linking.* The system is open to input from its members and from external sources (e.g., people, ideas, other information and knowledge resources). The process is flexible in that the planners are free to move about the various stages of planning as the situation demands. It is thoughtful. Many planning activities are designed to bring to consciousness various aspects of the system, the environment, and the potential for change. The process is based on human and organizational linkages in order to increase resources available for planning, organizational development, and change or innovation. The links also heighten the ability of the planning team to assess the needs of the system's various clients and identify problems either within the organization or in the interface between organization and environment.

The P/ICM represents an eclectic process, drawing on the various knowledge resources of organizational development, systems analysis, managerial psychology, organizational theory, systems thinking, and knowledge production and use.

144

Stage One. Stating the Organizational Mission (Goals and Objectives)

When the planning group or team has been identified and brought together, the first stage of the process for the organization is the collaborative development of an "organizational mission statement."

WHY A MISSION STATEMENT?

The purpose of the mission statement in the P/ICM is to help the planning team identify problem areas in need of immediate attention. It is important not to get bogged down in specifying goals and objectives in behavioral terms when developing the mission statement. Stating the organizational goals of a school or school system should not be a unilateral action of any single system member or role position. The P/ICM is designed for collaborative decision making among relevant actors both within the system and in the environment. Ideally, the planning group (change-agent team) should not make or appear to be making unilateral decisions concerning the organizational mission; however, the group can initiate action to begin building the set of organizational purposes into a mission statement.

A useful tool for building the mission statement is the process of "brainstorming" in small groups. This process is designed to generate all the potential purposes for the organization without editorial comment or critique. It is also a useful team-building tool. Members from diverse professional and nonprofessional backgrounds are free to define the organization's goals without constraint. Once the goal/objective identification process has been exhausted, the planning team comes together to share the raw data of their efforts. Redundant purpose statements are synthesized; clarifications of purpose elements are made; and subordinate statements are categorized under major umbrella headings, such as learning objectives for clients, curriculum content, professional competence, community competence, and environmental interaction. Once this has been done, the general headings and subordinate objectives can be included in a "preference survey." This survey can be used by the planning team to generate a priority data base among the potential elements in the mission statement. The team may wish to survey others, such as faculty/staff not on the team, parents and students, and community leaders. Once surveys are completed, the data should be collected and summarized for members of the planning team.

In diverse groups, consensus may not be reached immediately. The survey data should be analyzed and diverse interpretations discussed in planning team groups. Members differing with the majority should have opportunity to define and defend their positions. All members are given a chance to react to the survey data. Provision should be made for adding new members to the planning team when that is deemed appropriate. Critical questions should be raised about the various mission elements: (1) Can it be done? (2) How will we know when we have accomplished a goal? (3) Do we have the present resources available for achieving the goal? (4) What limits should be placed on the elements in the mission statement? (5) What further information is needed?

The mission statement should not only set forth the organization's purposes but should *identify the groups affected by those purposes*. In educational systems, employee groups and clients should be identified (e.g., teachers, administrators, parents, taxpayers, students, community leaders, governmental bodies).

A NEED FOR FLEXIBILITY IN EDUCATIONAL ORGANIZATIONS

There is a potential danger in starting the planning process with a mission statement. The process may get unnecessarily blocked in an attempt to build consensus around the goals and objectives. If a critical problem is already at hand, the P/ICM may need to be revised to start with the problem identification or awareness stage and build back to organizational mission at a later point. True believers in management by objectives (MBO) would have a great deal of difficulty with this deviation; however, the overall purpose of the P/ICM is to generate a collaborative problem-solving process in order to create a continuous self-renewing organization. Thus, the starting point in the planning process is relative to the situation at hand. Change planners should be free to decide the most productive planning process. Although the mission statement is a useful learning device and planning tool, potential pitfalls and dangers in the identification of goals and objectives may indicate a need to start with the awareness stage of the P/ICM. The P/ICM is designed to help organizational planners to clarify their thought. It is not designed to lock planners into preconceived notions and rules. The planning process ought to be as free from constraints on creative thinking and association as possible.

LIMITATIONS OF MISSION STATEMENTS

James March (1972) notes the usefulness of normative theories of action following values in organizations "given a consistent set of preferences"; however, he is also concerned with system members who are not sure that their present values are the ones they wish to act upon.

> Perhaps we should explore a somewhat different approach to the normative question of how we ought to behave when our value premises are not yet (and never will be) fully determined. Suppose we treat action as a way of creating interesting goals at the same time as we treat goals as a way of justifying action.

March is making the point that people sometimes need to act before they think. Thus, planning-team members should not always have to justify their strategies, plans, or actions by a given set of goals and objectives in a mission statement. Educational institutions have a relative set of goals, given the shifting composition of the institution and the demands of the client population. With this in mind, the planning and implementation processes in the change model can be used to define and redefine the organizational mission through discovery of goals and objectives.

The above statements seem to indicate that starting with a mission statement in the P/ICM would be an unnecessary exercise. What is being said is that there is a choice for the initial stage of the process. If the planning team starts at the awareness stage, it should not ignore the need for identifying purposes for the organization. Rather, that identification should be a continuous process throughout the planning and implementing stages of organization change and innovation. If the process starts with a mission statement, that statement should be recognized as a useful tool and not as a constraining box. Mission statements are meant to be flexible and revised as the need arises.

EXAMPLE

An example will be useful at this point. The change-target institution is a small independent school in the midst of a large metropolitan area. The primary client group for the school is a community of professional people living in and around a major health-service and think-tank center. The school receives most of its support from the center; however, the center is entirely supported by money from the federal government. The ages of the students range from four to sixteen years. Most of the students go on to other forms of education primarily in preparation for human service professions, such as health, medicine, education, government, and welfare.

The planning group for the school has surveyed the various clients to determine a set of priority goals for a mission statement. Those surveyed include parents, students, teachers, administrators, representatives from the center, and various educational agencies that work with the school's graduates. An initial round of survey returns indicates that the school's mission ought to include service to the broader metropolitan community and to a diverse student population representative of the broader community. As a result, a later survey included parents and community leaders from several neighboring areas.

The general mission was to provide students with a broad-based educational background including specific cognitive skills to aid them in later formal and independent learning. The school also should provide an acquaintance with various human service professions and some of the skills needed in working with people on an interpersonal basis. The mission statement remained incomplete for several reasons. The new survey material indicated a need to provide job skills for some of the children. The managers in the think tank wanted to wait for specific behavioral objectives before moving on. The team needed to be expanded to include representatives from the other neighboring areas. The team decided to move on to some pressing problems that surfaced during this first stage.

Stage Two. Awareness/Diagnosis: Problem Identification

The first actual step in the planned change process is the problem identification stage. Although listed as the second step in the P/ICM, the awareness/diagnosis stage is an alternative starting point. The organizational mission development stage is the other starting point and can be helpful as a clarifying and diagnostic tool in determining performance gaps. Problem identification is the initial proactive step in planning for change and is essential to the P/ICM process.

Premise 6-1. Planned change cannot occur unless the organizational members are aware of the need for change or innovation.

"Awareness" and/or "diagnosis" is the initial stage of many adoption models for consumers and change models for organizations. Although it may be called by different names (e.g., knowledge, perception, dissonance), the central theme is the awareness among group members of a need for change and renewal (Robertson 1971; Rogers and Shoemaker 1971; Zaltman, Duncan, and Holbek 1973; Schmuck et al. 1972; and others).

UNFREEZING AND INITIAL MOVING

Lewin (1952) discusses three conceptual stages of social change: unfreezing, moving, and freezing (refreezing). The awareness stage of the P/ICM is the first step in the "unfreezing" of an organization. Advocates of the problem-solving approach to innovation (Havelock et al. 1971) suggest that the unfreezing stage of organizational change starts with some form of dissatisfaction with the status quo. (This was discussed in chapter 2.) This dissatisfaction or feeling of dissonance is the initial part of the awareness/diagnosis stage of the P/ICM. The planning team takes *proactive* steps to move from this initial discomfort to problem identification.

The proactive planning team members have the task of translating the initial feelings of discomfort and awareness into a problem-identification statement. How might the planning group support this movement?

THE GATHERING AND USE OF DIAGNOSTIC DATA

The process of data gathering and analysis serves three purposes for the change process: (1) it provides an initial objective and/or impersonal (less threatening) data base to clarify and sharpen perceptions among organization members; (2) it allows the planning group to focus on the critical organizational problems(s) for priority action; and (3) it gives the group a focus for personal interaction that will allow members to surface, clarify, and deal with perceptions, biases, feelings, and communication blocks. The use of data, either perceptual or objective, moves the group toward a problem statement and allows the planning group to strengthen its abilities in communication and cohesion building. The latter is the part of the awareness stage designed to build functional working groups useful in planning and implementing organizational change.

The objective data base may already be available to school organizations. Unobtrusive measures such as attendance data, records of vandalism, logs of office visits, and materials inventories may be used in the initial data base. Test scores, grades, follow-up data on alumni, percentage of class entrants graduating, and so forth may also be used as data. These objective measures should be viewed as the first part of the data-collection process. They deal for the most part with the symptoms of organizational problems. Some of this is feedback from the environment on how well the organization is doing: parent satisfaction, successful continuation of education, job placement, and so forth. Additional data may be used from program evaluations, external research studies, and observational reports gathered previously.

SURVEY FEEDBACK AND PROBLEM IDENTIFICATION

There is a companion data base that hits more directly at the educator's perceptions of the health of the organization. This information is derived from perceptions by the organization's personnel and clients concerning organizational process and product. A widely used and very applicable tool for getting at these perceptions is a survey. There has been considerable writing about the use of "survey feedback and problem solving" as a strategy for organizational development. More recently this has been extended to school systems as a useful tool for initiating organizational change based on collective decision making (Miles et al. 1971; Coughlan, Cooke, and Safer 1972; Cooke, Duncan, and Zaltman 1974). The use of survey data as an intervention in the group planning and problem-solving process of P/ICM can be seen as the step taken to move the planning team from awareness to diagnosis.

The content of such a survey will be generated in the initial stages of planning action. Examples of items often covered by surveys are given in list 6-1.

The value of survey feedback as the stimulus for problem identification is that it not only provides understanding of the perceptions held by various members of the system and environment, but also provides for a legitimization and acceptance of the data. Survey feedback is designed to get the organization to make

FIGURE 6-1. The Awareness/Diagnosis-Problem Identification Stage, P/ICM

Awareness   Date Gathering and Analysis   Problem Formulation

(Unfreezing the organization)   (Initial Moving)

LIST 6-1.   A Sample of a Survey-Feedback/Data-Generating Inventory

Professional Work Environment
1. Professional/nonprofessional orientation
2. Cosmopoliteness/localness of the staff
3. Innovativeness of the organization
4. Decision-making authority structure
5. Open/closed system-environment interaction
6. Free/constrained communications flow among organizational members
7. Formal/informal decision-making pattern
8. Autonomy/dependence of school vis-à-vis central office
9. Conflict resolution/management strategies
10. Level of risk capital
11. Resource strength
12. Level of involvement in decision making
13. Client-centered/content-centered nature of instructional process
14. Support for change
15. Isolation/interaction of professional peers

Personal Attitude/Opinion Inventory
1. Organizational commitment
2. Innovativeness
3. Willingness to take risks
4. Decision-making style (independent, interactive, dependent)
5. Scope of professional role (narrow/broad)
6. Local/cosmopolitan orientation
7. Isolation/interaction with peers
8. Awareness of developments and innovations in the field
9. Curriculum content- or client-centered
10. Hygienic/motivation orientation for satisfaction

Environment Perceptions
1. The school is open/closed to the community and parents.
2. Community members participate in policy decisions for the school.
3. The school is willing to respond to the needs of the community.
4. The community is generally supportive of the change efforts of the school.
5. The school is able to use the resources of the community.

a self-analysis based on the members' *own* perceptions of the technology, structure, and processes of the organization. Coughlan, Cooke, and Safer (1972) discuss the value of feeding back survey data to groups rather than individuals. They comment on the benefits of broad-based problem solving, "pooling and exchange" of information among members in natural work settings, increased recognition of shared perceptions of problems, clarifying performance expectations of peers and subordinates, and "reciprocal pressures . . . [from] mutual expectations to implement decisions agreed upon by the group."

Miles et al. (1971) mention five beneficial outcomes of survey feed back and problem solving:

1. Acceptance of data
2. Increased linking among group members (and for group activities)

3. Clarification of own and others' positions
4. Practice of new behavior
5. Development of norms that support open, collaborative problem solving

They also suggest that the feedback data be used in group discussion meetings and that the discussion process be used to develop group interaction and decision-making skills. Members take responsibility for their own meeting agendas, the planning of group sessions, interpreting data, and making and implementing action decisions. Through the process of surfacing norms of behavior, barriers, supports, and constraints for change become clarified and dealt with. A group norm is developed around collaborative problem solving. When accompanied by more objective data, the survey information helps group members to increase acceptance of the problem and clarify reasons for success or failure.

When the data have been collected, fed back, analyzed, and discussed, the planning group should begin to list (brainstorm) all of the problems that might be dealt with in the organization. Redundant problem statements and similar concerns can be synthesized and categorized to determine whether the problems stated are causal or symptomatic. The group members should attempt to push back each problem to determine if they are dealing with a cause. This can be done by attempting to identify causes for each problem stated. When the group finds it difficult to do this, it is getting to the root problems to be dealt with. If the same root causal problem is given for many of those initially stated, priorities become apparent and the group begins the process of forming a problem-identification statement.

A note about linking is important here. The data collection, survey construction and application, feedback, and analysis may be difficult to use effectively the first time. The links to external change agents and those experienced in survey feedback and problem solving have been built into the P/ICM. The use of external resource people is an option for the planning team. If used, the external person should also play an educational role for the team so that future data gathering and analysis efforts can be accomplished by the team members.

A note here about awareness or diagnosis is directed at the need for a continual self-awareness and self-renewal mode for school systems. Although the process of evaluation for change efforts will be developed later, the diagnosis/ awareness (problem identification) stage of the P/ICM is the starting point for developing a continuous evaluation or "monitoring" process for the system.

NOTIONS OF A HEALTHY, INNOVATIVE ORGANIZATION

Premise 6-2. Organizational illness cannot be adequately diagnosed unless there is an understanding of organizational health.

The organizational mission statement and the survey data categories given in this and the previous stages of the P/ICM provide useful indicators of the system elements, environmental forces, and personal perceptions that could be monitored under a continuous planning process. However, there is an additional need to develop an "organizational health inventory" to be monitored constantly. The proactive planning process of the organization should not be left to the intuitive feelings of dissonance or dissatisfaction for future diagnostic efforts. Once the planning team has gone through the awareness process, it can begin to develop an organizational monitoring system through the use of the inventory of the healthy, innovative organization.

In addition to the indicators derived from the mission statement and survey inventory given above, the elements presented in list 6-2 will be useful in developing the organizational health inventory.

In many ways the P/ICM can be seen as an eclectic synthesis of many of these elements given for healthy, innovative organizations. Some of the elements are not applicable or will need adaptation for each situation, but in general they may be used as a guide in constructing an inventory for the continued monitoring of the organization so that awareness and diagnosis become an ongoing part of the school system.

Returning to our earlier example, the school planning team's initial feelings of dissonance between the desired and actual practice of the institution have unfrozen the organization in several ways. Providing students with basic skills to further their education did not seem to be enough. Although many of the younger children seemed pleased with their educational program, some of the older students complained of the "unrealistic atmosphere" and homogeneity of the student population. Data from graduates indicated that the school did provide a sound cognitive development for later learning; however, a significant number of graduates felt they were ill prepared to work in social service professions dealing with people from a broad spectrum of economic and cultural backgrounds.

The staff, while generally pleased with the operation of the school and the degree of freedom to innovate in their work groups, indicated a frustration with current policy regarding external activities of students, such as visiting resource centers and working with community agencies. In short, the staff felt isolated from other social service agencies which could enhance the educational program for students. Several faculty members on the planning team also indicated that the team meetings were among only a few opportunities they had to interact with professional peers outside of the work group (their teaching team).

The planning team used the survey technique both to identify problems and to clarify perceptions and feelings among planning participants. The growth of the planning team to include additional community leaders from the larger metropolitan area provided the team with some additional data concerning the external perceptions of the school. The school seemed to be viewed as an elitist institution exclusively available to the professional staff of the think-tank and health center. Previous efforts to include some low-income students from the surrounding urban area had failed, in part because of the elitist reputation of the school.

A positive revelation was the center's willingness to include students from families not directly associated with the professional staff of the center. They

LIST 6-2. Inventories of Attributes in Healthy Organizations

John Gardner *(Rules for Effective Self-Renewing Organizations,* 1965):
1. Recruits and develops talent
2. Built-in provisions for self-evaluation and criticism
3. Organizational structure is fluid
4. A means is available to avoid becoming prisoners of procedures

Richard Beckhard *(Improving Organizations,* 1966):
1. Decisions are made close to information source (regardless of locus)
2. Reward system supports (a) short-term production (teaching and learning), (b) growth and development of subordinates (technical staff or teachers), and (c) creation of viable work groups
3. Open communication system (facts and feelings freely shared)
4. Conflict over ideas, not personalities (win/win rather than win/lose)
5. Open system (free flow of communication and resources between system and environment)
6. Action-research orientation with feedback (data on performance) used to teach from experience
7. Balance between consultation from inside expertise and outside resources
8. Willingness to take risks
9. Tolerance for ambiguity

Victor Thompson *(The Innovative Organization,* 1969):
1. Uncommitted and unspecified resources (money, time, skill, and goodwill)
2. Provision and permission for diversity of input (experience and stimulation)
3. Balance between individuals' (members') commitment to and alienation from the organization
4. Deemphasis on usual extrinsic rewards
5. Emphasis on internal rewards of satisfaction, professional growth, and peer esteem (also in Herzberg 1966; Sergiovanni and Carver 1973)
6. An indulgent creative atmosphere of risk and mistake sharing
7. Collaboration (win/win) over competition (win/lose)

Mathew B. Miles *(Organizational Health: Figure and Ground,* 1965):
1. Goal focus (clear, accepted, and acted upon)
2. Communication adequacy (free and relatively distortion-free both within organization and between organization and environment)
3. Optimal power equalization (influence rests on competence rather than position)
4. Resource utilization (members are motivated to actualize their potential)
5. Cohesiveness (collaboration and commitment to organization)
6. Morale (feelings of well-being)
7. Innovativeness (movement to growth, development, and change)
8. Autonomy (proactive)
9. Adaptation (interaction with environment and self-correcting change)
10. Problem-solving adequacy (active coping with problems)

---

indicated a desire to include children of nonprofessional staff families; however, they would allow a number of other students into the school on a limited basis. (Notice that the diagnosis/awareness efforts already begin to move the planning team into resource identification.)

Stage Three. Objectives: Problem-solving Purposes

Following the identification of a critical problem for the educational system, the planning team should generate statements of what they would like to accomplish. Elements in a statement of problem-solving objectives should be given in terms that are useful for a later evaluation of the problem-solving effort, organizational change, or innovation.

The team may use several of the instruments given before for the initial generation process: brainstorming, force-field analysis, survey feedback, and so on. However, the team must take the data from these instruments and translate them into a statement of objectives indicating different or changed behavior for the members and/or clients of the system. Again, a word of caution is necessary. It is useful to remember James March's statement that not all strategies or actions must be justified in light of stated goals and objectives. The team should not get unnecessarily bogged down in the process of generating problem-solving objectives. It is a useful tool for the assessment of needs, the generation of alternative solutions, and the evaluation process; however, the team may wish to move ahead with other parts of the planning process and work back to this statement when alternative solutions have been generated.

The example school may have a variety of potential problems; however, given the working process of the planning team and the data review and assessment, the team is concentrating on the isolation of the school, the homogeneity of its student population, and the frustration of faculty with school/environment interaction. These problems seem to have a common thread in the need to diversify experiences for student clients in the educational program.

The specific objectives for the school include the following: (1) a student population that includes representation from a broad spectrum of the surrounding urban area in each student work unit; (2) increased time and incentives for teachers to work together in planning for the use of external social and material resources in the educational program; and (3) the involvement of various social and cultural groups in the planning and operational aspects of the school.

A Note on Need Assessment

The P/ICM indicates that need assessment is a significant part of several stages of the planning process. The client for which a need assessment is performed may shift with the specific need of the planning group. The need assessment process, discussed in detail in chapter 7, is mentioned here as both a significant part of the planning process and an ongoing effort throughout planning, adoption, and implementation efforts of organizational change. Although a formal need assessment is unnecessary for all stages of planning and changing, assessing needs is critical for the successful operation of social systems.

Need assessment is also a critical step in the linking process and a useful tool for recognizing the limitations of resources available within the organization or planning team. Additionally, the need assessment is already an active part of planning when the team has reviewed its own needs, expanded its membership, used external change agents and/or team-building resource people, used informational resources, and so forth.

As the team moves through the problem-solving objectives stage, concentration on the resources perceived to be unavailable within the team or organization will become important. Several general resource categories may be useful here: (1) knowledge/information resources, (2) human resources, (3) material/technology resources, and (4) power/authority resources.

The planning team must begin to establish a linking system with both general environmental forces and specific resource organizations. This linking system can be used to facilitate the identification of needs salient to team members and increase the awareness of resources previously unknown among organizational members. The inclusion of community and client-system members in the planning team is indicative of an ongoing systematic linking structure.

The movement of the planning process toward the resources/constraints stage calls for a systematic and well established network reaching out from the planning team to various resource-producing organizations in the environment. The following section deals with the development of such a network for the planning process and continued self-renewal of the organization.

The Linking Network: In Preparation for Identifying Resources and Contraints

THE NEED FOR LINKING CHANGE TARGETS WITH RESOURCES

Premise 6-3. The change/innovation process is enhanced by the establishment of viable links between the organization and resources within its environment.

The proactive planning team will enhance its ability to identify needed resources for the planned change effort through an established network of linkages with other educational and service systems. A body of knowledge is growing around the problems associated with the practical application of research findings and research and development efforts. Short (1973:237) sees this new realm of inquiry as directed toward the "improved coordination between the process of knowledge production and the process of knowledge utilization." Studies of the association between knowledge production and use (KP&U) have developed the concept of the "linking system" and "linking roles" associated with the systematic application of knowledge to practical problems in organizations. Havelock et al. (1971) and Rogers and Shoemaker (1971) deal with the problems associated with diffusion/dissemination and use of knowledge (D&U). The early studies by rural sociologists and the development of the U.S. Department of Agriculture's Cooperative Extension Service have been models for linking systems between knowledge production and knowledge application. The planning team can make use of this knowledge in determining the basis of their linking system with other knowledge production and practice institutions.

THE SCHOOL: A PRIMARY PRACTICE INSTITUTION

Premise 6-4. The school is the central practice institution for any collaborative interorganizational network for elementary and secondary education development (Florio 1973; Havelock et al. 1971).

The planning-team members can decide whether they want a temporary linking system built around the problem identified in the earlier stages of the P/ICM or a more permanent system for continuous relationships and linkages with resource organizations. It will be helpful to discuss some of the systematic ways of linking for both knowledge producers and users. Havelock gives four categories of linking forces: (1) communications media, (2) specialized linking roles, (3) temporary linking systems, and (4) permanent linking systems. Traditionally, the flow of knowledge from basic research to practical application for organizational problems has relied upon the individual scholars and graduates of professional schools to translate academic learning and research to the practice institutions (schools in education). KP&U and D&U studies have shown the weakness of such assumptions (Havelock et al. 1971; Guba 1972).

NORMATIVE DIFFERENCES IN EDUCATIONAL ORGANIZATIONS

Basic differences between the norms and values of knowledge-production institutions and those of the practice institutions have played up the difficulties in translating theory and research into practice. Much of the study of these problems has dealt with research and development efforts and the marketing of products. In education, these problems have significant implications for the planned-change process.

Premise 6-5. The existence of normative differences between knowledge-production organizations (universities, research centers, and laboratories) and the knowledge user (schools) in educational systems necessitates a linking system and broker roles between such organizations.

The broker role or institution acts as translator between research and user. The broker institution can bridge gaps in human interaction and language between the research scholar and practitioner in educational institutions. Professionals in the practicing institutions become involved not only as recipients of research and development products, but also in the formation of research and policies to improve educational practice. Broker systems would establish a continuous communication between knowledge producers and users and would blur the barriers between the two. Problems of the practitioner become the basis for the research, and problems of translation and application become part of the research process itself.

KNOWLEDGE SOURCES

The planning team may wish to establish a permanent or temporary linking system with knowledge-resource organizations. Not all of the links need be interpersonal, and the team may delegate certain roles to its members for the purposes of gaining knowledge for the planning efforts. Some of the potential knowledge sources are given in list 6-3.

LIST 6-3.   Some Knowledge-Resource Organizations

---

1. U.S. Office of Education
2. The National Institute of Education
3. State departments of education
4. Other local, state, and federal agencies
5. Mass media (radio, TV, press)
6. Community service organizations
7. Universities and colleges
8. Professional schools of education
9. Commercial producers of educational technology
10. Educational research and development centers and/or laboratories
11. Educational journals and publications
12. Professional associations
13. Scholarly discipline associations
14. Accreditation organizations
15. Business and industry (local)
16. Health and medical organizations
17. Local private and public schools (peers)
18. Local cultural institutions
19. Religious groups and churches
20. Citizen groups (community councils, parent/teacher groups, school/home associations, minority-organized groups and associations, other special interest groups)
21. Unions (teacher and other)

POTENTIAL LINKING PROCESSES

The linking process can take many forms, including (1) interpersonal ties, (2) cooperative activities, (3) collaborative planning, (4) reviewing of publications, (5) written or oral correspondence, (6) special information receiving and sending roles within the organization, (7) overlapping memberships, (8) retaining of consultants, (9) change-agent roles, (10) product or information presentations, and (11) the established linking system. A brief inventory of these linking functions among planning team and/or organizational members will reveal an "informal" linking structure already in operation within most educational organizations. The problem for the planning team will be to bring these informal links into the planning process as the team develops its needs, resources and constraints, and problem-solving strategies. Assigning team members to review the recent research on a problem area is but one way to increase the development of the linking structure. The establishment of a linking system may include the expansion of the planning team to include representatives from knowledge-production institutions. The organization may join or form an alliance or consortium of other schools and research- or knowledge-production institutions.

Another means of establishing a permanent relationship with a professional education school might be to develop a reciprocal agreement between the school and the university. In return for providing a site for action, field-based research, and clinical experiences for students, the school could gain several valuable resources from the university, including research and evaluation expertise, university faculty membership on the planning team, and in-service or professional development for school faculty. When this reciprocal arrangement is tied to the problem(s) identified by the P/ICM process, the linking network begins to approach the broker institution described above. Although not necessary for the linking process, special funding for research, development, and problem-solving efforts may be gained through the interaction with human resource expertise in proposal writing, scholarship, and publication of results of organizational development efforts. In short, the practice institution becomes part of the knowledge-production process.

MODELS OF LINKING SYSTEMS

The planning team should review the models of linking systems developed by Havelock et al. (1971) and Havelock and Havelock (1973): the research, development, and dissemination (RD&D), the social interaction (SI), the problem solver (PS), and the linkage process (LP) strategies for dissemination of innovations or knowledge.

The *RD&D model* is taken from more traditional R&D efforts and can be conceptualized as in figure 6-2. This is basically a linear model that views the practice institution as a passive receiver. The production, innovation, and development stages may involve the practice institution as part of the field-testing process; however, the strategy involves large-scale marketing and dissemination of a product.

FIGURE 6-2.   RD&D Perspective on Innovation Dissemination and Change

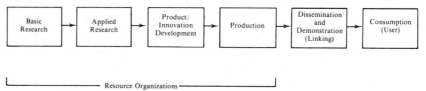

FIGURE 6-3. **Social Interaction Perspective of Innovation Dissemination and Change**

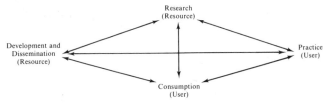

The *social interaction model* is much less systematic in that it relies on the informal linking structure of practice organizations and knowledge-production sources. Figure 6-3 describes the social interaction model.

The social interaction process is less a strategy and more a loose association among individuals involved in research, development, diffusion, practice, and consumption in educational systems. It has one advantage over the RD&D strategy in that it is not a unidirectional, linear strategy for dissemination. Communication, being informal and ad hoc, is often two-way. Research and development activities can come from problems informally identified from the interaction of practitioners and scholars. Connections are made through a series of reference groups and associations between resource and user organizations.

The *problem-solving strategy,* shown in figure 6-4, centers more on the user organization. Initiation of linking derives from some internal or external change agent (individual or group) that identifies a need for change; establishes a change relationship with resource and practice organizations and their members; clarifies or diagnoses problems, examines alternative strategies for change from identified resources and constraints; aids the transformation from adoption (intent) to implementation (action) of the selected strategy; and stabilizes (institutionalizing) the innovation.

In this perspective, the organization takes an initiating problem-solving mode and, with the aid of external change agents, actively seeks external resources and solutions following a problem diagnosis.

The linkage process is most closely analogous to the network proposed for the P/ICM. Through a temporary and more permanent linking system and planning team, the P/ICM elaborates the collaborative change process by a synthesis of both linking and planning efforts. Figure 6-5 outlines the linking network for the P/ICM. The model should be viewed as a potential system with elements to be used as appropriate in any given situation.

The planning team may initiate a temporary system of action research, collaborative action, or survey feedback and problem solving to generate the linking system. Members of the temporary system could include community members, parents, practice institution (school) professionals, members of professional school (university) faculty, and other resource institutions. A more permanent linking system could be developed out of this initial effort. As the process continues in an ongoing organizational planning and development effort, new resource members will join the planning team, others will leave, and informa-

FIGURE 6-4.   A Problem-Solving Perspective on Organizational Change and Linking (Need Reduction/Problem-solving Cycle)

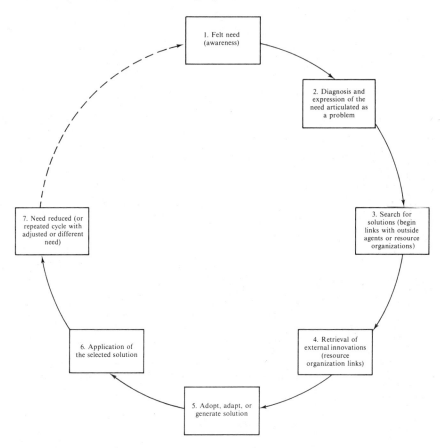

tional resources will change and expand. Informational input from impersonal media sources will be enhanced through the diverse membership of the planning team.

The linking network can be used in various parts of the planning process: awareness/diagnosis, need assessment, resource and constraint identification, generation of alternative strategies, professional and leadership development, decision making, and evaluation. The linking model could include representatives of peer groups in other practice institutions. It should be noted that a great deal of the linking process will come from the informal system/environment interaction of the P/ICM, with the more systematic aspects of the linking process coming in the generation of resources and constraints. This may be particularly applicable to the adoption or adaptation of externally developed innovations.

Reinvention of the wheel may be necessary in the process of developing

FIGURE 6-5. A Model of an Educational Linking Network for Planned Organizational Change

Source: Adapted from Florio 1973 and Havelock 1969.

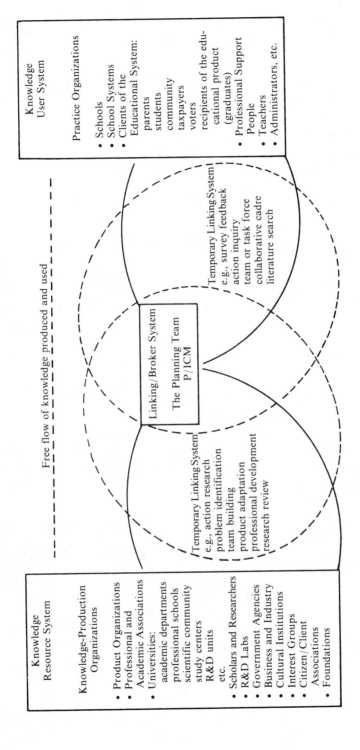

161

credibility among planning-team members; however, when trust is developed, well-developed innovations may be used and/or adapted for the problem at hand. In this sense, a review of other schools' or educational agencies' research and development laboratories, schools of education, and so forth would be a helpful part of the linking process. Expanding the planning team to include valuable evaluation, organizational development, research, and other human resource skills will be useful not only for generating alternative strategies for problem solving, but also for pilot-testing and evaluating such alternatives. R&D centers and labs have a significant experience in field-testing innovations, and many have inventories of existing innovations that may apply to the problem identified through the P/ICM.

The linking model in figure 6-5 indicates several categories of organizations, agencies, or people that fit into the general framework that distinguishes between the knowledge-resource system and the knowledge-user system. A brief clarification is necessary to avoid inflexibility. The dotted line along the top of the model indicates that practice organizations can play the knowledge-production role and that knowledge-production organizations are often knowledge users. The suggested categories are useful for descriptive purposes and are not intended to lock any institution or individual into one or the other of the general systems. The linking system is a reciprocal model, with knowledge use and production freely flowing among participating organizations and their representatives.

Stage Four. Resources and Constraints

The next step in the P/ICM is another awareness stage in the planned-change process. It is also a continuing part of the need assessment. When new ideas, innovations, or change strategies are brought to attention or when new barriers and resistances to problem solutions become apparent, new needs may be generated in the thinking of the planning team. This awareness stage is called the identification of resources and constraints. At this stage the task is to acquire knowledge about potential aids and barriers to problem solution. A *resource* can be defined as any person, tool, piece of equipment, bit of information, or other object that has potential for aiding the production process. Since the planning team is directing its efforts toward the solution of an identified problem, resources, as the term is used here, will be interpreted as anything that can aid in the solution process. Resources may also represent constraints, depending on the amount and quality of the resource. For example, the availability of money is a resource and its absence a constraint.

Resources can be classified under three general headings: human, informational, and material (including financial). Another useful typology distinguishes between resources useful in the *planning process* and those useful in the *technology* (methods used for achieving purposes) of the organization. Through the use of these latter two categories, the planning team can become aware of resources both immediately and potentially available for problem solutions. The planning team represents a wide pool of human resources available to the change process. Through the relationships and expanded membership of the team in the linking network, both the human and information/knowledge resources become greatly expanded. Material and financial resources are developed both through the work of the team and through the contacts made in the linking network.

Perhaps one of the most significant links for generating financial and human resources for the technological aspects of problem solution is the relationship with governmental and private foundations. Grants for implementing solutions are available for specific problem areas. Planning teams may delegate responsibility to specific members to review various "requests for proposals" (RFPs) from government agencies in the state and federal education units. Personal ties with people in Washington, state capitals, and foundation agencies become a part of the linking network. These contacts can lead to early awareness of relevant legislation and grants, thus enabling the team to prepare for writing and submitting proposals requesting funds and support services in the P/ICM process.

Product organizations, R&D centers and labs, and other innovation-producing agencies have a variety of material and process innovations available for review. The planning team may wish to adopt or adapt such innovations, curricular or structural, in the planned-change process. Contacts between the planning team and innovation-producing organizations are also desirable.

Premise 6-6.   Identification and clarification of resources, constraints, and resistance to planned organizational change increase the likelihood of developing successful planned-change strategies.

RESOURCE CATEGORIES FOR CHANGE IN SCHOOLS

A brief outline of some resource subcategories can be useful to the planning team. These are grouped in table 6-1 according to the three major resource types.

The knowledge of resources and their limitations or constraints should be supplemented by familiarity with barriers or "sources of resistance" to change (see chapter 2). Knowledge of these barriers and resisters will be useful for the planning team in various stages of the P/ICM: planning, testing/trial, decision making/adoption, implementation, control, and evaluation. Strategies for change must address not only the identified problem, but also these potential barriers.

As noted in earlier chapters, resistance should be viewed as both a positive and negative force in the change process. Resistance tends to protect the organization against unnecessary or harmful change and is thus positive. However, resistance can be negative when it arises from dogmatism, fear, ignorance, distorted perception, conformity, habit, parochialism, elitism, lack of communication, bureaucratic rigidity, ethnocentrism, or avoidance. The P/ICM provides for "studied resistance" through the knowledge building processes of diagnosis, resources/constraints, strategy building, testing/trial, and evaluation. Re-

TABLE 6-1. Some Resource Categories for Change in Schools[1] (limitations on resources represent constraints)

	RESOURCES USEFUL IN:	
	The Planned-Change Process	The Organizational Technology
I. Human Resources (*individuals with skills and talents*)[2]		
A. Group development and planning abilities	x	
B. Conflict-management skills	x	
C. Budget planning and resource-allocation skills	x	
D. Ability to analyze and recruit talent/expertise	x	x
E. Leadership ability	x	x
F. Information-retrieval and processing skills	x	x
G. Ability to generate alternative solutions to problems	x	x
H. Ability to assess and redevelop self	x	
I. Research, evaluation, and assessment skills	x	x
J. Ability to take risks	x	x
K. Ability to implement innovations	x	x
L. Managerial skills of balancing the needs of organizational members with organizational goals and objectives	x	
M. Knowledge of innovations and current research	x	x
N. Personal relationships outside of the organization	x	
O. Motivations toward innovativeness and change	x	
P. General feeling of efficacy	x	
Q. Ability to apply theory and research findings to practice	x	x
R. Time	x	x

II. *Technical Information/Knowledge Resources* (These are given as a separate category; however, they only become resources when possessed by members of the planning team or organizational members in addition to those cited above.)

A.	Research in the problem area identified		x
B.	Knowledge about products and innovations developed in the field	x	x
C.	Evaluation reports, product validation studies, case histories, and experiences of innovators	x	x
D.	Market studies and environment surveys: attitude and receptiveness of community and client groups to potential change and current practice in the school		x
E.	Awareness of organizational members' attitude and awareness re innovations and new practice in the field	x	x
F.	Knowledge of current demographic, economic, religious, political, and other social forces impacting school decisions		x
G.	Open communication channels within the school and between school and environment		x
H.	Operations knowledge of new methods of achieving tasks (technological)	x	x
I.	Feedback information (how well is the organization doing?)	x	x
J.	Knowledge of new sources of information (people, organizations, publications, indexes, inventories, *etc.*)		x
K.	Knowledge of new curriculum materials		x
L.	Knowledge of new organizational structures in schools	x	x

TABLE 6-1. *(Continued)*

	RESOURCES USEFUL IN:	
	The Planned-Change Process	*The Organizational Technology*
M. Knowledge of contracts and relationships flowing from formal agreements (e.g., collective bargaining)	x	x
N. Knowledge of self and perceptions of self by others	x	
O. Knowledge of the impact of particular innovations (i.e., attributes of the innovation: risk, cost, pervasiveness, etc.[3])	x	x
III. *Material Resources*		
A. Financial resources available	x	x
B. Space/facilities	x	x
C. Supplies	x	x
D. Equipment (teaching machines, audiovisual equipment, computers, etc.)	x	x
E. Packaged teaching aids and materials	x	x
F. Testing and evaluation instruments	x	x
G. Material resources for students and staff outside the school	x	x
H. Handbooks, instruction materials, and other printed materials to aid the use of innovative technologies	x	x

1. These are examples for description and should not be viewed as an inclusive list.
2. See chapter 2 for additional resources.
NOTE: This chart provides some descriptive categories in the process of bringing knowledge of resources and constraints to the planning team. Such an effort represents another step in the ongoing need assessment of the P/ICM.

jecting alternative innovations or strategies of change allows the planning team to move on to more realistic and potentially successful change efforts when the rejection is based on a sound knowledge foundation. *Time* is one of the most valuable resources. The planning team can ill afford random attempts to implement innovations that have not been developed in the light of the realities of the organization. However, the team need not abandon an innovation or change strategy simply because it may encounter resistance. Instead, the team, through the identification of levels of resistance in the sources found above, can develop strategies to deal with resistance. The testing/trial stage of the P/ICM is one attempt to reduce resistance when the change and/or innovation is unfamiliar to organizational members and their clients.

THE USE OF THE LINKING NETWORK: AWARENESS OF RESOURCES AND CONSTRAINTS

The linking network is a source of knowledge and human resources for the planning team. External change agents may be used to both introduce and pilot-test innovations for the organization. Change agents with expertise in making positive use of the forces for change, resources, and positive resistance can be included in the planning team. The team and planned-change process itself are designed to increase knowledge and lower negative resistance to organizational development. In short, the P/ICM activities (awareness, diagnosis, need assessment, resource and constraint identification, generating alternative solutions, testing/trial, and evaluation) are designed to make the organizational change process both informed and productive. The P/ICM, through the planning process and the linking network, is able to increase awareness of current and developing research, innovations, and knowledge. Translation and interpretation of information are accomplished through the broker activities of the planning team and its links to knowledge-production sources.

A brief review of the P/ICM will be helpful here. Notice that the model provides for a return to the problem-diagnosis and awareness stage of the planning process at different stages in the P/ICM. The resource/constraints stage of the process may reveal additional problems or concerns for the planning team. Throughout the need-assessment efforts, the planning team may need a periodic redefinition of the problem. The task of clarifying the central problem(s) of concern should be an ongoing effort. This does not imply that the entire process should be repeated for each of the revisions in problem definition. Rather, it is an attempt to clarify the purposes of planning for change. Strategies generated for problem solution, resource utilization, and implementation should be directed at a clearly defined problem. The review process indicated in the model is a tool for increasing flexibility. The team should not be locked into a rigid problem definition or inventory of objectives. As new information is generated and awareness increased, the team can easily refine its thinking to reflect the new knowledge and move to problem solving.

The objectives for the example school (e.g., diversity of student population;

increased teacher incentives and time for planning and use of external resources; and diversity of cultural and social groups in the planning and operation of the school) have outlined the need for a review of internal and external forces for and against change to meet those objectives. A complete list of resources and constraints developed would be superfluous here; however, it is important to note several significant resources, constraints, and barriers.

Resources include the vast human resource potential of both the think-tank/health center complex and the surrounding community. However, many of the complex personnel with potential for school involvement are already overcommitted and have little time for participation in problem-solving efforts. There are many available community leaders with expertise in understanding local social and cultural groups. However, there is some limitation on their motivation to invest time and energy with a school that will directly serve only a very small segment of their communities. Limitations on resources indicate constraints, and thus the planning group for the school will need to devise a strategy to address not only the problem-solving objectives, but also the resource-utilization needs of the school.

Involvement of teachers calls for valuable time and motivation resources. Time must be provided through external resources from the complex budget, and motivational resources will need to be provided internally through incentives in the organization. This brings the planners to a significant barrier. The management of the parent complex has not recognized the potential spin-off value of a diverse student population. Currently their willingness to broaden the student population to include children of nonprofessional staff is viewed as a fringe benefit to several employees; however, there is a significant problem in this area regarding the staff members who are not able to send their children to the school.

The teaching faculty of the school seems to be willing to invest time; however, there is little indication, thus far, of a lightened teaching load that would allow adequate time for planning and linking with external resources. The planning team has been freed from some of the daily duties to work on the identified problems. This represents a valuable resource. They have also been involved with meetings and symposia, presented at a local university, dealing with cultural pluralism in the schools. Several members of the planning team made contacts with university faculty and with faculty and principals of local public schools. There have been initial discussions about developing a network among local and public schools, the health/think-tank complex, and the university. One barrier is a vocal minority segment of the school faculty who do not see the value of getting involved with local public school people ''with all of their problems.''

The identification of these and other forces for and against problem solving and change provides the planning team with valuable information for the generation of alternative solutions. This knowledge, in any given situation, often brings to light additional problems for the organization. The P/ICM provides for flexible movement over the planning process. When a constraint or force against change is severe, the planning team may wish to redefine the problem or expand the problem-solving objectives to include the recently identified problem. In this manner, the problem-solving strategy-building process includes provisions for solving central problems and lowering constraints or barriers to the use of valuable resources.

Stage Five. Alternative Solutions

There are generally a variety of means by which problems can be addressed. Not all potential solutions are applicable or useful, given the specific nature, environment, and available resources of an organization. As noted in earlier chapters, schools have several unique properties. Furthermore, each school and school system has specific resources, constraints, and resistances that apply to any attempts to change the organization. The P/ICM provides the planning-team members with the structure for generating alternative solutions that fall within the range of their ability and that comply with the realities of specific school organization.

From having gone through the linking-system and knowledge-generation stages of the planning process, the planning team should already be aware of several strategies and potential solutions applicable to a specific problem. Innovations developed and tried in similar school organizations are valuable resources for the planning team; however, the team must build its own inventory of alternative solutions. Adapting previous change strategies and innovations to the specific school organization may be a first step in the alternative solution process.

PROCESSES FOR GENERATING ALTERNATIVES

The alternative solution stage of the P/ICM should be the most creative and broad-based stage of the planning process. Members may wish to break into small groups to review existing solutions, generate new ones, or develop eclectic innovations. They should be free from critical review in the early generation efforts. The planning team can then assemble potential strategies and solutions and begin a critical review of the alternative solutions. Gaps in solutions should be filled, and the planner or planning team should appraise the alternatives generated and select the most promising for testing or trial. A suggested process is presented in figure 6-6.

Stage Six. Testing/Trial: Demonstration

THE PURPOSE OF DEMONSTRATION

The testing or trial stages of planning can sometimes be a part of the alternative-generation stage. Testing a change strategy or innovation on a limited

FIGURE 6-6.   Building Alternative Problem-Solving Strategies

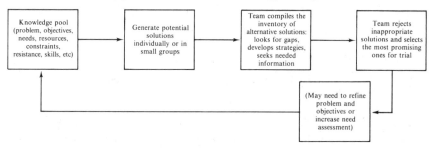

basis is a useful means of demonstrating an alternative to a current practice. When limited testing is not possible, owing to the nature of the change strategy or innovation, a trial stage may be used with a definite ending period. In this manner, the members of the organization participate in the change with the understanding that, after a given period of time, an assessment will be made to determine whether the value of the innovation warrants continued use.

SYMBOLIC AND BEHAVIORAL TESTING

Testing may be symbolic or behavioral (e.g., Zaltman and Duncan 1977). Symbolic testing involves a mental projection into the role of user without actually trying the change. Behavioral testing involves the actual use of the innovation on a limited scale. External evaluators may be brought in prior to the trial period to begin the evaluation process. The trial should assess not only the impact of the change on the problem at hand, but also its impact on the formal organizational structure, informal organization of human relationships, the environment, and individual members' perceptions. Unanticipated consequences should be reported and reviewed by the team. The testing/trial stage can be applied to each of the selected alternatives in the previous stage. This may include only one trial if the selected alternative is an eclectic approach derived from several other alternatives and is successful.

If none of the selected alternatives has a demonstrated usefulness and/or potential for success, the planning team should move back to the previous stages of problem identification, resources and constraints, or alternative generation. The results of the trial should indicate what alternative directions are most feasible.

In the example system, a problem centered on the involvement of parents in the planning and operational processes. The initial set of alternative solutions included paying parents to participate in the home-instruction component of the learning process; involving parents in curriculum-planning sessions to help develop the instructional process in which they would participate; offering special instructional programs for students that would mandate parent involvement as a prerequisite for student participation; hiring school/home-instructional liaison people to make periodic aid-and-review visits to students' homes; and setting aside time during the school day for parents to visit the school for instruction in child tutoring. The planning team, after a combination of symbolic and behavioral testing of each of the alternative strategies for increasing parent involvement in the home-based instruction of students, found that none of the alternatives proved successful. Either the strategy failed to increase parent involvement or the increased involvement failed to improve the instructional process. Assessment data from the trial periods and testing of alternatives revealed that, for some of the strategies, parents were unable to meet with the professional staff because of conflicting employment demands. Other strategies that increased the parent involvement were limited because parents needed training and knowledge in child development.

Using the increased information from their trial experiences, the planning team moves back up the planning process to the awareness/diagnosis stage to redefine the problem of parent involvement and to get at some of the basic home environment problems. Had the results revealed improved instruction when parents became involved, the planning team may have only had to develop further strategies to increase the involvement. When improvement came with strategies designed to involve parents in curriculum planning and tutoring instruction, additional strategies might address the time conflict problem. In short, the team needs to move up the planning process only as far as necessary to constructively use the additional information gained through the testing or trial assessment of alternatives.

TESTING AND THE TURNKEY PHASE

Testing/trial provides another useful part of the turnkey phase of the P/ICM. It facilitates the transfer of planning to the larger social system of the school. Members of the organization and clients participate on a limited scale or for a limited period of time in the innovative practice. They become familiar with the change and are able to participate in the assessment through reports on their perceptions and experiences. There is value, too, for system members not participating in the change effort: (1) they learn of the results from colleagues in the same school rather than from some distant source; (2) they are familiar with the organizational system with which the experience has been tried; (3) they interact with opinion leaders on a face-to-face basis; and (4) demonstration is viewed and assessed in the context of their own situation.

Thus, testing and trial of alternative-solution strategies provide data for revising and developing new alternatives. The problems encountered in the testing phase may indicate a need for further development of strategies. This does not imply a need to initiate the entire planning process a second time. It involves taking the information from alternative-assessment data to improve on the problem-solving strategy. The P/ICM indicates feedback loops for the planning team. This points up the need for the team members to be flexible as they move about the planning process to redefine, revise, redevelop, and expand their knowledge base for further planning. The testing/trial stage of the P/ICM not only provides the demonstration efforts for alternative solutions to problems, but also gives the planning team valuable data concerning future planning—problem identification, diagnosis, need assessment, resources/constraints, and developing and refining alternative solutions. This is what educational evaluators call formative evaluation (Bloom, Hastings, and Madaus 1970) or the use of assessment data in the formulation of new strategy and practice.

Stage Seven. Decision Making: The Adoption or Rejection of Alternative Solutions

The planning team is ready to make decisions regarding the adoption of solution strategies when it has adequate information regarding the potential success of an innovation or organizational change. Decision-making efforts have been a constant part of the planning process (e.g., deciding what the problem is; making priority decisions regarding objectives of problem solving; deciding who should be included in the planning process; deciding which alternative solutions should be tried). Here, however, decision making refers to the decision to adopt or reject a particular innovation or problem-solving strategy. Adoption (and, by implication, rejection) decisions are based on data available to the team. As mentioned before, when none of the alternatives proves adequate, a rejection decision indicates a need for further planning activities by the team.

It is important to remember that a decision to adopt is the culmination of an attitude-formation process in the planning team. Team members and/or other members of the organization and interested environmental actors review feedback data from testing and trial and decide upon a problem-solving solution.

THE ACTORS IN THE DECISION PROCESS: THE IMPACT ON IMPLEMENTATION

The decision-making stage of the planning process is critical for the implementation stage. The manner in which decisions are made and the people involved in such adoption decisions are critical to the planned change process. A review of premises 5-6, 5-7, and 5-8 indicates that movement from adoption to implementation of innovations requires that the significant actors involved in the implementation of innovations be included in the decisions to adopt those innovations or change strategies.

TURNKEY AND LINKING: AIDS TO INVOLVEMENT

Thus, the turnkey phase of the planning process requires that the planning team integrate its members and their knowledge resources with other members of the human subsystem of the school. The team may have already concluded that a specific innovation is the most appropriate; however, other members of the organization must also have the opportunity to review the alternatives and their evaluation data. Schmuck, Runkel, and Lanmeyer (1969) suggest involving all members of the organization in the systematic planned-change process, thus avoiding many of the turnkey problems. However, the planning team may not find this to be effective or practical. The planning team may wish to broaden involvement through earlier stages of the planning process. The linking network is one means of early inclusion. Organizational members are included as potential resources for the planning team. A *communications network* should be part of the planning process so that organizational members and significant people and agencies in the environment are also informed of the planning activities.

In summary, the decision-making process is enhanced through the implementation of the planning process of the P/ICM. (1) Organizational and environment members are included from a broad base. (2) Planning-team activities provide for communication and interaction with decision makers through linking and planning efforts. (3) Previously disenfranchised groups are represented in the organizational change process. (4) Information, assessment data, and knowledge are shared openly throughout the organization. The middle-range assumptions, premises concerning planning, organizational/environment interaction, resource utilization, and strategy building all emphasize the need for integrating planning-team efforts with broad-based team membership and for open communication and involvement within the organization and between organization and environment.

The problems identified in the example school centered on the isolation of both the student body and faculty from the diverse elements of the metropolitan area. Planning-team membership, the later alternative solutions, and demonstration (testing) efforts with regard to including parents in the operational process aided the team in crossing several of the barriers associated with the central problem. Additionally, the decision-making efforts concentrated on problems associated with implementation of a successful resource-use strategy as well as the central problems of isolation. In short, decisions were made by a diverse group of professional and nonprofessional participants in the educational process of the school and community. It should not be unusual to find that the P/ICM, when implemented through temporary systems and adequate turnkey efforts, addresses additional problems associated with the institution.

Schools, being labor-intensive organizations strongly reliant on human resources, are often burdened with problems of understanding and/or communication blocks. The P/ICM is specifically designed to incorporate diverse participation by people in the organization and its environment. This participation, when accompanied by adequate preparation and training for collaborative decision making, should break many barriers.

The last two stages of the P/ICM—implementation and control, and evaluation—are briefly treated here; however, the reader will want to read the fuller discussion of them in chapters 8 and 9.

The decision-making stage of the P/ICM concluded the formal planning for a specifically identified problem or set of concerns. However, in a self-renewing organization, planning is a continuous function of the leadership. The summative evaluation of the implemented change becomes formative data for the continuous planning process. The short treatment of the three management sections of the P/ICM reflect their use in the continuous planning efforts in self-renewing organizations.

Stage Eight. Implementation and Control

The decision-making process of the P/ICM provides the legitimation for the proposed innovation or organization change. Through the integration of planning efforts, preparation for implementation has been made. This is provided for in the turnkey phase of the planning process.

Gross, Giaquinta, and Berstein (1971) provide several general categories of barriers in the implementation of change in educational organizations:

1. *lack of clarity:* either (1) the lack of clarity of the role expectations for teachers in the implementation of the innovation, or (2) lack of clarity and understanding of the innovation and its expected or demonstrated benefits among organizational members;
2. *lack of capability:* (1) inadequate skills and knowledge among organizational members to carry out the innovations, or (2) lack of required materials, equipment and other resources required to implement the innovation;
3. *lack of compatibility:* inconsistancy of organizational arrangements operating and those needed to implement and sustain the innovation;
4. *lack of feedback:* failure to provide a mechanism to identify and deal with problems associated with implementation efforts;
5. *lack of commitment:* unwillingness to invest time and energy.

They make the further observation that, when these barriers are inadequately dealt with, organizational members who were initially supportive of change may develop resistance out of frustration.

Several premises could be generated from these barriers; however, let it suffice here to say that the implementation process calls for at least six elements in dealing with potential barriers in the transition from adoption to implementation: (1) an instructional period, (2) a training period, (3) adequate material and equipment support, (4) a feeling of ownership and commitment for the change, (5) adjustment of organizational arrangements to fit the change, and (6) provision for feedback data on both the change and the effort to implement it. Several of these are covered in the P/ICM.

To summarize, the implementation process is already underway in the P/ICM planning process through the turnkey phase. Organizational members further identify and deal with implementation problems through information and training sessions, decision making and review, and feedback on the operationalizing efforts. The planning team is responsible for developing ownership for the innovation beyond its own membership. The critical concepts for the planning team to deal with are (1) clarity (of responsibility and innovation), (2) capability, (3) resource adequacy, (4) compatability, and (5) commitment. The implementation process is improved when organizational members understand their roles and responsibilities needed for the innovation; the nature, purpose, and expected consequences of the innovation; and the skills needed for successful use and implementation of the innovation. Implementation is possible when adequate material and human resources are available or there are provisions for developing them within the organization; when there is compatibility between the organizational structure and the structure needed for the innovation; and when there is a feeling of ownership and commitment among the organizational membership for implementing the innovation.

The operationalization of the innovation or change strategy calls for the "refreezing" or *control* of the organization under the new or different set of circumstances. Several elements of the control process are mentioned here for their usefulness in the continuous planning of self-renewing organizations.

The control element most useful for the planning team is "feedback" on both the process and product of the change. Stufflebeam (1967) and Zaltman, Duncan, and Holbek (1973) pay particular attention to the feedback processes in both the planning and implementation of change efforts. Stufflebeam gives several kinds of feedback useful for the change process: context, input, process, and product evaluation or feedback.

- context feedback: continuous monitoring of the organization to identify unmet needs and problems.
- input feedback: information on the assessment of potential solutions or alternative strategies to reduce problems or needs.
- process feedback: information concerning the operations of the innovation to determine adjustments and modifications or problems encountered under the implemented change.
- product feedback: this is the essential evaluation component of the change process in which the impact of the innovation on the problem identified and the environment is assessed.

The feedback process is a continuous element in the planning effort. This feedback can take one or more of the several forms described above. Context feedback is used in both the problem-identification stage and the implementation stage of the P/ICM. The continuous monitoring of critical elements in the technical and human subsystems of the organization provide the planners with data for problem identification, diagnosis, strategy building and revising, redefining causal factors, and adjusting the organization to meet anticipated implementation and management problems.

Input feedback is a critical part of the attitude-formation stages of the planning process: generating alternative solutions, testing/trial and decision making. Feedback of this nature is also tied to the generation of resources and constraints through the linking network. Resources for decision making include available data on the proposed innovations or change strategies (e.g., evaluations from other attempts, case histories, participant observations).

Process feedback is perhaps most important for the control stage of the innovation. The P/ICM is designed to anticipate problems and barriers in the implementation of the innovation and to build strategies to reduce those barriers; however, few implemented changes are able to enjoy a trouble-free operation. The planning team can use feedback from both the human subsystem and the environment on the unanticipated problems generated through the operationalizing of the innovation.

Katz and Kahn (1966) refer to the most common form of feedback: externally (environmentally) generated information on the operations of the organization. Zaltman, Duncan, and Holbek (1973) include externally generated and internally generated feedback that can be used as a guide for implementation and change within organizations. The planning team may delegate responsibilities to organizational members to gather process feedback data during the early implementation of an innovation or change strategy. This feedback includes both the technical feedback on the operation or functioning of the innovation and the feedback from the human subsystem of the organization. The former may include information on the workability of the materials, equipment, and technologies involved in the innovation: adequacy, breakdown, clarity of responsibility, and so forth. The latter includes information on the perceptions of the organizational or affected environment members: authority structure, threat, uncertainty, satisfaction, human interaction, and so forth. The data collected through observation, survey, and log reports can be used to adjust the innovation or organization accordingly. In some cases, the feedback data on the innovation process may call for further changes and innovations to meet problems and needs. Product feedback is related to the evaluation of the innovation or change and will be covered in the next section.

In summary, a critical element of control is the feedback on the processes involved in the implementation and maintenance (refreezing) of the planned change. This information, derived from both the constant monitoring of key variables in the system and specific process monitoring, provides the planners with information to guide, adjust, and adapt to the realities of implementing planned change in a social context unique to a particular organization. The linkages with the immediate environmental forces and actors provide avenues for gaining feedback on the impact of the innovation during its operation. This also provides the planners with guidance data.

Stage Nine. Evaluation

Gross, Giaquinta, and Bernstein (1971) highlight a problem that has plagued project-evaluation efforts in education for a long time. This is the assumption by evaluators that an innovation or change that has been verbally adopted has therefore been implementated. This leads them to believe that evaluation efforts are assessing the impact of the stated change. However, there is often a critical gap between verbal adoption and actual implementation of organizational change.

The first step of the evaluation process is to determine what is being evaluated. Process feedback data is part of the evaluation process, as are the other forms of feedback available to the planning team. The evaluators of the planned-change efforts must determine whether they are evaluating the product of an implemented change or whether they are evaluating the ability of the organization to change from its previous way of doing things. A potentially sucessful innovation or change may be classified as a "failure" because there was no significant change in the organizational product (e.g., student learning, problem reduction, conflict resolution, environmental impact). When the lack of impact was due to a failure to implement the change, the evaluation efforts provide misinformation on the innovation unless the evaluator is measuring the degree of implementation as well as the product assessment.

The evaluation component of the P/ICM refers more to summative evaluation (Bloom, Hastings, and Madaus 1970) of the planned change. The distinction here is between the process evaluation and the product evaluation types given by Stuffelbeam (1967). Assessments of the potential strength of alternative solutions have been carried out in the testing/trial stage. The data from such evaluation efforts were formative (Bloom et al. 1970) in that they were used for developing change strategies, revising innovations, adapting the organization for change, and decision making. The summative evaluation of the innovation or planned change is to assess the impact of the innovation on the problem identified. Data on the achievement of the problem-solving objectives are generated through direct assessment of the product and the impact of that product on the environment. In schools, the product could be student learning, staff development, changes in the communication flow, shifts in the authority structure, parent involvement in student learning, and so forth. In short, the evaluation is the summary assessment of the results of an organizational change.

For the planning efforts of the organization, feedback on the evaluation process and its results becomes formative data for the continuous planning process. Specifics of evaluation plans and strategies are covered in a later chapter; however, it is important to note here the use of evaluation data in the identification and diagnosis of problems. The P/ICM indicates a feedback loop from the evaluation stage to various steps in the planning process: awareness/diagnosis, need assessment, resources/constraints, and alternative solutions. Depending on the substance of the evaluation results, the organizational planning members may need to return to devising additional or different strategies for solving the problem; however, in some cases, the team may need to diagnose new and different problems identified in the evaluation effort.

DANGERS OF LOCKING IN ON A PLANNING MODEL

There are several dangers in application of a "systems analysis" process of planned change. These dangers are not meant to indicate a negative stance for system planning for educational institutions. They are given here in the light of the ambiguities of educational systems regarding their goals, technology, and organizational structure. The dangers lie in the rigid application of any systems model. Sergiovanni and Carver (1973) provide three general dangers in the literal application of "systems engineering":

1. *Overplanning and overcommitment:* locking in on narrowly defined objectives and means of accomplishing them. The building of extensive, inflexible structures and facilities that influence the organizational arrangements long after they are needed.
2. *Emphasis on mechanistic dimensions:* overemphasis on centralization, stratification, formalization, specialization, and control. Limiting objectives to measurable or quantifiable results in turn limits the organizational flexibility and adaptability.
3. *Reduction of discretion:* overemphasis on bureaucratic goals to the limitation of the use of professional resources. Limitations on flexibility and discretion at the point of impact through the increase of management control decrease creative problem solving, adaptation to reality, open communication, professional judgement, and so forth.

The P/ICM is designed to increase flexibility in the planning process; however, a literal application of the planning model may unduly constrain the resources available to problem solving. As noted earlier, there are times when action may need to precede the goal formulation. In educational organizations, the problem-solving process may be ambiguous, and the planning team may wish to establish external links and communications networks to aid in both the problem identification and diagnosis process and in the need assessment. The P/ICM is designed as a general guide and should not indicate a lock-step approach to planning.

Flexibility is the essential concept in educational planning. The systems model is most helpful when certain precautions are taken to ensure flexibility and when a continuous awareness of the dangers of rigidity are taken into account. Key questions that should be raised are:

1. Are members allowed to communicate ideas openly and freely?
2. Are decision making and discretion allowed at all levels of the organization?

3. Are those most involved in the basic (teaching and learning) operations of the organization involved in revising and adapting innovations or changes?
4. Is feedback constantly viewed as a formative evaluation to be used in the redefinition of problems and objectives or the revising or refinement of alternative solutions?
5. Are the planning-team members allowed to move back and forth in the various stages of the planning process without undue limitation?
6. Are proper precautions being taken to avoid being locked in on a chosen alternative solution?
7. Are barriers dealt with as they appear rather than put aside for a "more appropriate stage in planning"?
8. Is planning viewed as a continuous process rather than a linear process leading to a culminating change?
9. Are summative evaluation data used as formative information in the continuous planning and organizational renewal process?

Other steps can be taken to increase the flexibility of the planning team. If the team is open to outside challenge and is willing to challenge itself and the planning process, the value of the P/ICM is increased.

PROBLEMS OF DEFICIENT PLANNING

The need for flexibility should not overshadow problems of omission in the planning process. Planning is an effort to cogently decide on future courses of action. Neglect of critical elements or misperception of significant variables affecting the organization can undermine otherwise careful planning efforts. Some of the causes of "deficient planning" are given in list 6-4.

LIST 6-4.   Causal Factors of Inadequate Planning (adapted from Kahneman and Schild 1966)

1. Neglect of the informal social subsystem (overemphasis on formal structure)
2. Neglect of the interdependence of groups in the social structure (overemphasis on a category scheme in analysis of the organization)
3. Use of stereotypes in attributing motives to target system of change participants (seeing motives as common for all human targets of change)
4. Mistaken belief in the commonality of perceptions or the ease with which misperceptions can be corrected
5. Underemphasis on the pressure to conform (collective authority—conformity through status-seeking acceptance, avoidance of conflict, etc.)
6. Neglecting the use of group or significant other forces acting on opinion leaders and other influentials (or failing to recognize that these forces exist for leaders)
7. Overemphasis on the forces for change to the neglect of the often more significant reduction of forces against change (the need to lower barriers and constraints)
8. Neglect of the change target participants' need to enhance their own status
9. Internal organizational pressure (or pressures from interested publics in the environment) for "quick and conspicuous action"

These sources of errors in planning stem from neglect or oversight by planning-group members. Many of them come from the push to move ahead rapidly and produce some tangible or at least salient change. Educational organizations have often been accused of jumping on bandwagons and succumbing to the latest fad. Many of these short-lived "innovations" fail because of poor planning or improper screening. However, many sound innovations fail because of the neglect of significant forces affecting the organization and its primary participants. The results of poor planning or neglect in the planning process become more evident in the transition period from planning to action or from adoption to implementation.

The conclusion of the planning discussion sets the stage for implementation of the planned change. The planning process is most active in the pre-implementation arena; however, it is a continuing function of the self-renewing organization. The implementation of the change calls for a refreezing or stabilization of the organization under the innovation or change. This does not imply that problem identification through feedback of the evaluation or system-monitoring instruments is neglected. Temporary planning systems can be set up to handle problems as they arise. Rotating and overlapping memberships of various organizational and environmental members in these temporary problem-solving systems increase the experience and skills necessary for adequate planning and collaborative decision making. Commitment in the organization is developed through such participation. The ownership of the change strategies and adopted innovations is increased. As members of planning groups invest time and energy in the problem-solving process, personal motivation becomes more congruent with the purposeful direction of the system. Dangers of overcommitment are reduced through a constant process of problem diagnosis. The P/ICM calls for a continuous series of activities centered on assessing client needs, diagnosing organizational ailments, linking with environmental forces and resources, analyzing forces for and against change, generating solutions, testing and experimenting, making decisions, implementing those decisions, managing changed systems, and evaluating and monitoring the system to provide feedback and identify other problems. Organizational self-renewal is based on the assumption that members look as objectively as possible at what they are doing and assess those actions in the light of what they believe they should be doing. The P/ICM provides a means for the basic self-awareness, diagnosis, planning, and action.

Summary

Chapters 5 and 6 provided a synthesis of the notion of planned change in educational organizations, including the development of system/environment linking for improved communications, use of available resources, and lowering resistance to change. The initial argument for planning is designed to motivate the educational organization to shift from being a reactive system responding to the random pressures and forces of the environment to being a proactive and interactive organization. Initiating change through the collaboration of organizational members and between human elements in the organization and the environment is a goal of such systems.

The Proactive/Interactive Change Model represents a guide for such an organization. It is designed not only as a problem-solving model, but as a continuous development and renewal process for the organization. The organizational leaders and change agents take steps for the preparation of the planned change to ensure broad representation in the planning process, discretion and flexibility in decision making, and increased awareness of the organizational structure and variables associated with the changing system. Skills are accounted for and provisions for developing needed abilities are made during the planning process. The authority structure is reviewed and revised to increase the resource information and implementation commitment needed.

The notes on temporary systems and risk are designed to develop the joint ownership and commitment needed for change strategies and innovations. The critical concept of involvement for commitment is developed to provide the planning team with guides for membership and process. The turnkey phase from a temporary or planning system to an organizationally implemented change is given to highlight the need to develop ownership for the planned change in organizational members and critical actors in the environment.

The critical concepts for the P/ICM are *open system, flexibility, system/ environment linking, informed/collaborative decision making, unconstrained human interaction,* and *multidirectional communications flow.* These concepts are derived from the recognition that educational systems are dominated by human technology. Schools are labor-intensive organizations with structure, management, instruction, curriculum, and other processes dominated by the human element. In short, the P/ICM is a problem-solving systems process with significant attention to individual need dispositions. The model also recognizes a need for individual treatment not only for students in educational institutions, but also personnel and directly involved client group representatives.

The P/ICM is designed to overcome many of the dangers of a strictly rational problem-solving and planned-change strategy. However, it is important to note some of those dangers for the potential planning team.

7

Client Need Assessment
RICHARD T. COFFING*

THE PURPOSE OF INITIATING EDUCATIONAL CHANGE is to satisfy better the needs of students, teachers, administrators, or others having an interest in the educational process. A proper *understanding* of these needs is essential if they are to be satisfied through imaginative program planning, implementation, control, and evaluation. However, sound information about people's needs *relative to a particular school setting* is seldom already available. It has to be gathered. And gathering good information about needs is the job of a process called *client need assessment*. The purpose of this chapter is to describe the basic concepts and procedures of client need assessment.

Why Assess Clients' Needs?

Educational changes are supposed to respond to and satisfy needs. Therefore, information about clients' needs becomes a critical prerequisite for making decisions. Too seldom, however, is that information available with the quality, representativeness, and richness of detail that is really useful for making decisions—and especially for making *planning* decisions. In a report on "the design of an alternative academic program for a suburban high school using directly obtained client needs data," Lehner (1973) observes that

---

*Richard T. Coffing is a private consultant in public administration, residing in Atlanta, Georgia.

Information about what teachers and students (and their parents) need is implicit in the school environment, since members of these groups interact with each other daily, but this information is often not available in an explicit form which could be used for decision making. In many schools, norms of the organization do not at present encourage individuals to be sensitive to or to seek out knowledge of others' needs (Sarason, 1971). The school focuses on certain areas of presumed need as defined by certain members of the enterprise—primarily administrators; the institutional emphasis on achievement in cognitive areas works against the development of any further sensitivity to needs.

It is generally accepted that the primary clients of schools are students—those people, young or old, eligible to be ''enrolled'' in the school curriculum. But to name the students as the only clients would be to ignore many others whose welfare is in some way affected by school programs: for example, parents, teachers, and future employers of present students. Thus, a realistic look will show that any school has many different clients to serve, directly or indirectly (Miles 1967).

Clearly, the direction that educational change should take is toward fulfilling those needs which are not being fully met now by school programs. If students are not reading well enough, for example, they should be given better opportunities to learn. Yet, this basic thrust of change will involve some serious complications. Meeting unmet needs requires new resources—time, money, materials, or equipment—or at least some shifts in existing resources. An existing level of need fulfillment—in mathematics, say, or extracurricular activities—may have to be sacrificed in order to improve reading. This means setting priorities and making hard choices.

Priorities and hard choices are nothing new, of course—especially in the current era of taxpayer resistance and tighter-than-ever budgets. Mentioning these conditions, however, serves to highlight the problems faced by persons making decisions about change. These *decision makers* as a group include teachers, administrators, planners, change agents, school board members, parents, ''community influentials,'' and—increasingly—students. To make good decisions, they must have good information. For decisions about need-fulfilling changes, information is needed about how clients' needs are *defined* and about the current level or *status of need fulfillment*. Good information may not guarantee good decisions, but it certainly helps. What are the alternatives: no information? bad information? too little information?

This discussion leads to the basic purpose for employing a process of client need assessment: *to provide useful information about client needs*. In other words, the purpose of client need assessment is to give relevant decision makers some information about client needs that is actually useful in making decisions. Usefulness for decision making is part of what ''good information'' means, because if information isn't useful, what is it? As defined here, usefulness includes criteria such as reliability, accuracy, relevance, focus, specificity, and understandability. More will be said about these criteria later in this chapter.

In most instances, data describing and assessing needs are not available when they are desired. The reasons are many, but perhaps most important is that processes for ongoing need assessment are generally lacking in most educational systems. In response, many educators have advocated adopting a set of systematic rules and procedures that can define clients' needs and that can assess how well these needs are being met. An ongoing assessment process can monitor changes in needs and changes in how well they are being satisfied. This type of ongoing need assessment should be central to all decision-making activity; it is thus useful at this point to discuss the basic concepts of client need assessment.

Basic Concepts

Experience has shown that certain concepts of client need assessment must be understood before the process can be carried out effectively. The basic concepts presented here are central to the methodology that follows. Note that these concepts are all implied by the purpose of client need assessment, which is to provide useful information about client needs.

WHAT IS A NEED?

One of the central concepts of client need assessment is that of a "need."

A "need" is defined here as *a concept, an idea, or an image of some desired set of behaviors and/or states; a "need" is a mental image of "what should be" according to the person or persons who hold the image.* [Coffing and Hutchinson 1974]

According to this definition, a need is first of all an idea, a thought, a cognition, This means that needs are aspects of people's mental experiences. Needs are "real" in the sense that all thinking is real. Secondly, a need is an idea about some set of behaviors or states that *ought* to exist even though those behaviors or states might not exist now. The objects of a need—that is, the things that "should be"—may be contemporary or future-oriented. For example, "I need a larger classroom" expresses a contemporary need; "I will need a larger classroom for next year's enrollees" expresses a future need.

This definition of a need differs in emphasis from the more prevalent definition of "need" in psychology, especially physiological psychology, in which need is a state of sensory deprivation. In this sense, hunger is a good state of need because at the time of hunger, the body is deprived of food. Similarly, the psychologist A. H. Maslow (1954) has theorized that people are motivated in accordance with a *hierarchy of needs* (see figure 7-1). As interpreted by R. G. Owens (1970), Maslow's theory holds that when the lowest order of needs in the hierarchy is satisfied, a higher-order need appears, and, since it has the greater

FIGURE 7-1.   Maslow's Hierarchy of Needs
Source: Adapted from Maslow 1954.

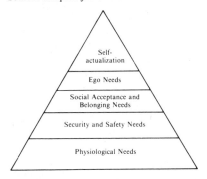

potency at the time, this higher-order need causes the individual to attempt to satisfy it.'' For purposes of client need assessment, decision makers must have specific information about ''what should be'' or a ''cognitive map'' of what is needed by their clients. Even if the decision makers were to learn where their clients were located on a hierarchy of needs—and this might be helpful to know—specific information would be lacking for making specific decisions about specific educational changes. Hence this chapter stresses the cognitive definition of needs.

A need, then, is a concept of ''what should be.'' As such, it is composed of specific *dimensions* or *attributes*. These dimensions or attributes of a need are the behaviors and/or states that define the need. A stylized diagram of the structure of a need-concept is shown in figure 7-2. In the figure, an unnamed, hypothetical need is shown to be composed of eleven dimensions, each of which is more specific than the need-concept as a whole.

WHAT IS NEED FULFILLMENT?

Needs can be met, partially met, unmet, or even overmet. Need fulfillment therefore is defined as the observed status of some state of affairs when measured in terms of the dimensions of a particular need. In other words, need fulfillment is a measurement of how well a particular need *is being met*. If a need means ''what should be,'' then need fulfillment means ''what is.''

For purposes of client need assessment, existing information on test results, personal growth, job placement, and so forth is not very meaningful unless and until the clients' needs are specified. Once the needs are specified, however, existing information relevant to the specified needs can be used to determine the status of need fulfillment; or necessary new information can be gathered. The most efficient, least wasteful gathering or selecting of information will take place after the client's needs have been specifically defined.

FIGURE 7-2. Diagram of Relationship between a Need Concept and Its Specific Component Dimensions

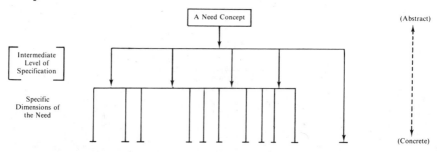

The discrepancies or "gaps" that exist between clients' specified needs and the status of their need fulfillment can become the most salient performance gaps to which educational changes should be directed. With good information in hand, the decision makers responsible for effecting responsive changes will be better able to keep up with, or ahead of, their clients.

In carrying out the client need assessment process, the participants will play several roles, and sometimes a participant will play more than one. These roles are "client," "decision maker," and "needs assessor."

WHO IS A CLIENT?

School programs affect the lives and welfare of many different people—not only students, but also the school staffs, the employers of graduates, and the taxpayers who support the schools. In any community, almost everyone is touched, directly or indirectly, by the educational system. Thus, almost everyone can reasonably be considered to be clients of the schools.

Those who are conducting the client need assessment—especially the intended users of the information—are responsible for deciding which types of clients should have their needs assessed by this process. Typically, the clients of concern for a school district-wide study will include students, parents, teachers, administrators, and as broad a cross-section of the rest of the community as feasible. Typically also, the client groups of concern will be further segmented into subgroups (for example, in relation to age, grade, or developmental level of the students) with differing needs.

WHO ARE THE DECISION MAKERS?

In client need assessment, the decision makers are simply the people for whom the information is gathered. Presumably, they are people who make decisions about educational change. They may or may not be people "in power," members of the "Establishment," or school administrators. The decision makers might be, for example, the steering committee of a community group seeking improvement of the schools, the management staff of a special project effecting some kind of change, a parent-teacher-student committee, a "change team" of teachers and administrators, the school board, a school principal, the superintendent of schools, or members of the school district's planning, research, and evaluation staff. Decision makers, in short, are those people who are expected to use information resulting from client need assessment in order to influence, plan, approve, direct, or evaluate educational change.

WHO ARE THE NEEDS ASSESSORS?

Needs assessor, a term like *planner, evaluator,* or *researcher,* names the role of the person technically responsible for carrying out the process. In actual practice, there may be one needs assessor or several working as a team. And needs assessors might wear additional "hats" in the process: they might be clients and they might be decision makers.

To be a needs assessor, one has to understand and be able to implement the concepts and procedures of client need assessment. Some background preparation in evaluation, measurement, or survey research is helpful in carrying out the role. The needs assessor might come from the community, might be on the school district staff, or might be hired as a temporary specialist.

Figure 7-3 shows the communication relationships among the three roles of client, decision maker, and needs assessor during the course of a client need assessment. The needs assessor is the *linking pin* or intermediary between the client and the decision maker. For instance, the needs assessor asks certain questions of the decision maker and receives from the decision maker some responses (e.g., responses that identify the particular clients of concern) which give *substantive* direction and guidance to the study. Also, the needs assessor asks certain questions and receives some responses from the clients (e.g., the clients' specific concept of their needs).

This chapter considers next two concepts or types of validity that are central to client need assessment.

WHAT IS CLIENT VALIDITY?

If a client explicitly acknowledges that certain information accurately represents his or her needs, then the information is considered to have "client valid-

FIGURE 7-3.   Communication Relationships between Client, Decision Maker, and Needs Assessor in Client Need Assessment

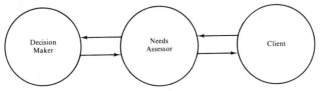

ity.'' One of the unusual and important features of client need assessment is that the needs assessor is encouraged to carefully review the specific need definitions with the client and obtain concurrence in the accuracy of the information before reporting it to the decision maker. (Some clients may be clearly incompetent to participate in this way—for example, mentally retarded persons. For them, substitutes or ''surrogates'' will have to be involved instead.)

The concept of client validity has certain implications for the methodology of client need assessment:

> If the data are to be valid from a client's perspective, there is the implication that, with respect to any domain, the methodology must provide for open-ended identification of the client's [needs]. Moreover, the methodology must provide for specific definitions of the [needs] from the client's perspective. . . . [Coffing 1973:29]

WHAT IS DECISION-MAKER VALIDITY?

If an item of information is used by a decision maker in making a decision, then the information has ''decision-maker validity'' (Hutchinson 1972). Decision-maker validity is dependent upon the decision maker's evaluation of both the information and the process by which the information is gathered. Accordingly,

> this suggests that the methodology should provide for open-ended identification of the decision maker's concepts of domains (of service or of program) and clients. It should respond to his priorities for obtaining data about particular combinations of clients and domains. And it should provide for obtaining the decision maker's approval or willing acceptance of the procedures employed to provide data. Without these provisions, there is the danger that the decision maker will ignore the data because he might believe that the data and/or the process lacks validity for his use. [Coffing 1973:29]

Taken together, the concepts of client validity and decision-maker validity

> suggest that the methodology must contain procedures which *objectively serve the subjective concerns of each party*. This implies that the client must be enabled to define his [needs] in terms of directly observable behaviors and states—in which form there would be minimal loss of meaning in the transmission of [needs] between client and decision maker. [Pp. 29–30; emphasis added]

It is thus very important for the needs assessor, especially, to understand the concepts of need, need fulfillment, client, decision maker, needs assessor, client validity, and decision-maker validity. Next are presented the basic procedures comprising the client need assessment process.

Basic Procedures

Conducting a client need assessment is something like piloting an airplane: in order to do either one successfully, a set of rules and procedures must be carefully followed. The crew members of a commerical jet, for example, go through elaborate checklists just to get the plane off the ground. They perform certain operations, get certain feedback about how the craft is responding to their operations, and then perform still more operations, get feedback, and continue through a prescribed sequence of activities. In fact, the complete flight can be described in terms of the deliberate, systematic interaction of crew and machine according to a largely predetermined pattern of actions. Contingencies such as weather, field conditions, weight of payload, mechanical functioning, and air traffic are all taken into account according to rules and procedures. The pattern leaves as little as possible to chance. Thus, the passengers are maximally assured of safety, comfort, and rapid delivery to their destination.

While the process of client need assessment does not involve a risk to people's lives as does an airplane trip, it does affect their *welfare* by the information it produces. The "destination" is reached when useful information is given to the people who will be making decisions about meeting clients' needs. To reach that destination, some basic rules and procedures of client need assessment should be carefully followed.

The process of client need assessment consists of six stages:

1. *Preparing* to do client need assessment
2. *Focusing* the effort
3. *Identifying* the clients, needs, and definers*
4. *Defining* the needs
5. *Measuring* the status of the needs
6. *Evaluating* the utility of the information

These six stages can be visualized as a cylical process as shown in figure 7-4. Each stage consists of a series of steps, and many of these steps are in turn composed of substeps and sub-sub-steps.

The cyclical nature of the process is emphasized here because in a system of planned educational change some of the assessment procedures should be repeated periodically. Figure 7-4 also shows that each stage is dependent in some way on the results of the prior stages. Thus, the status of needs is not measured until the clients' needs have been specifically defined. (Unfortunately, many educational need assessments in the past have attempted to do just that: measure the status of undefined or ill-defined needs. Usually the results have been unintelligible or, worse, misleading.)

In the sections that follow, the process is discussed and illustrated stage by stage, beginning with "preparing to do client need assessment." Although each stage is important, some are more complicated than others. Therefore, the chapter will give briefer attention to the simpler stages, while devoting greater attention to the more complex stages—particularly to the fourth and fifth stages: "defining clients' needs" and "measuring the status of the need."

Of the numerous studies that have been conducted using client need assess-

---

*"Definers" are people who, in a client need assessment, describe clients' needs in specific detail. Definers may or may not be the clients themselves.

FIGURE 7-4.   The Client Need Assessment Cycle

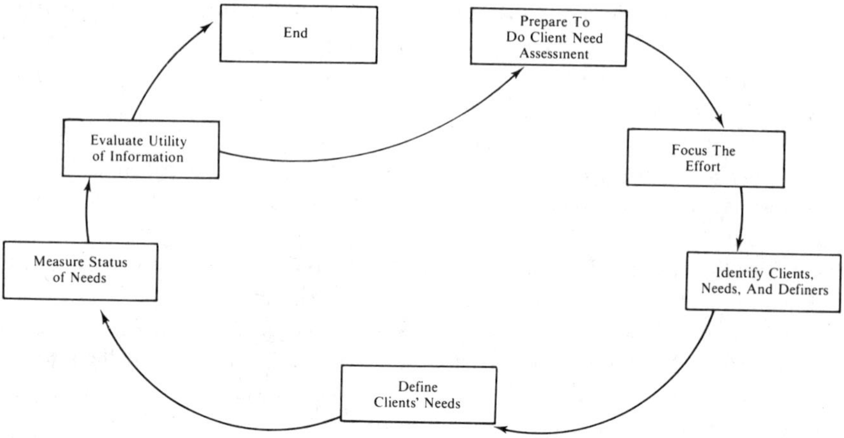

ment procedures, one will be drawn upon to provide a continuous example through the stages and steps of the process: Lehner's "Design of an Alternative Academic Program (For a Suburban High School) Using Directly Obtained Client Need Data (1973). Lehner's preface gives his personal perspective on why the study was undertaken, what it sought to accomplish, and how client need assessment became a part of that change effort:

> As a teacher at "Riverfield Junior High School" for five years, I had been aware that our graduates were dissatisfied with the high school they attended, "West Oldham High School" (WOHS). Inevitably, I became interested in changing that situation. Any practitioner knows, however, that it is extremely difficult to find acceptable ways of making a helpful intervention in the life of any educational institution, especially a neighboring one. Staff members are often protective of their own practices, and suspicious of "outsiders" whom they do not consider "experts"—an expert being someone more than fifty miles from home.
>
> The problems ordinarily attending any intervention were compounded in this instance by differences in the educational philosophies of Riverfield and West Oldham High School, the former having developed a somewhat controversial but nationally recognized innovative program. To make a successful intervention at WOHS, then [as a doctoral intern at WOHS on leave of absence from Riverfield JHS], I had to solve these problems and, more important, I needed a theory of action that would guide my efforts.... [Client need assessment methodology] suggested a theoretical approach to solving the expected intervention problems at WOHS.
>
> I saw that a direct client needs analysis could be expected to provide the data, and hence the credibility, that would be needed in an effort to design implementable alternative programs for WOHS. I would play an intermediary role, administering procedures that would help clients define their own needs and create programmatic responses to areas of deficiencies. While that role definition imposed constraints that were occasionally personally irritating, it did form a viable theoretical basis for action in what was to become the "Sharpe House Project."

The "Sharpe House Project" will be used to illustrate many aspects of client need assessment in the pages that follow.

STAGE ONE: PREPARING TO DO CLIENT NEED ASSESSMENT

Some educators want to "get on with it" before they really know what "it" is. Perhaps this helps explain why, over the years, education has been a ship's graveyard for innovations that failed to float. Client need assessment, like any other process of planned change, requires some preparation that can be summarized by the words *learning* and *linkage*. Learning refers to the fact that the needs assessor has to learn the concepts, rules and procedures of client need assessment, and linkage means establishing initial contacts with people who need what the process can deliver. Although not difficult, learning and linkage are sufficiently important to deserve special attention.

Step 1. *Learning the process.* Learning the process is largely a matter of reading about the basic concepts and procedures, perhaps discussing them with others, and then trying out the procedures under simple conditions, such as with one's family or with some members of a curriculum committee or change team. Initial trials should be conducted on a very small scale so that the needs assessor can directly *experience* the basic logic of the process without a lot of confounding variables. This chapter has been constructed to provide the basic information about the process and to give the reader some vicarious experience with it through brief examples of how the procedures can be used or have been used.

> In the "Sharpe House Project," Lehner learned about client need assessment by working with the author in adapting to Lehner's study the methodology described in early and uneven documentation of the approach. Moreover, he participated in a study of graduate students' needs relative to a university program in educational leadership and administration, and later during his own study he learned about the methodology through trial and revision.

Step 2. *Linking the process.* In the context of this book, preparation also means putting the process in touch with people who need what it can do. If the reader is already participating in a planned educational change effort, then the linkage is easily established. The process can then serve the people who are planning, implementing, controlling, or evaluating the larger set of change strategies. It is likely that the needs assessor will be one of those people. In any event, client need assessment has to be part of a larger programing effort.

> Since he was the designated "change agent," leader of the program planning effort, and needs assessor, too, Lehner in the "Sharpe House Project" was himself the link between the client need assessment process and the intended users.

The preparation stage should not be ignored. Otherwise, there is likely to be a failure to produce useful information, not because of the basic process but because of inadequate learning or linkage on the part of the needs assessor.

STAGE TWO: FOCUSING THE EFFORT

Client need assessment usually is not conducted overnight; it may take days, weeks, or even a few months to go through the cycle just once. While actual resources are scarce, the resource requirements for conducting an absolutely complete and continuous assessment of clients' needs could be almost limitless. So complex, different, and changeable are people's needs that it is possible to imagine spending so many resources that none are left for *meeting* needs. Therefore, some affordable balance has to be struck.

For this reason, the effort should become focused at the beginning, which means three things: first, identifying the principal intended users of information; second, identifying the actual resources (time, energy, materials) that can be made available for conducting client need assessment; and third, setting priorities for which of the decision makers (information users) the effort should be focused toward, considering the limited resources.

One preliminary issue is important, unavoidable, and tricky: who gets to identify the decision makers and resources and to set the priorities? In other words, who decides how the effort will be focused? This issue is important because it pertains to how the information-gathering effort will tie into any other planned-change activities; whoever decides on the focus will thereby play a gatekeeping or facilitating role in the larger change effort. The issue is unavoidable because *someone* has to set priorities when resources are limited. The issue is tricky because it is so easy to concentrate on the *planning decision makers* while forgetting *other decision makers* who might later be making crucial "go/ no-go" decisions about educational changes. Thus, whoever decides on the focus has to understand which decision makers are relevant and important, considering both the planned-change process and the education setting in which the change efforts are occurring. This person has to be familiar with the resource situation; in some sense, he or she should be someone who controls the availability of the resources.

The role involved here can be called "focus decision maker." If the client need assessment is an official activity of the school system, this role might conceivably be performed by a change team (as a group), a director of research and evaluation, a principal, the superintendent, the school board, or a citizen's committee—depending on the particular setting in which educational change is contemplated. If the client need assessment is not an official activity, but rather is independent of the school system, then the focus decision maker might be one or more leaders of the group involved. So who should be the focus decision maker in any given educational setting? The answer will vary for each specific context in which a needs assessor will be working.

When the focus decision maker has been selected, the needs assessor will then interact with that person (or group) in implementing the three steps of focusing the effort, as discussed next.

Step 1. *Identifying the relevant decision makers.* Identifying at the beginning those decision makers for whom information will be gathered enables the needs assessor to involve them directly in the effort. Their involvement will be crucial at the third stage (identifying clients, needs, and definers), the fifth stage (measuring the status of needs), and the sixth stage (evaluating the utility of the information).

> In the "Sharpe House Project" Lehner played the role of focus decision maker and he initially identified as decision makers everyone he and the people he talked with could think of who had anything to do with WOHS and Sharpe House. In priority-ordering the long list of decision makers, however, he focused on students and then finally decided that as leader of the change effort he ought to focus primarily on information concerns he had. Thus in this project the needs assessor was also the principal decision maker for whom the information was to be gathered. Later a planning committee would be involved, too.

The needs assessor asks the focus decision maker to create a list of all the decision makers (individuals and groups) for whom it would be desirable to gather decision-oriented information about clients' needs, considering the educational setting in which the planned-change efforts are to take place. Then the focus decision maker should assign a rank order to the decision makers on the list, based on the importance of their receiving decision-oriented information about clients' needs. Usually this rank-ordering step is facilitated by the following instruction:

> If such information could be provided to *only one* decision maker on your list, which one would it be? Assign rank number one to that decision maker. Now, for the remaining decision makers, if such information could be provided to *only one* of them, which one would it be? Assign rank number two to that decision maker. (And so forth, until the whole list, or a reasonable portion of it, has been rank-ordered.)

List 7-1 provides some hypothetical examples of the results of this step.

Step 2. *Identifying the available resources for conducting client need assessment.* In order to plan and carry out client need assessment, the needs assessor has to know the *kinds* and *amounts* of resources that can be made available. Further, the limitations or *constraints* on those resources must be known. Any assessment will have to be conducted within the limits of the scarce resources actually available.

Therefore, in this step the focus decision maker is asked to make a *list of resources* that can be used in the course of the effort. These resources will surely include the time of anyone involved directly in the process as well as the costs of supplies, postage, telephone, and transporation. The key people whose time availability should be estimated are the needs assessor and any decision makers for whom information is to be gathered. Additionally, the time of "definers" (the persons who will be asked to define needs) will have to be estimated—not necessarily at the beginning, but after they have been identified as part of the third stage of the process. The services of outside consultants may prove desirable, so funds for employing them might be included. The kinds and amounts of resources should be identfied, and any constraints or contingencies

LIST 7-1.   Examples of Generalized Decision-Maker Lists that Might Be Created by Different "Focus Decision Makers"

Hypothetical School Attendance Area List of Decision Makers (in no particular order)	Hypothetical District-wide List of Decision Makers (in no particular order)
1. School board	1. School board
2. Superintendent	2. Superintendent
3. Teachers	3. Parents
4. Students	4. Teachers
5. Principal	5. Students
6. Parents	6. Principals
7. Neighborhood association	7. Voters
8. PTA	8. Taxpayers
9. Student council	9. Central staff
10. Curriculum committee	10. Editor of the newspaper
	11. Most influential persons in town
Hypothetical Classroom	12. PTA
Level List of Decision Makers	13. School accreditation commission
(in no particular order)	14. State department of education staff
	15. Local businessmen
1. Teacher	16. School dropouts
2. Students	17. Teachers' union
3. Parents	
4. Principal	
5. Curriculum committee	

should be noted: for example, certain people's time might be available only before or after a certain date because of the school calendar or personal vacations. The listing of resources, in short, represents the focus decision maker's best preliminary estimates, recognizing that subsequent decisions will determine actual resource usage.

Step 3. *Allocating the available resources.* Usually, the resources are scarce and the relevant decision makers are numerous. In such cases, some apportionment of the resources is required to get the most value from the assessment effort. There are two ways in which resources should be allocated: first, across decision makers and, second, across stages in the process for each decision maker.

Ordinarily only a few decision makers should be directly involved in the initial cycle of the process; others can be involved later. If it is decided that there are sufficient resources only to provide some information to each of three decision makers, for example, then the question is: Should the resources be allocated equally across the three (i.e., one third for each), or should the allocation be unequal (say, 50 percent for the first priority decision maker, 30 percent for the second, and 20 percent for the third)? It usually takes more effort to serve a group decision maker than an individual decision maker. Knowing the process better, the needs assessor should advise the focus decision maker how far the available resources might be stretched and still provide useful information within a reasonable time period.

The next question is : Within the allocation for *each* decision maker, how shall the resources be apportioned among the remaining stages (three through six) of the assessment cycle? Here, the needs assessor should take the lead by working out and recommending the apportionments. A benchmark apportionment—to be adjusted according to the actual situation—might be 10 percent for the third stage (identifying clients, needs, and definers), 35 percent for the fourth stage, 50 percent for the fifth stage, and 5 percent for the sixth stage (evaluating the utility of the information). Table 7-1 illustrates a two-way resource allocation in which the focus decision maker has decided upon a 50–30–20 percent apportionment across three decision makers and a 5–40–50–5 percent apportionment across stages three through six for each decision maker.

The above percentages serve as guidelines for budgeting the available resources. However, because resources may vary for different decision makers, the budget is likely to differ somewhat from what the percentages might suggest. Table 7-2 shows a hypothetical budget that reflects the percentage allocations from table 7-1.

Step 4. *Scheduling the effort.* If the client need assessment effort will span more than a few days' time, then the needs assessor should develop a timeline or a network flow diagram in order to help plan and control the process. The availability of each decision maker must be determined before building the schedule. The school calendar and other considerations may enter as well. Figure 7-5 illustrates a timeline, assuming the information given in tables 7-1 and 7-2 plus information on when the decision makers will be available to participate.

Step 5. *Review and approval.* The results of the preceding four steps should be reviewed with the focus decision maker, and the needs assessor should make any changes that the focus decision maker thinks are necessary before undertaking the rest of the assessment effort. The focus decision maker's review and approval establishes a kind of contract with the needs assessor. It is advisable to reduce to writing the mutual understandings—especially the results of steps 3 and 4 as revised. This can be done in the form of a memorandum signed by both. In this manner, the client need assessment effort will have become focused on directly serving certain decision makers, using known resources.

STAGE THREE: IDENTIFYING CLIENTS, NEEDS, AND DEFINERS

In this stage the needs assessor works directly with each decision maker in order to establish exactly which clients and which client needs the decision maker most wants information about. Then the decision maker will be asked to name some people and/or some literature to serve as sources of need definitions for those clients. The principal steps of the third stage are shown in list 7-2.

Step 1: *Plan how this stage will be implemented.* At the very outset the needs assessor should arrange to meet with each decision maker, and the rest of

TABLE 7-1. Example of a Focus Decision Maker's Allocation of Total Resources by Percentage across Three Decision Makers and Four Stages of the Client Need Assessment Process.

STAGES OF CNA	FIRST PRIORITY DECISION MAKERS	SECOND PRIORITY DECISION MAKERS	THIRD PRIORITY DECISION MAKERS	TOTALS
Stage Three: Identifying clients	2.5%	1.5%	1%	5%
Stage Four: Defining	20	12	8	40
Stage Five: Measuring	25	15	10	50
Stage Six: Evaluating	2.5	1.5	1	5
Totals	50%	30%	20%	100%

TABLE 7-2. Example of an Allocation of Dollar Resources According to the Focus Decision Maker's Choices Shown in Figure 7-1.

STAGES OF CNA	FIRST PRIORITY DECISION MAKERS	SECOND PRIORITY DECISION MAKERS	THIRD PRIORITY DECISION MAKERS	TOTALS
Stage Three: Identifying clients, Needs, and Definers	$ 125	$ 75	$ 50	$ 250
Stage Four: Defining	1000	600	400	2000
Stage Five: Measuring	1250	750	500	2500
Stage Six: Evaluating	125	75	50	250
Totals	$2500	$1500	$1000	$5000

FIGURE 7-5.   **Example of a Timeline**

1 = Preparation
2 = Focus the effort
3 = Identify clients, needs, and definers for (a) DM #1, (b) DM #2, and (c) DM #3
4 = Defining for (a) DM #1, (b) DM #2, and (c) DM #3
5 = Measuring for (a) DM #1, (b) DM #2, and (c) DM #3

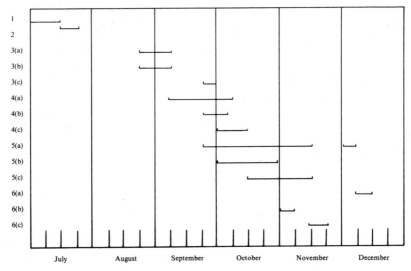

the stage should be planned in enough detail so that the effort can be kept on target in terms of budget and time. This may mean abbreviating some of the steps.

Step 2. *Determine the first (next) available decision maker's concerns in terms of "whose needs for what according to whom?"* If it is both practical and politic, and if their schedules permit, the needs assessor might arrange for two or three decision makers to go through this step together. This might enable each to have the perspectives in making certain decisions relative to the interests of each in having client-need information. If a joint meeting is not arranged, the needs assessor will meet the one decision maker who is available first. This first meeting typically lasts from one to three hours.

Step 2.1. *Prepare the decision maker for identifying the clients, needs, and definers.* In advance, if possible, or at the beginning of the first meeting, the needs assessor briefs the decision maker on the scope and focus of the need assessment effort and especially on the purpose of providing this decision maker with useful information about clients' needs. It often helps to give the main questions of step 2 to the decision maker ahead of time so that some answers or other relevant information can be brought to the meeting.

Step 2.2. *Ask the decision maker to identify the clients of concern.* Different decision makers typically are concerned about meeting the needs of different clients—or at least they categorize their clientele differently. An elementary school principal, for example, might be concerned about the categories of (1) all

LIST 7-2.   Principal Steps of the Third Stage in Client Need Assessment

1.   Plan how this stage will be implemented.
2.   Determine the first (next) available decision maker's concerns in terms of "whose need for what according to whom?"
   2.1   Prepare the decision maker for identifying the clients, needs, and definers.
   2.2   Ask the decision maker to identify the clients of concern.
   2.3   Ask the decision maker to identify the needs of concern.
   2.4.   Ask the decision maker to develop the combinations of client and need most important to have information about.
   2.5.   Ask the decision maker to identify the persons whose definitions the decision maker wants.
   2.6.   Ask the decision maker to review, revise if necessary, and approve the priority combinations of clients, needs, and definers.

students, (2) students by grade level, (3) new students, (4) handicapped students, (5) gifted students, (6) disadvantaged students, and (7) parents of each category of student. A parent advisory committee, however, might be concerned about the categories of (1) students with learning disabilities, (2) students from certain ethnic backgrounds, (3) students who are bused to and from school, as well as other student and parent categories. A teacher might be concerned about meeting the needs of (1) students in her or his classes and (2) their parents. Asking each decision maker to identify the clients helps ensure that each decision maker will get relevant information.

The clients named may be individuals (such as Mary Jones or Ms. Wilma Jones, Mary's mother), intentional groups (such as each sixth-grade class in our building), or conceptual categories (such as children with reading problems or sixth-graders' parents). Often the clients will overlap because the decision maker is concerned about the same people in different ways for different purposes. An individual student, for example, might be named (1) as an individual client, (2) as a member of Ms. Thomas's third-grade class, and (3) as a Chicano.

When feasible, the needs assessor should test the completeness of the decision maker's list of clients by asking ·the decision maker (1) to think about decisions that have been made or might be made in the future and about which clients those decisions pertain to, and (2) to consider the perspectives of one or more other persons (such as other decision makers or advisory groups) about who the clients of concern might be. If the decision makers are meeting as a group for this step, then they can simply compare lists as a test of completeness. (See list 7-3 for an additional test of completeness.)

Step 2.3. *Ask the decision maker to identify the needs of concern.* The decision maker will thus have created a list of the clients of concern to that decision maker, and the needs assessor next asks the decision maker what kinds of needs or what domains of service the decision maker is concerned about relative to the clients. This question can be approached in any of three ways. First, the decision maker might make a list of *kinds of needs* that pertain to any or all of the clients and that the decision maker is concerned about meeting (Coffing, Hodson, and Hutchinson 1973). For example, such a list might include counseling, individual tutoring, in-service training, instructional materials, learn-

LIST 7-3. An Additional Test of Completeness List of Possible Clients

- Students—by grade level
  - —kindergarten
  - —elementary
  - —junior high
  - —senior high
  - —technical school
  - —learning disabilities/behavior disabilities
  - —physically handicapped
  - —mentally retarded
  - —gifted
  - —homebound
  - —majority
  - —minority
    - —black
    - —native American
    - —Chicano
    - —Puerto Rican
    - —English as second language
  - —individual
  - —transfer
  - —disadvantaged
  - —dropouts
  - —all neighborhood
- Preschool children, handicapped
- Parents of each category of preschool children
- Adults
- Teacher aides
- Teachers of each category of students
- Teachers—by grade level
  - —First year
  - —tenured
  - —Master
  - —by department
- Preservice teachers
- Principals
- Central staff
- Clerical staff
- Custodial staff
- Maintenance staff
- Business staff
- Fund raisers
- Taxpayers
- School board
- School board members
- District residents
- District residents—by neighborhood
- District staff
- School staff
- Counselors
- School psychologists
- Prospective employers
- Prospective employees
- Community agencies
- Employers of enrolled students
- Classified staff
- Nonclassified staff
- Federal program coordinators
- Federal project directors
- Benefactors
- Alumni

ing, socio-emotional support, transportation, participation in decision making, professional growth, information, reading skills, individualized instruction, stability, and change. The list can get quite long. In a second approach, the decision maker might identify the *domains or service areas* of concern (Coffing 1973). This list usually will be much shorter because the service areas are broader in the decision maker's mind, and it may overlap the "kinds of needs" list. Some examples might be elementary education, special education, social studies, physical education, bilingual/bicultural programs, extracurricular activities, and psychological services. A third approach is to use the first two and then combine the lists—but it is useful to *ask the questions separately,* because experience has shown that separate questions will elicit more categories of concern than if the decision maker is asked to respond to both at once.

If it is feasible, the needs assessor should test the completeness of the list of needs or service areas. This can be done by asking the decision maker (1) to consider other people's identification of needs or services (from other decision makers, from an advisory group, or from some clients themselves), and (2) to consider all the programs and services the decision maker expects to make decisions about. (See list 7-4 for an additional test of completeness.)

LIST 7-4. An Additional Test of Completeness List of Kinds of Needs

- Cognitive—
- Affective
- Psychomotor
- Learning
- Instruction
- Space
- Equipment
- Facilities
- Learning resources
- Media
- Materials
- Transportation
- Health services
- Dietary services
- Clothing
- Food
- Shelter
- Supplies
- Professional growth
- In-service training
- Preservice training
- Information
- Counseling
- Supervision
- Testing
- Advice
- Positive self-image
- Good human relations
- Basic skills
- Daily living skills
- Social skills
- Tutoring
- Individualized instruction
- Alternative programs
- Participation in decision making
- Continuing education
- Technical skills
- Technical assistance
- Vocational skills

- College preparation
- Recreation
- Extracurricular activities
- Socio-emotional support
- Multicultural education
- Multilingual education
- Administrative support
- Data for decision making
- Research
- Planning
- Control
- Continuity
- Change
- Fresh ideas
- Released time
- Planning time
- Compensation
- Personal time
- Fringe benefits
- Satisfaction
- Organizationl health
- Coordination
- Cooperation
- Independence
- Involvement
- Choice
- Record keeping
- Financial support
- Knowledge of cultural heritage
- Help
- Self-direction
- Teaching others
- Helping others
- Competition
- Staff development
- Team work
- Tradition
- Tenure
- Administrative skills

Step 2.4. *Ask the decision maker to develop the combinations of client and need most important to have information about.* The needs assessor asks the decision maker to combine the lists of clients and needs into sets of phrases in the form *"whose need for what."* Some examples might be: "our Chicano students' need for bilingual/bicultural programs," "our parents' need for participation in decision making," "our teachers' need for in-service training," or "Mary Jone's need for reading skills." To develop the relevant combinations, the needs assessor can ask the decision maker to (1) look at the client list; (2) pick out the one client (an individual, group, or category) whose needs the decision maker most wants to have information about; (3) look at the list of needs and services; (4) pick out the need or service about which the decision maker most wants to have client information relative to the client who was selected; (5) write down that combination of client and need (or service) in the form "whose need for what"; and then (6) repeat the procedure in order to select a second combination, varying the need or the client or both, continuing until the list of combinations appears to the needs assessor to be as long as can be implemented in succeeding stages of the assessment effort. The needs assessor's experience and the particular circumstances will suggest when to stop.

Some examples of "whose needs for what" in the "Sharpe House Project" are shown in list 7-5.

List 7-5: "Whose Needs for What": Examples of Some Combinations of Clients and Needs

---

- •SH students' needs for learning and instruction
- •SH students' needs for guidance
- •SH students' needs for social and emotional support
- •SH students' needs for self-esteem
- •SH teachers' needs for self-determination
- •SH teachers' needs for professional growth
- •SH teachers' needs for success as a teacher/professional fulfillment
- •SH parents' needs for confidence about their childrens' college or vocation preparation
- •SH parents' needs for involvement in school

SH = "Sharpe House"

SOURCE: Lehner 1973:46ff.

Step 2.5. *Ask the decision maker to identify the persons whose definitions the decision maker wants.* Often the most important information for a given decision maker is the specific definition of particular clients' needs. As used here, *specific definition* means "definition by attribute"—that is, definition in terms of the behaviors and/or states that comprise the operational meaning of a concept (Hutchinson and Benedict 1970). If this is unclear, the reader may wish to review the earlier section on "what is a need?" and especially figure 7-2. Where does the needs assessor get the specific definitions that are pertinent to the particular clients and needs of concern to this decision maker? From sources (that is, definers) identified by the decision maker as people whose definitions the decision maker wants to have. These definers may be people in the local community such as parents, teachers, and students; they may be "experts" whose definitions are available through review of literature; they may be developers of standardized tests whose definitions are available in the form of their test items.

The decision maker is asked to identify one or more definers for each combination of client and need. A "definer" might be an individual, an intentional group (such as a parent advisory committee or a curriculum committee or a class of sixth-graders), or a conceptual category (such as taxpayers or professors of educational administration or students aged fourteen to seventeen). The decision maker may want more than one definition.

> Faculty members of a Special Education Department of an Eastern state college were developing a course for pre-service and in-service teachers on the topic of parent relations. The committee wanted information about "the needs that parents of handicapped pre-school children have for dealing competently with their children." Definitions were obtained from three definers: parents of pre-school handicapped children, pre-service teachers preparing for early childhood special education, and in-service special education teachers involved in early childhood programs in that state. [Weinthaler 1974]

Or the *clients* may be named as definers; for example:

> In the "Sharpe House Project," the change agent sought information from students and teachers. For example, students were asked to define their own needs for learning and instruction, and teachers were asked to define their own needs for self-determination. (See List 7-6.)

LIST 7-6. Examples of Some Combinations of Clients, Needs, and the Desired Definers as Chosen by a Decision Maker

DM's Priority	"Whose Needs for What According to Whom"
1	SH students' needs for learning and instruction as defined by SH students
2	SH students' needs for guidance as defined by SH students
3	SH students' needs for social and emotional support as defined by SH students
4	SH teachers' needs for self-determination as defined by SH teachers
5	SH teachers' needs for professional growth as defined by SH teachers
6	SH teachers' needs for success as a teacher as defined by SH teachers

SH = "Sharpe House"

SOURCE: Lehner 1973:52.

Some additional examples of definers are shown in list 7-7.

LIST 7-7. Some Examples of Definers: Individuals, Groups, and Categories

Some Individual Definers:
- Johnny (an individual student)
- Johnny's teacher
- Johhny's mother
- Johhny's counselor
- The school psychologist
- The home-school liaison person
- The coordinator of federal programs
- The principal

Some Group Definers:
- The change team
- The student council
- The English department faculty
- The teachers at Crocker Elementary School
- The Citizens Committee for Effective Schools
- The school board
- The students in Ms. Harris's 6th-grade class
- Participants at a public hearing

Some Categorical Definers:
- High school students
- Parents
- The community at large
- Graduates
- Employers
- Classified staff
- Taxpayers
- Professors of education

The decision maker's choices of definers should be tested for completeness and screened for feasibility. The latter ensures that the definers chosen are accessible to the needs assessor within the budget and time schedule for the effort.

Step 2.6. *Ask the decision maker to review, revise if necessary, and approve the priority combinations of clients, needs, and definers.* In the preceding steps, the decision maker will have produced a set of combinations of clients, needs, and definers in the form *"whose need for what according to whom."* Because some of these concerns may be more important or more urgent than others, the decision maker is asked to review and approve the list, and to set priorities or provide desirable target dates for when at least the need definitions would be useful. The needs assessor then establishes with the decision maker a relative emphasis among the concerns and a feasible time schedule.

As soon as each decision maker has identified a priority set of clients, needs, and definers, and the needs assessor and decision maker have worked out the schedule, then the process moves to the fourth stage for that decision maker.

STAGE FOUR: DEFINING CLIENTS' NEEDS

A need has been defined as a mental image of "what should be" according to the person holding that image. The specific or operational meaning of a need image is defined by the set of behaviors and/or states that comprises the need image in someone's mind. Therefore, the role of definer is to express as specifically and as operationally as possible the definer's image of a particular client's need. Accordingly, the needs assessor's task is either (1) to *locate* that operational definition, if recorded (in the literature or in a standardized test, for example), or (2) to *elicit* that operational definition, if not recorded, from the definer. The needs assessor then reports the definition to the decision maker and asks whether the status (fulfillment) of the client's need or any of its dimensions should be measured. (Measurement of need fulfillment is not undertaken *automatically* in client need assessment because experience has shown that need definitions alone can be very powerful. That is, with the operational definition in mind, the decision maker sometimes knows adequately, for his or her purposes, how well the need is being met, and resources will not have to be spent measuring the status of that particular need.) The principal steps of the fourth stage are shown in list 7-8.

LIST 7-8. Principal Steps in the Fourth Stage: Defining Clients' Needs

1. Plan how this stage will be implemented.
    1.1 Go to either step 2 or 3, whichever is appropriate.
2. Locate existing definitions of the client's need.
3. Obtain directly from the definer a specific definition of the client's need.
    3.1. Develop with the decision maker's approval an open-ended question, the "defining stimulus."
    3.2. Obtain definer responses to the defining stimulus.
    3.3. If the definer is more than one person, administer a second-round defining instrument.
    3.4. Conduct further defining activities if greater specificity is desired and if resources will allow.
    3.5. Recycle to step 2 or 3 if there are other definers for the same client and need.
4. Report the definition(s) to the decision maker.
    4.1. Compile the results of step 2 and/or step 3.
    4.2. Give the results to the decision maker.
    4.3. If measurement resources have been allocated for the fifth stage of client need assessment for this decision maker, have the decision maker choose which dimensions of the client's need should be measured to determine the status of need fulfillment.

Step 1. *Plan how this stage will be implemented.* The fourth stage may require intricate planning in order to keep within the budget and timeline. Instruments will be designed, tested, and administered, and the results will be analyzed and reported. Existing literature, reports, and records may be located and analyzed. Definers may be contacted and arrangements made for their participation. Accordingly, the needs assessor should (1) review the budget and timeline, (2) review the steps of this stage, (3) state specifically how each step and substep should be done, omitting those not feasible under the circumstances, (4) set a detailed schedule for implementing the steps and substeps, and (5) devise a contingency plan covering problems such as the unavailability of some definers.

Local decision makers for planned educational change will usually name local people as the most important definers: parents, students, teachers, counselors, administrators. These people's conceptions of "what should be" are usually considered more relevant for local decision making than the definitions of clients' needs found in literature, because the latter typically are much more general than would be useful for the specific decisions required in the local situation. On the other hand, some literature may be specific enough, particularly when "literature" includes standardized tests (of mathematics skills, for example) and survey-feedback questionnaires used in other, similar school settings. Depending upon whether the definer is some existing literature or some people from whom definitions will be elicited directly, the needs assessor uses either step 2 or step 3.

Step 2. *Locate existing definitions of the client's need.* Step 2 is used if the decision maker has named as "definer" some existing, recorded sources such as books, journal articles, research reports, standardized tests, or broader bodies of literature. To obtain definitions from these sources, usually the needs assessor interacts with written materials rather than with the author personally.

Depending on the nature of the written source material, step 2 entails either (1) a combination of information search and analysis or (2) analysis alone, if the source is specific and already available. Both possibilities can be costly in staff time, if not in dollar cost of source materials. If the resources of the study are too limited for step 2, then perhaps the decision maker should substitute other, more accessible definers and shift to step 3 for them.

Standardized tests and survey-feedback instruments are special cases, since (1) the test or instrument items constitute the need definition and (2) the results of administering the test or instrument constitute the measurement of need fulfillment relative to that definition. In fairness to the clients and the decision maker as well as to the developers, the needs assessor should make sure that the groups on whom the tests were referenced are very similar to the particular clients of concern to the decision maker. Culturally biased instruments are a particular danger to be avoided.

Several steps for conducting an information search are suggested in list 7-9.

The "analysis" substep requires the needs assessor to develop as detailed a description of the client's need as the literature will allow. Ideally, this description (definition) will be statable in terms of the directly observable dimensions or attributes of the client's need, prioritized according to the importance of those dimensions from the definer's perspective. Ideal completeness and specificity are

LIST 7-9.   A Brief Set of Steps for Information Search

1. Determine what resources (time, personnel, etc.) are available for conducting the information search.
2. Plan how to carry out the following steps without exceeding the available resources.
3. Identify possible sources of the desired information, e.g., existing information systems such as ERIC, university libraries, reports of previous need assessments in the school system.
4. Estimate which possible sources are most likely to yield the desired information.
5. Determine which of the likely sources should be checked first (or next), given the available resources.
6. Gain access to the first likely source.
7. Screen the existing information in that source, identifying the most useful information.
8. If resources remain for the information search, repeat steps 5–7 for the source that should be checked next.

seldom possible from a literature review. Nevertheless, the needs assessor extracts from the source whatever definition is there, being careful to retain the author's language and avoid "contaminating" the author's conception with the needs assessor's interpretations. Thus, the product of step 2 should be a list of dimensions in priority order. From step 2, the needs assessor skips to step 4. (The first-time reader of this chapter should continue with step 3, the more frequently used step for obtaining specific definitions of clients' needs.)

Step 3. *Obtain directly from the definer a specific definition of the client's need.* This step is used when the decision maker has named as definer an individual or group from whom a definition must be *elicited* because it does not already exist in record form.

> In developing a metropolitan regional "Education Center for the Arts" which would provide special programs in the visual and performing arts for gifted high school students, the design team determined which guidance services for the students were most needed according to the eligible students themselves and the Center staff.
>
> Preparatory to seeking federal funding assistance for desegregation programing in the schools of a medium-sized city, the district's central staff developed a number of client need assessment designs. In one design, fourteen special reading teachers were asked to define their students' needs for specific reading skills.

For any combination of client, need, and definer ("whose need for what according to whom"), the basic defining substeps of step 3 are (1) designing an appropriate open-ended question (also called the defining stimulus) and a protocol (e.g., an interview schedule) for presenting this stimulus to the definer; (2) obtaining the definer's response to the stimulus; (3) analyzing the results into discrete dimensions or items of need; (4) if the definer is a group or category of persons, constructing and administering a second-round survey instrument; and

(5) if time and resources allow and if it is important, repeating the above substeps with some of the *dimensions* or items of need requiring further specification in order to measure their status. Various inquiry methods may be used to present the defining stimulus and obtain the definer's response: face-to face individual interview, group interview, telephone interview, hand-out or send-home survey, mail-out survey, or public hearing.

Step 3.1. *The defining stimulus*. Since the purpose of step 3 is to elicit the definer's mental image of the client's need, the definer must be allowed great initial freedom to express the image. Prompting and providing examples should be minimized in order to avoid contaminating the definition at the outset. The initial defining stimulus should therefore be open-ended; it should not dictate in detail what the definer should say. Of course, the defining stimulus also must fit the circumstances of the particular need assessment, which means that it must (1) refer to the given client and need being defined in this instance, (2) be understandable by the definer, and (3) have the decision maker's approval.

> In the ''Sharpe House Project'' the following defining stimulus was used to elicit from teachers a definition of *their needs for success as a teacher:* ''Imagine that you are working in a school where your needs for success as a teacher are being completely fulfilled, where you are achieving the kind of professional fulfillment you really need and want. In that (imaginary) situation, what are the things that would be happening that would indicate to you that you are achieving the kind of professional fulfillment you really need and want? List those things in the space below.''
>
> In a metropolitan regional ''Education Center for the Arts,'' students' and staff members' definitions of *students' needs for guidance services* were elicited using the following defining stimulus: ''Imagine that the ECA students' needs for guidance services are being completely met. Look at this situation in your mind—what is going on, what students are doing, what other people are doing, and where it is happening. Then in the space below write a list of all the things you see in the situation that tell you that ECA students' needs for guidance services are being completely met in the situation.''

The foregoing examples will help illuminate the rules for designing a defining stimulus as outlined by Coffing, Hodson, and Hutchinson (1973:A-33, A-34), which in turn are based on a methodology for ''operationalizing fuzzy concepts'' invented by Hutchinson (Hutchinson and Benedict 1970). The rules for designing a defining stimulus are as follows:

1. Given a decision maker's desire for definitional information relative to a particular combination of client and need as defined by a particular definer, the needs assessor asks the decision maker to say a few words about *how the information is likely to be used.* The decision maker's purposes for having the information will help the needs assessor do the next step, below.

2. The needs assessor develops a *hypothetical situation* appropriate to the decision maker's purpose and in which the client's need is said to be completely fulfilled. Additional instructions are added to cause the definer to identify and write down (or tell the needs assessor) everything the definer visualizes in the situation (as constructed in the definer's mind) that indicate to the definer that the client's need is completely fulfilled in the situation.

3. The decision maker's approval of the defining stimulus, perhaps after modifications are made in it, is obtained; the decision maker is asked to consider: "Will this stimulus work? That is, *do you think it will produce information that you want and can use in decision making?*"

While designing the stimulus, the needs assessor should remember that the whole purpose of the stimulus is to elicit the definer's image as completely as possible without exceeding the boundaries of the client and the need of concern to the decision maker. If the stimulus is too broad—that is, if it is not focused on the actual decision-making requirements of the, decisionmaker—it will produce definitions the decision maker may find irrelevant or beyond the realm of his responsibilities. That unfortunate result could be frustrating, if not angering, to the decision maker, to the definers whose definitions were solicited, and to the clients who understand that their needs are going unheeded.

In addition to the stimulus, the needs assessor prepares (when appropriate) an interview schedule, a questionnaire format, or other contextual material to be given to the definer, including a letter or memorandum or other presentation that (1) gives reasons why the definer is being asked to participate in the client need assessment and (2) thanks the definer for participating.

Step 3.2. *Definer responses.* After the decision maker has approved the defining stimulus, the needs assessor arranges for the definer's response. Various inquiry methods might be used: face-to-face individual interview, group interview, telephone interview, hand-out or send-home survey, mail-out survey, or public hearing.

The responses should be collected in list form. However, a few definers will describe the clients' needs narratively in paragraphs or in compound statements; these must be analyzed by the needs assessor into discrete, unitary dimensions of need. If possible, the definer can help or at least approve the analysis of such items. The resulting lists from all definers are then combined (except for exact duplicate dimensions) into a composite list. List 7-10 shows the narrative response of one definer in the "Sharpe House Project," and list 7-11 shows dimensions from the definer as analyzed and compiled by the needs assessor.

If the definer is an individual, the needs assessor next asks the definer to assign a rank order of importance to the dimensions and even a weighting if their number is relatively few—say, a dozen or less. Then the needs assessor goes to step 4, reporting. If, however, the definer is a group of people, a second-round survey instrument is required, as described next.

Step 3.3. *The second-round instrument.* Group or categorical definers must be given an opportunity to respond to the total combined set of dimensions. This is accomplished by designing and administering a second-round instrument.

An interesting way to handle the second-round instrument is at a group

LIST 7-10. A Defining Stimulus and One Definer's Response to It

A DEFINING STIMULUS FOR THE PHRASE"STUDENTS' NEEDS FOR LEARNING AND INSTRUCTION ACCORDING TO THE STUDENTS":

Construct in your mind a hypothetical or imaginary learning situation with people in it, materials, equipment, space, etc. In this situation you are receiving instruction, you are learning, and it's the kind of instruction, the kind of learning, that you really need and want.

As you observe this situation in your mind, what are the things that tell you that you are really learning, really receiving the kind of instruction that you need? Write down what you see happening in this situation; try to get as much out of the situation as you can, making your list as complete as possible.

ONE DEFINER'S WRITTEN RESPONSE TO THE DEFINING STIMULUS:

The situation would be as follows: some person, age not important as long as he was open, enjoyable, and knew something to communicate with others, would spend time with a person or persons, teaching. In many ways it would be Athean-like (*sic*). There would be educational facilities available, but their use not mandatory. Time would be spent in nature discussing botany, geology, compositional English, geometry incorporated with maps and geography, and also time spent on survival and finding one's way by the stars.... [The definer's narrative continued for a page and a half.]

SOURCE: Lehner 1973:53, 56.

LIST 7-11. A Needs Assessor's Analysis of the Definer's Narrative Response Shown in Figure 7-10

- The person teaching me is open.
- The person teaching me is enjoyable.
- The person teaching me knows something to communicate with others.
- The age of the person teaching me is not important.
- The person teaching spends time with me.
- The teaching/learning situation is Athean-like (*sic*).
- Educational facilities are available.
- The use of educational facilities is not mandatory.
- We are spending time in nature discussing botany.
- We are spending time in nature discussing biology.
- etc.

SOURCE: Adapted from Lehner 1973:56.

meeting: if the number of definers is small—say, ten or less—the instrument can be constructed in front of them on a blackboard, on a strip of brown wrapping paper tapped to a wall, or on a series of flip-charts. But if the group size and the number of dimensions so dictate, a subsequent meeting or a written survey will be required.

LIST 7-12. Part of a Second-round Instrument

SHARPE HOUSE SURVEY OF STUDENTS' NEEDS

Introduction. I would like to use this survey to find out whether you're getting what you need as a student at West Oldham High School. In a previous round of interviews with students, I have determined that most of the needs of Sharpe House students fall into three main categories: (a) learning and instruction, (b) guidance, and (c) social and emotional support. The purpose of this survey is to determine exactly what your needs are in each of those three categories.

The items in this survey were written by randomly selected students in Sharpe House—perhaps you or one of your friends were one of them. The lists are long, because I wanted them to be as complete and as accurate as possible. I am depending on your patience and your helpfulness to make the results of this survey meaningful and useful. Thanks.

I. What do you need?
    A. *Learning and Instruction.* Imagine that you are attending a school where you're really learning and getting the kind of instruction you need and want. In that (imaginary) situation, which of the following things would be happening? Please check all the statements that are part of *your needs* for learning and instruction, *whether or not they currently are happening at West Oldham.*

    ____ 1. I'm thinking through a book I'm reading.
    ____ 2. We spend time in the city learning the organization of the city.
    ____ 3. Students are not competing for grades.
    ____ 4. I am not dissecting line-by-line books I read (in English, for example).
    ____ 5. Our curriculum includes academic subjects, and emphasizes practical usage.

      .   .
      .   .
      .   .

    ____ 216. Most kids do not learn unless they want to.

II. Which needs are most important?
    B. Please go back over the list you have just completed, and examine each one of the items you have checked. Some of them are more important to you than others. Please pick out the ten most important parts of your need for learning and instruction, regardless of whether or not they are currently happening for you at WOHS. Put a circle around the *numbers* of those ten items.

III. Are you getting what you need at WOHS?
    C. This is the last step, but it is extremely important. Please examine each of the circled items (your most important needs) on your list, and decide whether that item is currently happening for you at WOHS. Then rate each item according to this code, putting the number to the left of the check:

    ____ 1. It's not happening at all.
    ____ 2. It's happening, but there's not enough of it.
    ____ 3. I'm completely satisfied on this item.
    ____ 4. There's too much of it going on, more than I need.
IV. The End. Thank you for your thoughtfulness and your patience. Have a happy day.

SOURCE: Adapted from Lehner 1973:149–50.

List 7-13.

SHARPE HOUSE PROJECT PRELIMINARY REPORT ON STUDENTS' NEEDS

    A. *Sharpe House Students' Needs for "Learning and Instruction" According to Sharpe House Students (59 Respondents)*

    Responses to the second-round defining instrument were scored as follows:

        1 point each time an item was identified as needed.
     10 points each time an item was identifed as one
          of the ten most important needs

The following list of needs is presented in priority order according to the tabulated combined scores of each item across all respondents:

Points	Item (Dimension) of Need
297	I can go to class and enjoy it.
253	I am enjoying my courses as a group.
231	I do not feel pressured.
217	My teachers care about me as a human being.
201	Traveling is an integral part of the program.
200	I am learning to think independently.
183	The process of learning is not competitive.

    .   .
    .   .
    .   .

SOURCE: Adapted from Lehner 1973:197ff.

The second-round survey utilizes the defining stimulus and some additional instructions; an example is shown in list 7-12. Note that the instructions call for priorization of a certain number of dimensions by each definer. By scoring these "most important" dimensions more heavily when the results are tallied, we get a priority-ordered list of dimensions (see list 7-13 for an example). A frequently used weighting system in scoring the second-round results gives 1 point for each item chosen by each definer as one of the ten most important dimensions of the client's need. The needs assessor should determine the weighting system, considering the number of definers and the number of dimensions in the survey.

    Step 3.4. *Further defining:* In the preceding substeps the definers will have "broken down" the client's need into a set of more specific dimensions that, taken together, represent the defining image of that need. The thrust of those substeps is to arrive at the most specific level of definition: directly observable behaviors or states. Reaching this level is important because there the dimensions are objective—they have the same referents from the perspectives of different people.

Yet the most specific level of definition for some dimensions probably will not be reached during the open-ended and second-round defining. This is to be expected, because most needs relative to education are conceptually complex, and it is difficult in one or two rounds to elicit all the specific behaviors or states that define them. This doesn't mean the initial breakdown lacks utility. On the contrary, the initial definitions usually are reasonably adequate for the decision maker's use. But the decision maker may want more specific definition of a given client's need, especially when the dimension is both unclear *and* very important. When this is the case, the needs assessor repeats the preceding supsteps (defining stimulus design and administration, second-round instrument for group or category definers). Combined with the previous definition, the result is a more specific definition of the client's need.

Step 4. *Report the definition to the decision maker.* The definitional information from the preceding steps should be represented to the decision maker in list form, arranged by rank and weight. The presentation should include the decision makers' name, the combination of client, need, and definer being reported on, and any problems encountered that might affect the quality or utility of the information. While separate reports might be made for each combination of client, need, and definer, it helps to combine into one document different definitions of the same client and need. For example, a single document might be used to report parents', teachers', and students' definitions of students' needs for counseling. This way, the decision maker can more easily compare and contrast the different definitions.

In the report also, if measurement resources are available, the needs assessor asks the decision maker to note any dimensions whose status he wants measured.

STAGE FIVE: MEASURING THE STATUS OF THE NEED

The fourth stage provided definitional information about the client's needs, about "what should be" from the point of view of the definers. The next logical step (often but not always taken) is measuring how well the specified needs are being met. Measuring involves observing whether and to what degree the defined dimensions of "what should be" are actually present, or are actually happening, in the real world. The observed status of "what is" can then be compared with the definition of "what should be"; any discrepancies between the two suggest the existence of performance gaps which the decision maker may want to take steps to close.

In the "Sharpe House Project" the needs assessor asked the students and the teachers to observe the status of their own defined needs. For each dimension, the clients were asked to say whether:

1. It's not happening at all.
2. It's happening, but there's not enough to it.
3. I'm completely satisfied on this item.
4. There's too much of it going on, more than I need.

When the decision maker wants status information, and when there are resources available for measurement, then the needs assessor develops and implements a measurement plan with the approval of the decision maker. According to Coffing and Hutchinson (1974:21), an appropriate measurement plan

> may involve simply the collecting of status data already in existence. It may involve gathering new data by the implementation of existing observational techniques, tailor-made for this inquiry.
>
> Within the available resources, the plan must attempt to maximize the quality of the information in terms of reliability and validity. The [decision maker's] approval of the plan helps to assure that utility will be ascribed to the resulting information.

The principal steps of the fifth stage are shown in list 7-14.

LIST 7-14.   Principal Steps of the Fifth Stage of Client Need Assessment

1. Plan how this stage will be implemented.
2. Choose an observational technique.
   2.1. Consider further defining, if necessary.
   2.2. Think of an ideal way to observe the dimension(s).
   2.3. Develop or adapt a practical observational technique as close to the ideal as is feasible.
      2.3.1. Come as close to the ideal as possible.
      2.3.2. Consider all threats to validity, etc.
      2.3.3. Consider available resources.
   2.4. Examine and/or test the technique.
      2.4.1. Conceptually examine the technique.
      2.4.2. Pilot-test the technique.
   2.5. Revise as necessary.
   2.6. Develop rest of measurement plan, e.g., recording device, schedule of observations, analytical techniques.
   2.7. Obtain decision maker's approval.
3. Implement measurement plan
   3.1. Carry out observations.
   3.2. Analyze the data.
4. Report the results to the decision maker.
5. Make transition to another stage or step.

Step 1. *Plan how this stage will be implemented.* Again, the resources for measurement will surely be limited, so the needs assessor should carefully plan the fifth stage. Moreover, if the measurement process appears to require skills beyond the needs assessor's expertise, then a measurement consultant might be called in to help.

It may be necessary for the decision maker to prioritize the dimensions for purposes of allocating the measurement resources. For example, the decision maker may want to measure only three dimensions, and their relative importance is 70 percent, 20 percent, and 10 percent; or the decision maker may desire measurement of 150 dimensions of equal importance. Knowing these priorities, the needs assessor can decide how much time and effort to spend on designing the measurement of each.

Step 2. *Choose an observational technique appropriate for the dimension.*
An "observational technique" is a way of observing the presence or absence of a
dimension in a given setting. One such technique is to ask the definers to report
on the degree of fulfillment of the dimensions they have defined. In the "Sharpe
House Project," for example, the definers (who were also the clients) were asked
to say for each dimension whether it was met ("It's happening now"), partially
met ("It's happening, but there's not enough of it"), unmet ("I'm completely
satisfied on this item"), or overmet ("There's too much of it going on, more than
I need"). Asking the definers to be observers of need fulfillment is a relatively
easy technique to implement; it can often be done during the second round of
defining (see the fourth stage, step 3). But asking the definers to be observers is
sometimes not appropriate (for example, if they could have no experience of the
local school situation) and raises questions about the reliability and validity of the
information. Still, it may be the most practical technique in a given assessment.

Step 2.1. *Consider further defining.* Given one or more dimensions of need
about which the decision maker wants status information, the needs assessor
should consider whether the dimension is sufficiently specific to be observable.
If it is not, then further defining is required, either by the definer (if that is
practical), by the decision maker, or by the needs assessor (as a last resort). For
example, the dimension "there should be a reasonably small number of dropouts
from Simpson High School" is difficult to measure as stated; it might be further
defined to say that "the dropout rate at Simpson High School should not exceed 2
percent in the tenth grade, 5 percent in the eleventh grade, and 10 percent in the
twelfth grade." The latter statement gives more specific meaning to the former
and makes the dimensions more observable.

A rule-of-thumb test for specificity of a dimension is: "If you were to send
someone else out to see whether this dimension were happening, would he bring
back exactly the same information you would bring back if you went to look? If
you don't think so, then you should consider defining the dimension further"
(Hutchinson and Benedict 1971).

Step 2.3. *Develop, adapt, or select an observational technique.* This substep and those immediately following may require the services of a measurement
specialist. Since one may not be conveniently available in many cases, some
guidelines for the needs assessor can be discussed. The first consideration is;
What would be an ideal way to observe the dimension if there were no resource
limitations? The needs assessor should try to think of an ideal observational
technique for the dimension. Three criteria for the ideal are suggested: first, how
can the dimension be observed *directly;* second, how can it be observed *un-
obstrusively;* and third, how can it be observed under natural rather than artificial
conditions? (Coffing, Hodson, and Hutchinson 1973:38–42 and A-46 to A-71).

An absolutely perfect means of observing probably cannot be devised. Often
the ideal is impractical. But the act of *imagining* the ideal helps the needs
assessor visualize the standards of quality that should be approximated in the
actual observational technique. The practical technique, in other words, will
necessarily involve sacrifices of quality. The needs assessor and the decision

maker should both understand how far the practical technique differs from the ideal, because their understanding of those discrepancies will help them judge how well the information can be relied upon for making decisions. Thus, the affordable technique may be somewhat obtrusive, may require somewhat artificial conditions, and may involve somewhat indirect observation. (An enlightened, entertaining discussion of measurement is to be found in Webb et al. 1966.)

In moving from an ideal to a practical observational technique it is also important to consider the threats to the accuracy of the information and how they can be minimized or eliminated. Campbell and Stanley (1966) discuss this problem for certain kinds of research. Threats to accuracy are those aspects of a proposed observational technique that might prevent true observation of the dimension. Suppose, for example, that one dimension to be observed is the attendance rate of students in a certain ethnic group and that the observational technique calls for someone in the central office to calculate a rate based on a master list of the student members of that ethnic group and on teacher reports of absences. The threats to accuracy of that technique might include (1) inaccuracies in the list of ethnic membership, (2) errors in the teachers' reports, and (3) errors in the central recording of information. As another example, suppose a questionnaire is used to collect teachers' observations of a number of dimensions related to teachers' needs for self-determination; and further suppose that the questionnaire's instructions are not clear about the confidentiality of the individual responses. One threat to accuracy, certainly, would be that some teachers might expect some administrators to make negative judgments about the teachers personally if the questionnaire were answered accurately. Another common threat to accuracy relates to ambiguous instructions in a questionnaire; different respondents may interpret the instructions differently and thus may not answer the question that the questionnaire's developers assume is being asked.

Step 2.4. *Examine and/or test the technique.* The technique's design can benefit from other people's perspectives and from pilot testing. The needs assessor should at least show the technique to someone else—a colleague, some students, a measurement specialist—and ask her or him to point out potential problems. The technique should also be tried under circumstances similar to the intended implementation to find out whether the technique delivers the information intended.

Step 2.5. *Revise, if necessary.* If examination or pilot testing has revealed problems that can be overcome or at least reduced to a tolerable level, then the needs assessor makes the necessary revisions.

Step. 2.6. *Develop the rest of the measurement plan.* A measurement plan is a complete design for observing the status of one or more dimensions, and it may include a description of the recording device (e.g., how the data will be recorded), the time schedule of observation, a plan for sampling the dimension if the observation cannot be continuous or if it cannot include all the clients at once, and any techniques that will be used to analyze the "raw" results and convert them into a form more meaningful for the decision maker.

Step 2.7. *Obtain the decision maker's approval.* This substep cannot be overemphasized, because it helps ensure that the information will actually be used. The decision maker is asked to review and approve the plan. If the decision maker sees problems that, if unsolved, would cause the decision maker to ignore the information, then revisions are necessary. With the decision maker's concurrence, the process moves to the next step.

Step 3. *Implement the measurement plan.* The plan is implemented according to the schedule, the observations are made, and the data are gathered and analyzed. Note that the needs assessor also documents any deviations from the plan that may occur and any problems that may occur. This additional information will help the decision maker judge the validity of the information for use in decision making. Problems also are documented in order to modify similar measurement plans so that recurrence of the problems can be avoided.

Step 4. *Report the results to the decision makers.* The results of measurement are compiled in tabular, graphic, or narrative form as may be appropriate under the circumstances. Deviations from the plan and other problems are described. The approved measurement plan may be appended to the report. The needs assessor prepares a written or oral presentation, depending on the decision maker's desires and the resources available for reporting. The needs assessor delivers the report and offers to answer any questions about how the information was gathered, compiled, and reported. When the measurement report is combined with a defining report (i.e., when the definers have been asked to say whether and to what degree each dimension is happening), then the presentation resembles that described for step 4 with the addition of the status responses. Table 7-3 shows a partial set of information from the "Sharpe House Project."

Step 5. *Make transition to another stage or step of the process.* If more measurement is to be done, the needs assessor cycles back to the appropriate step of the fifth stage. Otherwise the next stage in sequence is evaluating the utility of the information.

STAGE SIX: EVALUATING THE UTILITY OF THE INFORMATION

Client need assessment is conducted in order to give useful, relevant information to decision makers. Therefore, the needs assessor should evaluate its success in accomplishing this purpose. Three criteria are suggested: efficiency, completeness, and focus. As explained by Coffing, Hodson, and Hutchinson (1973):

"Efficiency" can be defined roughly as the ratio of data reported. For example, if the decision maker used 40 data items out of 100 data items reported, the efficiency of the needs analysis would be 40:100 or 40%.

"Focus" can be defined as the relationship between data used and the importance of decisions according to the decision maker. In other words, focus represents the extent to which the needs data were useful for the most important decisions.

"Completeness" can be defined as the extent to which the application has provided needs data for the decisions for which the decision maker wanted needs data.

TABLE 7-3. Partial Set of Information from the "Sharpe House Project"

A. *Sharpe House Students' Needs for "Learning and Instruction" According to Sharpe House Students (59 Respondents)*

Students' Ratings of Need Fulfillment:

1 = It's not happening at all.
2 = It's happening, but there's not enough of it.
3 = I'm completely satisfied on this item.
4 = There's too much of it going on, more than I need.

POINTS	ITEM (DIMENSION) OF NEED	Rating (percentage of respondents)				
		1	2	3	4	TOTAL
297	I can go to class and enjoy it.	17	53	30	0	100
253	I am enjoying my courses as a group.	17	47	36	0	100
231	I do not feel pressured.	27	36	27	10	100
217	My teachers care about me as a human being.	10	63	27	0	100
201	Traveling is an integral part of the program.	42	27	31	0	100
200	I am learning to think independently.	10	42	42	6	100
183	The process of learning is not competitive.	32	36	22	10	100
.	.	.	.	.	.	.
.	.	.	.	.	.	.

SOURCE: Adapted from Lehner 1973: 197ff.

Given those definitions, an ideal way to evaluate utility would be to keep a complete *log of the decision maker's decisions* (and their priorities) over a period of time, all data about needs (from any source) *used* in those decisions, and all other data about needs *desired* by the decision maker *but not available*. This log could be compared with information reported by the need assessment, and the needs assessor could calculate efficiency, completeness, and focus. Although this ideal would be impractical in virtually every real situation, it suggests some practical questions the decision maker can be asked:

1. Which information from the entire client need assessment process have you been able to use and which information do you expect to be able to use in the future?

2. With respect to the decisions you make, how completely has the client need assessment met *your* requirements for useful information about clients' needs?

3. Has the information from the client need assessment been most useful in making the really *important* decisions as opposed to the trivial decisions you have had to make?

Answering these questions can be easier if the decision maker has been asked to keep some kind of log. Just the request, in fact, usually causes decision makers to be more aware of decisions they make and information they use.

Where there seems to be a lack of efficiency (a lot of information is reported that is not used), a lack of completeness (much more information is required than may be provided), or a lack of focus (the information tends to be less useful for important decisions than for trivial ones), then the needs assessor and the decision maker should together examine the work that has been done, including the choices the decision maker has made at various steps, in order to determine where the performance of the effort can be improved.

Moreover, if the decision maker does maintain a log (even if only a list of, say, a dozen decisions made in the past two weeks), then the needs assessor can ask: Which clients and which of their needs were affected by each of those decisions? This question may help identify some clients or needs that have been omitted from previous consideration in the client need assessment or that in practice have assumed a greater importance than the decision maker originally thought.

The client need assessment has now reached the end of one cycle. In this chapter, six stages have been discussed and many illustrations have been given—some are hypothetical, many are actual examples of how the methodology has been applied in educational settings. It is reasonable to conclude this presentation by quoting one change agent's expectations as he began a client need assessment, expectations which he affirmed were realized during the effort:

> [A client need assessment] could be designed to identify some important needs of teachers and students and parents. Obtaining these data would encourage members of

the organization to think and talk about their own needs and the needs of others in the organization; this process could serve to heighten awareness of new information among all groups and thus help reduce the barriers established by existing institutional norms. And the kind of information brought out by this process could reasonably be expected to have the "disconfirming" effect, in Shein's terminology, on individuals in the organization, as their "definition of the situation" and their "image of others in the situation" are enlarged by their new knowledge of others' needs. [Lehner 1973:9]

Summary

This chapter began with the premise that relevant decision makers must have the type of information about client needs that is "good information," that is, information which is useful in making decisions. The gathering of such information is termed client need assessment, and the basic procedures involved in this cyclical process are presented in six stages. The first, or preparatory, stage involves learning the assessment process and linking the process with the people who need its benefits. In stage two, effort is focused through identification of relevant decision makers and available resources, allocating resources, and scheduling the effort. At that point, a review of progress should take place with the focus decision maker before continuing to the next stage. In stage three, the assessor identifies clients and client needs through consultation with each decision maker, who is also asked to suggest sources of information on need identification for each client. With the above information, the assessor can proceed to the fourth stage, which is the actual defining of clients' needs. The definitions are then reported to the decision maker. In stage five, the status of the need is measured through an observational technique appropriate to the dimension. This stage could involve refinement of the definition and revision of the measurement technique, and the decision maker's approval should be obtained before the final measurement is done. The results are then reported to the decision maker. Stage six, the evaluation of the utility of the information, completes the cycle.

8

Implementation and Control

IMPLEMENTATION IS AN ESSENTIAL COMPONENT of the P/ICM. Early change-related activities such as planning are directed toward achieving implementation. Most of the remaining change-related activities, such as evaluation and control, are directed toward sustaining the implemented change by altering, if necessary, the way in which a change has been implemented. This chapter is concerned with implementation and control, stages 8 and 9 in the P/ICM schema. The focus of this chapter is on what occurs *after* the decision to adopt a change has been made. The central questions are: What can be done to put the change into effect with best results? What can be done to ensure continued effective implementation? Actually, these questions have been addressed frequently in earlier chapters, most noticably 5, 6, and 7. Careful need assessment and planning and the related problem-definition and solution-generation activities are crucial to the success of the implementation stage.

Zaltman and Duncan (1973, 1977) identify two basic stages in the adoption process. First is the initiation stage, which involves knowledge-awareness of a change, attitude formation, and a decision to adopt or reject. The second general stage is implementation, which is concerned with the process by which the organization integrates the change into its ongoing operation. Our concern here is primarily with the second stage.

The implementation stage involves an initial substage, itself called implementation, at which the organization implements the change on a *trial* basis to determine if it is practical. A second substage, called continued-sustained implementation, will occur if the trial is favorable.

During the trial substage, responsibilities are assigned and time schedules and deadlines are established and clearly communicated. Communication among all affected parties is important in detecting and working through unanticipated consequences. It is usually desirable to institute a change on a trial basis, particularly if there is considerable concern about the change or even opposition to it. Individuals who are reluctant to see a change made permanent will often agree to a trial period if no commitment is made to continue the change. It is necessary, of course, to clearly define the duration of the trial and to realize that the results obtained during a trial period may not totally reflect what the experience would be if the change were permanent. Not all the benefits or difficulties will necessarily become evident in a trial situation. The trial experience enables members of an educational system to evaluate the pros and cons of a change. It also affords the change planner an opportunity to gain more legitimacy for the change or solution. Further, it provides feedback that may serve as a basis for modifying the solution and the way it is put into operation. Full-scale operation may involve establishing new positions or altering existing roles to encompass new activities while eliminating other activities.

At the continued-sustained implementation stage, a solution becomes routinized. Dilemmas that individuals may have faced with respect to the change or solution tend to be resolved at this point. However, full-scale adoption may not always occur. The timing of change may be poor. For example, teachers are less open to change at the end of a school year than at the beginning. Financial or human resources to fully implement the change may not be available. There may be no evidence after the trial that the solution is sufficiently beneficial. Unanticipated negative consequences may have occurred during the trial. These and many other reasons may result in a decision to discontinue a trial or prevent full-scale implementation.

In the following sections, we discuss conditions that affect the implementation of change, matters relating to control, and the process involved in continued-sustained implementation of change.

Implementation

Conditions affecting implementation include organizational characteristics, change-planner skills, and the nature of the change, as well as a series of factors described by the "A VICTORY" model of implementation discussed below.

ORGANIZATIONAL CHARACTERISTICS

The structure of the organization or system that has adopted a change will have a strong impact on the implementation of the change (Zaltman et al. 1973; Zaltman and Duncan 1977). The very structures that facilitate the initial predecision and decision stages make the implementation stage difficult. Similarly, structural characteristics that facilitate implementation make initiation difficult. This paradox was discussed in chapter 3 and need not be continued here. However, it is useful to discuss three characteristics of organizational structures that affect implementation. The first is *complexity,* which refers to the number of occupational specialities within the organization, the professionalism of people in those specialties, and the extent of differentiation of the task structure. *Formalization* refers to the degree of emphasis placed on following specific rules and procedures. *Centralization* refers to the locus of authority and decision making: at what level are decisions made and how many members of the organization participate in the decision-making process?

The importance of these characteristics can be illustrated by reference to a three-year study sponsored by the National Institute of Education. This study involved the testing of a special problem-solving mechanism using survey feedback to identify and clarify problems, generate solutions, and implement solutions. A unit school district with twenty schools was the test site. Problems could be identified at the school building level or at the district level. Responses to the problems could involve (1) teachers at the individual school level or on a district-wide level, (2) special-education teachers not primarily involved in any one school, (3) principals, (4) assistant superintendents, (5) the superintendent, (6) nonteaching building staff, or (7) any combination of people mentioned.

At the district level, the organization is complex. There are many different roles that could be affected by a given change. It thus became necessary to discuss with most of the people how an accepted change could be put into effect to be of maximum value to the user of change. Because of the large number of persons and perspectives, the implementation of change at the district level was a long process. This was later compensated for by temporarily making the school district less complex. An implementation team was established which consisted of two teacher representatives, principal representatives, a nonteaching-staff representative, a special educator assigned to a building for purposes of the study, and a member of the superintendent's staff. Thus, because complexity was a hindrance, a switching rule was developed which made the implementation situation less complex. That is, fewer roles and fewer people were charged with the task of putting a change into effect.

The school district lacked a formal structure that would facilitate the implementation of change. Thus, a provision was made to clearly identify ways a proposed solution to a problem could be implemented. The solution, if accepted, could then be put into effect in a relatively straightforward way. An implementation plan was thus ready at the time the adoption decision was made, instead of having to be developed afterward. Actually, the implementation plan gave decision makers a better sense of what the change or problem solution involved and so made it easier to reach a decision. The plan was prepared by teachers at the school building level and by teachers, principals, and sometimes staff from the superintendent's office. The implementation was in effect a formal procedure.

In general, a highly centralized structure facilitates implementation. Fewer people are involved in the decision about how the change is to be implemented. This does not necessarily mean that better implementation results from a highly centralized authority, but rather that it can proceed more quickly. For the most part, decisions were made in a highly centralized way: the school principal had final say in individual school matters, and the superintendent had final say as to whether and how district level changes were implemented.

CHANGE-PLANNER SKILLS

The change planner concerned with implementation should possess several skills. It would be rare to find anyone who has all of these skills, but the change planner should approximate them to some degree. First, the change planner should be able to negotiate and achieve conflict reduction. This is particularly important if, in the implementation process, one person or group receives fewer resources than another person or group seen as competitive. A department within a school, for example, may perceive another department as receiving preferential treatment in the number of faculty positions made available.

The change planner must also be able to predict the effects of results of a particular action (or of not taking action). The vice-president for academic affairs of a large university in Boston, Massachusetts, correctly perceived a strong negative reaction among members of the school of education when he selected someone from outside the school (and outside the university) to direct a new education research center that was organizationally independent of the school. To reduce the feelings of alienation and threat experienced by members of the school of education, he influenced the new director to select his associate direct from among existing school-of-education staff, and to be liberal and quick in extending joint appointments to several members of the school of education. (It might be added that in this case there was a fairly large minority in the school of education who did favor the appointment of an outside person.)

Third, the change planner must be able to create enthusiasm and trust. Enthusiasm is particularly important to help compensate for the extra ''start-up'' costs often associated with something new. At the early stages of implementation, meetings may have to be more frequent. Unless people are enthusiastic, their attendance may drop off, the meetings may become less fruitful, and the implementation effort may be less effective. Care must be taken not to let unrealistic expectations develop about how rapidly benefits of the change will be realized. Enthusiasm will be dampened very quickly if substantial immediate benefits are expected but are not forthcoming. A change planner can often keep enthusiasm high in the absence of immediate benefits by communicating his or her own enthusiasm.

A fourth skill is the ability to organize and arrange people and resources effectively. The planner must know whom to delegate particular responsibilities to and what kind and amount of resources must be allocated to enable individuals to carry out their responsibilities. He must be sensitive to various personalities and know something about the interpersonal relations that exist among colleagues. For example, he should recognize that people who do not get along with each other in general should probably not be placed together in a small group to achieve some task. The planner must be able to identify leaders and others who are task-oriented and should assign important responsibilities to them. Thus, diplomacy and political finesse are important traits.

A fifth and related ability is to provide access to important financial and nonfinancial resources. This involves knowing where and how resources can be obtained. Many school systems have individuals whose responsibility it is to monitor the availability of external resources, including state and federal as well as private-foundation sources of money. This function also involves identifying experts and data sources. Thus, the planner involved in implementation must generally have a wide network of interpersonal contacts on professional matters.

It is important for change planners both within and outside the organization to be sensitive to different roles affecting the change process. In implementing change it is necessary to consider who the *gatekeepers* are. For example, school principals may be gatekeepers who relay information from superintendent to teachers. The information may consist of instructions for carrying out a new grade-reporting system or a new method for teacher and staff self-appraisal. In studying the role of gatekeepers in education, one of the authors found that the manner in which the principal of the school passed on the instructions was a critical factor in differentiating between schools that implemented a change easily and successfully and schools that experienced difficulty and limited or no success. Principals who opposed the self-evaluation process tended to relay the information less accurately and with fairly evident disapproval and thus were more likely to have problems with the new system. In contrast, principals who supported the new system were more accurate and enthusiastic and had greater success with it. Unfortunately, in this case, the school principals were the only channel between the superintendent and teachers. Thus, the gatekeeper may be a key person in implementation and should be ''won over'' by the change planner, in this example, the superintendent.

It is also necessary to consider who the *influencers* are. The influencer is a person who helps shape the attitudes and/or behavior of users. The influencer need not be directly involved with the change, but may nevertheless affect its success. Special-education personnel may oppose a new reading program that a principal is implementing. Their opposition may dampen teacher enthusiasm and hence the effectiveness of the program. Teachers in this case are the users (although the students and even the principal can be users here as well). The users, then, may or may not be influencers and may or may not be gatekeepers. A teacher using a new reading program on a trial basis in another (pilot) school within the same district may be a user, a gatekeeper, and an influencer with respect to implementing the new program in another school or in the entire district. Note that in this example the *decision maker* is not the user, gatekeeper, or influencer, but rather the school principal or possibly the district superintendent.

In general, when implementing change in an organization, it is necessary to identify the key roles of influencer, gatekeeper, decision maker, and user. Furthermore, it should be realized that one person may fill more than one role. A fifth role has been suggested, namely the *affectee* or person who experiences the consequences of a change. For example, students will be affected by the change as well as teachers. Teachers at higher grade levels may also, with some time lag, be affected by techniques and programs used by teachers in lower grade levels. Parents of students are also affected less directly.

Finally, the change planner must have the ability to distinguish between those variables or factors which can be manipulated and those which cannot and must therefore be adapted to. This is discussed at length later in this chapter when we focus on the control of change. However, the issue of *controllability* is important at the implementation stage as well, since control is simply a continuation of implementation.

THE NATURE OF THE CHANGE

The nature of the change or innovation is an important variable in the initial and continued implementation process. As noted above, some aspects of change can be altered by the change planner, while relatively unalterable aspects must be adapted to. Some examples will illustrate this point. First, the more *pervasive* the innovation—the more it affects many people or groups within an organization—the more important it is for the change planner to continue to interact with a broad spectrum of people in the school system in order to be alert to and help prevent potential problems. This is based on the assumption that the larger the number of people affected by a change, particularly in different areas of the organization, the greater the likelihood that someone will have an unsatisfactory experience with the change.

The more *complex* a change, either in terms of the basic idea behind it or in terms of its actual operation, the more important it is to undertake educational activities both before and after it is implemented. The important point is that efforts to enhance understanding of the change should continue after implementation, perhaps even on a permanent basis. Thus, frequent workshops or seminars on new computer programs or other technology may be held. For example, periodic orientation programs and user training in library resource use are conducted by university libraries, particularly for disadvantaged persons who may be especially lacking in experience in using libraries and may perceive them as complex systems.

Divisibility is another important attribute of a change. This refers to the degree to which a change may be tried in a limited way. Thus, a university may try an evaluation-free method of conducting classes in only a limited number of courses. When there is considerable opposition or uncertainty about a change and the change is divisible, it is good practice to implement it in a limited way but in a context, such as a school or grade or course, where the chances of success are greatest. It will typically be easier to introduce a change on a system-wide basis after a limited but sucessful trial in one part of the system.

Reversibility refers to the degree to which the pre-implementation situation can be reinstituted if a change is discontinued. In the case of evaluation-free courses, this could be (and in fact has been) done relatively easily. On the other hand, attempts to discontinue an organizational development program have sometimes created considerable conflict between proponents and opponents, a conflict not present before the implementation of the program. Of course, some changes are not amenable to trial in either a limited or a temporary way. Thus, *trialability* becomes another important dimension.

THE A VICTORY MODEL

A checklist of implementation considerations that are particularly useful at the initial implementation stage has been developed by staff of the National Institute of Mental Health (1973; see also Davis and Salasin 1974). Before presenting the checklist we shall give a brief description of the model behind it. The model attempts to identify factors affecting the fate of a given change after an adoption decision has been made.

The Model.   The behavioral formula upon which A VICTORY is based is as follows:

$$B = E_s + T + S_e + [(P + H_s) D \times C] - I, \text{ where}$$

B is the desired *behavioral* change,
E_s is an individual's *self-expectancy* (values, life style, etc.),
T is the timing,
S_e is the stimulus conditions (environmental factors affecting the individual),
P is the *pattern for behavior* (information/skills needed to perform the desired response),
H_s is *habit strength* (the tendency to do certain things because of a previously learned association between those activities and pleasant consequences),
D is *drive* or motivation,
C is the *capacity to perform the behavior,* and
I is the *inhibitors* of the desired behavioral response.
A translation of the general behavioral model into the A VICTORY paradigm is described below:

B = A VICTORY, where
B = *Behavior* (the desired program change)
A = *Ability* (resources or capacity required to execute the desired change)
V = *Values* or self-expectancy
I = *Information* about the idea
C = prevailing *Circumstances* or stimulus conditions
T = *Timing*
O = *Obligation* (felt need or motivation)

R = *Resistances* or inhibitors to the change
Y = *Yield* or habit strength (felt rewards or benefits)
[Adapted from NIMH 1973: 27–28]

The model elements are by no means discrete, and a good deal of interaction among them may be expected. Advocates do believe, however, that all of the variables that may affect a change endeavor are subsumed within its parameters. They also feel that, although the model is intended to explain the behavior of an individual, it is equally applicable to groups of individuals, which are more often the target of educational and other social change programs.

The A VICTORY technique has been and is currently being employed in a variety of social-service settings including community mental health centers, hospitals, and community change programs (Davis and Salasin 1974). The authors are unaware, however, of any applications of the model in educational settings. We believe that it is a potentially powerful tool for effecting change in educational systems.

As a hypothetical example, the A VICTORY technique could be applied to the problem of improving the quality of college teaching (the target behavior change). One vehicle for this improvement might be a course on teaching and instructional techniques for doctoral candidates who plan to pursue careers as college or university professors. Data could be gathered on the effectiveness of such an approach by providing students who have completed the course with an opportunity to teach a college course (or at least a segment of one). For the purpose of comparison, other graduate students who did not receive the treatment (the course on college teaching) would also be provided with a comparable teaching experience.

Ability. The institution of a course on college teaching in a given graduate school would require several kinds of resources: (1) a faculty member (or members) with the requisite skills to teach the course, (2) funds to free his/her time to pursue this end or to hire an appropriate outside person, and (3) graduate students willing or able to participate.

Values. University faculty members and administrators should perceive the merit of the innovation, as teaching is a very important function of the present and future professor's role. Faculty review committees generally consider evidence of "good teaching" second only to "scholarship" in their promotion considerations. For similar reasons, graduate students should be receptive to the idea. The question remains, however, whether administrators and faculty members would view the innovation as important enough to warrant freeing the necessary resources in terms of time and money as opposed to giving only token resource support.

Information. If one or several graduate institutions were to offer the course and gather data on its effectiveness, it would be necessary to disseminate information and data to other potential users. Traditional avenues of diffusion employed by educators would be appropriate, such as the publication of articles in educational journals and the presentation of papers at meetings of professional organizations. Although it seems reasonable that these diffusion activities would reach a fairly large number of potential users, little is known about their impact on professional practice.

Circumstances. The environment or physical facilities of a university are certainly amenable to such an innovation. Classrooms, audiovisual aids, textbooks, and library resources are already available. Providing graduate students with an opportunity to teach may be a problem in some institutions. Other means of assessing program effectiveness may be devised, however.

Timing. It would probably be best to introduce the innovation during a period of relative stability for those who would be affected. Receptivity would likely diminish during periods of change or stress.

Obligation. Another factor would be the intrinsic motivation of relevant parties to offer the new course—whether or not they perceive the existence of a performance gap and, if so, the degree to which they feel the course would close the gap.

Resistances. An obvious source of resistance would be budgetary and/or faculty time constraints. Since resources are never unlimited, judgments would have to be made regarding the relative importance of the course on college teaching versus all other possibilities for expending the finite quantity of time and energy. External funding sources could be explored, however. Another source of resistance might be faculty sensitivity to the emphasis on "teacher accountability." If they perceive that their support of this innovation might be construed as tacit approval of a university or department policy on student or peer evaluation of teaching, opposition is likely.

Yield. The results of the studies comparing the "teaching success" of graduates who have completed the course with that of comparison groups would provide some evidence of the success of the innovation. If the research efforts are carefully designed and executed—if they are replicated in a variety of university settings—and if the results are generally favorable to the notion that "training" can improve college teaching "ability," then the promise of the innovation is enhanced.

The A VICTORY Checklist. For those who seek to develop a change plan that employs the A VICTORY model, the following (NIMH 1973:30) can provide further insight into the components of the model:

ABILITY
- Are staff skills and knowledge appropriate to accommodate the desired change?
- Are fiscal and physical resources adequate for the change?

VALUES
- Is the change consonant with the social, religious, political, and ethnic values of the beneficiaries?

- Is the change consonant with the philosophies and policies of the program supporters?
- Is the change consonant with the personal and professional values of the staff?
- Is the top person in the organization in support of the desired change?
- Are the characteristics of the organization such as to render change likely?

INFORMATION
- Is information on the desired change clear?
- Does information about the idea bear close relevance to the improvement needed?
- Is the idea behind the desired change one that is "tryable," observable, of demonstrated advantage, etc.?

CIRCUMSTANCES
- Are conditions at this setting similar to those where the idea was demonstrated to be effective?
- Does the present situation seem to be conducive to successful adoption of this particular plan?

TIMING
- Is this a propitious time to implement this plan?
- Are other events going on or about to occur which could bear on the response to this change?

OBLIGATION
- Has the need for this change been ascertained through sound evaluation?
- Has the need for this change been compared with other needs in this program?

RESISTANCES
- Have all reasons for not adopting this change been considered?
- Has consideration been given to what may have to be abandoned if this plan is launched?
- Has consideration been given to all who would lose in this change?

YIELD
- Has the soundness of evidence about the benefits of this proposal been carefully assessed?
- Have possible indirect rewards for this change been examined?

Control

What happens in a healthy, self-renewing organization after the change or innovation has been implemented? The proactive/interactive organization must be prepared to continually assess its performance not only in the light of its problem-solving objectives, but also in the light of new contingencies within and outside the educational system. Through collaboration among its members and between itself and its environmental forces (e.g., client groups, interested publics, governing bodies), the healthy organization continually reviews the impact of a specific change on various parties and how the impact compares with their expectations.

When the impact of a change is judged to be negative or insufficient, the exercise of control becomes necessary. Control refers to activities responsive to results of monitoring a specific change and activities responsive to results of a continual assessment of performance over time. Those activities involve the systematic manipulation of some variables, such as staff size, human-resource expertise, and so on, to maintain or achieve a particular level of performance in some part of the educational system. The variables that the change planner may adjust or manipulate may or may not be within the educational system. For example, when a school is the target educational system, teachers concerned about a problem area such as reading may attempt to have the district office hire an additional reading specialist or acquire more time of an existing specialist in the district. This is the adjustment of a variable outside the immediate system. Alternatively, a teacher within the school may obtain special training or, if he or she possesses that training, may be given more time to deal with reading problems.

Control requires that the educational system (1) set forth standards for its objectives, (2) assess actual performance in the light of the standards set for objectives, (3) analyze the cause of any discrepancy between actual and intended performance, and (4) adjust performance to close any observed gaps. These four elements are shown in figure 8-1.

Figure 8-2 represents a plan-control process by which the change planner considers where it will be necessary to make adjustments in order to bring actual performance in line with intended performance. Assume for purposes of illustration that the performance of a curriculum innovation is judged to be unsatisfactory. This would be determined by evaluation research (discussed more fully in chapter 9). The educator should ask first whether the measures of performance used are accurate and measure the correct items. If not, he may find that he is trying to adjust for a performance gap that does not exist. If, on the other hand, he determines that the performance gap is indeed real, it becomes necessary to ask whether one or more of the other factors—implementation, plan, objectives, and so on—could be at fault.

IMPLEMENTATION

Of most concern in this chapter are the questions: Is it the implementation that is at fault? Are the strategies and tactics being used appropriately? Were the most important criteria for selecting strategies considered explicitly? Chapter 3 discussed these concerns at length and we shall return to some of them shortly.

FIGURE 8-1.   Four Elements of a Control System
Source: Bell 1972. Used by permission.

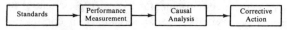

What has not been previously discussed to any significant degree is the concept of causal analysis, which is a necessary foundation for implementing change and undertaking corrective action. Causal analysis involves developing a picture of what factors influence what other factors. This serves as a guide to selecting factors to control in order to achieve a change in some other factor. In developing such a picture it is necessary to separate those variables or factors that can be altered from those that cannot be altered by the change planner. These latter factors are those to which the change planner must adjust. Control variables must be identifiable, accessible, and, of course, manipulable. These three criteria can be defined as follows:

1. *Identifiability:* The feature or organizational variable is both observable and operational in light of resources, constraints, and other real-world considerations.
2. *Accessibility:* The variable can be addressed, seen, and approached by the significant organizational members involved in the control process. There are communication channels between the organizational members and those individuals associated with the variable (or channels could be built through the linking network).
3. *Manipulability:* The variable is identifiable and accessible, and the organizational members have the resources and "leverages" to "put the variable to work." "The practitioner must weigh factors within his agency structure that may place restrictions on his capacity to manipulate the given variable." (Rothman 1974:554)

For example, the successful use of a curriculum innovation may depend upon such uncontrollable variables as student's present intellectual capacity and the degree of reinforcement received in the home.

Consider the case of the DUSO kit, which is intended to Develop Understanding in Self and Others among preschool and early-grade-school children. Controllable factors might be advance training for teachers in the use of the DUSO kit, the degree of preparation students receive prior to using the kit, and the nature of their debriefing at the end of sessions with the kit.

The association of independent variables (e.g., training), sometimes called impact or causal variables, with dependent variables (e.g., performance or results) is thus the essential task of the causal analysis phase of control. The change planner can then undertake the necessary corrective action. Such action might include group sessions for training teachers in the use of an innovation. In the case of DUSO, this would also cover the procedure for preparing students for the use of the kit.

FIGURE 8-2. A Plan–Control Process

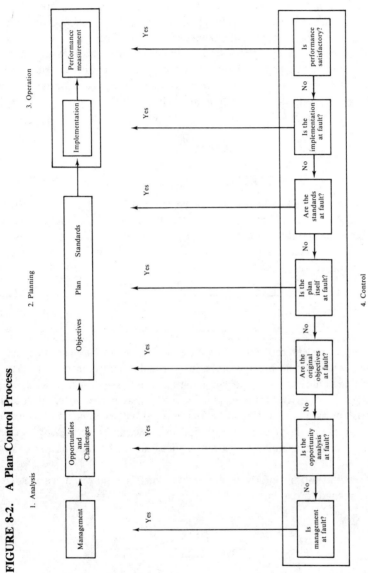

INFERENCE TREES: A TOOL FOR CAUSAL ANALYSIS

Developing *inference trees* is a useful process for change planners to use in connecting independent variables with dependent variables. Such efforts are designed graphically to visualize causal variables for a given outcome or performance gap and, as much as possible, to indicate their relationship to each other as well as to the dependent variable. Two basic types of inference trees are helpful. One involves *longitudinal prediction,* or the chain of events that must take place in order for the expected outcome to occur (Zaltman, Pinson, and Angelmar 1973). The other involves *point-in-time analysis,* which is descriptive of multiple variables impacting the result simultaneously.

The basic longitudinal inference tree is depicted below.

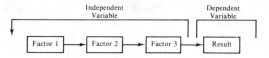

For the DUSO kit, Factor 1 may be the level of interest among students and/or teachers in the use of the kit. Factor 2 may be student (or teacher) preparation for the use of the kit. Factor 3 may be debriefing after the use of the kit. Thus, poor learning of basic psychological and sociological concepts (the result) could be shown as:

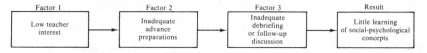

Low teacher interest and motivation could lead to careless preparation of students, which would prevent proper use of and involvement with the kit. Poor preparation could render the debriefing session useless because of an inadequate experience base derived from the kit. The reader may have a different structure of relationships as well as different factors in mind with reference to this example. This is precisely the reason for drawing inference trees—to clarify one's own thinking and to reexamine one's initial ideas about the reasons for success or failure.

The point-in-time inference tree helps clarify causal variables that are not directly related to one another. For example:

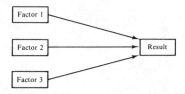

Factor 1 could represent teacher innovativeness, factor 2 students' basic abilities, and factor 3 the clarity of the teacher guide that accompanies the kit. Thus, poor performance of students with the kit could be expressed as:

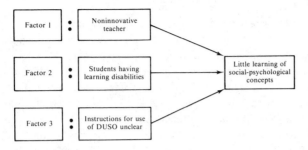

In the short run, student learning disabilities (factor 2) are an uncontrollable factor. The reader may or may not find factors 1 and 3 controllable. In several actual instances involving the kit, these were controllable factors and variables.

There are several variations on the two basic types of causal models. One is a combination of both basic types. For example:

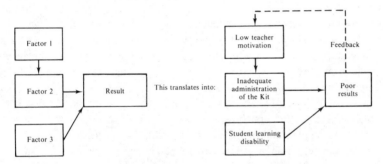

The reader can imagine the number of variations that could occur when the number of factors increases and when more than one result occurs.

Several considerations should be kept in mind when developing inference trees in causal analysis.

1. Is the causal chain comprehensive? Are all the relevant factors presented?

2. Have time considerations been taken into account? For example: Are variables operating simultaneously taken into account? Student learning disabilities and teacher motivation may exist at the same time, whereas the adequacy of kit administration follows teacher motivation. As indicated by the dotted feedback line, the poor results may reinforce and thereby lower teacher motivation still further. In this instance a given state of results may temporarily precede and bring into existence a change in teacher motivation.

3. Are there unrelated independent phenomena (variables) occurring at different points in time?

4. Are there times when variables interact and other times when they do not? Does teacher motivation interact with kit administration only when the teacher perceives the principal or school psychologist as being indifferent to the use of the kit? Will strong interest expressed by the principal overcome low teacher motivation?

5. Are there variables that are essential for the obtained result to have taken place? Adequacy of administration of the kit may be essential no matter what teacher motivation and student abilities are.

6. Are there variables that are "sufficient" for a particular result but not essential? It is possible that, even in the absence of student disabilities, low teacher motivation to innovate with the use of the kit would still ultimately produce poor results. On the other hand, the same results might occur even with highly motivated teachers if students were seriously handicapped.

7. Are there spin-offs or latent consequences of variable sets that can impact the results at a later time or even mitigate the resulting events?

8. Which variables are most easily manipulated in the event results produce serious performance gaps? Student learning disabilities may not be manipulable in the short run. Teacher motivation might be manipulated by offering incentives for effective use of the kit, assuming that the disabilities of students alone were not sufficient to produce poor results. Alternatively, if proper administration of the kit is essential and if teachers cannot be motivated to use it effectively, then administration could be controlled by having a specialist (perhaps a psychologist employed by the district) administer the kit. This would interrupt the impact of teacher motivation on the results obtained in using the DUSO kit.

Once again, the use of causal analysis—that is, thinking in terms of "what influences what"—helps the change planner develop more explicitly the set of relevant variables or factors, how they are relevant and related to one another, and which factors can and cannot be changed in the short run.

The implementation process may falter because inadequate attention was devoted to the various considerations that successful programs must satisfy and the implications of each consideration for the choice of basic strategies. The change planner can exercise control in the ongoing implementation process by manipulating (1) the perceived need for change; (2) the degree of commitment to change among people in the educational system; (3) the system's capacity to change; (4) the time involved in the change process; (5) awareness of the presence of a change program; (6) the dynamics of particular decision stages; (7) the magnitude of the change; (8) the systems and the way members of educational systems are classified and responded to; (9) the sources and levels of resistance; (10) the unintended/unanticipated/dysfunctional consequences of change; and (11) the nature of the change. These considerations, discussed briefly below, are not exhaustive. Rather, they are simply representative of some of the most important things a change planner may control to create educational change. These must be considered in all aspects of the control process but particularly at the implementation stage. Many of these will be familiar to the reader as a result of reading chapters 2, 5, and 6. (A more detailed discussion of these potential control factors can be found in Gross et al. 1971 and Zaltman and Duncan 1977.)

Perceived Need for Change   Making an educational innovation available does not guarantee that it will be used. The proposed change must be linked clearly to a felt need for change among educators, and it is important that they believe that the need can be met without undue social, psychological, or financial cost.

When the client group does not perceive a need or experience a performance gap, power strategies may be the most appropriate approach to control, since there will be no particular motivation for voluntary change. While initiating change through a power approach—for example, through instructions from the superintendent for all teachers and other staff to participate in an organizational development program—it may be desirable to be pursuing manipulative and rational strategies to identify the need for change so that change may be continued voluntarily later on.

Degree of Commitment   Having a felt need is important in the change process. Equally important, however, is a commitment or strong intent to undertake remedial action. In general, the lower the educator's motivation to solve a problem or satisfy a need, the easier it must be made for him to use an innovation not yet adopted. The lower the degree of commitment, the greater the need to exercise control through power strategies or perhaps manipulative strategies to heighten effective commitment by controlling the perception of a situation. A rational strategy would be less likely to affect commitment. One effective control technique for increasing and maintaining commitment is to link advocated practices to interpersonal relationships, thus making educational innovations a vested part of the educator's social setting. This is especially important for maintaining commitment.

Capacity to Change   The change planner often has to exercise control by enlarging the capacity of the system to undertake change. This capacity is a function of at least three factors. One factor is a general openness to change. Are administrators and other educators willing to experiment and take risks? A second factor is knowledge or awareness of innovations. Frequently when an individual (or a system) is open to change, he will generally be aware of innovations relevant to him. A third factor is available resources, both human and financial, for identifying, acquiring, or building and implementing change. When all three factors are present in the desirable degrees, a rational strategy is generally all that is needed to induce (partially control) at least the trial of an innovation.

Time Requirements   In many instances where groups or individuals are ready to implement change, a rational change strategy may produce change relatively quickly. Thus, those persons for whom innovation-related information is already relevant or useful but simply not available could change their practices rapidly if the change planner brought the information to their attention. Such rational strategies that help inform educators about the nature and severity of a problem and bring potential solutions to the attention of adopters are appropriate when the need for change is not urgent.

The use of a power strategy may cause a backlash of resentment. However, when the need for change is urgent and a commitment to change is not present, a power strategy is indicated.

Educator Awareness of a Change Program   Rational strategies do not work simply by virtue of their having made an innovation available to educators. Consumers must be aware of the availability of solutions to problems. Also, they must clearly understand the behavior required by a change or innovation, or there may be resistance at the trial or adoption stage. Ambiguity is often due to inadequate efforts by the change planner to clearly communicate the nature of the change. Rational strategies are important for creating awareness of an innovation and informing people of the most appropriate way to obtain the innovation and related information concerning the effective use of the innovation. Training system members to use and participate in the linking network increases their ability to initiate and implement change in a rational way.

Stages in the Change Process   Social and individual change has been described by many people as an unfolding sequence of stages. Chapters 3, 5, and 6 discussed this in some detail. Although many different sequences of stages have been offered, there is general agreement that different change strategies are differentially relevant for particular stages. There is also agreement that the early stages usually require problem-recognition efforts, while later stages require solution-generation and implementation efforts. Rational strategies are the most appropriate means of control at the early stages for creating awareness of an innovation and, together with manipulative strategies, for identifying a need or problem that the innovation is supposed to address. Manipulative strategies become increasingly important control techniques at the evaluation and trial stages of adoption for structuring in favorable ways the interpretation of information and experience. If resistance occurs, then a power strategy may become desirable for moving the client into the adoption stage.

Magnitude of the Change   The larger or more significant the advocated change, the greater the inducement to change needs to be—that is, the stronger the control effort necessary. The change planner needs more power over the variables affecting the target system and must generally undertake all kinds of strategies.

It is useful to distinguish between the magnitude of the initial change and the magnitude of the continued change. A new authority structure may require considerable psychological adjustment at first but little additional effort after the initial period of implementation. However, some changes require much effort over a long period. An example is integration in the Boston school system, which required that police be more or less permanently assigned within school buildings.

Segmentation of the Educational System   Educational systems often differ from one another in their needs and even in the way the same needs are best satisfied. Accordingly, it is often desirable to cluster consumers into meaningful groups and to distinguish between different groups. One study (Kasulis 1975) reports that different kinds of information about curriculum innovations should be presented to teachers who differ in the way in which they use information. This suggests a manipulative strategy. Similarly, the change planner should consider whether the same information about organizational structure innovations should be presented in the same way to teachers, administrators, and other educational staff. In one project involving an organizational development innovation, it was learned that teachers and principals had different concerns and information needs and hence had to be approached differently. For example, teachers wanted to increase their voice in decisions and were concerned about whether or not the OD project would allow for this. Special emphasis was placed on this feature of the project by the persons introducing the project. Principals, on the other hand, were concerned that they not lose any control or authority. Considerable control effort was necessary during the early phases of the project to explain how the project could in fact increase principal control even with greater participation of teachers in particular decisions (Duncan, Zaltman and Cooke 1975).

Anticipation of Sources and Levels of Resistance   Resistance to change may be found in the form of cultural barriers, social barriers, and psychological barriers. These three general sources of resistance are highly interrelated, as was indicated in chapter 2. The change planner must anticipate both the source and level of resistance and must develop contingency plans, should resistance occur. More important, by anticipating resistance, the change planner can develop and implement strategies to avoid or minimize undesirable conflict and resistance. Both rational and manipulative strategies are appropriate control techniques in this regard (Watson 1973). For example, the foot-in-the-door technique appears to be an effective manipulative approach with regard to curriculum innovations. A comparison of innovative and noninnovative elementary schools in three Chicago-area school districts showed that principals who had their teachers try curriculum innovation on a limited, clearly defined trial basis were much more successful in introducing enduring change than were principals who tended to require or encourage immediate, full-scale change. In the latter case, the changes were often perceived as being imposed and as very disruptive, while in the former case the changes were perceived as more voluntary and as less threatening and less disruptive. The use of temporary systems can aid this small-scale foot-in-the-door strategy.

Unintended/Unanticipated/Dysfunctional Consequences   Planned change may yield intended and unintended consequences. The unintended consequences may or may not have been anticipated and may or may not be dysfunctional from the educator's standpoint. Many change programs fail or achieve less than full impact because unfortunate unintended effects occurred that were not anticipated. Examples of such effects or consequences are *confusion* about the change (which leads to selective filtering out of information associated with the change) and *mistaken assumptions* that the change is more or less advantageous than it actually is. This stresses the importance of rational strategies to enhance educator information or knowledge. On the other hand, when dysfunctional consequences occur, a power-strategy mode of control may be necessary. In one OD program, teachers decided to convert into a teacher lounge a room used informally by the secretarial staff as a luncheon area. When the secretaries protested vigorously, the high school principal had to reverse unilaterally the teacher group decision.

Nature of the Innovation   One of the most important considerations is whether to control or manipulate the innovation or change itself to improve acceptance and impact. Several manipulations can be inferred from a discussion of innovation attributes by Lin and Zaltman (1971). When encountering resistance to or low effectiveness of the change, the change planner can attempt to (1) implement the change incrementally in a step-by-step process; (2) make it easy to return to prechange conditions, thereby reducing the adopter's perceived risk of a wrong decision; (3) decrease the real or apparent complexity of the change in terms of its use as well as its understandability; (4) lessen the impact of the change on valued interpersonal relationships; (5) improve the unique advantage of the change and add others; (6) decrease the financial or other costs to increase the cost/benefit ratio; (7) make the change available on a trial basis; (8) co-opt users or potential users in the process of adapting the change to the unique situation of the users; (9) stimulate word-of-mouth communication about the change; (10) facilitate actual use of the change; (11) clarify what the change is and what it does; and (12) make the change more compatible with the organizational structure of the school and the values of its members.

STANDARDS

Whether or not implementation is the source of difficulty, it is desirable also to ask if the standards are at fault. Standards are the *levels* of performance objectives agreed upon as necessary for successful problem solving or accomplishment of the change intentions.

Standards can be related to both process and product outcomes. Process outcomes are related to the intended changes made in the educational system, and product outcomes are the results of those changes in the system. In the case of schools, for example, an innovative student performance evaluation system may have a process standard of 70 percent of the faculty operating with the new system after the first year of its availability in the district and 100 percent after the second year. The product standard would be the improvement in student learning made possible by more precise measurements of student academic strengths and weaknesses.

As noted earlier in the book, successful change efforts act as pathfinders and stimuli for further change and self-renewal efforts. Therefore, it is important to set the standards at a level that has reasonable chance of achievement. It is also important not to set unreasonable objectives that cause dysfunctional behavior among organizational members. For example, a performance contracting experiment used such extreme rewards as portable radios and television sets for students who met or exceeded performance standards on achievement tests. On the other hand, there is some evidence that high expectations can induce strong achievement efforts. If motivation is to come from successful efforts to achieve a goal, the goal must be placed low enough so that there is a reasonable chance of success and high enough so that achievement requires a significant effort and results in a sense of accomplishment. It is essential that the performers in the organization perceive the standards as attainable. In setting standards for performance under an innovative program, it is often desirable to place the standard within some "range of tolerance." In the example of the performance review process, if only 60 percent of the faculty of a school put the new system into operation, a 10 percent plus or minus range of tolerance would allow the organization to experience a relative degree of success and retain a certain dissonance so that motivation to reach the higher standard is improved.

In setting standards for control it is essential to choose standards related to features of the organization that are *identifiable, accessible,* and *manipulable.* These features were defined earlier and include the available organizational resources, current or recently changed programs, organizational structural characteristics, costs, abilities, and so forth.

The identification of such features is aided in the resource/constraint stage of the P/ICM. Associating standards with manipulable variables also aids in the testing and trial stage of the P/ICM. In short, the planning process involves the reality or feasibility testing of intended change and the problem-solving objectives and standards that the innovation addresses. Unreasonable standards simply add to frustrations and feelings of impotence among system members vis-à-vis their environment. For example, a public school would be unreasonable in applying certain standards of student achievement prior to entry. Neighborhood public schools have little choice in selecting student clients. In fact, political constraints may even prevent student-selection choices for within-school programs. Constraints on financial resources may preclude the full implementation (process standards) of an innovation. Product standards must be reasonable in light of limitations on the implementation of change. On a broader scale, constraints on the measurability of standards have caused severe problems in the implementation of state-wide accountability plans for public school systems. Public expectations for associating student learning on cognitive tests with teacher performance are not reasonable, given the current state of the art of educational evaluation.

THE PLAN

After considering whether standards need adjustment, the change planner must next ask whether the general plan itself needs adjustment. The several premises and other considerations discussed at length in chapters 5 and 6 should be reconsidered in the light of the actual performance of the change, the standards used, and its implementation. The following questions are among those which should be asked about the plan.

1. Is the plan sufficiently comprehensive—that is, does it take all necessary factors into account?
2. Is the plan sufficiently detailed? Is there too much or too little detail?
3. Does the plan distinguish between variables that could be easily manipulated and those that could not?
4. Is the plan based on sound information? Are major assumptions of questionable validity made? Does the plan contradict the major premises in chapters 5 and 6?
5. Does the plan take into account the various conditions in which intervention would be most effective? Is the timing of activities carefully considered?
6. Does the plan consider the various criteria for selecting particular strategies and objectives? Is the information that is available about the problem situation clear enough to determine which strategies and tactics are most important?
7. Does the plan conform to the objectives set? Does the process of planning unwittingly involve an alteration of the original objectives?
8. Does the plan require resources, both financial and nonfinancial, not available to the change planner?
9. Does the plan involve excessive "political" compromise at the expense of effectiveness?
10. Does the plan contain both short-run and long-run considerations?

If any of these questions cannot be answered satisfactorily, it is generally indicated that the element of planning must be addressed. If most or many of the questions are answered unsatisfactorily, the plan may have to be totally revised, or the entire planning process may need to be reenacted.

OBJECTIVES

After the plan is reviewed, the objectives of the change must be studied for possible problems and appropriate remedial activity. "Objectives are the specific endpoints for the programs which are to bring realization of goals" (Blum 1974:29). There are several questions that the change planner can ask to help diagnose problems relating to objectives.

1. Are the objectives too broadly stated to provide guidelines for planners, implementers, and evaluators?

2. Are there sub-objectives that identify "points of impact and what is to be accomplished at each point"? (Rothman 1974:29).
3. Are the objectives realistic in the light of available resources?
4. Are the objectives realistic in terms of legal, social, and other constraints?
5. Are there hidden agendas in the objectives? That is, are there unstated objectives that are as important as, or more important than, the stated formal objectives? To what extent are the hidden objectives structuring the formal objectives and thus altering the stated objectives in unrealistic ways? If hidden agendas predominate, should there even be an evaluation of the formal agendas?
6. Are the objectives consistent with the belief and value system of those persons or groups whose thinking and/or behavior is to be altered by the change?
7. Are there too many objectives? Too few?
8. Are different objectives in conflict and possibly preventing the successful implementation of any of the respective objectives?
9. Is there a guide as to which objectives have highest priority and should be implemented first?
10. Is there a distinction between long-run and short-run objectives? If so, does the evaluation reflect this distinction?

After considering the adequacy of objectives, it may be necessary to reexamine the initial need assessment or opportunity analysis for possible problems. This topic has been treated extensively in chapter 7 and will not be developed here.

MANAGEMENT

Many programs fail as a result of wrong assumptions made by the managers of change. When this is diagnosed, the change planner must exercise control by correcting such assumptions and modifying the change process accordingly. The five most common and serious misassumptions are discussed below.

Rationalistic Bias   This problem is characterized by the belief that individuals are guided by reason and are rational according to conventional criteria. The manager or change planner assumes that all he needs to do to create change is to present information and knowledge regarding change to the intended educators. The tenuous assumption here is that when rational individuals are presented with the rationale for a change, they will accept it. Ignored is the fact that what educators consider rational for themselves is not necessarily what the change planner believes is rational for them. Thus, a change planner may inappropriately perceive his task as less complex than it actually is.

Poorly Defined Goals   Change attempts are often characterized by poorly defined goals. Educational goals or objectives are frequently stated only in diffuse and ambiguous ways. Is the intention of the change planner to change awareness? Knowledge? Attitudes? Behavior? All of these? In the short or long run? Is the intended change instrumental—that is, is it a means of achieving another goal? Or is it ultimate in that no further goals are sought? A dysfunctional consequence of poorly defined goals is that they are likely to create ambiguity, uncertainty, and anxiety for those persons who are going to be affected by the change. Ambiguity among educators about the use of information may create frustration or even tension, which in turn could lead to avoidance of that information. Similarly, ambiguity can lead to the wrong use of information. If goals are poorly defined, the change program cannot be evaluated in terms of its effectiveness in accomplishing those goals. The change planner in education should have an explicit goal statement, like that discussed in chapter 6, addressing issues such as what changes(s) is expected of what groups(s) within what period of time. Without explicit statements of this nature, evaluation is difficult, and therefore appropriate remedial or control activities to improve the performance of the innovation cannot be readily designed.

Poorly Defined Problems   Problem definition is an intricate and highly partisan task. Too often symptoms are mistaken for causes of problems, thus resulting in the misdirection of remedial efforts, in effective use of resources, and increases in levels of frustration experienced by all parties involved in the change. For example, at one level of analysis, deficient reading may be diagnosed as the problem. At another, more specific level of analysis, poor reading is a symptom having its own unique causes, such as the absence of reinforcement at home of what is being taught in school. It seems more fruitful for the change planner to take the latter approach and determine what home and school factors are responsible for poor reading, their order of magnitude, and which student groups are involved. The subjective viewpoint of a single change planner highlights the need for multiple inputs of problem percepts. This is achieved by the team approach of the P/ICM.

Overremphasis on Individuals   Another major difficulty in creating successful educational change is the common assumption that individuals behave in a vacuum and are not influenced by those around them. Change programs geared to changing the attitudes and/or behaviors of the individual student, teacher, or administrator often forget that the individual's behavior is affected quite dramatically by the interpersonal environment. If a teacher is asked to change behavior and is not supported or reinforced by other teachers and administrators, then behavioral change is unlikely to occur or to be maintained if it does occur. Thus, control efforts that neglect the social and physical context of the situation in which change takes place are missing some of the important causes of behavior.

Technocratic Bias   Technocratic bias is the overemphasis on *development* of a change program without an accompanying plan for *implementation*. There are many examples of educational innovations in which very substantial expenditures were made in product development and testing but very small financial and other resources were allocated to the preparation of a plan for implementing the product or service. Many illustrations of this are provided by Turnbull et al. (1974). For example, some developers of simulation games, individually guided instruction, and other innovations have made exhaustive efforts to develop products and services, but dissemination of them was very restricted because of inadequate marketing or implementation plans. A major reason why school desegregation is proceeding slowly is that court ruling and legislative action do not reflect consideration of how to implement that objective.

An Educational Organization Information System

A major assumption of figure 8-2 and the discussion of it is that information is available to enable the change planner to determine where changes are necessary in the various analysis, planning, and operations stages. Information is the most critical element of the control process. The systematic flow of information is vital to the guidance of the educational system. Chapter 9 discusses at length the research process of evaluation research, which focuses primarily on the task of providing information about the impact of a change. However, it will be useful here to discuss the notion of a general organization information system (OIS).

A good organization information system will be one that not only facilitates control and evaluation of specific changes, but also alerts the organization to the important changes in its environment, as well as within its own boundaries, that may represent new problems and new opportunities. Thus, an effective OIS in an educational setting should provide the five types of reliable feedback mentioned in chapter 6: (1) *content feedback;* (2) *input feedback,* or data assessing alternative potential solutions to the problems caused by a change; (3) *process feedback,* or information about how the change is occurring; (4) *product feedback,* or information about the success of the change in satisfying its intended objectives; and (5) *environmental feedback,* or information about developments outside the immediate change setting that could affect the change process.

List 8-1 presents the basic sources of information that can provide the necessary feedback data for control within and external to an educational setting. The perspective is that of a district-level educational system. In order to make effective use of data from these sources for control purposes, the following seven activities (adapted from Cox and Enis 1972:19) must be performed:

1. Assembly: the search for, and gathering of, educational data from sources such as those in list 8-1
2. Processing: the editing, tabulating, and summarizing of data
3. Analysis: statement of the program implications of the data

LIST 8-1.   Sources of Educational Information for Use in an OIS

Sources Within the District	Sources External to the District
1. The District as a System	1. Consultants
Operations	2. Constituents
Kindergarten, elementary schools	3. Government Agencies
Junior and senior high schools	Federal
Vocational training institutions, etc.	State
Services	Local
Special education, diagnostic	4. Published Sources
testing	news media
Vocational guidance, organ-	association newsletters
izational development experts,	scholarly journals
etc.	books
2. Other operations	5. Syndicated Services
Superintendent, business manager, associate	ERIC
superintendents, school board	NTIS
3. Other Service Groups	6. Nonprofit Organizations
Teacher association (unions), parent-teacher	foundations
groups, maintenance, etc.	citizen groups
4. Intrasystem Committees	professional societies

4. Evaluation: statement of the amount of faith or confidence that can be placed in the accuracy of the data
5. Storage and retrieval: the indexing and filing of data
6. Dissemination: routing useful information to the proper decision maker
7. Use: converting the implications into actions

Figure 8-3 presents a simplified and idealized or prescriptive organization information system for the educational change planner. The change planner would monitor both internal and external sources of information relevant to an initiated or contemplated change. The assembled information would then be processed, analyzed, evaluated, and stored. When a performance gap is identified—that is, when measures of performance fall below desired standards (see figure 8-1)—appropriate information is retrieved by the change planner for his own use, or it is disseminated to another relevant person. The information user should undertake a causal analysis of the situation and use the data in a manner suggested by the causal analysis. Use of the data is a control activity. The consequences of the control effort should then be assessed in the light of existing information from both internal and external sources.

The following example of an organization information system is a synthesis of the experiences of two small universities that attempted to change their public image. One school had been established as a two-year college and had recently converted to a four-year college. The other school had also been a two-year college but had changed to a four-year program several years earlier. Collectively, the two schools performed all the functions in figure 8-3, although individually they did not. Thus, the example will be presented as if a single school were involved.

FIGURE 8-3.   An Idealized Organization Information System

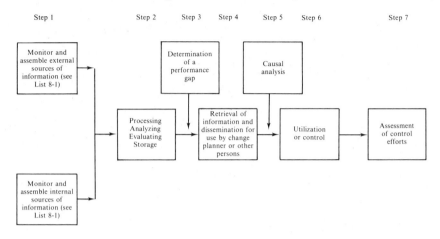

The particular problem of concern to this college was that it was being perceived as a local school serving local community needs and very limited in its course offerings, although in fact the course offerings were better than average for a college of its size. The school was very concerned with how to attract students from a broad geographical base. Data concerning this problem was obtained from both internal and external sources. Internal sources included records of applicants and a yearly survey of how incoming students percieved the school. A record was kept of the community and state of residence of all applications received, regardless of their ultimate disposition. This information was assembled each summer. These data covering a four-year period were prepared for a special meeting of the college board of trustees (processing). There had been no change over a four-year period in the (very low) number or proportion of applicants from outside the immediate geographical area of the college (analysis). The data were considered by the school administration to be a good indicator of the geographical range of appeal of the college (evaluation). The college president, upon the advice of his assistant for planning and development, decided to gather external data consisting partly of a survey of a random sample of high school teachers serving as advisors to college-bound seniors. The sample was drawn from a six-state area surrounding the college's location. These data, describing teacher/advisor knowledge and opinions about the college, were also processed, analyzed, evaluated, and in effect stored pending the trustees' meeting. The college administrators indeed felt there was a serious gap between the information about the college that nonlocal high school students and teachers actually had and the information the college felt they should have. This determination of a gap was presented to the trustees (retrieval and dissemination to relevant persons). These data, along with other information from internal and external sources, were analyzed at length by college administrators and trustees (causal analysis and use).

Summary

This chapter discussed implementation and control. Implementation is generally the process by which the organization integrates change into its ongoing operations, and control is the means by which it sustains the implemented change. Organizational characteristics, change-planner skills, and the nature of the change are all conditions that affect implementation. The A VICTORY model presented a comprehensive view of variables that may affect a given change. Control involves the systematic manipulation of some variables, such as staff size, human-resource expertise, and so on, to maintain or achieve a particular level of performance in some part of the educational system. A general organization information system should provide five types of reliable feedback important to control of change and identification of new problems and opportunities.

9

The Evaluation of Educational Change Programs*

EACH EDUCATIONAL CHANGE EFFORT should have an evaluation function as a major component of the undertaking. Ideally, a specific person or team should be assigned this task at the outset of the project. We shall refer to such a person or team as the evaluator. The major task of the evaluator is to coordinate and facilitate an orderly evaluation process. This involves several activities:

1. Understanding the objectives and interrelationships of all components of the change effort
2. Identifying the criteria for measurement of the effectiveness, significance, and efficiency of the program's component activities—e.g., improved leadership, less teacher turnover, parental involvement
3. Setting standards or levels of performance within established criteria
4. Determining how to obtain the needed data
5. Planning how to implement the evaluation program
6. Identifying possible sources of assistance outside the school system
7. Overseeing the analysis of evaluation data, particularly to ensure its usability
8. Establishing awareness of the possible contact with evaluation efforts of similar programs
9. Preparing reports on the results of the evaluation

These evaluation activities have been conceptualized in different ways. Two such conceptualizations—one somewhat general and the other more specific— are presented here.

*This chapter was coauthored by Laura Klemt, School of Education, Northwestern University.

A team of professional evaluators (Dornbusch and Scott 1975) has identified four components of the evaluation process. First, there is the task of *allocating*. A task must be assigned before it can be evaluated. (This does not refer to situations where the overall evaluation might conclude that responsibility for a given task was never clearly assigned and hence was not performed.) Allocation, then, is the task of determining *who* is to be evaluated for performing *what task* toward *what goal* and perhaps *how* the task is supposed to be performed as well as *for whom* within an organization.

A second aspect of evaluation is *criteria setting*. Criteria are essential in evaluating the performance and/or outcome of a task. First, it is necessary to determine what aspects of a responsibility should be part of the evaluation. Should classroom discipline be considered along with student proficiency? What is the relative importance of each criterion? Typically, not all aspects of a role or task can be evaluated. A subset of the full range of attributes must be selected. Once a set of job responsibilities is selected, it is necessary to determine the relative weights that should be assigned to them. There is a natural tendency to place greater emphasis on the most easily measured task responsibility. A college dean may be evaluated disproportionately more on the level of funds brought to his school, although the vice-president for academic affairs may never openly say that this has greater weight than other aspects of the dean's work. How much weight should be given to the impact of a curriculum innovation on classroom discipline relative to its impact on the academic performance of students? How much weight should be given to the benefits of school integration relative to its limitations? After establishing relative weights, it is necessary to set standards and transformation rules. For example, what is considered to be a poor or a good or an excellent performance and outcome? What reduction in organizational anxiety or conflict represents a positive improvement as a result of an organizational change program? Moreover, how are the indicators of conflict of learning transferred into measurable units? How does one convert teacher turnover into a score that will reflect improvement or deterioration in the school or district environment? Setting standards involves the process of determining levels of performance within the given criteria. For example, if improved reading scores for students in a new instructional program is the criterion for successful change, the level of improvement must be set as a standard to determine the relative success given the costs of starting a new program.

After determining what aspects of an educator's task are to be evaluated and determining what values are to be measured, it is necessary to decide which information is to be used. This *sampling* decision has two dimensions. First, what indicators will be used to reflect the level of performance achieved? Second, what methods will be used to obtain information about the level of performance? With regard to the first question, will the amount of time spent by a teacher with slow or fast learners be an indicator of performance? With regard to the first question, will the amount of time spent by a teacher with slow or fast learners be an indicator of performance? Will the number of innovations attempted by a teacher be used as a measure of performance, or will courses taken during the year at an accredited school be one of the indicators of performance? The second basic question concerns what measures will be used to reflect the values achieved on these indicators. Thus, what will constitute a trial of an innovation? Should the number of credit hours taken be used as a measure of a teacher's professional advancement, or should grades received be considered also? Will teacher classroom performance be assessed through a visitation of the department chairman or the school principal or through a standardized questionnaire completed by students? If visitations are used, how frequent should they be? Should advance notice be given? Should the teacher be informed about the criteria the visiting evaluator is using?

The process of assigning an evaluation to a performance is what Dornbusch and Scott refer to as *appraising*. This involves making a judgment that some performance does or does not equal or exceed a standard and that it is good or bad. A major problem in appraising is the absence of a good frame of reference. Does one make a judgment on the basis that a given improvement of students in some academic area was not very likely to happen by chance? Does one compare a performance with another very similar situation in which the change or innovation was not used? The task of establishing a frame of reference within which to make an appraisal is very difficult and yet very critical.

Dornbusch and Scott present a model of the evaluation process that reflects the four basic concerns discussed above. This model is shown in figure 9-1.

Another overall but more specific conceptualization of evaluation research has been suggested by Wortman (1975:565). This is presented in figure 9-2. Basically, his model states that there are three major interacting sets of components. One set, the *organizational components*, consists of the sponsors or advocates of the evaluation effort and the people or groups who conduct the evaluation, whose efforts are being evaluated, and who are influenced by whatever it is that is evaluated. The second set, *theoretical components*, involves the values of various organizational members, the theories being tested, the intention or goals of the change, how they are to be put into operation, what they in fact become

FIGURE 9-1.   A Model of the Evaluation Process
Source: Dornbush and Sanford 1975:144. Used by permission.

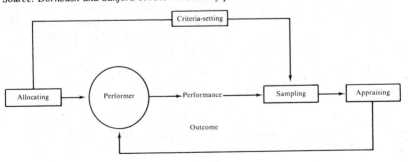

FIGURE 9-2. A Model of Evaluation Research
Source: Wortman 1975:565. Used by permission.

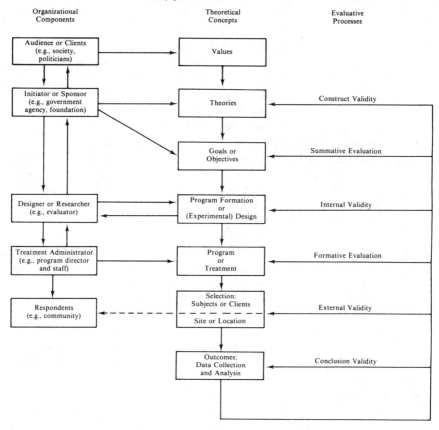

when put into operation, the people and places being affected, and finally the outcome. The *evaluative process,* the third set of components, involves such considerations as whether the ideas being tested have been faithfully derived from theory (construct validity). For example, "if remedial education is thought to close the gap between the haves and have nots, is Head Start appropriate remedial education, and do reading-readiness test measures reflect the goal of closing the gap?" (p. 565). Next an evaluator might ask whether a program had an effect and whether that effect was indeed desired. ("After all, Head Start provided nutritional meals and day care facilities.") The next issue concerns internal validity. Did the program organizers correctly deduce the actual program from the basic concept of Head Start? Given that the basic idea of Head Start was deduced correctly, was it implemented in the most effective way so as to allow the theoretical remedial force of Head Start an opportunity to have its impact? This refers to formative evaluation. External validity concerns how representative the people, places, and other factors in the program are. Can they also be assumed to represent other situations where the change could be implemented? Conclusion validity simply asks whether the data have been collected and analyzed in a way that places great confidence on their interpretation. All aspects of the evaluative process are discussed in greater detail later in this chapter.

Fundamental Concepts of Educational Evaluation

Both the general and the more specific conceptualizations of evaluation suggest a number of fundamental concepts or issues of educational evaluation. It will be useful to discuss each of these before proceeding with a discussion of the major types of evaluation.

FORMATIVE AND SUMMATIVE EVALUATION

The terms *formative evaluation,* and *summative evaluation,* coined by Scriven (1967), were first applied to problems of curriculum evaluation, although they apply to nearly all types of changes in educational institutions. They refer to two fairly broad roles of evaluation that can be distinguished by temporal characteristics. Formative evaluation performs its function primarily during developmental stages, when a curriculum or other program is being designed, pilot-tested, and revised. The role of formative evaluation is thus associated strongly with program-improvement decisions. Summative evaluation refers to a broader analysis of the final product of the developmental process and thus is associated primarily with adoption, continuation, and rejection decisions. However, the two processes are not mutually exclusive. Data from formative evaluations can be useful in making judgments about a product's value, performance, merit, and so on. It is perhaps even more common for summative data to be used for making adjustments in the operations of an already functioning program. Indeed, it is wise to reap as many benefits as possible from any evaluation effort. This is advisable from an economic as well as a quality-control perspective.

DESCRIPTION AND JUDGMENT

The formal process of evaluation requires some minimum involvement in measurement and data-collection activities. Typically, the evaluator's function includes the development and application of appropriate data-gathering instruments (tests, questionnaires, observation systems, etc.) to assess the degree to which certain goals have been achieved. Furthermore, the evaluator is often expected to interpret the data that are collected—to pass judgment on the merit or worth of the program under consideration. Thus, the evaluator can have two obligations to fulfill: to describe and to judge a program. In fact, Stake (1967) reasons that description and judgment are the two most fundamental activities that comprise an educational change evaluation.

Of the two activities, the judgment of a program is perhaps more often avoided. The evaluator may view himself as unqualified to make value judgments. He may reason that, since he is a measurement specialist (as is often the case) and not an expert in the content area of the program being evaluated, subjective issues such as the importance or worth of the program or its various components are beyond the realm of his expertise. In other words, he feels more able to describe than to appraise.

This inclination is furthered by the educator/client's natural apprehension about the evaluation activity. No one enjoys being criticized. The education researcher's fear that an uncomplimentary evaluation may endanger funding, the regard of his colleagues, or even the very existence of the program is generally not unfounded. In fact, summative evaluations are undertaken to make decisions related to these very issues; e.g., is performance contracting superior to other alternatives? (See Carpenter-Huffman et al. 1974.) Is performance contracting or school busing worth the present investment in terms of personnel, money, and other resources? In this context, it is quite understandable that an evaluator may choose the path of least resistance, stopping short of passing judgment. However, because of the critical importance of the questions considered during the process of summative evaluation, an evaluation is incomplete until they have been answered (Stake 1967). These questions are part of the cost/benefit analyses necessary in using evaluation data to determine the relative benefits of a change program. This is why standards are set in relation to the social, economic, and organizational costs incurred in the change process.

INTERNAL VERSUS EXTERNAL EVALUATION

Although a rather strong case has been made for a broad-based approach to the evaluation of educational programs, something more needs to be said about staffing considerations. That is, who should conduct the evaluation? Is it best to assign responsibility to an existing member of the organization or program structure (internal evaluation), or is it more advantageous to seek a less biased party (external evaluation)?

Very often a school chooses the external evaluation route, especially if there is no available insider who possesses appreciable evaluation experience and skills. Other advantages of this route include a greater degree of objectivity and perspective unclouded by prior close involvement with the program and its personnel. Thus, an external evaluator is more likely to bring greater methodological expertise and more objectivity to an evaluation. He is likely to feel less constrained in communicating his findings, particularly those which might cast a negative light on the program.

However, the external evaluator is unlikely to know a great deal about the nature or content area of the program under consideration. He will almost certainly lack firsthand familiarity with the program's goals, objectives, and history. Some view this as potentially advantageous (e.g., Scriven 1972); however, an internal evaluator is less likely to overlook subtle aspects of the program that might be as important as the more obvious aspects (Suchman 1972). An external evaluator is less likely to be aware of a conflict between a school principal and a department head that would decrease interaction between them in a project demanding close cooperation, for example.

Further, an outsider is likely to experience less cooperation from program staff members who fear the consequences of an unfavorable evaluation. It is helpful for the external evaluator to proceed cautiously in his relationships with staff members. It is necessary for him to strike a balance between cultivating a cooperative atmosphere and maintaining objectivity. This problem manifests itself in internal evaluations as well, but it is usually of lesser magnitude.

Whether an internal or external evaluation is used, or both, certain problems can be anticipated and measures taken to minimize them. Perhaps the most significant preventative action that can be taken is to nurture a collaborative atmosphere. If the staff members are given the opportunity to participate in the planning stages of the evaluation and in the decision making, they are likely to experience fewer anxieties. Their resistance to the notion of being evaluated should be somewhat reduced, resulting in their increased cooperation. Another benefit of the participative approach to evaluation planning and decision making, especially in formative evaluations, is that staff members are likely to be more receptive to the implementation of changes suggested by an evaluation when they have played a role in the process. The temporary system evaluation team, involving organization members and external evaluators, is a mechanism designed to facilitate this collaborative evaluation effort.

REACTIVE EFFECTS OF EVALUATION

The concept of reactivity in program evaluation pertains to any effects that the evaluation activity itself may have on the program being evaluated or the data being collected. The act of evaluating an educational program will nearly always have some unanticipated or undesired effects on the functioning program. Thus, the evaluator must take care not to mistakenly identify artifacts of the evaluation process as program effects. Several examples of common reactive effects of measurement include (1) the "guinea pig" effect, (2) role selection, (3) real changes in the characteristic being measured attributable to a prior measurement, and (4) response sets (Webb et al. 1966).

The guinea pig effect is observed when teachers are aware that they are being evaluated. This awareness may affect their behavior. In other words, they may behave somewhat differently during the test or observational period than they would normally.

The role-selection effect is related to the previous concept in that the educator being observed or tested behaves in a manner consonant with his perceptions of the evaluator's expectations. In this sense, the role-selection effect seems to be a specific instance of the guinea pig effect.

The third type of reactive effect, a real change in the characteristic being measured, occurs frequently in evaluation designs that employ more than one measurement of the same characteristic over time (e.g., a pretest-posttest design.) In this instance, the exposure to the pretest may be responsible for some of the improvement on the posttest. For example, teachers may stress subject matter that they know will appear in a test to evaluate a curriculum innovation.

And finally, a response set refers to an individual tendency to respond to certain types of questions or other stimuli in a consistent although meaningless manner. A specific example of this phenomenon is the "acquiescent-responder effect." The acquiescent responder tends to consistently respond positively to items requiring positive-negative discriminations. One solution to this problem is to design instruments that include equal numbers of questions phrased in each direction. For example, an instrument used to assess student perceptions of teaching effectiveness might include both of these items:

The teacher provided assistance to those students seeking extra help.
Strongly Agree   1   2   3   4   5   Strongly Disagree

The student having difficulty with the subject was pretty much on his own.
Strongly Agree   1   2   3   4   5   Strongly Disagree

In these two items, the most favorable responses would be 1 and 5 respectively.

Other factors that may affect the validity of the measures taken are associated with the person or persons responsible for collecting and scoring the data. It is well known, for example, that interviewees respond differently when interviewed by someone of the same or differing sex, race, or age. The competence, and even the expectations, of the data collector may also impact the final results.

There are two ways of dealing with the problem of reactivity in evaluation. One is to attempt to eliminate many of the undesirable effects by employing nonreactive or unobtrusive measures (Webb et al. 1966). The other is to be aware of possible reactive effects in order to rule them out later.

The first solution relies heavily on the use of records, hidden observations, and other less direct sources of information. Webb and his associates delineate three basic sources of nonreactive data: physical traces, archives, and observations. Examples of physical trace measures include estimates of wear-and-tear and program-related equipment and the utilization rate of other disposable program materials. The evaluator may also choose to examine archives or records pertaining to student attendance, the use of relevant library materials, records from instructor conferences, and recent promotions of program participants, to name a few. Observational data are invaluable in terms of identifying discrepancies that may exist between what a program purports to do and what it is in fact doing. Observations by humans can be supplemented by mechanical devices such as movie cameras, and tape and videotape recorders.

Of course, observations cannot be considered unobtrusive if participants are aware that they are being observed. If properly conducted, however, observations can be less reactive than tests or interviews. A recommended procedure is to ignore data collected during the first few days of observation. After this initial adjustment period, the data should be a reasonably valid reflection of what occurs "normally." Because of ethical considerations, the alternative of conducting observations without the participants' knowledge is rarely justified.

Since the art of unobtrusive measurement is not sufficiently advanced to meet all needs of most programs, the evaluator should be keenly aware of the spectrum of possible reactive effects. Furthermore, he should pause before attributing an interesting evaluational finding to the treatment or program under consideration. Only after all the reactive effects have been carefully examined and ruled out can the evaluator draw such a conclusion with a reasonable degree of certainty.

COMPARATIVE AND NONCOMPARATIVE EVALUATION

As discussed earlier, a critical step in the design of evaluation studies is to decide on the criteria by which to judge the program. Perhaps the most fundamental issue is deciding whether to compare the program's performance with that of competing programs or the same program in other settings (comparative evaluation) or to judge the program solely in terms of its performance in the present environment (noncomparative evaluation). For example, should the impact of a problem-solving training program for a school district be compared with that for other districts which used the same training program, or should it be judged simply on how well it performed within the specific district? The choice is essentially between relative or absolute standards for judgment. When relative standards are employed (comparative evaluation), the problem of equivalence must be dealt with. How can one determine the true similarities of programs designed to do somewhat different things, or of the same program implemented at different sites? One must somehow avoid the "apples and oranges" syndrome. When absolute standards are elected, one is faced with the difficult task of deciding what aspects of the program are most important and what level of performance is acceptable.

CONSIDERATIONS IN EVALUATION RESEARCH

Evaluators should consider several factors if they are to be of assistance to the educators involved in a change program. First, *objectivity,* while probably impossible to achieve fully, should be sought. Evaluation activities must minimize subjectivity and must be as straightforward and factual as possible. Second, evaluation studies should be concluded at a point where the results can be fed back into the change effort early enough to remedy any problems. Thus, *timeliness* is important. Third, the results of evaluation research should be useful or *applicable*. The answer to the "so what?" question about evaluation data should be easy. Fourth, the feedback should not be presented in a jargon or format that is difficult to understand. Results should be easily *communicated*. Fifth, the conduct of the research should follow procedures that generate valid and reliable information.

Several factors should be kept in mind in preparing to conduct an evaluation. First, the evaluator must be concerned with the *objectives* of the evaluation effort. What is the purpose of the evaluation? Will the evaluation provide new and needed information that could result in new policies and new ways of implementing a change? Given the design of the evaluation, are appropriate *methods* being used? While a particular method may be ideal in some objective way, is it really suited for the particular circumstances under which a change is occurring? Is it really suited for the kind of change being intended? Is the sampling plan accurate? Are the questions being asked appropriately for the study in question? Is there perhaps an excess amount of data being collected? Still another concern should be *data processing*. Are the procedures for the statistical manipulation of the data that are to be gathered clearly stated? Are qualified personnel available to do the analysis required for meaningful results? Another consideration is whether the full array of possible answers are allowed for. That is, do the questions and analytical techniques permit the evaluator to come up with answers to all plausible questions that could be asked? *Finances* are yet another factor. Are travel, personnel, supplies, and other resources budgeted in a realistic way? Are there unnecessary items? Are there items that are underbudgeted or not allowed for at all? To the extent possible, *cost-benefit* studies might be made of the evaluation effort as well as for the target system being evaluated.

Still another consideration is the *nature of the task* characteristics (Dornbusch and Scott 1975:145ff.). The more *complex* the task, the more complex the evaluation process. For example, if the task being evaluated is that performed by an organizational development expert hired by a school district, then it is necessary to evaluate the highly complex array of activities that expert may engage in. Each activity may involve many considerations, and cause and effect connections may be very difficult to establish. Another aspect of the task is the *clarity of goals*. How clearly defined are the end states the organizational development expert is expected to achieve (criteria and standards)? How clearly defined are the emotional security states a child is to achieve after participating in an emotional development program in kindergarten? The less clear the goals are, the less clear the evaluation will be. The frequency with which *unpredicted events* may occur in the performance of tasks is important, too. This involves in part a distinction between focusing on outcomes and focusing on performance. For example, scores on standardized tests among students in a particular school may have declined over a three-year period. Does this mean that the quality of teaching in that school declined over that three-year period? The answer could be yes if one focused only on outcomes. However, an unpredicted change in the task of teachers could have occurred, such as a major change in the composition of the students. A substantial change in the character of the student body may have occurred because of demographic changes in the neighborhood. Faced with a new challenge, a teacher may have actually performed better, but there may be little indication of this without controlling for student motivation and abilities.

Organizational arrangements are another source of possible difficulty. As indicated in an earlier chapter, the classroom is typically treated as the private preserve of the teacher, particularly in higher education. The *visibility* of the teaching task is thus not great, which is one reason administrators place considerable weight on student course and instructor ratings. Of course, work by administrators is often less visible still and hence difficult to evaluate as well. *Costs* associated with various programs or efforts are also difficult to see. We are speaking here of nonfinancial costs such as strain, anxiety, loss of self-esteem, and other invisible social and psychological costs. *Savings* on these costs are also difficult to assess; they are no more visible than cost increases. In some organizational settings, tasks may be performed jointly by two or more persons. This complicates evaluation considerably. An administrator may perform poorly because of constraints set by less competent colleagues on whom his or her work depends. The example referred to earlier, in which a change in student population could reflect poorly but inaccurately on teachers, is another instance of this. Team teaching shares some of the problems when the team as a whole is evaluated, rather than each member separately. Related to this is the *separation of outcomes*. It is often difficult to attribute particular aspects of an outcome to individual members of a team responsible for achieving the final product. In general, it appears that under conditions of team arrangements, the greater the visibility of performances, the more likely performers are to accent evaluations.

Another factor associated with organizational arrangements concerns the frequency with which performance evaluations are made known to those being evaluated. This factor is a difficult one to cope with. The more frequent the evaluations made, the more feedback there is to enable performers to improve their work and receive encouragement and reward. On the other hand, frequent evaluation may be perceived as interference, as indicating a loss of autonomy, or as evidence of low confidence of the evaluators in the performers. Still another difficulty concerns the number of different persons involved in the evaluation. It is difficult to determine a priori how many evaluators would be too many in a given situation. However, when many evaluators are involved, communication and coordination among them is difficult, and evaluations may be incomplete or even incompatible if no consistent assumptions and criteria are used. This problem is more likely to occur at district levels and at the level of the university at large. In general, there should not be more evaluators than there are needed areas of evaluation expertise. If one evaluator is sufficiently competent to perform two or more evaluation services, it may be desirable to have him do so. This should not be done at the cost of reducing too much the variety of perspectives a multimember evaluation team can provide.

Major Types of Evaluation

Once the evaluator has a clear grasp of the problem he faces, he can choose from among several types of approaches, which fall into two categories: focused evaluation and unfocused evaluation.

FOCUSED EVALUATION

An investigation designed to test certain hypotheses or to determine how well a program performs with respect to predetermined standards (relative or absolute) can be classified as a focused evaluation. It is focused in the sense that the evaluator and/or client have identified needs that must be met or questions that must be answered.

The high degree of precision and validity attainable in well-designed experiments makes the experimental approach to educational evaluation a very attractive option. In the experimental model, the evaluator attempts to link effects with causes, either by determining from a number of possible explanations the one which is most likely, or by determining if a particular treatment had the predicted effect. By systematically manipulating possible causes, the evaluator can determine which of several possibilities is associated with the effect or how various levels of a cause relate to the effect (e.g., Does the new curriculum result in greater learning than the old curriculum?) However, the rigid requirements and assumptions for true experiments can rarely be satisfied outside of the laboratory. As an alternative, the quasi-experiment can be employed which answers the same type of questions, but is allowed to deviate from some of the strict requirements of a true experiment.

As the discussion below will make apparent, there are times when even a quasi-experimental approach is not feasible. Furthermore, experimentation cannot answer many of the questions which concern the educator, (for example, what kinds of communication patterns exist among the project staff members or between teachers and students?). For this reason, several additional focused evaluation models will be presented which have greater flexibility and wider applicability.

Experimental and Quasi-Experimental Evaluation Research   The fundamental requirement of a true experiment is the random assignment of subjects or participants to experimental and control groups. The experimental group tries the new program; the control group continues to use the old program or engages in totally unrelated activities for the duration of the experiment. The performance of the two (or more) groups on the criterion variables(s) is compared to determine if statistically significant differences exist that can be attributed to the experimental treatment. For example, in one study (Coughlan et al. 1972), an organizational development program for elementary schools was being tested. Certain schools in the district tried the program. The investigators measured with questionnaires the "organizational climate" of the experimental schools before and after the program was tried. Other schools, both within the same district and outside the district, had their organizational climate measured at the same time as the experimental schools even though they did not participate in the OD program. The control-group schools were selected to be as similar as possible to the experimental schools. The results of the questionnaires showed that greater improvements in organizational well-being occurred in the experimental school than occurred in the control schools. These differences in improvement were attributed to the OD program.

A critical concern is with the *internal validity* of the experiment, "the basic minimum without which any experiment is uninterpretable" (Campbell and Stanley 1966:5). Internal validity refers to the degree of certainty with which the experimenter can conclude that the observed differences (or lack thereof) result from the treatment rather than from extraneous variables. A few of the threats to internal validity are history, maturation, testing, and mortality (Campbell and Stanley 1966). The threat of history concerns events that take place during the experiment other than those experiences provided by the experimenter. A school strike or the resignation of a key person in a trial program or the firing of a superintendent are examples. Different experiences of experimental and control-group members may influence their behavior on the criterion measures. The obvious fact that time has elapsed from the beginning to the end of an experiment may also pose threats to internal validity. Factors such as hunger, fatigue, boredom, and increased age contribute to the maturation factor. The potential problem of testing, discussed earlier, refers to the effects of an earlier measurement experience on a later one. And, finally, experimental mortality refers to differences that are attributable to differential loss of subjects in experimental and control groups (e.g., "bright" students may drop out of one group more than the other).

Another concern, usually less pressing, is with the *generalizability* or *external validity* of one's findings. An administrator contemplating the adoption of an educational program at a variety of sites and with different types of students would be more concerned with this issue than an educator desiring information on a program's performance or value in one particular setting. When generalizability is deemed important, the evaluator should be certain that the experimental participants are representative of the population to which generalizations will be drawn.

The Discrepancy Approach   This widely recognized evaluation method came out of the early work of Ralph Tyler (1942, 1950), who defined evaluation as the process of assessing the degree to which educational objectives have been achieved. The term *discrepancy evaluation* (Provus, 1971) is quite appropriate since the evaluator is concerned with identifying the distance between desired and obtained program goals and objectives, a form of performance gap.

The focus of discrepancy evaluation has broadened considerably since the appearance of Tyler's early works. In addition to discrepancies in student achievement, the evaluator is encouraged to look for attitudinal outcomes, a form of spin-off effects, as well as discrepancies in process variables. The importance of the feelings and attitudes of participants cannot be denied. Goals relating to process might include a comparison of the actual operation of the program with what was intended. Program participants may be functioning rather differently from what was expected. Deviation from the values espoused by program planners may be found in individuals responsible for program implementation. This information is useful in program resolution at an early stage. Finally, discrepancies may exist in the interaction of intents, process, and outcomes. For example, certain program components that are not operating as planned may be adversely (or positively) affecting other components or outcomes.

Figure 9-3 depicts the various stages involved in conducting an evaluation of this nature. After the roles of evaluation (referring to a hierarchy of decision-making needs) and relevant program objectives have been identified, an evaluation plan is developed, refined, and implemented. The data are then analyzed, allowing the necessary comparisons and decisions to be made. The evaluation is useful to the extent that the chosen goals are truly comprehensive and the measurements used a true reflection of those goals.

An example of the discrepancy approach is provided by a southern school of business that wanted to improve the quality of its M.B.A. enrollees. In terms of figure 9-3, they assigned to the evaluation effort the task of determining how much, if at all, the quality of students improved (the criterion outcome) as a result of their efforts to attract better masters-level business students. Among the several criteria established for making judgments, a major criterion was the increase in average scores of enrollees on the Admission Test for Graduate Study in Business. An average increase of twenty-five points was sought for the next

FIGURE 9-3.   Steps in a Discrepancy Evaluation

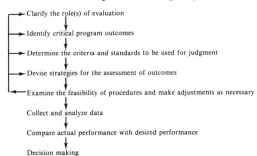

entering class over the average of the entering classes for the past three years. The strategy was very simple since the scores for all students were available. We will not go into the problems and outcomes of this evaluation effort, since it is mentioned here simply to illustrate a discrepancy evaluation. It might be stated that an improvement did occur, but not of the desired magnitude, thus leaving still some discrepancy between desired and achieved goals.

Discrepancy evaluation is indeed more flexible than the experimental mode. New aspects may be incorporated as the evaluation proceeds; goals may be deleted or emphasized more or less. Some goals are more difficult and time-consuming than others to measure, especially those requiring precise instrumentation. This approach is recommended for situations where answers to specific questions are sought. The results will be somewhat more equivocal than those of an experimental evaluation, but a more comprehensive array of outcomes can be examined. If factors other than program outcomes are more important, or if a more complete program description is desired, the evaluator should entertain the more comprehensive model described next.

Program-Audit Model   The program audit is a mechanism for assessing the process of a change program. Program audits are *assessments of the intent* to operationalize components of the change or innovation. For example, many of the compensatory education programs funded by the federal government claimed to provide additional human and material resources for students of low-income families. These resources were supposed to be directed at the needs of the target learners and were to be additional to the resources already provided by the school systems. Teams of program assessors (auditors) were sent into school districts with compensatory programs to find out if these intentions and program purposes were in fact being accomplished. Initial reports showed that federal funds were being used to replace the school system's own in order to save the district money. This led to government regulations demanding that districts make schools eligible for compensatory programs comparable to other schools in the district before additional resources were provided.

Accreditation of professional schools often used a form of program audit to assess the programs being reviewed for recognition. Usually the target organization develops a self-study that includes a statement of mission, goals, and objectives; a description of program processes designed to meet goals; and descriptive data concerning facilities, faculty, students, graduates, and so forth. Following the preparation of the self-study, the accrediting body sends an auditing team to the institution to assess the accuracy of the study. A similar process has been used by research and development centers when reviewing the organizations using their innovations. They "audit" the institution to see if minimal processes have been operationalized in order to implement the innovation. As noted before, many change or innovative programs have been adopted on paper but have not had sufficient resources, processes, or structure to adequately implement an intended change.

The "Countenance" Model   Data collection to determine goal achievement is the primary concern of the discrepancy approach. By definition, its focus is almost entirely on outcomes. However, it is relatively insensitive to outcomes that are not anticipated. This is a serious limitation, particularly for formative evaluation. The model provides gradations of yes-no answers to the question "Is the program working?" It offers fewer potential answers to the question "Why or why not?"

Stake (1967) suggests that the "countenance of educational evaluation" should include a broader spectrum of data resources, including *antecendents* and *transactions* as well as outcomes. Antecedents are conditions that exist for individuals and organizations before the implementation of a new program. Insight into antecedent conditions is important to both program planning and the design of a sound evaluation plan. Educational programs are based on certain assumptions about the existing behaviors, attitudes, and so forth of those who will participate. If these assumptions are inaccurate, the new program may prove to be inappropriate for the intended purposes.

Knowledge of antecedents is invaluable for avoiding false conclusions. For example, consider a program that has been designed to teach skills A and B to an 80 percent criterion standard. Twenty participants complete the program and take an achievement test, but only a few achieve the desired level. The evaluator concludes that the program did not meet the expectations. Few explanations may be ruled out, however, without additional data. Some knowledge about the performance level of the participants before the program was implemented (antecedents) would narrow the range considerably. It could be that the average level of performance was 5 percent before and 75 percent after the instructional sequence. If that were so, it would indeed be misleading to conclude that the program was a failure.

Transactions are the innumerable events or interpersonal encounters that take place during the instructional program. Some knowledge of transactions, usually obtained by means of observation, can be extremely helpful. In the hypothetical example given above, knowledge of transactions may provide suggestions for program changes so that the desired criterion may be achieved in the future. Observational data may uncover interpersonal problems or deficiencies in program implementation.

Figure 9-4 depicts a framework useful for recording and processing information pertaining to antecedents, transactions, and outcomes. First of all, the evaluator obtains and records descriptions of the educator's intent as well as corresponding descriptions of what was actually observed. The process of establishing "congruency" between intents and observations is essentially the same as in the program-audit model. It entails the estimation of distances or discrepancies between the two. The difference between the two models lies in the range of congruencies examined.

For program-improvement decisions, establishing "contingencies" or casual relationships among antecedents, transactions, and outcomes is particularly im-

FIGURE 9-4.   A Representation of the Processing of Descriptive Data

Source: Stake 1967. Used by permission.

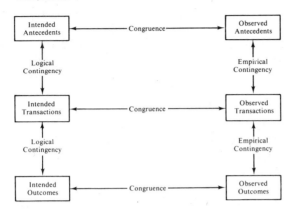

Descriptive Data

portant. Logic is used to demonstrate contingencies among intents. For example, a subject-matter expert may judge that a given activity or transaction is appropriate for effecting a given outcome. Empirical evidence is required, however, to establish contingencies between observed antecedents, transactions, and outcomes. Pretest and posttest scores would provide empirical evidence that a given transaction resulted (or did not result) in the desired outcome or that a relationship exists between antecedents and transactions.

Use of the countenance model provides an evaluation that is less precise than the experimental approach and more time-consuming than the discrepancy model, but the resulting data can serve a wide range of decision-making needs.

A Typology for Decision Making   A multifaceted model will be offered next to highlight the scope of possible information needs for decision making. The context-input-process-product (CIPP) evaluation model (Stufflebeam et al. 1971; Stufflebeam 1974*a*) can be viewed, to some extent, as a synthesis of the models that have come before.

Context evaluation serves its function in the management of an ongoing program. It bears the greatest similarity to the discrepancy model. Context evaluation is concerned with the identification of incongruencies between what is intended and what is observed with respect to intermediate program goals and objectives. Information gained through context evaluation is useful in guiding program-modification decisions, including both immediate and long-range changes.

Information that plays a role in the selection and development of educational programs is gained through *input evaluation*. These concerns were not addressed to any great extent by the other models. Input evaluation answers questions about the feasibility of competing strategies in achieving desired goals: the availability of required materials, technology, and personnel; the relative costs of competing strategies; and the advantages and disadvantages of each strategy.

Process evaluation is similar to formative evaluation and can also be viewed as an extended version of context evaluation. As the name implies, data are gathered on an already functioning program regarding issues other than goal attainment. Interpersonal relationships, staffing patterns, and adequacy of space and equipment may be investigated. When operating at an optimal level, process evaluation provides the program manager with reasonably continuous feedback which is useful in troubleshooting and making short-term program improvement decisions.

Finally *product evaluation* is nearly synonymous with summative evaluation. The overall impact and success of the program is assessed to guide termination/ continuation decisions.

Table 9-1 provides a framework for using the CIPP model. For each of the four types of evaluation activities, three steps are involved: (1) *delineating* the information to be obtained, (2) *obtaining* that information through measurement activities, and (3) *providing* the decision maker with the information found. The first step usually involves collaboration between evaluator and decision maker; the second and third are usually the responsibility of the evaluator. A given evaluation plan may include one or all four types of evaluation, depending on needs.

The "decison-making" cells in table 9-1 were explained in the above paragraphs. Each type of evaluation serves different decison-making needs; a summary is provided in table 9-2. And, finally, the cause of "accountability" can be served by this model through the detailed records maintained for all phases of program development and implementation. The records and evaluation reports can be made available as the need arises.

The CIPP model illustrates the benefits of an evaluation component at every stage in the evolution of an educational innovation. Systematic evaluative information is beneficial, if not essential, at program-planning stages (input evaluation), throughout the various implementation phases (context and process evaluation), and at each point thereafter where a continuation/rejection must be made (product evaluation).

UNFOCUSED EVALUATIONS

An unfocused evaluation is one in which few issues, goals, or objectives have been prespecified as being especially significant (with respect to the evaluation effort). This may seem a contradiction in terms, since evaluations are executed to provide useful information for decision making. It is not at all contradictory, however, if one considers that data obtained in focused evaluations may in the long run turn out to be less critical than other data that might have been collected.

The notion of *goal-free evaluation* was conceived in an effort to deal with the

TABLE 9-1. A Framework for Designing CIPP Evaluation Studies

TYPES OF EVALUATION

Stages in Evaluation	Context Role		Input Role		Process Role		Product Role	
	Decision Making	Accountability	Decision Making	Accountability	Decision Making	Accountability	Decision Making	Accountability
Delineating			(What questions will be addressed?)					
Obtaining			(How will the needed information be obtained?)					
Providing			(How will the obtained information be reported?)					

SOURCE: Stufflebeam 1974a: 123). Used by permission.

TABLE 9-2. A Summary of Decision-Making Needs Served by CIPP

TYPES OF EVALUATION	PRIMARY DECISION-MAKING NEEDS SERVED
Context	Day-to-day management decisions; program improvement decisions
Input	Program selection, development, and implementation decisions
Process	Program improvement decisions
Product	Continuation/termination decisions

problem of unanticipated program side effects, or spin-offs. *Responsive evaluation* is seen as a means of communicating information that is tailored to the unique needs, values, and interests of the persons involved in a particular program. The *adversary approach* is also useful when questions of personal values are a high priority.

Goal-free Evaluation   Goal-free evaluation (Scriven 1972, 1973) was devised because of the difficulty in separating those program effects which are intended from those which are unanticipated. Nearly all evaluators, regardless of their philosophy, would acknowlege the importance of seeking data on unanticipated side effects. Scriven reasons, however, that learning about actual effects is far more useful than learning of failure or success with respect to planned ones. To be more specific, the knowledge that a program did an excellent job in some clearly delineated areas can be a good deal more informative than the knowledge that it failed to achieve its broader, perhaps unrealistic, goals. It follows that evaluations should be designed to maximize the likelihood of uncovering those actual effects.

The goal-free evaluator (GFE) must strive to maintain objectivity and avoid being indoctrinated by project affiliates. He must postpone becoming acquainted with expressed program objectives (and even inferring them) as long as possible. The evaluation should be conducted without forming close associations with project staff that would inevitably lead to a loss of independence. It becomes evident that the GFE cannot be a member of the project staff.

Scriven suggests that the GFE be brought in very early in the program-implementation phase. The project manager should give the evaluator (1) an extremely brief description of the program—for example, "It is a four-week instructional sequence designed to teach arithmetic skills"—and (2) a sample of program materials with goal statements extracted. From this limited information, the basic evaluation plan is conceived.

Evaluative data may include a detailed analysis of program materials, descriptions by participant-observers, interviews with program participants (e.g., teachers and students), and an analysis of tests and test results. Tests that assess a range of outcomes broader than those specified in program objectives are highly desirable in goal-free evaluations. The emphasis is on changes in the individuals who are the target of a program, especially changes that can be reliably traced to the program. Changes in attitudes, values, and motivation as well as behavior may be highlighted.

Goal-free evaluation seems to be especially useful in the summative context in helping to judge the merit or worth of an educational product and making a cost-benefit analysis of a change program. Scriven argues, however, that GFE can also play an important role in program-improvement decisions. If unanticipated side effects can be uncovered in the formative stages, changes can be made to foster the favorable ones and eliminate those which are unfavorable.

It should be noted that goal-free evaluation is not advocated (by Scriven or his critics, e.g., Stufflebeam 1974*b*) as a replacement for other approaches. It is a strategy that can provide additional benefits when used to supplement other approaches. An internal evaluator might also be employed to follow a goal-based strategy, since the GFE may fail to pick up some of the important planned effects.

Responsive Evaluation   Because of time and monetary constraints, few evaluations can be truly comprehensive. No single effort can possibly achieve all of the goals of evaluation that have been outlined previously. The evaluator and program manager must necessarily examine their needs and priorities and devise a strategy that best fits their requirements, given the constraints.

The limitations of a "preordinate approach," typified by the discrepancy evaluation model, have already been discussed in some detail. A concentration on outcomes reduces one's awareness of and sensitivity to the pervasive activities and value perspectives of an educational program. The responsive evaluation model (Stake 1975, 1972) has been offered as an alternative to other perspectives to be used when a fuller program description is deemed to be more important or of greater utility. It emphasizes the *process* of education at the expense of a full analysis of the *product*. According to Stake, a sharp focus on only a few program goals or decisions cannot be classified as an evaluation of "the program."

When an integrative reflection of a total program is desired, a responsive evaluation approach should be considered. "An educational evaluation is *responsive evaluation* if it orients more directly to program activities than to program intents; responds to audience requirements for information; and if the different value-perspectives present are referred to in reporting the success or failure of the program" (Stake 1975: 14). Thus, an evaluation of this nature is highly situation-specific. Results are not intended to be generalized to other programs or individuals.

To conduct a responsive evaluation, a good deal of time must be invested in gaining familiarity with the program and with the values and interests of those who are involved. The primary activity is observation. Information may be communicated by means of a formal report, although natural means of communication are more often employed. With the assistance of the observers, program descriptions, case studies, product displays, scrapbooks, films, photographs, and judgments may be compiled or collected. The judgments or "expressions of worth" should reflect the entire spectrum of opinion on the issues. Some measure of reliability and validity is achieved by collecting various interpretations of the "accuracy," "importance," and "relevance" of the findings. In cost-benefit analysis, responsive evaluation is very useful in identifying who incurred what costs and gained what benefits.

After becoming acquainted with the program and its environment, the evaluator can compile a list of issue questions to provide a framework for the data-collection activities. Questions may pertain to values, procedures, facilities, and scope. The "issues" concept replaces that of "objectives," its more parochial counterpart. And to provide additional structure in the representation of data, the framework put forth in the countenance model may be used.

Figure 9-5 depicts some of the events that take place during a responsive evaluation. The events are expressed on the face of a clock, although it is not meant to suggest that they will occur in that prescribed order. Each activity is likely to be repeated several times during the evaluation process.

A responsive evaluation provides information by which the decision maker may form his own judgments concerning the program. It strives to provide a reflection of the program in its entirety, a picture that is perhaps quite different from that which would be revealed by a more detailed examination of selected components. Once again, the model is not advocated for all situations. If precision of measurement or definitive answers to pressing questions are required, one of the goal-based models would be selected. The responsive approach may still be entertained, however, as a supplement to other models.

The Adversary Approach   The adversary approach, borrowed from the field of law, is offered as a substitute for previous methods of interpreting and reporting evaluative data. It does not stand as a fully prescriptive model, since the methods by which the data are collected are not dictated. Any combination of previous strategies for obtaining information may be used.

T. R. Owens (1973) suggests that for educational decision making, the adversary approach is more viable than either a criminal or civil court model. It provides a reasonably flexible forum by which the strengths and weaknesses of a program may be analyzed and judged. The decision maker may serve as judge, jury, and representative for the prosecution and defense. Depending on the circumstances, each of these roles may be assumed by different parties. Several of the attributes of the adversary-proceedings model offered by Owens are given as follows:

1. The rules for conducting the proceedings provide a good deal of latitude.
2. Evidence may be evaluated freely, provided that it is considered to be relevant by the hearings officer.

FIGURE 9-5.   Prominent Events in a Responsive Evaluation
Source: Adapted from Stake 1975:20.

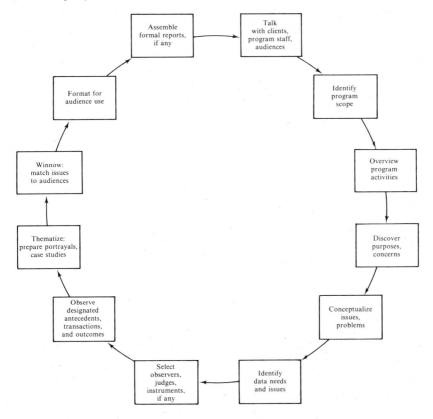

3. A request can be made of both the prosecution and defense to make available the relevant facts, means of proof, and names of witnesses prior to the trial.

4. The defendant may elect to acknowledge or challenge the various charges before the proceedings begin.

5. Witnessess may testify before or during the trial and be cross-examined without excessive restraint.

6. The search for relevant facts is facilitated by pretrial meetings between hearings officer, defense, and prosecution.

7. Other interested parties may also participate in the proceedings. [pp. 296–97]

The adversary model is particularly applicable to innovation-implementation decisions, whether the innovation being contemplated is a new textbook or a full-scale educational program. The values, procedures, and probable effects on both the individuals and the system may be debated. The model provides a means by which various interpretations of information collected may be obtained.

For example, let us assume that a new reading curriculum has been implemented on a limited basis in an elementary school district. An evaluator was retained early in the school year to collect data on its success and impact. The district's reading coordinator and the various principals (the decision makers) have opted for an adversary-proceedings approach to weigh the evidence that has been collected. Toward the end of the school year, the reading coordinator selects two of the participating teachers to prepare arguments, one for the new reading program and one against it.

The adversary and advocate are free to consult the evaluator, other teachers, students, parents, and so on in the preparation of their respective cases. They may choose to collect additional data with or without the assistance of the evaluator. Written briefs are submitted to the trials officer (the reading coordinator) and made available to interested parties prior to the formal proceedings. To supplement evidence presented and the testimony of witnesses solicited by both prosecution and defense, other concerned individuals may be allowed to present their views (e.g., parents, teachers, administrators). In this case, the reading coordinator would be a logical choice for the trials officer and the principals for the jury. After all of the evidence has been presented, they may then deliberate and make the necessary continuation, expansion, termination and/or program-improvement decisions.

Summary

The chapter began with a discussion of general issues that must be considered in any educational evaluation. It is necessary to entertain these fundamental questions before choosing a viable evaluation strategy: Why, when, how, and for whom should the evaluation be conducted?

An array of evaluation theories and methodologies were detailed which can be used to provide answers to a wide range of questions that concern decision makers. The models in the section on focused evaluations include strategies for determining if relationships exist among program components (objectives, process, and outcomes). A combination of these strategies may be devised to meet the specific information demands of just about any program at any phase, provided that those needs can be clearly specified in advance.

There are some advantages, however, to an evaluation perspective that is less intent on providing clear-cut answers to prespecified questions. For this reason, four additional models, called unfocused evaluations, were introduced. One might choose one of these approaches if there is greater concern for picking up unanticipated program effects or for learning something about the program's impact in a larger sense than whether or not its objectives have been realized. The last two of these models provide an alternative process of judging a program and a means of facilitating continued program adoption, respectively.

A very limited evaluation budget may dictate a choice of only one of these models. Under severely constrained circumstances, the program manager must be especially careful to choose the one that meets the highest-priority needs. If more time, personnel, and resources are available, a plan may be devised to inform a broader range of decisions. Obviously, resources are never infinite, so allocations should be contingent upon the relative importance of the issues. The evaluation scheme to be followed may be totally focused, totally unfocused, or some combination thereof, depending on what is thought to be of greatest utility.

Educational programs can be extremely costly in the broadest possible sense of the term. If a new program provides appreciable benefits, a sound evaluation should help to identify them. If it fails to fulfill its promises, these shortcomings should be uncovered so that appropriate changes can be made or the program discarded. The decisions are much too important to be made inadvisedly.

PART IV

Self-Renewal in Educational Organizations

10

Knowledge Use for Educational Change

KNOWLEDGE AND RESEARCH USE is one of the most vexing problems in all sciences. Indeed, it has been termed the Achilles heel of social research. A demand for substantive results of social science research in the form of policy, practice, and production is ever present among funding sources and interested publics.

Concern over the problem of knowledge use in education has increased greatly in recent years. The use of new ideas, products, services, practices, and other innovations is a major ingredient in the process of educational change. It is therefore important to address the issue of knowledge production and use here.

Accumulated personal experiences or observations of the experiences of others are an important source of data for developing and guiding educational change programs. Change-oriented individuals or organizations must be able to *acquire* new information produced by others and also acquire new insights from various past or current experiences. Creators of change must also be able to *translate* new information into change programs or innovations applicable to an existing situation. The material in this chapter provides a background for considering the questions: (1) How can individuals or groups desiring change acquire information about change in general or concerning a specific change problem? (2) How can relevant information be translated into action principles and change programs?

Most work on knowledge use concerns the improvement of processes for disseminating knowledge rather than the translation of knowledge or research into action principles and change programs. Additionally, the literature in this area is written primarily from the disseminator's standpoint or from the standpoint of some third party, such as an agency or person researching the problems of knowledge production and use. This chapter will take a different perspective—that of the educator who wants to create change in an educational organization. The principles, generalizations, and findings are designed to be useful for obtaining information pertinent to needed change and for generating from the knowledge and data available a large array of plausible action implications.

What Is Knowledge Use?

Knowledge production and use (KP&U) is the process by which knowledge is formulated or produced and then used to some advantage. The systematic study of this process is fairly new to education. No common definition of KP&U is shared by all. However, for managers of educational change in organizations with knowledge production and/or use missions, it is generally thought of as a process in which knowledge produced by research, theory building, strategy testing, conceptualizing, hypothesizing, observing, professional practice, and other means is translated into useful forms by or for an individual or group. A more narrow view of KP&U is the "theory into practice" process, or the use of research findings for problem solving. These two conceptualizations are parts of the KP&U activities in education.

These subconcepts of KP&U imply that certain individuals and organizations are knowledge producers and other individuals and organizations are knowledge users or consumers. This is one of the serious conceptual limitations in planned change. The separation of the knowledge producer and consumer in a conceptual sense has resulted in unnecessary barriers between individuals and organizations. Some of these are status barriers, others are language barriers, and still others derive from the establishment of territorial domains by those calling themselves researchers or theory builders and those calling themselves practitioners or "doers."

These individual, group, and organizational separations have had a debilitating effect both on the development of knowledge and on thinking or theory building in education. The isolation of individuals and organizations is a significant theme in the literature of educational KP&U. Such isolation blocks the growth of knowledge and the collaborative development of educational practices through the use of broadly based data sources.

The research-use processes are greatly enhanced when the user and the researcher have an open relationship. Rogers, Lin, and Zaltman (1973) define research use as "a process by which users' needs are determined and communicated to researchers, leading to research designed to meet the needs, and eventually to new knowledge based on research which is communicated to answer their needs." This definition implies the need for direct and open communication between the researcher and user. It does not preclude a case in which the researcher and the user are one and the same.

Although it is clear that some organizations and individuals will view either knowledge production or knowledge use in the development of educational practice as a primary role, more enlightened concepts of KP&U processes view all organizations involved in the educational activities as involved in both knowledge production and use.

Several components are involved in research use. These components are shown in Figure 10-1 and are defined briefly below.

1. Need assessment involves identifying (1) who the users are, (2) their readily expressed or felt needs, (3) latent needs, and (4) needs that may develop in the relatively near future.
2. The translation of needs into research questions involves redefining problems or difficulties stated by users.
3. Conduct of usable research involves doing research related to user needs in a manner amenable to users' capacity to act upon research.
4. Creating an innovation (e.g., new information or knowledge) memory bank (or inventory) involves gathering the results of research, synthesizing them, storing them, retrieving them as necessary, and formating the new knowledge in a way that facilitates user interpretation.
5. Implementation of innovations or new knowledge involves helping users put the new knowledge or research results into practice.
6. Evaluation and research involves the constant improving of all earlier components.

As noted, unless the ultimate user is also the producer of knowledge, he has been involved in step one, to provide data for need assessment, and thereafter is not involved again until steps 5 and 6.

However, the concept of schools as self-renewing organizations requires that at least two improvements be made in present practice. First, where knowledge is produced as a separate process, the intended users should be linked to all components. The resource linking network of the Proactive/Interactive Model (described in chapter 6) is designed to aid such collaborative processes between researchers and organizational problem solvers and to stimulate the two-way flow of knowledge and data between knowledge producers and users. Second, continuous self-renewal implies that, at least at some level, practitioners must also be knowledge producers. If they do not actually conduct the research or carry out the development activities that provide the basis for change, they still

FIGURE 10-1.   Components of Research Use
Source: Rogers, Lin, and Zaltman 1973:13.

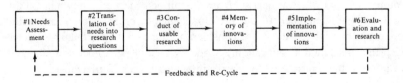

must develop the knowledge base necessary for their own problem-identification and solution-generation phases.

Clearly, from the point of view of the practitioner, an essential use of knowledge and data is in the initial change process of awareness and diagnosis. As pointed out in chapter 6, organizations need to be "unfrozen" and change movement needs some initiation force. One of the methods described there is the use of survey feedback for problem identification. Survey-feedback and problem-solving techniques are designed to enhance the self-directed change/innovation abilities of educational practitioners. By systematically looking at their own perceptions of organizational operations and climate, educators can initiate change processes in their own organizations. Duncan, Zaltman, and Cook (in progress) have studied and tested this approach extensively and found it to be an effective technique for solving a wide range of problems. Hand, Estafen, and Sims (1975) suggest that it is effective primarily in making the work environment better able to satisfy human needs rather than changing group performance in a short period of time.

The following example highlights the notion that practitioners are also knowledge producers. It is presented in detail to permit the reader to use the same or similar forms and methods for collective decision making in his own setting.

A Survey-Feedback and Problem-Solving Example

A three-year field experiment sponsored by the National Institute of Education examined the joint use of survey feedback, problem solving, and collective decision making (Duncan, Zaltman, and Cooke, in progress). Since the experiment was rather complex, only part of it will be described here.

At the start of the experiment, a questionnaire covering several different categories was administered to the principals (as well as the teachers) of twenty schools from one school district. The intent of the questionnaire was to learn what the principals thought about a wide range of issues in which they were involved.

Exhibit 1 identifies the various categories of possible problems and the percentage of principals responding favorably to each category. It can be seen, for example, that only 35 percent felt they had an adequate voice in the program, in contrast to 71 percent who felt that staff relations were adequate or good. Each category in exhibit 1 is an index derived from a set of larger questions. For example, category 11 was derived from the thirteen questions shown in exhibit 2. These data are fed back to the principals in the format shown in exhibit 3. Looking at exhibit 3, we can see considerable variation. Less than 20 percent of the principals felt that outstanding work by school personnel was adequately rewarded in the district. At the same time, more than 75 percent felt that they

EXHIBIT 1.   Principal Feedback Survey: Summary Profile

Number in group: 20 — PERCENTAGE FAVORABLE RESPONSES

Category	Item	Percentage Favorable Responses
General Administration	1. Administrative practices	(51%)
General Administration	2. Work load	(57%)
General Administration	3. Materials & equipment/Buildings & facilities	(53%)
Educational Program	4. Educational effectiveness	(66%)
Educational Program	5. Evaluation of students	(39%)
Educational Program	6. Special services	(47%)
Educational Program	12. Students	(56%)
Interpersonal Relations	7. School-community relations	(51%)
Interpersonal Relations	8. Supervisory relations	(60%)
Interpersonal Relations	9. Staff relations	(71%)
Interpersonal Relations	13. Principal relations	(42%)
Interpersonal Relations	14. District office-principal relations	(41%)
Career Fulfillment	10. Voice in educational program	(35%)
Career Fulfillment	11. Performance & development	(49%)
Career Fulfillment	15. Reactions to survey	(75%)

(Scale: 0 10 20 30 40 50 60 70 80 90 100)

were encouraged frequently enough to attend outside professional conferences and workshops.

This survey feedback constitutes research data. Principals meet periodically and discuss the underlying causes of the various problems reflected by the data. When a collective decision is reached on how best to solve a particular problem, they implement the solution (assuming it is within their control). If the solution requires district-level action, a meeting is held with the superintendent or other central office staff.

EXHIBIT 2. Principal Survey Category 11: Performance and Development

Number	Item		Percentage of Favorable Response
1	Outstanding work by school personnel is adequately rewarded in this district.	A	18.2
2	I'm rarely told whether or not I'm doing good work.	D	22.7
3	I do not understand how my work performance is evaluated.	D	27.3
4	I am seldom encouraged to attend outside professional conferences and workshops.	D	77.3
5	My work here provides me with ample opportunity for personal growth and development.	A	54.5
6	Men and women in this district have equal opportunities for promotion and advancement.	A	68.2
7	This district too strongly emphasizes "professional development," graduate study, attending conferences, etc.	D	86.4
8	Our procedures for evaluating faculty members seem to be effective.	A	63.6
9	Our procedures for evaluating administrators seem to be effective.	A	18.2
10	Our procedures for evaluating nonprofessional staff members seem to be effective.	A	40.9
11	Our teacher in-service education programs genuinely promote staff development.	A	31.8
12	Teachers have insufficient voice in the selection of in-service educational programs.	D	40.9
13	This district provides adequate in-service education for principals.	A	45.5

EXHIBIT 3. Principal Survey Category II: Performance and Development

Overall 47.6% Favorable

Percentage Favorable Responses

	Percentage Favorable (X)	Unfavorable	Undecided
1. Adequately rewarded work	~15	68.2	13.6
2. Not told about quality of my work	~25	77.3	0
3. Evaluation of performance	~30	59.1	12.5
4. Seldom encouraged to attend workshops	~72	18.2	4.5
5. Work provides growth opportunity	~52	40.9	6.1
6. Equal opportunity	~62	18.2	13.6
7. District emphasizes "professional development"	~77	9.1	4.5
8. Effective evaluation procedures (faculty)	~57	31.8	6.2
9. Effective evaluation procedures (administration)	~22	72.7	9.1
10. Effective evaluation procedures (nonprofessional)	~42	50.0	9.1
11. In-service programs promote development	~37	54.5	13.6
12. Teachers have insufficient voice	~42	40.9	17.0
13. Adequate in-service education for principals	~42	50.0	4.5

To facilitate the principals' effective use of the data feedback in their group problem-solving meetings, the project staff conducted an intensive two-day training session at a site outside the school district. Among the areas covered in this session were procedures for feeding back data to the group by the elected "group facilitator," guidelines for the conduct of feedback sessions, and problem-solving thinking and guidelines. Exhibit 4 presents feedback guidelines or procedures; exhibit 5 describes guidelines for the feedback sessions. Exhibit 6 describes a reflective-thinking problem-solving sequence, and exhibit 7 describes selected problem-solving guidelines.* The reader should find many of these materials helpful in a variety of group problem-solving settings.

*Exhibits 4 through 7 were developed by Robert Cooke, Robert Duncan, Emmet McHenry, Monty Mohrman, Susan Mohrman, and Gerald Zaltman.

EXHIBIT 4. Feedback Procedures

Favorable versus Unfavorable Responses: The information is fed back in terms of the percentage of *favorable, unfavorable,* and *undecided* responses. A favorable response is one that indicates positive feelings about the issue being tapped by the item. If the item is worded positively (e.g., "In general, I approve of school-board policies"), an Agree response is favorable. If the item is negatively worded (e.g., "It is sometimes difficult to obtain substitute teachers"), a Disagree response is favorable.

In interpreting the information that is fed back, it is important to keep in mind that the scores indicate percentage of responses that were favorable, rather than percentage of responses in agreement with the item.

Wording of Items: As you look back over the items, you may notice that some are worded more strongly than others. Thus, at face value it may appear that an unfavorable response to one item is a stronger negative comment than an unfavorable response to another. Also, it is possible that on some items there may be disagreement about whether a particular response really is a negative commentary on the work situation.

It is best not to let the discussion focus on the particular wordings of items, but to concentrate on deciding whether the issue raised in the question is indicative of an underlying problem that merits the attention of the problem-solving group.

Summary Profiles: The Summary Profile presents the percentages of favorable response in each category. There are two ways of thinking about these percentages. First, they can be thought of as indicating the average number of favorable responses in that category—i.e., on the average each principal answered, say, 60% of the items in that category favorably. So, if the category had 10 items, on the average 6 items were responded to favorably.

The second way to think about the percentages is in terms of the total number of possible positive responses. In a particular category there are x number of items (say, 10) which are answered by y number of people (say, 20). Thus, there are x times y total possible answers ($10 \times 20 = 200$). The percentage tells us what percent of this total was answered.

The Summary Profile is useful in detecting general areas that are perceived as comparatively favorable or unfavorable. It *may* be used to help decide which categories to focus on first in the feedback of the detailed results. However, one should bear in mind that, even in categories with a highly favorable overall response rate, there may be several items that had very unfavorable responses and that may indicate underlying problems which could be important to the group members. Therefore, it is useful to look at every category individually.

On the left side of the Summary Profile the categories are grouped into four general areas: *General Administration, Educational Program, Interpersonal Relations,* and *Career Fulfillment.* This is one way to delineate the major areas being tapped by the questionnaire, and it is possible that the pattern of category scores within these areas might provide useful information to the group in directing its feedback and problem-solving activities.

Detailed Profiles: A profile of the items in each category is also presented. For each item, three pieces of information will be fed back:

1. Percentage favorable responses
2. Percentage undecided responses
3. Percentage unfavorable responses

EXHIBIT 4. *(Continued)*

In interpreting each category and the individual items within the category, several things should be kept in mind:

There are *several possible interpretations* that can be ascribed to an item. Bringing these interpretations out in the discussion can enhance the ability of the group to determine the underlying problem, if there is one.

Most of the items in the questionnaire represent *symptoms* of a problem rather than the problem itself. One of the principal reasons for having group discussion is to get at underlying problems.

The *pattern of responses within a category* may provide useful information in determining underlying problems. It is helpful to notice not only which items are unfavorable, but also those that received favorable responses. Each item score is data that may be helpful in focusing in on the problem area and its subcomponents.

The items in the questionnaire are stated in general terms. The meaning of the responses only becomes clear when the group can deal with *what it is in their work situations that caused the group members to respond the way they did.*

The items or the problem areas that they relate to will vary in *salience or importance* to the group and its members. Group discussion is a way to determine which problems the group perceives to be important enough to commit itself to the problem-solving process.

EXHIBIT 5. Guidelines for the Feedback Sessions

---

1. *Your suggestions:* An attempt is made to have the total group contribute to the discussion.

2. *Diagnose problems first, suggest solutions later:* Initial stress is placed on problem definition and specification; the generation of solutions is deferred. Suggestions and options are solicited regarding whether the survey results reveal problems and, if so, specifically what they are.

3. *Group feels . . . :* Group members are encouraged to say, "Perhaps the group feels this way because . . ." rather than "I feel so because . . ." to keep the discussion on a less personal level. This rule was designed to help the members express their thoughts as members of the group rather than as isolated individuals.

4. *Titles, not names:* To keep the discussions "objective" and "factual," the emphasis is on organizational roles and relationships rather than on personal and interpersonal problems. Group members are encouraged to use job titles or organizational functions to be performed rather than names.

5. *No leader evaluation:* The principal leader is encouraged not to evaluate member contributions. The objective is to have all members contribute their ideas and opinions without the feeling that their statements will be judged by the leader as "good" or "bad."

6. *Minutes, but no names:* The group monitor records the ideas expressed during the meetings but does not mention any names. Individual principals or a subcommittee of the group are invited to review the minutes later to determine whether they accurately reflect the group's thinking.

EXHIBIT 5. *(Continued)*

7. *Understandable specification of problems:* The statement of problems must be precise and understandable to people in other parts of the system.

8. *Disagreement as source of ideas:* The leader and members should perceive members' disagreement as a source of ideas rather than as an obstacle to problem solving.

EXHIBIT 6. Reflective-Thinking Problem-Solving Sequence

1. *A Felt Difficulty.* The logical process of problem solving begins with an awareness of a problem. This first step involves the following procedure:

   Phrasing the problem. The question must be worded so that it cannot be answered by yes or no.

   Definition of terms. All words in the statement of the problem must be clear.

   Limitation of the subject. Unless prediscussion meetings are held to phrase the question, it will be necessary to limit the subject at the beginning of the problem-solving session.

2. *Analaysis of the Problem.*

   Background. New problems without precedent require little time for this step. However, most problems have histories, and the facts uncovered by the group will accelerate the problem-solving process.

   Causes and effects. Group participants must be able to demonstrate any relationship of cause and effect that they propose as solution for the problem.

   Test to be applied to group's causal reasoning:
   a. Does the alleged cause produce other effects?
   b. Does the alleged cause actually produce the effect?
   c. Do other modes of reasoning support an alleged causal relationship?
   d. Can the alleged cause be verified?

   Goals. The goals set forth during the analysis of the problem actually constitute the criteria or requirements for a satisfactory (optimum) solution.

3. *Finding Possible Solutions.* All solutions to a problem should be considered by the group. The seemingly "impossible" solution or far-fetched suggestion often contains the germs of ideas that can be modified and adopted into workable solutions.

4. *Evaluation of Proposed Solutions and Choice of Best Solution.* The solution should accomplish the following:

   a. It should meet the needs of the group.
   b. It should lessen or eliminate the cause of the problem.
   c. Its advantages must outweigh its disadvantages.
   d. It must work. (Smile.)

5. *Applying the Solution.* The final step is to devise a plan of action that will implement the solutions.

EXHIBIT 7. Problem-Solving Guidelines

1. *Subproblem identification:* The objective is to identify and delineate problems and to break these down into their key components. The leader is responsible for moving the group from the symptom to the problem to the subproblem definition.

2. *Basic reasons and causes:* In an effort to identify underlying organizational dynamics, each subproblem is analyzed for its specific reasons and causes.

3. *Multiple alternatives:* The group is encouraged to identify a number of possible solutions for each problem rather than arrive at just one or two remedies.

4. *Decisions later:* As ideas for improvement are generated, it is understood that solutions will not be evaluated immediately. Final evaluation of alternatives and selection of the "best" solution are postponed until alternatives have been carefully examined.

5. *Avoidance of financial remedies:* The group is discouraged from only generating solutions that simply require "more money." Attention is directed toward proposals that involve a more efficient use of existing resources. As part of the process, the group is encouraged to engage in a "cost-benefit analysis" of proposed remedies.

6. *Positive statements:* The principals are asked to offer suggestions in the form of positive statements. For example: "Communication between the school board and the principals can be improved by . . ." is preferred to "The school board doesn't let us know about. . . ."

7. *Action to take:* After alternative solutions are evaluated, the group selects what it perceives to be the best course of action. This includes steps to be taken at the school level within the purview of principal authority as well as those recommendations to be communicated up the line to the policy committee for approval.

8. *Written communications:* Decisions requiring legitimation at the policy committee level should be forwarded in written form. The problem and proposed solution should be clearly stated, with responsibilities delineated.

9. *Request response:* Matters forwarded to the policy committee can be accompanied by a request for action by a certain time. This can be done inoffensively by saying something like: "We would like the response of the policy committee three days before our next principal group meeting, which will be on . . ."

10. A timetable is kept of the action program initiated for each problem analyzed. This includes starting dates, interim progress reports, and completion dates.

11. *Follow-up on results* Periodically, each problem area is reviewed by the principal leader or the group to determine what has been done, how well solutions have been implemented, and overall results.

The survey-feedback process is one way to link the knowledge production and use activities. Other types of temporary systems (see chapter 5 for background on temporary systems) are also useful. For example, action research and cooperative action inquiry, both similar to the Rogers, Lin, and Zaltman research-use model, provide for interaction and collaboration between researchers and practitioners. Collaborative action centers on the following activities:

1. defining the problem area
2. retrieving research findings from both the problem target institution and other sources external to the institution
3. deriving implications from research for problem solving or program change
4. making decisions for change strategies and programs

The task force or team approach provides for various role types and functional expertise in knowledge production and use within the temporary problem-solving group.

These temporary linking systems are designed to lower individual and organizational barriers to knowledge use. A more permanent or ongoing linking network is advocated for the healthy self-renewing organization following the P/ICM processes of organizational change.

Why Research Is Not Readily Used

Before we proceed further, it is necessary to highlight some of the major reasons why educational research is not as widely used in educational practice as it could be. All of the following reasons concern a communications gap between researchers and practitioners.

1. One reason why research use is a problem is simply that it is not trusted. Practitioners who lack sophistication in research technologies are understandably reluctant to act upon information generated through processes they cannot evaluate.

2. Researchers often do not have policy or practice relevant information ready when the decision makers need it. This may be due to the sometimes considerable amount of time required to mobilize research resources and conduct a carefully designed study. If the practitioner cannot defer taking action until sound research is made available by social scientists, he will simply not make a research request at all. Thus, the challenge is to find ways of reducing the gap between the recognition of an information need by practitioners and the production of that information by researchers. One possible solution is to develop a technology for forecasting educational policy questions.

3. The practical relevance of existing social science research or knowledge may not be evident to either practitioners or researchers.

4. Practitioners may not know of the existence of research findings whose decision-making implications are self-evident. Similarly, researchers may not be aware of practitioner needs that they can clearly connect with their work. Thus, another challenge is to develop effective mechanisms for fostering interaction between researchers and practitioners.

5. Some researchers, especially those in academic institutions, are better rewarded for doing research without direct policy relevance. There are institutions in which action research is not considered as respectable as theoretically oriented research. The task here is to find ways to persuade not only theoretically oriented experts in education, but also similarly oriented sociologists, political scientists, and anthropologists, that practice settings are good contexts in which to develop and test theories.

6. Practitioners have been unable to translate their information needs into problems attractive to researchers, especially those in academic settings. Perhaps we need training mechanisms in our education courses and workshops that will develop skills in classifying practical problems in terms of theoretical issues. This has the advantage of helping the practitioner who does his or her own research to know where to look for relevant ideas about problems.

7. Many practicing educators fail to pass along information about the application of new or developing theories to other professional peers, researchers, and disseminators.

These reasons for the limited use of research in education settings highlight the need for linking systems and networks in educational change and development. As noted in chapter 6, the use of linking systems and linking roles will greatly enhance the KP&U process. Managers of educational change, change agents, researchers, and others, have developed a number of perspectives on the linking of organizations and individuals involved in KP&U. Some of these are noted below.

Some Perspectives on Knowledge Use

Rogers, Havelock, and Clark and Guba provide useful and interesting overviews of the KP&U process. Rogers's (1973c) conceptualization, presented in figure 10-2, features the direct and indirect interaction between three social systems involved in the research-using subsystem of the KP&U macrosystem: (1) the research system, including researchers, (2) linking systems, which translate clients' needs to researchers and diffuse innovations to clients, and (3) the client system, which recognizes needs for research and thus leads to its initiation, and which later adopts resulting innovations.

Havelock and Havelock (1973) offer a somewhat different perspective. In their conceptual framework, there is initially a user self-servicing effort that, when inadequate, results in need processing. Need processing begins with sens-

FIGURE 10-2. Paradigm of the Research Utilization Process
Source: Rogers 1973.

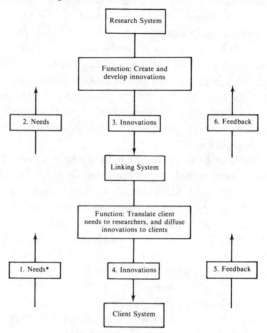

Function: Recognize the needs for research, and adopt innovations

1. Flow of user needs (for information) to linkers.
2. After interpretation and clarification, these needs are transferred to the research system.
3. Researchers attempt to provide needed information for users' needs, either from accumulated knowledge or via newly originated research.
4. Linkers distill and interpret this new information (innovations) for users.
5. Feedback from users to linkers on the adequacy of the new information in meeting their needs.
6. Linkers convey users' feedback to researchers, perhaps leading to further user needs and recycling of the entire process.

ing and assessing the unmet need and ends with the transformation of that need into researchable problems. Solution builders work on these problems and eventually deliver solutions and provide consultative assistance to users. Related to solution processing is what the Havelocks refer to as microsystems building. Solution builders (knowledge sources) interact in close and immediate ways with solution users (knowledge users), thus creating a new system consisting of organizational linkage. An even larger system may exist, the macro system, which functions to create widespread awareness of problems common to both solution builders and solution users. Government agencies such as the National Institute of Education and the Office of Education, professional associations, and other such bodies often serve this function in the larger national education system.

Clark and Guba (1975) criticize existing educational policy growing out of the research-development-dissemination-adoption perspective for diffusion of innovations. The RDDA perspective is a unified systems perspective, and federal policy growing from it is inadequate, given the realities of the KP&U processes and entities in education. The RDDA perspective can be seen in the Havelock model of RD&D (see figure 6-2), with "consumption" being analogous to "adoption" as an end point. The failure of state and federal educational policy growing out of the RDDA perspective has created a number of problems, including (1) unachievable objectives, (2) failure to consider individual and organizational missions in the KP&U process (often placing KP&U activities in low priority), and (3) overcentralizing and overcontrolling of programs in the KP&U process (Clark and Guba 1975:6). Rather than a system tied together through common purposes and aspirations, Clark and Guba describe educational KP&U from a *configurational perspective*. They include a broad range of individuals and organizations loosely forming the educational KP&U arena.

> The configurational perspective is roughly analogous to the concept of a community. The variety of institutions and individuals concerned with and functioning in educational KPU are more likely to consider themselves to be related to one another in a community sense rather than an organizational one. [p. 8]

The configurational perspective provides a useful picture of how organizations and individuals operate in relation to KP&U.

A. Not sharing a common conception of necessary or desirable KPU outputs.
B. Viewing KPU activity as subordinate to their primary activity.
C. Functioning essentially independent of one another.
D. Playing overlapping roles in relation to KPU.
E. Maintaining no binding authority relationship to one another.
F. Operating with no functional flow across organizational boundaries.
G. Sharing minimal activity relationships. [p. 9]

The Clark and Guba perspective is very useful not only in pointing out the current state of the national educational KP&U area, but also in pointing out the need for the development of both temporary and permanent linking systems among educational agencies. It is clear that linking systems and linking roles would be useful in closing some of the obvious gaps among individuals and organizations noted above.

In addition to the overview perspectives provided above, there are several models for linking systems more applicable to the change-target institutions. The following perspectives are commonly found in the literature on organizational change and linkage: (1) research, development, and dissemination, (2) social interaction, (3) problem solving, (4) change-planner systems, (5) broker institutions, and (6) ombudsmanlike organizations.

The *RD&D model* of linking networks, similar to the RDDA perspective, is presented in chapter 6 as a linear model of KP&U viewing the change-target organization as the passive receiver of educational knowledge, innovations, and products. The *social interaction* concept, also presented in chapter 6, is more analogous to the configurational perspective of the educational KP&U macrosystem. Loose linkages, often ad hoc and with little systematic effort, bring together individuals and organizations in the KP&U processes—research, development, diffusion, practice, and so on.

The *problem-solving perspective* (see chapter 6) is similar to the problem-solving systems analysis process with the addition of a "retrieval" phase for external knowledge/innovation seeking and linking with resource sources.

The *change-planner systems perspective* presents a similar problem-solving linking strategy and KP&U model for organizations. The Cooperative Project for Educational Development (COPED) provides an example of a collaborative network of schools and universities using a process of planned change designed around organizational problem solving and linkages to external resource institutions. A seven-stage model describes the basis for such an approach: (1) developing a need for change, (2) establishing a satisfactory relationship between change planner and target system, (3) clarifying the target-institution (client-group) problem, (4) identifying alternative plans of action for problem solving, (5) choosing an alternative and introducing it to the client system, (6) stabilizing or institutionalizing the innovation or implemented change, and (7) achieving a terminal relationship.

The *knowledge-broker system* and *ombudsman organization* are similar to the eclectic linking strategy that follows. As noted earlier, there is a strong need to translate knowledge for the change-target institution. The broker system and ombudsman organization provide the change-target institution with specific people and agencies that provide linkage and translation roles. They can be found as part of the following eclectic linkage system and strategy. The reader is urged, however, to consult the excellent work done by Sam D. Sieber and his colleagues (Sieber et al. 1972; Sieber and Louis 1973; Sieber 1973) for a complete discussion of the use of field agents in education. This work borrows heavily from the agricultural extension agent program.

AN ECLECTIC MODEL OF KNOWLEDGE/RESOURCE UTILIZATION

The P/ICM provides for linkage at various stages of the change process. The linking model presented in figure 6-5 (page 161) provides for

1. linkages between knowledge-producing and knowledge-using systems
2. a free flow of knowledge produced and used (and freedom for members of various systems to shift roles)

FIGURE 10-3. A Model of an Educational Linking Network for Planned Organizational Change

Source: Adapted from Florio 1973 and Havelock 1969.

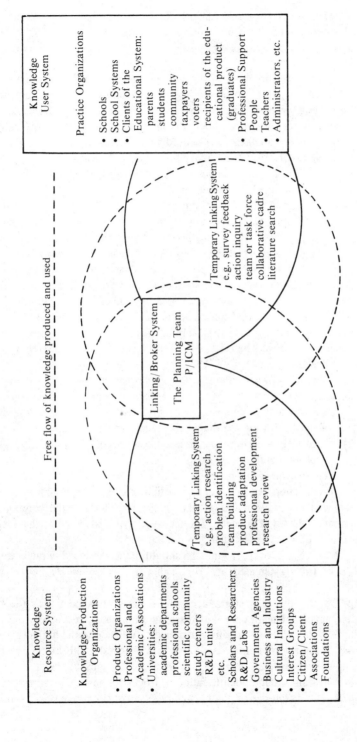

Knowledge
User System

Practice Organizations

• Schools
• School Systems
• Clients of the
  Educational System:
    parents
    students
    community
    taxpayers
    voters
    recipients of the edu-
      cational product
      (graduates)
• Professional Support
  People
• Teachers
• Administrators. etc.

Free flow of knowledge produced and used

Temporary Linking System
e.g., survey feedback
action inquiry
team or task force
collaborative cadre
literature search

Linking/Broker System

The Planning Team
P/ICM

Temporary Linking System
e.g., action research
problem identification
team building
product adaptation
professional development
research review

Knowledge
Resource System

Knowledge-Production
Organizations

• Product Organizations
• Professional and
  Academic Associations
• Universities:
    academic departments
    professional schools
    scientific community
    study centers
    R&D units
    etc.
• Scholars and Researchers
• R&D Labs
• Government Agencies
• Business and Industry
• Cultural Institutions
• Interest Groups
• Citizen/Client
  Associations
• Foundations

3. a linkage/broker system (the P/ICM planning team, a more permanent change/organizational monitoring function)
4. a variety of other temporary systems that should arise on an ad hoc basis

The various roles involved in the linkage process can include many of the following labels: conveyor (of knowledge and innovations), consultant, trainer, leader, innovator, defender, knowledge builder as linker, practitioner as linker, user as linker, integrator, developer, disseminator, diffuser, broker/translator, social engineer. The labels are often used to describe the various actors in the KP&U process involved in the linking function or "retrieving basic or applied knowledge, deriving practical implications from it, and distributing it to people who need it and can use it." (Short 1973:255).

The P/ICM approach to knowledge use builds upon the works of Rogers, Havelock, Glaser, Argyris, Guba and Clark, and other scholars who have participated in the development of concepts, practices, and other knowledge of the KP&U processes in social systems. While building upon this work, we are also making extensive additions of new elements or considerations growing out of the principles derived from the various sources of knowledge dealing with planned change in educational organizations. A series of detailed steps is presented below which is both descriptive and normative with regard to the process whereby a problem is recognized and a solution applied. An illustrative example follows the presentation of the steps. The reader is also urged to consult Lazarsfeld and Reitz (1975) and Kilmann and Mitroff (1976).

Step 1. Initially a *performance gap* or disturbance of the status quo occurs; a gap is created between what the preferred performance of the system is and what the actual performance is. This step corresponds to the following P/ICM processes and stages: (a) awareness/diagnosis: problem identification (performance gaps), (b) need assessment (determining client needs), (c) linking (gaining diagnostic problem-identification skills).

Step 1.1. An *index or measure of performance* of a curriculum unit, administrator, teacher, organizational function, etc. should be identified which is accurate and not confounded by phenomena unrelated to the component of the educational system of concern. The measure should also be one that responds rapidly to change in the particular component.

Step 1.2. Levels of performance should be established which are considered to be (a) very inadequate, (b) inadequate, (c) adequate, (d) very adequate.

Step 1.3. Levels of performance should be established which the school system is capable of achieving with varying amounts of resources, e.g., with more funds, with additional technical expertise, with additional human resources (and from a variety of human capital resource pools), with human resources outside of the educational scene. (This step corresponds to the initial P/ICM resources/constraints stage: identification of forces for and against change, etc.)

Step 2. The difference or gap between the actual performance of some component of the educational system and what the component is capable of performing with available or readily acquired resources is judged to have *reached or exceeded a critical threshold*. This step corresponds to the following P/ICM stages: (a) resources/constraints (emphasis on aids and forces for and against achieving objectives), (b) objectives (problem-solving purpose identification), (c) statement of organizational mission (where applicable goals and objectives have been given), (d) linking (search for potential resources that can be realistically incorporated), and (e) need assessment.

Step 2.1. It is necessary to define the capability of the component under consideration. That is, in addition to its actual performance, what is its potential performance level?

Step 2.2. It is also necessary to determine how realistic an expected or desired level of performance is, given possible limited resources for component improvement and possible inherent limitations in the component itself. Built-in constraints on resource use should be given.

Step 3. The *reason(s) for the gap* between actual and desired performance is determined. This is a problem-definition task (see Zaltman and Burger 1975; Zaltman and Duncan 1977). This step corresponds to the following P/ICM stages: (a) awareness/diagnosis, (b) resources/constraints, (c) linking, and (d) need assessment.

Step 3.1. It is necessary to determine whether there are possible explanatory variables that function in time periods considerably removed from the period when performance gaps are first noted.

Step 3.1.2. Whether there are possible explanatory or causal variables related to a performance gap at certain times and not at others is determined.

Step 3.2. The most plausible explanatory variables are selected. Plausibility is established by virtue of logic, past experience, past research, and soundness of the underlying theory or model.

Step 3.3. It is necessary to determine whether variables among the most plausible set are (a) sufficient but not necessary, (b) necessary but not sufficient, (c) both necessary and sufficient, or (d) neither necessary nor sufficient.

Step 3.4. It is also necessary to determine relationships among the causal or explanatory variables and between these variables and the problem symptom.

Step 4. *A decision is made to close the performance gap*. Priorities for problem solving are made. This step corresponds to the following P/ICM stages: (a) objectives (problem-solving purposes identified), (b) resources/constraints, (c) linking and the initial formulation of alternative solutions, and (d) alternative solutions (mental reality testing of alternative courses of action in the light of resources and constraints identified).

Step 4.1. Variables that can and cannot be influenced by the educator are identified.

Step 4.2. Possible actions to be taken by the educator are identified and matched with those variables that can be changed by the educator and those to which the educator must adapt.

Step 5. *A search is made for ways to close the performance gap* (use of resource linking networks).

Step 5.1. Existing knowledge about the relevant variables identified during step 3 is assessed.

Step 5.1.1. Existing knowledge should be assessed for its help in understanding how the important variables or factors relate to one another and contribute to the performance gap.

Step 5.1.2. Existing knowledge should be assessed for its relevance in guiding the educator in his manipulation of certain variables and adaptation to others.

Step 5.2. It should be determined whether new knowledge is necessary for steps 5.1.1. and 5.1.2. and readily obtained through new research, existing research, evaluation studies, and other data sources.

Step 6. A solution or set of solutions is selected for trial. This step corresponds to the following P/ICM stages: (a) alternative solutions (attitude formation), (b) initiating the turnkey phase, and (c) testing/trial (demonstration).

Step 6.1. The trial stage occurs when solutions are put into effect on a small scale or in only a subunit of the organization.

Step 6.2. All members of the organization are involved in review of the demonstration or in trial efforts.

Step 7. At the conclusion of the trial stage it is necessary to decide whether to (a) implement the change on a permanent and/or full scale, (b) explore other potential solutions, (c) wait until better solutions become available through further research and development, or (d) work back up the planning and knowledge-use process to discover errors or to redefine and identify critical factors affecting problem solutions. This step corresponds to the following P/ICM stages: (a) decision making (adoption/rejection), (b) turnkey phase, (c) implementation or (d) further alternative building, (e) awareness/diagnosis (problem reformulation), (f) further need assessment, and (g) linking.

This basic procedure has been used quite successfully in several educational settings for both curriculum and organizational development change. One of the most interesting applications occurred in a school district in southern Illinois. This district had been experiencing exceedingly high teacher turnover in its elementary, junior high, and senior high schools for several consecutive years and had been sharply criticized by departing teachers—and by some who stayed on—for being extremely conservative in educational and administrative practices. Indeed, there was considerable evidence, gathered by a consultant team, that students in a neighboring school district that had essentially the same community culture performed better on standardized tests and in their first year in post–high school educational programs.

Although the problem was district-wide, we shall concentrate in this example on the behavior of a newly appointed junior high school principal. During his first two years, the new principal was very successful in attracting and, through strong personal persuasion, in keeping innovative teachers. The influx of these new teachers disturbed a characteristic pattern in which innovative teachers left after a year and conservative teachers stayed on. The school principal deliberately created this disturbance in the status quo, which caused much resistance and led to the resignation of three conservative teachers. As a result of the *planned imbalance* favoring innovative teachers, a consensus developed that the school should be more venturesome than it was (step 1). This consensus was carefully developed by the principal. During his second and third years at the school, he established several task forces (with overlapping membership); these were temporary systems that essentially were charged with the responsibility of performing steps 1.1 and 1.3 with regard to various aspects of the school's operation. Summaries of each task-force report were prepared and circulated among the school personnel. Collectively, the various summaries made it abundantly evident that the school needed considerable overall remedial attention. They were presented to the district superintendent and clearly showed him which difficulties in the junior high school exceeded what acceptable levels of trouble (step 2). The principal, along with the superintendent and his staff, agreed that students, teachers, and other staff personnel were basically well qualified and could perform much better (step 2.1). It was also agreed that for some problems financial resources were readily available, partly from local funds but also through state and federal programs. The principal felt strongly that his staff did indeed have the training and motivation to improve specific problems; in fact, he stated that he had worked very hard for over two years to attract and keep highly competent staff in the belief that the school district could acquire and provide the resources they needed to function more effectively (step 2.2).

Although the staff identified several problems, one of particular importance was the apparent professional isolation of the regular and special-education teaching staff. Exposure to new developments in the education field generally was quite low for the district as a whole, but less so for the junior high school staff. In fact, the junior high staff subscribed to a much larger average number of professional journals than teachers in any other school. Still, the teachers felt they needed more contact with innovative developments. Thus, a very specific performance gap was identified, namely, a gap between actual and desired contact with new developments in education. The relative lack of contact was felt to have a stultifying effect on the ability of teaching and nonteaching staff to innovate.

The lack of contact in previous years had apparently resulted from a lack of interest among the staff, including the former principal. In a very real sense, there was no performance gap at that time. Consequently, no provision, financial or procedural, existed to facilitate contact with sources of new information. This caused some degree of frustration among most of the current teachers.

The principal decided (step 4) to make this problem among the first difficulties he tackled. He was able to obtain some additional but limited funding from the central district office as well as from a federal foundation. He reallocated certain funds over which he had control and established a fund to be used by teachers for such purposes as attending conferences and symposiums, bringing in special persons for workshops or general staff counseling, visiting regional R&D laboratories, and so forth. A committee of four teachers administered the fund, and, in the event of deadlocks in allocation decisions, the principal cast the deciding vote.

The decision to establish the fund (called the "fun fund" by critics) and to have it administered primarily by teachers was not arbitrary or based on intuition. The principal had made several phone calls and had written several letters to principals of schools both in and out of the state who were known to be innovative (step 5). In addition, a consultant on educational change spent two days visiting with the staff and advising the principal on a broad range of issues. In fact, the consultant had suggested the names of many of the persons the principal contacted by telephone and letter. The consultant was very supportive of the idea to establish the fund and allow the staff to help decide how the money would be spent. He cited a number of cases in which such a plan had been effective and was able to provide a good explanation of why it should work well for this particular school. Essentially, the principal and the consultant performed step 5.1. The fund was actually established several months before the federal support became available (step 6). The fund was to run for a period of eighteen months on a trial basis. After approximately fourteen months it was considered so successful that it became permanent (step 7), and other schools in the district had begun similar efforts (dissemination within district).

Aids and Barriers to Organizational Collaboration

"There is a high relationship between self-perception of potency to influence one's environment and openness to learn from it" (Lippitt 1974). The more reciprocal the influence of knowledge exchange is perceived to be among individuals in the KP&U process, the more likely that knowledge will be constructively used in the planning of change.

By their very nature, organizations are conservative. They take on the *survival* characteristics of humans in many ways. To protect themselves from chaos and disintegration, the organizations must maintain some steady state, or *stability*. They have goals and objectives that form the *purpose* for their existence and participants that form their *membership*.. All of these entities come into play when an organization works with its environment or other organizations.

These components of organizations can act as a filtering system for messages, ideas, and innovations flowing both into and out of the organization. The ability of messages to flow freely and without distortion within a resource/knowledge-sharing network of organizations will depend on the balance between (1) the organizations' "drive to maintain order and certainty," which "tends to create structures, hierarchies, requirements, and screening procedures which act as barriers to knowledge flow," and (2) "the drive to innovate and improve," which tends to lower the barriers to knowledge flow (Havelock et al. 1971). A discussion of some influences that tip the scale in the balance between maintenance and change follows.

BARRIERS TO INPUT

As noted by Havelock et al. (1971), there are a number of barriers or inhibitors to the flow of research, ideas, innovations, programs, and other information into an organization. Some are described more briefly in chapter 2 as sources of resistance to change. However, they take on special significance for the more specific process of information flow. These are also barriers to the linking and collaboration process, which is greatly dependent on the free and accurate flow of information to open institutions.

Internal stability and the need to preserve it highlight the naturally conservative state of an organization. New information can be disrupting to the organization's "steady state" and thus may be ignored or distorted so that it no longer appears new or different.

Donald Schon (1967) points out that while new knowledge may appear disruptive to the steady state of an organization, it is also a potential threat to the informal structure of the organization. This informal structure, held together by *social relations,* may often be more important to members than the formal structure, and thus participants may fight harder to protect it. Team teaching is an example of an innovation that threatens to disrupt both the internal steady state of schools and informal social relationships in schools.

Stanley Seashore (1967) points out that groups often establish a *uniqueness of language* or a separate language in order to distinguish their identity or enlarge their sense of importance. This creates "communication differentials" or "coding barriers" for those not in the group. The jargon used in the field of education is often called educationese. The use of such catch terms as *interface, linking, role conflict, diffusion,* and *feedback* in this book may create coding barriers for some readers unless their meanings are made clear by their context. Even within the same field, different organizations have different language. Those engaged in research have a language not often used by practitioners. A researcher who has spent most of his professional life with other researchers may not know that not everyone understands the difference between a *chi-square* and a *t score* or between *mode, median,* and *mean.*

The fear of some outsider bent on doing harm is more prevalent in the highly competitive organizations of our society. In these organizations, a "win or lose" psychology permeates the interorganizational relationship. This fear that new information or ideas may be hidden threats to survival may cause organizational paranoia. This may change the quality controller, previously mentioned as a potential linker, into a negative force in organizational development. Although schools are not usually characterized by an intensely competitive atmosphere, their institutional paranoia is remarkable. Perhaps this paranoia stems from the competition for control, rather than from competition with other educational institutions. This competition for control extends to the three areas of government (local, state, and national), to professional groups (e.g., teacher association, administrator groups, and institutions of higher education), and within the organization and its environment. A current example centers on program budgeting systems. Program Planning Budgeting Systems (PPBS) was originated by the U.S. Department of Defense in order to secure tighter central (and civilian) control over the military expenditure in the 1960s. Although PPBS can be effectively used to either centralize or decentralize an operation (as with school systems), the concept has aroused fear that PPBS is a hidden move toward the federal takeover of local school operations. Local anti-PPBS groups have formed to block its entry into schools.

Personal threats to members of organizations are another source of resistance to new knowledge. New ideas and innovations often imply that the old ways are less efficient, antiquated, or counterproductive with regard to organizational goals. Individuals who for years have been advocating or participating in traditional methods of operation may feel severely threatened by innovations. The concept of organizational development carries with it the undercurrent theme of individual development as well. Community groups and champions of certain innovations have been known to call for the ouster of tradition-bound educators, causing deep anxiety feelings among such organizational members. This has been called the "devil theory" of organizational change. This theory implies that change will occur when the resistors (devils) are gotten rid of. More enlightened change strategies call for staff development efforts rather than exorcism. A more recent (OD) outlook is designed to provide alternative methods within organizations, thus allowing members options and a chance to observe the innovation in the local situation before deciding to try it themselves.

Institutional loyalty and pride are two more barrier-producing characteristics in organizations. In interviews with potential members of a school/university consortium project, school personnel commented that they though the concept of a collaborative network was a good one; but many remarked that "the [other institutions] will have much more to gain [from us] than we will from being part of such a project." (Florio, 1973a). Local pride in an organization is important for maintenance; however, when pride is extended to the belief that the only useful new knowledge is that which comes from members in the organization, institutional loyalty can have a serious stagnating effect on the organization. Organization members need to believe that an innovation has a good chance of improving the current situation before they adopt it and work for its implementation. There is also a serious barrier when *status differences* exist among potential collaborating organizations. Cultural and class differences are a part of this barrier-producing phenomenon. The more stratification there is within an organization, the less likely it is that innovations will be readily adopted. It follows that the more stratification between interacting organizations on social, cultural, and intellectual levels, the more difficult it is to collaborate in the planning and implementation of innovations. The practice and theory-producing organizations have some problems with status differences, as pointed out by Richard Schmuck (1968:150) in describing university and school interaction: "School administrators are viewed by researchers as being unsophisticated, anti-intellectual, and dependent, while researchers are viewed by educators as wanting to base everything done in the school on research and as 'having their heads in the clouds.'"

The *economic condition* of school systems has serious potential for inhibiting the flow of information to systems. In order to be adopted, innovations often have to be site-tested. Learning about and trying innovations often require the support of risk capital, a pool of funds, or other resources that are not committed to the operation and maintenance of the organization. Having risk capital, however, in no way guarantees the adoption of innovations. In a study of several Pennsylvania and West Virginia school districts, Richard Carlson (1965: 83–85) found no correlation between dollars spent per pupil in school systems and innovativeness. This finding refutes a number of earlier suppositions; however, Carlson's study may show that the other barrier and support factors will undercut the economic one even when the risk capital is present.

Another example of barrier-building potential is the *socialization* process of new members of the organization. Membership in an organization naturally separates the insiders from the outsiders. The socialization of the neophyte into a "don't rock the boat" attitude is not uncommon in educational institutions. This socialization into acceptance by established members of an organization can become a serious barrier to the flow of new ideas and innovations.

AIDS TO INPUT

The phenomena in organizations that facilitate entry of information are often a matter of realizing that it is more rewarding to change or that the status quo is more uncomfortable than some other structure or process. Even with many of the barriers to change and innovation, the present society and the rate of change in it make the introduction of new knowledge and information also important for survival. Present pressures to change and adapt have forced school systems to be more outward-looking.

Among the most powerful of aids to input of information and innovation is the *value system* of the organization that is *constantly seeking to improve*, is less satisfied with the status quo, and *rewards* the successful pursuit and application of innovative ideas. In education, innovative values are difficult both to measure and to achieve. In the building of a value system that rewards innovation, nothing succeeds like success. For example, the use of temporary systems in schools often provides an initial effort to create organizational innovativeness: "As change agents and organizational development strategies are perceived to be relevant to the school's needs, . . .administrators will be motivated to initiate and contribute to temporary system activities" (Cooke and Zaltman 1972:14).

Likewise, Coughlan, Cooke, and Safer (1972) found in a recent (OD) study that both school administrators and faculty participants in a "control group" also wanted to join in future organizational development projects: "Aside from increased observability of the results of the interaction, the motivation of these individuals possibly increased as a product of competitive, conformity, or 'bandwagon' factors."

A *change in leadership* can also have an effect on the openness of organizations to information and innovation. Griffiths (1964) agrees with Carlson's statement that "the number of innovations [in school systems] is inversely proportional to the tenure of the chief administrator" (quoted in Miles 1964). Both authors also agree that the amount of change in an organization is greater under new leadership when that leadership comes from outside the organization. This fits Carlson's (1972) description of a career-bound, as opposed to a place-bound, administrator with his progressive outlook.

Crisis or the perception of a crisis that has a potential threat to the organization is another motivating force for lowering barriers to information. When an innovation accompanies a crisis and has the appearance or historical implication of easing that crisis, the crisis becomes a great aid to the change process. A change in the "nonbureaucratic" head of an organization or reference group leader in a subunit may be perceived as a crisis, according to Etzioni (1964:56). Innovations are more easily introduced to "counteract deterioration or ward off challenges" during the transition period between leaders.

Schon (1967) points out that crisis may not always be accidental. A characteristic of many successful change planners is the ability to introduce deliberate crisis. This can take the form of a planned imbalance between the real and the ideal situation.

The uncomfortable feelings aroused by a real or potential crisis often create an atmosphere that encourages acceptance of new information. A comfortable organization is much less likely to seek outside information than one that has been disturbed by an awareness of a performance gap or a pending crisis (Bennis 1966a; Lippit et al. 1958). Mark Chesler and others advocate the use of crisis situations as growth opportunities. They call for individuals in organizations to occupy roles whose function is to encourage and facilitate "adaptive growth" for the institution and its members as a response to crisis situations (Chesler in Havelock and Havelock 1973).

The outward-looking organization often provides incentives to members for the *examination of other organizations*. Such examinations enable members to determine what is available in the field and to view demonstrations of innovative practices. Meetings, conferences, courses, conventions, site visits, demonstrations, participation of task-force teams, and temporary problem-solving systems are less direct ways of lowering the barriers to outside information flow. This *awareness* of new knowledge about innovations can be accomplished either by examination of an outside organization or by entry into or visitation of the organization by nonmembers. This includes the entry of leadership from outside the organization.

Both in-service and preservice *training* are important for the introduction of information into an organization. The new member of an organization can bring in both new and current information and experiences he or she has had in other positions.

As mentioned earlier, the ability to invest *risk capital* in innovations may have an effect on the flow of information and innovative processes into an organization. The *capacity* to both retrieve information and experiment with innovations may not ensure innovativeness; however, it may be essential to break the conservative pattern of less venturesome districts.

The *external change planner* has potential for bringing into an organization a variety of informational input; however, he may run into many barriers if he is not familiar with the organizational coding, values, self-perception, and environmental forces. When using an external agent or consultant it is essential that the contracting parties have a clear understanding of what is involved in and expected from the relationship. Kintzer and Chase have suggested the guidelines shown in list 11-1.

LIST 11-1. Practical Guidelines for Clearer Understanding Between Consultants and Clients

The school should request a proposal letter covering the following:

1. A definition of the problem to be solved
2. The objectives, scope, and nature of the project
3. The areas to be investigated
4. The program to reach objectives
5. The general methods to be used
6. The personnel to be assigned various tasks
7. The estimated length of time for the project
8. The estimated fees and method of billing
9. The qualifications of the consultant and other staff to be employed
10. References

The consultant's work should be monitored by determining the following:

1. If the project started on time
2. If any substitutions have been made in the personnel originally assigned to the project
3. If the principal consultant is actively involved
4. If the task is being conducted without undue conflict with the school system
5. If the data-collection procedure is biased in favor of initial predisposition
6. If the project is being delayed or slowed down to use up surplus time and funds

SOURCE: Kintzer and Chase 1969.

For school systems, there is another phenomenon that may encourage organizational openness. The *invader* in the educational marketplace may bring alternative practices and structures. Recently, "performance contractors" and "alternative schooling" organizations have tried to break into the monopoly of the conservative school system. One example is the Southern School in the Uptown neighborhood of Chicago. The school provides an alternative learning environment for youngsters from low-income families. Following the success of the Southern School, a number of public schools in the area formed "outposts" or "branches" with alternative learning environments.

In addition to the invaders and the external agents, the importing of human resources with expertise not held by organizational members can provide an opportunity for obtaining new knowledge and information on innovative practice.

The degree of success of change planners and new personnel in making organization members more open to information will be significantly affected by what Rogers and Shoemaker call homophily—the "degree to which pairs of individuals who interact are similar in certain attributes, such as beliefs, values, education, social status, and the like." Rogers and Shoemaker go on to say:

> In a free-choice situation, when a source can interact with any one of a number of receivers, there is a strong tendency for him to select a receiver who is most like himself.
>   ... When they share common meanings, a mutual subcultural language, and are alike in personal and social characteristics, the communication of ideas is likely to have greater effects in terms of knowledge gain, attitude formation and change, and overt behavior change. [Rogers and Shoemaker 1971:14,15].

Many organizations have internal knowledge-seeking subunits or roles. These departments or entities are oriented toward systematic research and development. The R&D unit in an organization carries two functions: the internal assessment of program and policy, and the external retrieval of new information and ideas. Katz and Kahn (1966) suggest that such units should be located near the bureaucratic top of an organization, reporting directly to the chief administrator. In this way, R&D personnel are perceived to have high status, and access to information will be easier. This may appear to run counter to Rogers's comments in that large status differentials may prevent the members of the R&D subunit from having effective interaction with others in the production part of the organization. They may even be viewed as a threat to the members' organizational survival. However, if the organizational subunit leader and/or respected authority figures legitimize the R&D unit, knowledge seeking and development within organizations take on increased credibility. Credibility is also enhanced when front-line performers of organizational tasks, such as teachers, participate in R&D groups and temporary problem-solving systems.

The concept of *professionalism* may provide a means of lowering barriers to information flow. This concept implies that the members of a profession are interested in furthering the profession itself as well as their own careers and organizations. Affiliations with and memberships in professional societies and an interest in keeping up with the literature are manifestations of the concept.

Fifteen Principles for Effective Knowledge Use

Although far from exhaustive, the principles for effective knowledge use given here represent the most basic considerations derived from the authors' own experiences and a review of the literature on the subject. The principles are presented from the standpoint of the user, although they are relevant to groups who fund and/or conduct research knowledge dissemination efforts and diffusion of innovations.

Principle 1. The educational system should provide, at various levels of the system, for a knowledge-use function.

This may be operationalized as a knowledge-use team established on an ad hoc basis as a particular problem arises. It is preferable, however, to have such a team on a permanent basis in which it systematically monitors the research and development activities in various areas of concern to the school system. The knowledge-use team should also have input from a problem-diagnosis team. There should be some overlap in membership between the two teams. Problem diagnosis is necessary to sensitize the knowledge-use team to specific problems or performance gaps. The team should exist in a formal way (especially at the district level) and appear on an organizational chart, and budgeting provision should be made to enable the office or team to function effectively. Ideally, knowledge-use teams should have members from different organizational levels, substantive areas, and, possibly on an "as needed" basis, people from outside the system.

Principle 2. The initiator of change should show a general willingness to alter his own operation or behavior.

There are two dimensions to this principle. First, the initiator of change should present himself or herself as flexible in a general way and thus be a role model, at least to a limited extent, for knowledge use. Second, when the knowledge being used as a basis for change involves change by the initator, he should demonstrate his willingness and intent to change as early as possible, even though the required adjustments on his part may not be necessary until much later in the change process.

Principle 3. Resources (broadly defined) should be available to implement change based on knowledge.

Resources are broadly defined here to include human, time, material, knowledge, and fiscal elements with the capacity to aid in the production of knowledge and for problem-solving processes of an organization.

A practice followed by one district superintendent in upstate New York is to have a specific line item in his budget allocated to the trial of new ideas resulting from advances in educational research and development. This "innovation fund" has facilitated some of the most successful educational changes in curriculum matters in his district. Knowledge of the availability of these funds has greatly heightened the sensitivity of teaching and nonteaching staff to new programs or ideas being reported in the journals, presented in professional conferences, or otherwise made known.

Principle 4. Resources should be available to develop staff capabilities for change.

In-service workshops or workshop days are not at all uncommon in schools. These workshops are often intended to improve teachers' abilities to change by increasing the knowledge foundation on which they build their activities. However, special change programs may require special skills not readily found in the school system anticipating or undergoing a specific change. Poorly planned or executed in-service workshops can be counterproductive when they fail to address themselves to the organizational problems perceived by the target audience. Thus, funds should be established for consultant services, for example. As noted above, not all resources are necessarily linked with funds. A major organizational development program being tried on an experimental basis in a large school district north of Chicago was very dependent upon key teachers, principals, and superintendent-office administrative staff with training in small-group dynamics, problem solving, and survey-feedback techniques. A major commitment was required by the school district superintendent to permit key individuals release time to participate in training programs. Additionally, a commitment was needed (and made) to let school out early for a number of days, thereby providing *time resources* for teachers and others to participate in the organizational development program. The very fact that such a commitment was made by the superintendent increased motivation in the district to participate. Thus, even *motivation* can be considered an important nonmonetary resource. The lack of these human resources acts as a significant constraint upon organizational innovativeness. This is especially so in labor-intensive institutions such as schools.

Principle 5. There should be a general sensitivity to the various constituents who could be affected by a change program.

Potential constituents include students, teachers, administrators, community leaders, and the school board. For example, in one elementary school participating in an organization development program based on survey feedback, a team of research users translated certain data they acquired into an action program involving the school librarian. Unfortunately, the librarian was not consulted prior to the change, and she resisted. She should have been consulted, not only to minimize potential resistance or conflict, but also so that she could contribute her special perspective to the interpretation of the data and formulation of a response to the problem that was uncovered.

Principle 6. It is necessary to establish a basic belief among members of the school system that research and new knowledge can improve existing and prospective change efforts.

As indicated earlier, a distrust of research exists among practitioners in all fields. Such distrust is not without foundation; hence, it is difficult to create an openness to research or a belief that research can benefit the school system. One way to establish such openness is to involve teachers in research efforts. Another way, largely unexplored, is to train teachers in methods for translating research into action. This will be discussed later in this chapter. Perhaps a lesson can be learned from another setting. Several business organizations have a monthly joint meeting to discuss selected research findings from the published literature. The basic question they pose is "What do these findings, if they are accurate, mean in terms of any of our present or future efforts?" Perhaps regularly scheduled meetings focusing on specific issues could be held to discuss the relevance of current research to the specific issues of concern to the school system, whether at the department, building, or district level. Such professional growth activities avoid the problem of individual bias and personal isolation.

Principle 7. The practice of continually translating program needs into researchable questions and projects should be encouraged.

In order to interact effectively with researchers or experts, practitioners must adapt somewhat to their thinking and way of organizing their knowledge. This should not be a one-way process, but realities are such that researchers do find it difficult to think in terms of practitioners' needs in addition to thinking in terms of research questions. Thus, in dealing with researchers or people familiar with research, a department chairman, teacher, or administrator should be prepared to ask a series of research questions. For example, rather than asking how unexcused absences can be minimized, they should ask what factors contribute to unexcused absences and which of these factors can be manipulated and how they can be manipulated by the school system to reduce unexcused absences. This enhances both the articulation of problems and the two-way linking system previously described.

Principle 8. Experiences with any change should be evaluated by persons with different perspectives, and the evaluations should be translated into recommendations for continuing and/or altering the change program. However, one person or group should be responsible for the evaluation and recommendations, while being careful to communicate with persons affected by the evaluation.

Every change should be treated as an experiment and monitored for suggestions that indicate a need for modification and redefinition. It is very important to have people who are expressing criticism or concern also suggest remedies that would make the change program work better. This helps create an open, constructive attitude toward change. Flexibility is enhanced when the target organization is open to such constructive review and input.

Principle 9. Research staff in an educational system should be trained to be sensitive to the need for developing and expressing the practical implications of their work. Care should be exercised to select research topics that are relevant to specific practitioner problems rather than topics that are of special theoretical or methodological interest.

This is not to say that theory and methodology are inappropriate in an educational system, but rather that they should be of secondary concern when they do not have an immediate bearing on school-system problems. When researchers are hired on a temporary basis, it should be made explicit that the research should help provide answers to specific problems. Action-research projects should seek, also, to articulate potential theory growing out of contemporary practice.

Principle 10. Research, teaching, and other staff should be rewarded for breaking out of the bounds of current practice and daring to be different.

A private secondary school in New York City has a special committee to review yearly all curriculum changes initiated by teachers during the preceding year. The teachers involved in the changes judged to be most innovative *and* successful are guaranteed total financial support from the school for attending any regional or national professional conference. At the time of this writing, the committee has been meeting for three years, and certain problems have begun to surface. One problem is that too many changes are being attempted without adequate advance study to assess their soundness and probable success in that particular school. Another problem is the difficulty of evaluating a change after it has been in effect for one year or less. Indeed, the nature of change in curriculum matters makes it difficult to assess under the best of circumstances. In general, however, the staff favors the program, and the school is working with a consultant to address the problems beginning to develop.

It is important to stress that using new knowledge does not need to result in significantly different programs. A small change in methods or means can produce major changes in results. For example, a teacher using a simulation game to teach consumer economics asked students to verbalize their behaviors as they proceeded through the game. The teacher found that students' understanding of their own behavior and the amount of learning taking place increased substantially. The teacher had gotten the idea for this practice in a discussion with a psychologist friend who had commented about the effect of verbalization and behavior on learning. Such practices highlight the advantages of two-way influence in resource-knowledge-sharing networks.

Principle 11. Mistakes in the research, translation, or implementation processes should be identified and the lesson(s) learned from them made clear. However, there should be a general understanding that mistakes are quite likely—perhaps inevitable—and should be viewed in a constructive spirit rather than in a spirit of criticism and blame.

Just as crisis can be used as an opportunity for growth, errors and mistakes in knowledge use can be used to broaden perspectives, increase awareness of resource constraints, and point out the areas needing more research. Some of the most effective research or knowledge-use programs in education and elsewhere have a formal stage in which problems or mistakes are identified. Having a formal stage for this activity in effect legitimizes the making of errors: it says, in effect, that errors are expected. Great care must be exercised, however, in performing the mistake-analysis function. It should be carried out in as depersonalized a fashion as possible. This is enhanced when the knowledge-use efforts are shared among a variety of organizational participants.

Principle 12. Research-project priorities should be based on the potential projects have for effective use as well as on the importance of the problem.

It is particularly important when establishing a new program or plan for knowledge use in education to have early successes to encourage further knowledge use. This does not mean that major problems cannot be dealt with at the outset. If resources permit, projects should be undertaken both where early success is possible and where success will be longer in becoming evident. Separate task forces can be established for each type of project or problem. When this is not possible, it is generally desirable to first have a knowledge-use effort that can be concluded early with a high probability of success, and then follow up with an effort where the magnitude of the problem requires a more difficult undertaking with less certainty of successful results. The demonstration effect of the first effort helps sustain enthusiasm during the more protracted effort required by the larger problem.

Principle 13. Continuous two-way communication between researchers and users should occur at all stages of the knowledge-use or action-research project and program implementation.

To the extent possible, users of research knowledge and projects should be consulted in the formulation of research questions, questionnaires, statistics to be used, and so forth. Similarly, two-way discussion between researchers and users is desirable when research results are being translated into practical applications by users.

Principle 14. Special incentives should be provided to motivate teachers, administrators, and other staff to use such internal resources of change knowledge as (1) teacher/researcher discussions and idea presentations, (2) in-service training, (3) curriculum supervisors and organizational development specialists, (4) library facilities, (5) research-evaluation staff, (6) media specialists, and (7) student discussions and idea presentations.

Considerable resources for change can often be found within the school system. Often, these resources are overlooked or the potential for developing such in-house expertise is not fully realized. Use of such resources can stimulate their development. A teacher or administrator who has some expertise in organizational development or a special curriculum matter may, if consulted or used as a resource, voluntarily act to enhance such expertise because of the rewarding experience of being asked for advice or opinions. The articulation of theory developed in the practices of organization members enhances self-esteem and respect for the theoretical bases of sound practice.

Principle 15. Special incentives should be provided to motivate teachers, administrators, and other staff to use such external resources as (1) state education agencies, (2) federal agencies, (3) universities and colleges, (4) professional associations, (5) ERIC, (6) regional educational laboratories, (7) foundations and other private sources, (8) consultants, and (9) publishers.

One incentive that has worked in a few schools is to allow teachers two or three half-days of release time every four to six months (at the cost to the school for a substitute teacher) to be used specifically for visiting or otherwise responding to the information obtained. Financial support is generally necessary to pay for long-distance telephone calls, the purchase of materials, and the costs of outside advisors. This resource allocation for the development of staff not only increases the constructive change processes of the organization, but also legitimizes external resources available to the organization but previously unused.

Summary

This chapter began with a discussion of knowledge production and use, emphasizing the need for an open relationship between the researcher and practitioner or user. The survey-feedback and problem-solving example demonstrated in detail how the practitioner also can be the knowledge producer. This would eliminate the communications gap between the two roles. The seven reasons why research is not readily used all concern this gap.

Several perspectives on knowledge utilization were presented as a background for a step-by-step guide to a descriptive and normative approach to planned change in educational organizations. Each step was illustrated in the case example of a Southern Illinois school district.

The needs for stability and survival, the purpose, and the membership of an organization can act as filters to messages, ideas, and innovations, thus affecting the balance between maintenance and change. Various aids and barriers to the free and accurate flow of information can have a great impact on organizational collaboration. Internal stability, jargon, institutional loyalty and pride, and the socialization process were among the barriers to input that were discussed. Some aids to input included values supporting change, new leadership, a crisis, awareness of new knowledge, and external resources. Finally, fifteen principles concerning organizations' attitudes, values, resource commitments, and use of research were presented. These principles represent the most basic considerations leading to effective knowledge use.

11

Basic Principles for Educational Change

THIS CHAPTER SUMMARIZES the most essential guidelines or principles a change planner should follow in any change effort. These principles are derived primarily from the discussions in previous chapters and are organized accordingly. A few principles not explicit in any of the chapters have been added for completeness. The sources for these added principles are given in the event the reader wishes to pursue them more formally.

Several observations should be made at the outset. First, the nature of social change in education is such that it would not be difficult to find a situation in which a particular principle does not apply or is even contraindicated. The principles do apply, however, to the great majority of educational situations. Second, we should be somewhat surprised if the reader finds the principles stated too generally or too specifically. For most principles we attempted to strike a middle range which would not be so abstract that it offered no real guidelines or so specific that the reader would find it difficult to translate into a meaningful form. Third, in addition to viewing these principles as action guidelines, it is also possible to treat them as propositions to be tested and used to construct a theory. We invite the reader to engage in this useful activity, which permits the derivation of still more principles. Finally, most of the principles contain no startling revelations. Various more or less straightforward principles are presented here despite their obviousness. It is surprising how often one takes leave of one's common sense when enacting something new. A checklist of the obvious is essential for even the most seasoned change planner.

CHAPTER 1

Principle 1-1. The change planner should be sensitive to societal trends and values. Changes that are not congruent with these must be expected to generate resistance both inside and outside the school system.

Principle 1-2. Any change that involves public review of the teacher's classroom behavior must be expected to generate resistance among teachers.

Principle 1-3. Any change that involves the sharing of classroom control must be expected to generate resistance among teachers.

Principle 1-4. Other things being equal, teachers will welcome changes that help them serve a diversity of student needs.

Principle 1-5. Any change that requires teachers to violate an existing norm or to behave differently must be expected to generate resistance among teachers.

Principle 1-6. Other things being equal, teachers will welcome changes that they believe will increase their achievements with students.

Principle 1-7. The change planner should consider and, where possible, collaborate with all of the groups that could importantly influence and/or be affected by change. He should look for opportunities for support and assistance from influential sources; he should try to forsee conflicts and take action to prevent them.

Principle 1-8. The change planner must collaborate with groups and persons who must approve or at least allow change as well as those who will actually initiate and implement change.

Principle 1-9. Other things being equal, changes that promote resource sharing will be supported by external influence groups and by administrators within school systems.

Principle 1-10. The change planner must consider the perspective and vantage point of anyone whose evaluation of the change effort will influence its continuation. Specifically, he must consider how that perspective will influence judgment regarding success or failure.

Principle 1-11. The change planner's own perspective is not broad enough if he has not considered opportunities and potential problems as they may arise from (1) aspects of the organizational climate, (2) the nature of the organizational environment, (3) characteristics of individuals, and (4) attributes of the change itself.

CHAPTER 2

Principle 2-1. The change planner can manipulate performance gaps by raising actual performance and/or by lowering expectations to accord with actual performance.

Principle 2-2. The change planner should prevent the development of unrealistically high expectations for the changed organization.

Principle 2-3. It is timely to introduce an innovation or change when expectations in the social system (school, district office, community) have risen beyond performance in the area of concern.

Principle 2-4. New personnel can be used as a source of solutions for improving performance as well as a means of increasing upward expectations.

Principle 2-5. Personnel training is a means of closing performance gaps by improving performance.

Principle 2-6. Knowledge use is a means of closing performance gaps.

Principle 2-7. The change planner can use other groups that are performing better as a reference stimulus to improve the performance of his group.

Principle 2-8. The change planner can use pressure from external sources to stimulate change in his group.

Principle 2-9. The change planner must be sensitive to a group's past failure to improve performance as a source of resistance to undertaking new remedial efforts.

Principle 2-10. Resistance to change should be used creatively by the change planner as an opportunity to learn more about his potential adopters.

Principle 2-11. The change planner should distinguish between resistance to a particular solution to an acknowledged problem and resistance to the idea that a problem exists. Different change-agent activities are involved in each case.

Principle 2-12. The change planner should distinguish between sources of resistance that can be overcome in the short run and those that can be overcome only in the long run or perhaps not at all.

Principle 2-13. The change planner must realize that a change that is resisted by some people may be attractive to others. Consideration must be given to presenting change differently or presenting different changes to people who respond differently to the original change.

Principle 2-14. The change planner should determine whether a particular factor (such as norms, personal attitudes, or characteristics of the setting in which change is to occur) works to hinder or facilitate change or both.

Principle 2-15. The change planner must realize that some sources of resistance, such as fundamental values and beliefs, are deeply rooted in culture and are extremely difficult to alter. Typically, the change planner must adapt *his* behavior to fit these values, beliefs, motivations, etc.

Principle 2-16. The change planner should realize that he may be coming from a different culture (e.g., from a university setting to an elementary school setting) and that the administrator, teacher, or others for whom he is serving as change planner may be very sensitive to cultural differences. Moreover, some of these differences may be viewed favorably, while others may be viewed unfavorably. The change planner must anticipate these reactions.

Principle 2-17. Highly standardized and routinized methods for handling various problems may serve as a barrier to organizational change.

Principle 2-18. Poor communication within schools and among schools in the same or neighboring districts may constitute important barriers to change.

Principle 2-19. The change planner must be prepared to encounter resistance if the proposed change would (1) disrupt a cohesive social group, (2) violate strongly held norms, (3) enhance the power of one clique or group over another, or (4) require a broader frame of reference than that currently possessed by the group.

Principle 2-20. If an organization or social system is highly complex (i.e., if it has many different roles or positions), the change agent will find the initiation of change easy but its implementation difficult. At the implementation stage it would be desirable to simplify the organization temporarily by grouping similar roles and having each group implement the change as a unit.

Principle 2-21. If an organization is highly centralized (i.e., if authority is at the top and not delegated), the initiation of change will be difficult but its implementation relatively easy. Hence, at the initiation stage the change planner might consider a temporary decentralization of authority whereby a change team may be given the authority to decide whether or not to accept a change.

Principle 2-22. The change planner should try to identify gatekeepers and disseminate information through them.

Principle 2-23. The change planner should be careful to present change in such a way that power elites are not threatened.

Principle 2-24. The change planner should be on the alert for attempts by leaders to alter the change in a way that is more favorable to themselves but that has undesirable consequences for the organization as a whole.

Principle 2-25. Change will be implemented more quickly if change is introduced from the top down rather than the bottom up. However, the change planner should also try to create openness to change at the grass-roots level and be alert to resistance when change is from the top down.

Principle 2-26. The change planner should identify the patterns whereby individuals or groups selectively and systematically avoid, seek, and retain information. The change planner can then present his change-related information within the normal information systems used by individuals or groups.

Principle 2-27. The change planner should undertake joint problem-defining activities when his perception of the problem differs from that of the individual or group.

Principle 2-28. To prevent some forms of resistance, the change planner should make clear the nature of the change and the required behavior for initiating and implementing the change.

Principle 2-29. Resistance can be minimized further if the change planner can determine what expectations exist concerning his role in the change as perceived by others and develop a consensus if disagreement exists or if expectations differ.

Principle 2-30. The change planner should be sensitive to—and attempt to minimize—feelings of uncertainty and anxiety among clients concerning their performance and evaluation when the advocated change is in effect.

Principle 2-31. The more the intended change requires nonconformity and lessening of commitment to a group or institution, the greater is the need to use special incentives such as money or other valued commodities as added inducements to change.

Principle 2-32. Different forms and sources of resistance, such as those discussed in chapter 2 (including tables 2-2 and 2-3), may manifest themselves at different times in the decision-making process. The change planner must be alert to new expressions of resistance as the client moves from one decision stage to another.

Principle 2-33. One particular source of resistance will be the nature of the innovation or change itself. Different attributes of change and innovation may be differentially important at different decision-making stages. Thus, the change planner must be differentially sensitive to various attributes of the change as his client moves from one decision stage to another.

Principle 2-34. As implied in several principles cited above, the change planner must be particularly sensitive to different types of errors on his part at particular decision stages. For example, at the problem-perception stage, the change planner must make the problem situation very salient to clients; at the awareness stage he should attempt thorough coverage of potential adopters with appropriate communications; at the comprehension stage he must make certain that his client understands the messages disseminated by him. (See table 2-2 for additional concerns.)

Principle 2-35. The self-renewing school will provide resources (time, money, etc.) to enable its members to acquire and test innovations.

Principle 2-36. The self-renewing school will create an atmosphere in which the act of experimentation is rewarded as well as the achievement of positive outcomes. Successful innovation should be widely publicized in the community and to the school board as a partial step toward creating a sense of pride and enthusiasm concerning innovative activities. Acknowledgments of successful innovation from sources outside the community are especially useful to disseminate within the educational system and community generally. This may stimulate others to be innovative who in the past were reluctant.

Principle 2-37. The central office should delegate authority (more than is typically found) to innovate to individual schools within the district.

Principle 2-38. A mechanism (e.g., a policy or program group) should be established at the district level to enable representatives from individual schools to address common problems and make remedial recommendations to the central office (Cooke, Duncan, and Zaltman 1974).

Principle 2-39. In an open organization, some role ambiguity and lack of role consensus deliberately fostered by top leaders may stimulate creativity and the pursuit of several differently valued objectives.

Principle 2-40. ''Persons involved, teachers, board members, and community leaders should feel that the project is their own—not one devised and operated by outsiders'' (Watson 1973).

Principle 2-41. ''The project should have wholehearted support from top officials of the system.''

Principle 2-42. ''Participants should see the change as reducing rather than increasing their present burdens.''

Principle 2-43. ''The project should accord with values and ideals that have long been acknowledged by participants.''

Principle 2-44. ''The program should offer the kind of new experience that interests participants.''

Principle 2-45. ''Participants should not feel that their autonomy and their security are threatened.''

Principle 2-46. ''Participants should join in diagnostic efforts so they can agree on the basic problem and feel its importance.''

Principle 2-47. ''Proponents should be able to empathize with opponents, to recognize valid objections, and to take steps to relieve unnecessary fears.''

Principle 2-48. ''Innovations are likely to be misunderstood and misinterpreted, so provision should be made for feedback of perceptions of the project and for further clarification as needed.''

Principle 2-49. ''Participants should experience acceptance, support, trust, and confidence in their relations with one another.''

Principle 2-50. ''The project should be open to revision and reconsideration if experience indicates that changes may be desirable.''

Prinicple 2-51. ''Readiness for change gradually becomes a characteristic of certain individuals, groups, organizations, and civilizations. They no longer look nostalgically at a Golden Age in the past but anticipate their Utopia in days to come. The spontaneity of youth is cherished and innovations are protected until they have had a chance to establish their worth. The ideal is more and more seen as possible.''

CHAPTER 3

Principle 3-1. The change planner must consider constantly how the external environment affects his behavior and that of others in attempting to create change.

Principle 3-2. The change planner should be aware of his own customary approach to change and determine if it is appropriate to the particular circumstance he is in.

Principle 3-3. Any attempt to change should be developed and presented in a way that appears consistent with the values and goals of the larger society.

Principle 3-4. If possible, major educational changes should be introduced when major changes are occurring in the larger society.

Principle 3-5. The change planner must try to identify the particular sources of influence in society that are most relevant to the change being attempted.

Principle 3-6. The change planner should try to connect a desired change with an unmet need of one or more interested groups.

Principle 3-7. Different phases of the individual or group adoption process may require different activities by the change planner.

Principle 3-8. The core stages of adoption that the change planner should consider are problem recognition, awareness, interest, information seeking, comprehension, evaluation, attitude formation, legitimation, trial, decision, implementation (adoption/rejection), and confirmation or reconsideration.

Principle 3-9. The change planner and client must decide at what stages the change planner should be most active; how long he should be available after a change has been initiated; and how problems in terminating the relationship can be minimized.

Principle 3-10. A distinction must be made between the initiation of change and the implementation of change. Initiation activities and implementation activities in an organization involve different behaviors for both adopters and change planners.

Principle 3-11. Different organizational structures have different effects on the adoption of innovations by organizations. Moreover, the effects of any given structure may differ according to the adoption stage. (See table 2-2.)

Principle 3-12. Different structural characteristics of organizations interact with particular decision-making stages, producing different decision-making modes—for example, participative versus authoritarian modes. Change is effected more slowly when a participative approach is employed, but resistance will typically be less than in an authoritarian situation.

Principle 3-13. Various models of change or innovation adoption should be used as guidelines by the change planner, although one model may be stressed if it is particularly appropriate to a given situation.

Principle 3-14. The change planner should try to "leave behind" for the clients the necessary skills to continue the change.

Principle 3-15. The change planner should expect resistance to actually implementing change and should prepare specific strategies and tactics to overcome such resistance.

Principle 3-16. The change planner should take into account very explicitly various criteria pertinent to the selection of change strategies. The change planner must also consider alternative strategies available to him.

Principle 3-17. The change planner must consider the consequences of his change strategies. These consequences may be intended or unintended, functional or dysfunctional.

Principal 3-18. Often, change has to be introduced step by step over time, rather than on a large scale in a short period of time.

Principal 3-19. Although it is important for the change planner to consider people as individuals, he must also remember that individuals exist in and are influenced by organizations and the larger society.

Principle 3-20. The change planner should realize that his perceptions of a situation are likely to differ, initially at least, from those of the client.

Principle 3-21. The change planner must have a full understanding of and interaction with various forces for and against change, both within and external to his organization.

Principal 3-22. Power strategies are perhaps the easiest to apply. Compliance does not rest on the nature of the change itself. However, power strategies are not necessarily the best over the long run.

Principle 3-23. The success of a power strategy rests on the extent to which the sources of power are really valued or important or compelling.

Principle 3-24. The success of a manipulative strategy rests on the strategist's knowledge of the target system as well as on his skill in manipulating the environment to favor change.

Principle 3-25. The success of a rational strategy depends very much on getting the user to accept change for itself rather than for some other reason. Thus, the change must be tied clearly and directly to perceived needs.

Principle 3-26. The change planner must take care that his messages about the desirability of a change are transmitted through various channels with high fidelity, that is, with a minimum of distortion.

Principle 3-27. It is often desirable to use different combinations of strategies where the relative importance of any one strategy is partly influenced by the decision-making stage of the client or intended users of the change.

Principle 3-28. Different strategies emphasize different kinds of knowledge about clients.

Principle 3-29. Different strategies vary in their financial cost.

Principle 3-30. Different strategies require different degrees of commitment to change by the change planner and by the client or target group. Commitment may be expressed in a variety of ways and may not be directly connected with the particular change being accepted or implemented. However, the more closely the commitment to change is connected to the change itself, the more self-sustaining will be the resultant change behavior.

CHAPTER 4

Principle 4-1. The change planner must provide a level of information that is necessary for motivating and guiding change.

Principle 4-2. The motivating information should be made readily available.

Principle 4-3. The change planner must give special attention to the fact that many educators are relatively isolated from one another and that this is a major roadblock to information transfer even within a school building.

Principle 4-4. Contact must be fostered between innovative and noninnovative educational systems.

Principle 4-5. The change planner can foster contact between an educational system and an innovation through such tactics as use of direct mail, advertising, articles and booklets, demonstration, salespeople, field agents, telephone, meetings, action research, confrontation, workshops, information systems, and training manuals.

Principle 4-6. The change planner can foster change by expressing the change in the form of a tangible product or definable procedure. This may involve a totally new product or procedure or a modification of one already in existence.

Principle 4-7. The change planner should involve potential users early in the development of a product or procedure and continue this involvement throughout the development process.

Principle 4-8. The potential user should be made to feel that he has contributed significantly to the research and development process.

Principle 4-9. The change planner should also involve users in the decision-making and trial stages of the adoptive process.

Principle 4-10. Potential users should be trained by the change planner or other appropriate party to train others to implement change. Thus, trainees become trainers.

Principle 4-11. If possible, the change planner should try to obtain public endorsements or early commitments from key persons in the educational system.

Principle 4-12. Special training of potential users is often needed for successful implementation of significant change.

Principle 4-13. Both trainers and trainees should be provided with adequate incentives to succeed.

Principle 4-14. "R&D delivery strategies aimed at bringing research findings, knowledge and products to the schools have less potential for change than those strategies that emphasize strengthening the capabilities of the school districts to actively be responsible for their own improvement." (Temkin and Brown 1974:22).

Principle 4-15. The change planner can help install and support change by subsidizing change, helping the system to locate funds, conducting preservice and in-service classes on the use of an innovation and on planning skills, providing help in problem solving, establishing a feedback system for monitoring the change, setting up temporary systems, and building networks among users and potential users.

Principle 4-16. Legal actions can be used that range from coercion to facilitation; however, the more coercive the tactic, the more vigilance is required, because of the increased likelihood of resistance.

Principle 4-17. The change planner must understand that different tactics are differentially important depending on his goals, the educational system's goals, the change situation, the nature of the change object, the stage in overall change process, and so forth.

Principle 4-18. The change planner must be concerned with the stability of the change. Will the tactic operate in the manner predicted?

Principle 4-19. The change planner should be concerned with the degree of interpersonal contact the tactic requires and whether adequate personnel exist for the tactic.

Principle 4-20. The change planner should be concerned with the degree of feedback he needs and is able to obtain with respect to any particular tactic.

Principle 4-21. The change planner should also be concerned with the degree of interpersonal contact required when he must be one of the interacting parties. Does the change planner have enough time for such a highly interpersonal approach?

Principle 4-22. The change planner should be concerned about the level of activity a particular tactic may require either on his part or on the part of the educational system. Level of activity may vary between the initiation and continued implementation stages.

Principle 4-23. The change planner should consider the degree to which a tactic should leave room for the educational system to act. How much of the educational system's actions does the planner want to structure?

Principle 4-24. The change planner must determine whether a given strategy can be used only once or a few times. If the tactic is nonrepeatable, he must determine the most appropriate time to apply it.

Principle 4-25. The change planner must determine how difficult a given tactic is to initiate and then to sustain. Does the planner or educational system have the requisite resources?

Principle 4-26. When selecting a tactic, the change planner should assess its potential coverage in terms of the number of individuals or groups it will (and is designed to) affect.

Principle 4-27. The change planner should also take into account the immediacy of tactic impact. How quickly must a result be shown?

Principle 4-28. The change planner must consider the availability of resources, financial and nonfinancial, to both the change planner and the educational system.

Principle 4-29. The more a tactic involves the use of an actual experience with a change, the more effective it will be.

Principle 4-30. Direct mail is relatively high in stability, activity, potential coverage, immediacy, and user convenience. It is a good tactic to use in situations where the audience is large and divided and is not inclined to seek the information.

Principle 4-31. Advertising in the mass media is useful in situations where there is a low tolerance for risk associated with ambiguity, where the educational system is large and divided, and where the message has special significance for the educator. This approach is especially effective in reaching opinion leaders.

Principle 4-32. Use of articles, books, and reports is good for a mass and/or divided audience when the message has special meaning, when the message is relatively complex, and where potential users of the change are motivated to seek information and are change-oriented.

Principle 4-33. Demonstrations are useful when complex information must be conveyed or when a change is perceived to be complex, when resistance is expected, and when the decision maker is close to a decision.

Principle 4-34. The use of salespeople is most appropriate for an advocacy position, for getting practitioners to take a particular action, and for situations where the audience is relatively small, clustered, and easily reached.

Principle 4-35. Field agents are more effective in renewal efforts than in advocacy efforts, and are especially appropriate in presenting new practices effectively and helping educators integrate new practices with existing practices.

Principle 4-36. The telephone is appropriate when the change planner and/or user needs immediate action.

Principle 4-37. Meetings are most appropriate at the very early or very late stages of the decision-making process.

Principle 4-38. Action research is useful where a system is complacent and needs very credible data to stimulate remedial efforts. Action research is useful at all stages of the change process.

Principle 4-39. Confrontation may be useful when quick action is necessary before the educational system can respond with resistance.

Principle 4-40. Workshops are appropriate when personal contact is important.

Principle 4-41. The use of information systems designed for change is appropriate when the educational system is receptive to change and self-motivated.

Principle 4-42. Training manuals are good for efficiently conveying specific information aimed at a particular form of change, and where the potential users are numerous and widely dispersed.

Principle 4-43. Product-development tactics are good in situations where the change is limited in scope and not too complex and where the convenience of the potential user is a major consideration.

Principle 4-44. User-involvement tactics are good for complex messages and where the change planner can be flexible in responding to user suggestions.

Principle 4-45. Legal tactics are good for effecting change in a highly specified form and over a large group with high user convenience.

Principle 4-46. Subsidizing change is appropriate in an advocacy situation where change may be needed very quickly by the change planner.

Principle 4-47. Preservice classes are appropriate for renewal efforts rather than advocacy efforts.

Principle 4-48. In-service classes are appropriate for advocacy efforts and where limited skills need to be taught to effect a particular change.

Principle 4-49. Consultants are particularly useful where the decision-making group is small and/or cohesive and has moved beyond the initial decision-making stage of change.

Principle 4-50. A feedback system is useful in the early stages of change to identify performance gaps and in later stages to assess the impact of the change.

Principle 4-51. Temporary systems are effective for introducing change in a receptive educational system and where change is complex and perceived as risky.

Principle 4-52. The individual school building should be allowed to adapt an imposed change to fit its own unique needs and circumstances.

Principle 4-53. ''In attempting to affect formal organizations (from the inside or from the outside), the practitioner should not operate as though organizations have a single, limited goal that guides all their activities. The practitioner should attempt to identify the various goals and goal configurations of the organization, the manifest as well as latent ones. The organization may be differentially vulnerable to attack or influence, or open to coalitions, based on subgoals'' (Rothman 1974:133).

CHAPTER 5

Principle 5-1. The change planner must prepare the organization for the change-planning process.

Principle 5-2. The change planner must move his client group toward a proactive and interactive relationship with the environment and away from inactive and reactive environmental relationships.

Principle 5-3. The change planner can achieve some degree of control over both internal and environmental or external forces if proactive and interactive management modes are followed.

Principle 5-4. The change planner must have clearly defined (preferably written) goals and objectives. However, this is not always possible when goals and objectives are not commonly agreed upon.

Principle 5-5. The exact nature of the problem should be stated explicitly (preferably in writing).

Principle 5-6.   A need assessment analysis must be conducted.

Principle 5-7. Various resources and constraints should be inventoried.

Principle 5-8. If intentional change is to occur in educational systems, planning must occur within the unit most closely associated with the client group.

Principle 5-9. The primary planning unit should be linked throughout the planning process with other units in the school system and with units in the environment external to the school system.

Principle 5-10. Before initiating the planning process, the change planner must determine the following: what the unit of change is; who the relevant people are in that unit; how decisions are made in that unit; who should be involved in the planning process; what the scope of the decision-making authority of the planning group should be; how expert planners are in problem diagnosis and problem solving; what additional skills planners need; what can and cannot be changed in the social structure and functioning of the relevant unit; what the unit of change is; who from the environment should be involved in planning; and how risk-aversive the change unit is.

Principle 5-11. The degree of acceptance, satisfaction, commitment, and follow-up action with regard to planning decisions is positively related to the degree of involvement that members of the system feel they have in the decision-making process.

Principle 5-12. Constructive participation and involvement cannot occur unless system members (1) believe their participation will lead to action and (2) are able to perform relevant tasks in the planning process.

Principle 5-13. People involved in follow-up activities should be part of the planning process to ensure that proper action follows the planning decision.

Principle 5-14. Authority structures in an organization, whether collaborative or highly authoritarian, should not be altered without adequate advance preparation for easing individuals into or out of authority positions. It is important to consider the history of the organization before redesigning its authority structure.

Principle 5-15. Educational organizations may need to break authority patterns and develop unused abilities through assistance from external agents.

Principle 5-16. The planning team should develop a list of elements within the organization (such as morale and communication patterns) that might be altered as a result of the implementation of change. Similarly, elements characteristic of the relationship between an organization and its environment (such as cooperation with other groups and financial support) that might be altered as a result of a change should be inventoried or listed.

Principle 5-17. The planning team may be used as a temporary change in authority structure to facilitate the initiation and implementation of a specific change or to facilitate a more permanent shift from an authoritarian structure to a collaborative decision-making structure or vice versa.

Principle 5-18. The decision-making process should involve not only members of the educational system concerned, but also members of that system's environment who have potential for facilitating or blocking the change effort.

Principle 5-19. A risky plan should be introduced after the successful initiation of an earlier plan.

Principle 5-20. The change planner must minimize perceived negative consequences of initiating a change program if active involvement of the client system is to be obtained.

Principle 5-21. The change planner should plan in such a way that the failure of the change cannot be attributed to any one individual. This will enhance the willingness of individuals to assume risk.

Principle 5-22. The decision concerning who is to be actively involved in the initial planning stages should be based on an assessment of the net benefits of including a particular person and the cost of not including that person.

Principle 5-23. The preparation for planning should consider (1) how to reduce risk associated with being involved in a planning process concerning change and (2) how to assist planning-team members in coping with risk.

Principle 5-24. The change planner should consider using temporary systems as a means of reducing risk, establishing ties with the environment, and testing new role definitions.

Principle 5-25. The P/ICM should be used flexibly. The change planner should start at the stage he considers most important and cycle forward or backward as appropriate.

CHAPTER 6

Principle 6-1. Generally, the first activity of a planning team should be the development of an "organizational mission statement" identifying problem areas in need of immediate attention and general goals and objectives. At this initial stage, objectives need not be stated in behavioral terms.

Principle 6-2. The organizational mission statement should be developed on a collaborative basis to the extent possible.

Principle 6-3. The mission statement should identify the groups affected by the organization's purposes.

Principle 6-4. The P/ICM model should be used flexibly. Special circumstances may make it desirable for the planning team to begin at a stage subsequent to the organizational mission statement.

Principle 6-5. The planning team should translate the discomfort or dissatisfaction of educators into a problem-identification statement.

Principle 6-6. Planned change cannot occur unless the organizational members are aware of the need for change or innovation.

Principle 6-7. Planning should be based on empirical data whenever possible. The survey-feedback approach is an effective procedure for acquiring and using empirical data.

Principle 6-8. Organizational illness cannot be adequately diagnosed unless there is an understanding of organizational health.

Principle 6-9. A statement of problem-solving objectives should be developed by the planning team.

Principle 6-10. A need-assessment activity should be a significant part of several stages of the planning process. (See chapter 7.)

Principle 6-11. The change/innovation process is enhanced by the establishment of viable links between the organization and resources within its environment.

Principle 6-12. The school is the central practice institution for any collaborative interorganizational network for elementary and secondary education development.

Principle 6-13. The planning team should identify the various human, technical, and material constraints and resources affecting the planning, implementation, control, and evaluation phases of change.

Principle 6-14. The normative differences between knowledge-production organizations (universities, research centers and laboratories) and the knowledge-use organizations (schools) in educational systems necessitate a linking system with broker roles between such organizations.

Principle 6-15. Resistance should be viewed as both a positive and negative force in the change-planning process.

Principle 6-16. The planning team should draw upon outside parties or agencies with whom it has established linkages and use such resources to help identify other resources and constraints the planning team may encounter.

Principle 6-17. The planning team should establish an inventory of several potential problem solutions and alternative strategies for their implementation relative to particular problems of concern.

Principle 6-18. The process of testing possible solutions should also be used as a process to generate additional alternative solutions.

Principle 6-19. The testing or trial should include an evaluation of the impact of the change on aspects of the situation unrelated to the problem of concern as well as its impact on the problem being addressed.

Principle 6-20. The change planner should assess the impact of the way or manner in which a decision is made on the overall planned-change process.

Principle 6-21. Identification and clarification of resources, constraints, and resistance to planned organizational change increase the likelihood of developing successful change strategies.

Principles 6-22. The change planner should be wary of underestimating how assertive he should be (Rothman 1974:75).

Principle 6-23. The change planner should respond differently to different role orientations present among the client group. For those who are professionally oriented, he should stress the consonance of the change with professional values and standards; for those who are bureaucratically oriented, he should stress the consonance of the change with current policies and norms of the organization; for those who are client-oriented, he should stress the consonance of the change with clients' clients (Rothman 1974:83).

Principle 6-24. The change planner should view his client group as creative people who are implementors of change, and he should convey this view to them.

Principle 6-25. The change planner can increase resources and innovative activity in his organization by developing joint programs with other groups. This can be done most readily by having a diverse professional staff, a decentralized organizational structure, and good internal communication, and through the use of temporary systems.

Principle 6-26. "As organizational goals are influenced, the practitioner should continually evaluate the dominant goals in the organization" when planning for change (Rothman 1974:135).

CHAPTER 7

Principle 7-1. Client need assessment is essential to the understanding of the current state of client needs and as a basis for making useful decisions.

Principle 7-2. The change planner should establish an ongoing need-assessment process in all areas of the educational system.

Principle 7-3. The recognition of a need stimulates the desire to innovate, and hence the recognition of needs is essential for creating change.

Principle 7-4. The needs assessor should carefully review the specific need definitions with the client and secure the client's concurrence in the accuracy of the information before the information is reported to the decision maker.

Principle 7-5. The methodology used by the needs assessor should be readily identifiable by the decision maker to permit him to make evaluative judgments about procedures used.

Principle 7-6. The methodology used by the needs assessor should be applied to services and programs of importance to the decision-maker.

Principle 7-7. The methodology used by the needs assessor should yield data in a form readily usable by the decision maker.

Principle 7-8. Before undertaking need assessment, the assessor should become very familiar with its basic formal procedures.

Principle 7-9. The needs assessor should be careful to address needs of interest to decision makers.

Principle 7-10. Assessment efforts must be focused by specifying who the intended users are, what resources are available for conducting the assessment, and, given limited resources, who among potential users are the most important decision makers.

Principle 7-11. The person or group that decides on the focus of the need-assessment effort should be someone in a position to (1) understand which decision makers are relevant and important and (2) be familiar with and perhaps control the availability of resources for use in need-assessment activities.

Principle 7-12. Decision makers for whom a need assessment is being conducted should be involved in all stages of the assessment effort.

Principle 7-13. The needs assessor should identify all resources available for the assessment activity.

Principle 7-14. There is no a priori basis for deciding whether to allocate limited resources first to different decision makers (in equal or varying proportions) and then to different stages in the need-assessment process (in equal or varying proportions) or vice versa.

Principle 7-15. If the client need assessment effort will span more than a few days' time, then the needs assessor should develop a timeline or a network-flow diagram in order to help plan and control the process.

Principle 7-16. The needs assessor should work directly with a decision maker in order to establish which clients and which client needs the decision maker most wants information about.

Principle 7-17. The needs assessor should express as specifically and as operationally as possible his image of a particular client's need. He should plan this activity carefully, taking into account existing definitions of client needs and obtaining from definers their definitions of needs.

Principle 7-18. It is necessary to determine whether a performance gap exists by comparing the satisfaction status of a need as currently observed with the definition of what level of satisfaction is desired or considered possible.

CHAPTER 8

Principle 8-1. Every change program should involve an information system to assess management activities, the nature of opportunities and challenges, objective setting, planning, implementation of programs, and performance.

Principle 8-2. The plan-control process should be undertaken periodically.

Principle 8-3. It is helpful to think in terms of causal imagery when planning and exercising control.

Principle 8-4. When exercising control, the change planner should consider such factors as client's perceived need for change, commitment to change, resources available for change, and the nature and magnitude of the change.

Principle 8-5. An organizational information system should be established to facilitate the exercise of control and evaluation as well as to identify new problems and opportunities.

Principle 8-6. An organizational information system should take into consideration information from outside as well as inside the educational system.

Principle 8-7. Care must be taken not to make district-level decisions that help stimulate laggard schools but stifle or discourage the more creative, innovative schools. Working individually with problem schools is preferable to issuing a district-wide policy or decision intended for a subset of schools only.

Principle 8-8. The change planner should continually review the impact of a specific change on various people and groups and determine how that impact compares with the expectations of all parties involved.

Principle 8-9. Rationality in a change program should be defined in terms of the frame of reference of the parties affected, not that of the change planner.

Principle 8-10. The goals of a change program should be stated very explicitly to facilitate implementation efforts, evaluation efforts, and control activities.

Principle 8-11. The exact nature of educational problems must be fully described before explicit goals can be stated and appropriate remedial programs developed and launched.

Principle 8-12. Educational change planners must recognize that individuals exist in an interpersonal environment and seldom think or act in the absence of considerable influence from some past, ongoing, or anticipated interpersonal event.

Principle 8-13. Implementation considerations are equal in importance to the task of developing an innovation; indeed, implementation constraints and opportunities should be considered in the development of an innovation.

Principle 8-14. An innovation should be presented to educators as being in direct response to a strongly felt need that they believe can be satisfied without undue social, psychological, or financial cost.

Principle 8-15. An innovation should not be introduced unless educators have or can readily acquire the necessary capacity—cognitive, social, and psychological—to accept it.

Principle 8-16. The lower the degree of commitment to change among educators, the easier the change planner must make it for them to adopt. Alternatively, the lower the degree of commitment among educators, the greater the effort that must be made by the change planner to heighten commitment.

Principle 8-17. The introduction of an innovation that is to be instrumental in achieving some larger objective, such as improved organizational procedures, should be accompanied by an awareness campaign identifying both problems and solutions.

Principle 8-18. An instrumental innovation (an innovation intended to help gain acceptance of another innovation or good) should be linked with one or more stages in the overall process whereby educators achieve the intended ultimate goal. The instrumental innovation should be introduced as educators approach that stage.

Principle 8-19. The greater the magnitude of change required for the adoption of an innovation, the greater the need for inducement or incentives beyond so-called rational justifications.

Principle 8-20. The salient attributes of an innovation as perceived by educators should be determined, and alterations in innovation design and communication plans should be made if necessary to minimize dysfunctional attributes and capitalize on positive attributes.

Principle 8-21. When designing an innovation and developing a program to gain its adoption and diffusion, it is highly desirable to determine whether the intended adopters can be segmented into meaningful groups that might benefit from a differentiated innovation and/or implementation plan.

Principle 8-22. Diagnosis of potential cultural, social, and psychological sources of resistance to change should be undertaken early in the process of planning for educational change so that strategies can be developed for reducing resistance.

Principle 8-23. Effective planned educational change requires a carefully orchestrated plan in which great care is given to the timing of each event in terms of when it occurs relative to other events as well as the period required for it to have an impact.

Principle 8-24. An effective change program should have an evaluation-research component built in to permit constant evaluation of the program's impact. This in turn would lead to changes over time to improve the functioning of the program. Evaluation research should begin well before the implementation of the program with at least two benchmark surveys.

Principle 8-25. Prior to the full-scale implentation of a program, a limited trial (or pilot program) should be undertaken.

Principle 8-26. Every effort should be made to identify potential undesirable consequences of a change program and to develop contingency plans for countering these consequences should they materialize.

CHAPTER 9

Principle 9-1. No program of change should be initiated without a plan for its evaluation.

Principle 9-2. Evaluation must be considered well before the change program is launched.

Principle 9-3. Because of time, monetary, and other constraints, comprehensive evaluations are seldom possible. The change planner must examine his needs and priorities in the light of the various constraints and devise a strategy that best fits his requirements.

Principle 9-4. Formal evaluation is necessary for improving an implemented program (formative evaluation) as well as for making decisions to continue or discontinue a program or innovation (summative evaluation).

Principle 9-5. An external or outside evaluator is likely to bring greater methodological expertise and objectivity to an evaluation.

Principle 9-6. An external evaluator may feel less constrained in communicating his findings, especially those that are unfavorable to a program.

Principle 9-7. Compared with an internal evaluator, an external evaluator will often lack familiarity with the program's goals, objectives, and history and is likely to overlook important subtle aspects of a program.

Principle 9-8. There is no universal rule of thumb suggesting that an internal evaluator is preferable to an external evaluator or vice versa; the specific situation should determine whether an insider or outsider *or both* should undertake the evaluation.

Principle 9-9. It is most important to develop a collaborative relationship between the evaluator (external or internal) and the staff involved in or affected by the change. Staff members should be given the opportunity to participate in the planning stage of the evaluation and decision making. This increases staff receptivity to proposed changes in a change program.

Principle 9-10. Great care must be taken not to allow the effects of the ongoing evaluation to become confused with the effects of the change that is being evaluated.

Principle 9-11. The greater the availability of alternative changes to accomplish given goals and the greater the competition for funds in general, the more useful it is to evaluate a change effort by comparing it with possible substitute or alternative allocations of funds.

Principle 9-12. When program improvement is the primary concern, non-comparative evaluation seems to be a better choice.

Principle 9-13. In addition to looking for changes in specific processes, evaluation research should also be sensitive to changes in attitudes and values associated with process outcomes.

Principle 9-14. The design of sound evaluation should be based on insight into the conditions and assumptions made at the outset of the change program.

Principle 9-15. Evaluation must take into account unique, special interpersonal or other events at a societal level which may have occurred during the period over which a program is being evaluated and which are not likely to recur.

Principle 9-16. Context evaluation that is concerned with identifying gaps between what is intended and what is observed in a program is especially useful in guiding program-modification decisions.

Principle 9-17. Input evaluations that concern the possibility of competing strategies for achieving a given goal are also desirable while a program is ongoing.

Principle 9-18. Systematic evaluation is necessary at all stages of educational change, starting with program planning (input evaluation) and continuing throughout the various implementation phases (context and process evaluation) and at each point thereafter where a continuation or rejection decision must be made (product evaluation).

Principle 9-19. Evaluations should be designed to uncover favorable and unfavorable but unanticipated outcomes of a change. This is especially useful in judging the value of an educational change.

Principle 9-20. Principle 9-19 requires an external evaluator who must try to minimize any loss of independence due to personal involvement with project staffs and their tasks and goals.

Principle 9-21. A responsive evaluation—one oriented more to program activities than to intents—may be best when an integrated reflection of a total program is desired. (See figure 9-5 for events in a responsive evaluation).

Principle 9-22. The adversary approach to evaluation is particularly applicable to innovation-implementation decisions and is desirable when a full range of interpretation of information should be obtained.

Principle 9-23. When strong resistance to change is expected, transactional evaluation can be an effective means of channeling criticism into constructive forms and generating feasible alternative change programs.

Principle 9-24. The transactional evaluator should be particuarly skilled in interpersonal communication as well as instrument development and data analysis.

CHAPTER 10

Principle 10-1. The application of new knowledge, whether as an idea or product, should be done in such a manner that minimal disruption of the overall formal and informal social system of the change occurs. Particularly important is the impact of the change on existing informal, interpersonal social relationships.

Principle 10-2. Information about the change or innovation should be cast in terms of the vocabulary used by educators as opposed to that used by developers and outside change agents. This highlights the need for broker systems and translator roles between knowledge-producing and knowledge-using organizations.

Principle 10-3. Every effort should be made to lessen the perceived threat of knowledge from an outside agent and to stress the commonality of the agent's goals and activity with those of the school teachers, administrators, and staff.

Principle 10-4. New knowledge and implied change should be presented as a means of increasing school loyalty and pride, particularly if the change to be implemented originated with a much more prestigious organization.

Principle 10-5. Any knowledge that requires substantial financial outlays should not be initiated unless funds are clearly available and earmarked for the tasks of soliciting and implementing new knowledge and maintenance of the change that knowledge may imply. (Otherwise, the knowledge can create unachievable expectations.)

Principle 10-6. Responsibility for major change should not be assigned to a new member of the school system unless that person has extensive authority or is working in collaboration with members who do have such authority and/or acceptance by the more established organizational members.

Principle 10-7. Infusion of new knowledge and associated changes should be attempted first in an organizational subsystem (department, school, district) whose members are open to change and are dissatisfied with the status quo, and where successful innovation or change is rewarded. The more innovative entity can then serve as a role model for departments, schools, and districts that are less change-oriented.

Principle 10-8. New information requiring or implying change may best be introduced by new leaders, who will be expected to bring new ideas independently of whether or not the ideas are sought out by members of the school system.

Principle 10-9. The introduction of new knowledge is most acceptable when a real or potential crisis is evident and the new knowledge is believed to represent a way of solving the crisis or aiding the development of the organization and its members.

Principle 10-10. New knowledge can often be gained very quickly by having teachers and/or administrators observe an application of the knowledge in another similar school or district. In-service and preservice training as well as participation in professional meetings by teachers and administrators can also infuse new knowledge into a school system.

Principle 10-11. It is desirable to invest risk capital in resources that enhance the school system's ability to retrieve information and experiment with the implications of information received.

Principle 10-12. External change agents as well as new permanent or temporary members of the system should be used as a source of new knowledge.

Principle 10-13. It is very desirable to have a special group whose members are carefully selected to serve as a new knowledge-search team on a permanent basis or at least on a temporary basis in response to a problem.

Principle 10-14. Teachers and administrators should be strongly encouraged to develop a strong sense of professional identity through participation in conferences, membership in professional associations, and periodic reviews of professional literature.

Principle 10-15. The accumulation of knowledge is necessary to facilitate the development of innovation, and hence the self-renewing school system will provide means for its members to acquire more of existing knowledge and participate in the development of new knowledge.

Principle 10-16. An educational system should have an adaptation mechanism—that is, some individual or group using a specific process that enables the system to adapt innovation or change to fit its specific situation. Alternatively, an educational system should be flexible enough to adapt itself to a nonmodifiable innovation or change.

Principle 10-17. A research basis for an action principle should be provided (Rothman 1974:557).

Principle 10-18. Research generalizations should be converted into their specific applied form and presented with an example of their implementation in a context and language relevant to practitioners (Rothman 1974:557–59).

Principle 10-19. The practitioner should be provided with appropriate definitions, qualifications, and elaborations necessary to clarify or amplify his use of research finding(s). This includes identifying potential pitfalls in using the data. Tips for avoiding the pitfalls should be given, too (Rothman 1974:561–67).

Principle 10-20. The practitioner should develop, or be provided with, alternative applications (tactics) of a research finding that are possible within the framework of a given intervention strategy.

Principle 10-21. Encouragement, reinforcement, and optimism, especially from peers, should accompany the initial attempts of a practitioner to use knowledge to introduce change in the school system (Rothman 1974:569). The change agent should not respond solely to role stereotypes but should be aware that individuals also modify their formal role specifications. These modified or informal role attributes must be considered to be as important as the formal role attributes.

Principle 10-22. The educational system should provide for a knowledge-use function at various levels of the system.

Principle 10-23. The initiator of change should show a general willingness to alter his own operation or behavior.

Principle 10-24. Resources (broadly defined) should be available to implement change based on knowledge.

Principle 10-25. Resources should be available to develop staff capabilities for change.

Principle 10-26. There should be a general sensitivity to the various constituents who could be affected by a change program.

Principle 10-27. It is necessary to establish a basic belief among members of the school system that research and new knowledge can improve existing and prospective change efforts.

Principle 10-28. The practice of continually translating program needs into researchable questions and projects should be encouraged.

Principle 10-29. Experiences with any change should be evaluated by persons with different perspectives, and the evaluations should be translated into recommendations for continuing and/or altering the change program. However, one person or group should be responsible for the evaluation and recommendations, while being careful to communicate with persons affected by the change.

Principle 10-30. Research staff in an educational system should be trained to be sensitive to the need for developing and expressing the practical implications of their work. Care should be taken to select research topics that are relevant to specific practitioner problems rather than topics that are of special theoretical or methodological interest.

Principle 10-31. Research, teaching, and other staff should be rewarded for breaking out of the bounds of current practice and daring to be different.

Principle 10-32. Mistakes in the research, translation, or implementation processes should be identified and the lesson(s) learned from them made clear. However, there should be a general understanding that mistakes are quite likely—perhaps inevitable—and should be viewed in a constructive spirit rather than in a spirit of criticism and blame.

Principle 10-33. Research-project priorities should be based on the potential projects have for effective use as well as on the importance of the problem.

Principle 10-34. Continuous two-way communication between researchers and users should occur at all stages of the knowledge-use or action-research project and program implementation.

Principle 10-35. Special incentives should be provided to motivate teachers, administrators, and other staff to use such internal resources of change knowledge as (1) teacher/researcher discussions and idea presentations, (2) in-service training, (3) curriculum supervisors and organizational development specialists, (4) library facilities, (5) research-evaluation staff, (6) media specialists, and (7) student discussions and idea presentations.

Principle 10-36. Special incentives should be provided to motivate teachers, administrators, and other staff to use such external resources as (1) state education agencies, (2) federal agencies, (3) universities and colleges, (4) professional associations, (5) ERIC, (6) regional educational laboratories, (7) foundations and other private sources, (8) consultants, and (9) publishers.

References

ALTMAN, TAMARA C., AND L. A. SIKORSKI. 1975. *A Study of the Dissemination of SM 3-12, "Your Chance to Live."* Final Report prepared for DCPA by Far West Laboratory (January).

ARGYRIS, CHRIS. 1965. *Organization and Innovations.* Homewood, Ill.: Dorsey Press.

————. 1970. *Intervention Theory and Method.* Reading, Mass.: Addison-Wesley.

ATKIN, J. M. 1969. "Behavioral Objectives in Curriculum Design: A Cautionary Note." In *Current Research on Instruction,* ed. R. C. Anderson et al. Englewood Cliffs, N.J.: Prentice-Hall.

BALDRIDGE, J. VICTOR. 1974. "The Impact of Individuals, Organizational Structure, and Environment on Organizational Innovation." Stanford, California: Stanford Center For Research and Development in Teaching, Research and Development Memorandum, No. 124.

BALDRIDGE, J. VICTOR, AND TERRENCE E. DEAL, eds. 1975. *Managing Change in Educational Organizations.* Berkeley: McCutchan.

BARNARD, CHESTER. 1938. *The Functions of the Executive.* Cambridge: Harvard University Press.

BARNES, L. B. 1969. "Approaches to Organizational Change." In *The Planning of Change,* ed. W. G. Bennis et al., 2d ed. New York: Holt, Rinehart & Winston.

BARNETT, HOMER G. 1953. *Innovation: The Basis for Cultural Change.* New York: McGraw-Hill.

BECKARD, RICHARD. 1966. "An Organizational Improvement Program in a Decentralized Organization." *Journal of Applied Behavioral Science* 2.

BELASCO, JAMES A. 1973. "Educational Innovation: The Impact of Organizational and Community Variables on Performance Contracts." *Management Science* 20, no. 4 (December), part 1.

BELL, MARTIN. 1972. *Marketing: Concepts and Strategies.* New York: Houghton-Mifflin.

336

BENNIS, WARREN G. 1966*a*. *Beyond Bureaucracy.* New York: McGraw-Hill.

———.1966*b*. *Changing Organizations.* New York: McGraw-Hill.

BENNIS, WARREN G.; K. D. BENNE; AND R. CHIN, eds. 1969. *The Planning of Change,* 2d ed. New York: Holt, Rinehart & Winston. (3d ed., 1976.)

BENNIS, WARREN G., AND P. E. SLATER. 1968. *The Temporary Society..* New York: Harper & Row.

BENZEN, MARY M., AND KENNETH A. TYE. 1972. "Effecting Change in Elementary Schools." *The Elementary School in the United States.* 72d Yearbook of the National Society for the Study of Education. part 2, ed. J. Goodlad and H. Shane. Chicago: University of Chicago Press.

BERMAN, PAUL, AND MILBREY WALLIN McLAUGHLIN. 1974. *Federal Programs Supporting Educational Change.* Vol. 1: *A Model of Educational Change.* Santa Monica, Calif.; Rand Corp.

BLAKE, R. R., AND J. S. MOUTON. 1964. *The Managerial Grid: Key Orientations for Achieving Production through People.* Houston: Gulf Publishing.

———. 1974. "Designing Change for Educational Institutions through the D/D Matrix." *Education and Urban Society* (February).

BLANZY, J. J. 1974. "A Change System for Education." *Educational Technology* 4, no. 14, pp. 45–47.

BLOOM, BENJAMIN S. 1968. "Learning for Mastery." *U.C.L.A.–C.S.E.I.P. Evaluation Comment* 1, no. 2.

BLOOM, B. S.; J. T. HASTINGS; AND G. F. MADAUS. 1970. *Handbook on Formative and Summative Evaluation of Student Learning.* Pittsburgh: American Institution for Research.

BLUM, HENRIK L. 1974. *Planning for Health.* New York: Human Sciences Press.

BLUMBERG, A.; J. MAY; AND R. PERRY. 1974. "An Inner-City School that Changed— and Continued to Change." *Education and Urban Society* (Sage Publications), vol. 6, no. 2 (February).

BLUMBERG, A., AND R. SCHMUCK. 1972. "Barriers to Organizational Development Training for Schools." *Educational Technology* 12, no. 10 (October).

BRACHT, G. H., AND G. V. GLASS. 1968. "The External Validity of Comparative Experiments in Education and the Social Sciences." *American Educational Research Journal* 5:437–74.

BUSHNELL, DAVID S., AND DONALD RAPPAPORT. 1971. *Planned Change in Education: A Systems Approach.* New York: Harcourt Brace Jovanovich.

CAMPBELL, DONALD T. 1972. "Reforms as Experiments." In *Evaluating Action Programs,* ed. C. H. Weiss. Boston: Allyn & Bacon.

———. 1974. "Quasi-Experimental Designs." In *Social Experimentation as a Method for Planning and Evaluating Social Programs,* ed. H. W. Rieckem et al. New York: Academic Press.

CAMPBELL, D. T., AND J. C. STANLEY. 1966. *Experimental and Quasi-Experimental Designs for Research.* Chicago: Rand McNally.

———. 1973. "Experimental and Quasi-Experimental Designs for Research on Teaching." In *Handbook of Research on Teaching,* ed. N. L. Gage. Chicago: Rand McNally.

CARLISLE, D. H., et al. 1971. *The Instructional Planning Team: An Organizational Arrangement to Accomplish Planning, Teaching, and Evaluation in a School: A Pilot Study.* Berkeley: Far West Laboratory (February).

CARLSON, RICHARD O. 1965. "Barriers to Change in Public Schools." In *Change Processes in the Public Schools,* ed. R. O. Carlson et al. University of Oregon: Center for the Advanced Study of Educational Administration.

————. 1972. *School Superintendents: Careers and Performance.* Columbus, Ohio: Charles E. Merrill.

CARPENTER-HUFFMAN, P.; G. E. HALL; AND G. C. SUMNER. 1974. *Change in Education: Insights from Performance Contracting.* Cambridge: Ballinger.

CARROLL, JOHN B. 1968. "Basic and Applied Research in Education: Definitions, Distinctions, and Implications." *Harvard Educational Review* 2, no. 38, pp. 263–76.

CARTER, FAUNOR AND HARRY SILKERMAN, 1965. *The Systems Approach, Technology and the School,* Professional Paper SP-2025, Santa Monica, California: Systems Development Corporation, April.

CHIN, ROBERT. 1967. "Basic Strategies and Procedures in Effecting Change." In *Educational Organization and Administration Concepts, Practice and Issues,* ed. E. L. Morphet et al. Englewood Cliffs, N.J.: Prentice-Hall.

CHIN, ROBERT, AND KENNETH D. BENNE. 1969. "General Strategies for Effecting Changes in Human Systems." In *The Planning of Change,* ed. W. G. Bennis et al., 2d ed. New York: Holt, Rinehart & Winston.

CHIN, ROBERT, AND LOREN DOWNEY. 1973. "Changing Change: Innovating a Discipline." Chap. 17 in *The Handbook of Research on Teaching,,* ed. N. L. Gage. Chicago: Rand McNally.

CHORNESS, M. H., et al. 1968*a.* "Decision Processes and Information Needs in Education: A Field Survey." ERIC ED-026-748.

CHORNESS, M. H.; C. H. RITTENHOUSE; AND R. D. HEALD. 1968*b.* "Use of Resource Material and Decision Processes Associated with Educational Innovation: A Literature Survey." Berkeley: Far West Laboratory.

CHURCHMAN, C. W. 1971. *The Design of Inquiring Systems: Basic Concepts of Systems and Organizations.* New York: Basic Books.

CLARK, DAVID L., AND EGON G. GUBA. 1967. "An Examination of Potential Change Roles in Education." Essay six in *Rational Planning in Curriculum and Instruction,* ed. Ole Sand. Washington, D.C.: NEA-CSI.

————. 1975. "The Configurational Perspective: A New View of Educational Knowledge Production and Utilization." *Educational Researcher* 4, no. 4 (April).

CLIFFORD, GERALDINE. 1973. "A History of the Impact of Research on Teaching." In *Second Handbook of Research for Teaching,* ed. R. M. W. Travers. Chicago: Rand McNally.

COFFING, RICHARD T. 1973. *Identification of Client Demand for Public Services: Development of a Methodology.* Unpublished dissertation, University of Massachusetts, Ann Arbor: University Microfilms, File No. 73-31, 073.

COFFING, RICHARD T.; WILLIAM A. HODSON; AND THOMAS E. HUTCHINSON, 1973. *A Needs Analysis Methodology for Education of the Handicapped: Version I.* New Haven: Area Cooperative Educational Services.

COFFING, RICHARD T.; AND THOMAS E. HUTCHINSON. 1974. "Needs Analysis Methodology: A Prescriptive Set of Rules and Procedures for Identifying, Defining, and Measuring Needs." Paper presented at the annual meeting of American Educational Research Association, Chicago.

COLEMAN, JAMES S. 1963. "Systems of Social Exchange." Mimeographed. Baltimore, Md.: John Hopkins University (February).

COLEMAN, JAMES S., et al. 1966. *Equality of Educational Opportunity.* Washington, D.C.: U.S. Office of Education.

COLEMAN, JAMES S. 1973. "Conflicting Theories of Social Change." *Processes and Phenomena of Social Change,* Gerald Zaltman. ed. New York: Wiley Interscience.

CONEY, R., et al. 1968. *Educational R&D Information System Requirements.* Berkeley: Far West Laboratory.

COOKE, ROBERT; ROBERT DUNCAN; AND GERALD ZALTMAN. 1974. "Assessment of a Structural/Task Approach to Organizational Development in School Systems." Paper presented at the annual meeting of the American Educational Research Association (April). Chicago Ill.

COOKE, ROBERT AND GERALD ZALTMAN. 1972. "Implementing the Change Agent Team Concept." Paper presented at the Annual Meeting of the American Educational Research Association. Chicago, Ill.

COOKE, ROBERT. 1971. "Social Organization of Schools: The School as a Formal Organization." *The Encyclopedia of Education,* vol. 8. New York: Macmillan Co.

————. 1972. "Strategies for Organizational Innovation: An Empirical Comparison." *American Sociological Review* 37 (August): 441–54.

COUGHLAN, ROBERT J.; ROBERT A. COOKE; AND L. ARTHUR SAFER. 1972. *An Assessment of a Survey Feedback–Problem Solving–Collective Decision Intervention in Schools.* DHEW Final Report, Project No. O-E-105, Contract No. OEG-5-70-0036(509) (December).

COX, KEITH, AND BEN M. ENIS, 1972. *The Marketing Research Process.* Pacific Palisades, Calif. Goodyear Publishing Co.

CRANDALL, DAVID P. 1972. *Relationship between Innovativeness and Selected Elements of Group Structure.* Paper presented at the annual meeting of the American Educational Research Association, Chicago.

————. 1974. "Fostering Change from Without: A Practical Perspective." In *What Do Research Findings Say about Getting Innovations into Schools: A symposium,* ed. Temkin and Brown. Philadelphia: RBS.

CRONBACH, L. J. 1963. "Evaluation for Course Improvement." *Teacher's College Record,* no. 64. pp. 672–83.

DAVIS, HOWARD, AND SUSAN SALASIN. 1975. "The Utilization of Evaluation." in *Handbook of Evaluation Research,* E. L. Struening and M. Guttentag, Eds., Beverly Hills, Calif.

DEAL, TERRENCE E. 1975. "An Organization Explanation of the Failure of Alternative Secondary Schools." *Educational Researcher* 4, no. 4 (April).

DENHAM, CAROLYN. 1971. *Title III in Massachusetts: An Evaluation.* Boston: Department of Education.

DERR, C. B. 1972. "Successful Entry as a Key in Successful Organizational Development in Big City School Systems." In *The Social Technology Of Organizational Development,* ed. W. W. Burke and H. A. Hornstein. NTL Institute. Washington, D.C.

DERR, C. B., AND A. DEMB. 1974. "Entry and Urban School Systems: The Context and Culture of New Markets." *Education & Urban Society* 6, no. 2 (February).

DORNBUSCH, SANFORD M., AND W. RICHARD SANFORD. 1975. *Evaluation and the Exercise of Authority.* San Francisco: Jossey-Bass.

DOWNS, ANTHONY. 1966. *Inside Bureaucracy.* Boston: Little, Brown.

DREEBEN, ROBERT. 1970. *The Nature of Teaching: Schools and the Work of Teachers.* Glenview, Ill.: Scott, Foresman.

DRUCKER, PETER F. 1973. "On Managing the Public Service Institution." *The Public Interest,* no. 33 (Fall).

DUNCAN, ROBERT; GERALD ZALTMAN; AND ROBERT COOKE. 1975. "Organizational Development Programs in Schools." Unpublished working paper (March).

————. In progress. *An Evaluation of a Survey Feedback Approach to Organizational Development in School Systems.* Preliminary Report to the National Institute of Education.

EATON, J. W. 1962. "Symbolic and Substantive Evaluative Research." *Administrative Science Quarterly* 4: 421–42.

EBEL, R. L. 1973. "Evaluation and Educational Objectives." *Journal of Educational Measurement* 10: 273–79.

ECKENROD, JAMES S. 1975. "Report on the Model of Curriculum Diffusion for the BSCS Human Sciences Program." Paper presented at the annual meeting of the American Educational Research Association, Washington, D.C.

EIBLER, H. J. 1965. "A Comparison of the Relationships between Certain Aspects of Characteristics of the Structure of the High School Faculty and the Amount of Curriculum Innovation." Ph. D. dissertation, University of Michigan, Ann Arbor.

EICHHOLZ, GERHARD, AND EVERETT M. ROGERS. 1964. "Resistance to the Adoption of Audiovisual Aids by Elementary School Teachers." In *Innovation in Education,* ed. M. Miles. New York: Teachers College Press, Columbia University.

EISNER, E. W. 1967. "Educational Objectives: Help or Hindrance?" School Review 75: 250–60.

ETZIONI, AMITAI, AND EVA ETZIONI. 1964. *Social Change: Sources, Patterns and Consequences.* New York: Basic Books.

FAR WEST LABORATORY. 1974. "A Statement of Organizational Qualification. for Documentation and Analysis of Organizational Strategies for Sustained Improvement of Urban Schools." Submitted to Program on Local Problem Solving, N.I.E. San Francisco: Far West Laboratory.

FESTINGER, LEON. 1957. *A Theory of Cognitive Dissonance.* Evanston, Ill.: Harper & Row.

FLORIO, DAVID H. 1973*a*. "Organizational Cooperation for Educational Development." Ph. D. dissertation, Northwestern University, Evanston, Ill.

————. 1973*b*. "The Urban Teacher as a Potential Consumer." Paper presented at the annual meeting of the Association for Consumer Research panel on "Broadening the Concept of Consumer Behavior" (November).

FOSTER, GEORGE M. 1962. *Traditional Cultures and the Impact of Technological Change.* New York: Harper & Row.

FREY, N. 1969. "The Ethics of Change: The Role of the University." *School Guidance Worker* (October), pp. 1–12.

FULLAN, MICHAEL, AND GLENN EASTABROOK. 1970. *Problems and Issues Defining School Innovativeness.* Paper presented at the annual conference of the Ontario Educational Research Council, Toronto, Canada.

———. 1973. "The Process of Educational Change at the School Level: Deriving Action Implications from Questionnaire Data." Paper presented at the annual meeting of the American Educational Research Association, New Orleans (February).

GARDNER, JOHN, 1965. "How to Prevent Organizational Dry Rot." *Harpers* June.

GETZELS, J. W.; M. LIPHAM; AND R. F. CAMPBELL. 1968. *Educational Administration as a Social Process.* Evanston, Ill.: Harper & Row.

GIDEONSE, HENDRIK D. 1974. "The Locus of Control and Decision Making in Educational Research Management: An External Viewpoint." In *What Do Research Findings Say about Getting Innovations into Schools: A Symposium,* ed. Temkin and Brown. Philadelphia: RBS.

GILES, MICHAEL W. ; DOUGLAS S. GATHIN; AND EVERETT F. CATALDO. 1974. "The Impact of Busing on White Flight." *Social Science Quarterly* 55, no. 2 (September).

GRIFFITHS, DANIEL E. 1964. Administrative Theory and Change in Organization." In *Innovation in Education,* ed. Mathew B. Miles. New York: Teachers College Press, Columbia University.

GRINSTAFF, L. 1969. "New Ideas: Conflict and Evolution." *International Journal of Psycho-Analysis* 50: 517–28.

GROSS, N.; J. B. GIACQUINTA; AND M. BERNSTEIN. 1971. *Implementing Organizational Innovations: A Sociological Analysis of Planned Educational Change.* New York: Basic Books.

GUBA, EGON G. 1967. "The Development of Novel and Improved Strategies for Educational Diffusion." Proposal submitted to the U.S. Commissioner of Education (April).

———. 1972. "The Failure of Educational Evaluation." In *Evaluating Action Programs,* ed. C. H. Weiss. Boston: Allyn Bacon, pp. 250–66.

HAGE, GERALD, AND ROBERT DEWAR. 1971. *The Prediction of Organizational Performance: The Case of Program Innovation.* Paper presented at the annual meeting of the American Sociological Association, Denver, Colorado (September).

HAGEN, EVERETT E. 1962. *On the Theory of Social Change.* Homewood, Ill.: Dorsey Press.

HALL, GENE E., AND WILLIAM L. RUTHERFORD. 1975. "Concerns of Teachers about Implementing Faculty Teaming." Paper presented at the annual meeting of the American Educational Research Association, Washington, D.C.

HAND, HERBERT H.; BERNARD D. ESTAFEN; AND HENRY P. SIMS, JR. 1975. "How Effective Is Data Survey and Feedback as a Technique of Organizational Development? An Experiment." *Journal of Applied Behavioral Science* 2, no. 3 (July–September), pp. 333–47.

HARTLEY, H. J. 1968. *Educational Planning-Programming-Budgeting.* Englewood Cliffs, N. J.: Prentice-Hall.

HAVELOCK, R. G., AND M. C. HAVELOCK. 1973. *Training for Change Agents.* Ann Arbor: Institute for Social Research, University of Michigan.

HAVELOCK, R. G., et al. 1971. *Planning for Innovation through Dissemination and Utilization of Knowledge.* Ann Arbor, Mich.: RUSK/ISR.

HAWKINS, WILBUR D. 1968. "Some Factors Which Contribute to Successful Educational Innovation." Ph.D. dissertation, University of Southern California, (January).

HAWLEY, WILLIS D. 1974. "Dealing with Organizational Rigidity in Public Schools: A Theoretical Perspective." Unpublished paper, Yale University.

HEIDER, FRITZ. 1958. *The Psychology of Interpersonal Relations.* New York: Wiley.

HENCLEY, S. P., AND J. R. YATES. 1974. *Futurism in Education: Methodologies.* Berkeley: McCutchan.

HENZBERG, F. 1966. *Work and the Nature of Man.* New York: World.

HILL, M. J.; M. C. HAVELOCK; AND R. G. HAVELOCK. 1971. "Phase Orientations to New Knowledge." Chap. 10, pp. 1–89, in *Planning for Innovation through Dissemination and Utilization of Knowledge,* ed. R. G. Havelock et al. (Ann Arbor: Center for Research and Utilization of Scientific Knowledge).

HOMANS, GEORGE C. 1974. *Social Behavior: Its Elementary Forms.* New York: Harcourt Brace Jovanovich.

HOOD, PAUL. 1974. User Profiles unpublished paper, Far West Laboratory for Educational Research and Development, San Francisco, Calif. (August).

————.1975. "The Relationship between Purposes for Seeking Educational Information, Sources Used, and Type of Position of the User." FWL (September).

HORNSTEIN, HARVEY; BARBARA BUNKER; WARNER BURKE; MARION GINDES; AND RAY LOWICKI. 1971. *Social Intervention: A Behavioral Science Approach.* New York Free Press.

HOUSE, ERNEST R. 1974. *The Politics of Educational Innovation.* Berkeley: McCutchan.

HUGHES, LARRY W. 1965. "Organizational Climate Found in Central Administrative Offices of Selected Highly Innovative and Non-Innovative School Districts in Ohio." Ph. D. dissertation, Ohio State University, Columbus.

HULL, WILLIAM L., AND RANDALL L. WELLS. 1972. *The Classification and Evaluation of Innovations for Vocational and Technical Education.* Center for Vocational and Technical Education, Ohio State University, Columbus.

HUTCHINS, C. L., et al. 1970. *Final Report on the Elementary Science Information Unit: A Pilot Program to Improve Information Flow between Research and Development and Practice in Education,* Berkeley: Far West Laboratory.

HUTCHINSON, THOMAS E., AND LARRY G. BENEDICT. 1970. "The Operationalization of Fuzzy Concepts." Monograph. School of Education, University of Massachusetts, Amherst.

JACKSON, P. W., AND E. BELFORD. 1965. "Educational Objectives and the Joys of Teaching." *School Review* 73: 267–91.

JANOWITZ, MORRIS. 1969. *Institution Building in Urban Education.* Chicago: University of Chicago Press.

JOHNSON, DAVID W. 1969. "Influences on Teachers' Acceptance of Change." *Elementary School Journal* 52 (December): 142–53.

JOHNSON, J. A. JR., et al. 1973. *Biasing Effect of Teachers on Low-Income, Urban Black Children during the Early School Years.* Berkeley: Far West Laboratory (October).

JONES, GARTH N. 1969. *Planned Organizational Change: A Study in Change Dynamics.* New York: Praeger.

KAHNEMAN, D., AND E. O. SCHILD. 1966. "Training Agents of Social Change in Israel: Definition of Objectives and a Training Approach." *Human Organization* 25, no. 1 (Spring).

KASULIS, JACK. 1975. "Cognitive Structure, Segmental Analysis, and Communication Effectiveness: A Field Study of Cognitive Complexity Theory." Ph. D. thesis, Northwestern University, Graduate School of Management, Evanston, Ill.

KATZ, D., AND R. KAHN. 1966. *The Social Psychology of Organizations.* New York: Wiley.

KELLER, FRED S. 1968. "Good-bye Teacher . . ." *Journal of Applied Behavior Science* 1: 79–89.

KELLEY, E. F. 1973. "Can Evaluation Be Used to Cut Costs?" pp. 34–41 in *School Evaluation: The Politics and Process,* ed. E. R. House. Berkeley: McCutchan.

KELMAN, H. C. 1966. "Processes of Opinion Change." *Public Opinion Quarterly* 25: 57–78.

KEMIS, S. 1974. "Telling It Like It Is: The Problem of Making a Portrayal of an Educational Program." Mimeographed. University of Illinois at Urbana-Champaign.

KERLINGER, FRED N. 1969. "Research in Education." Pp. 1127–1144. in *Encyclopedia of Educational Research* (4th ed.), ed. R. L. Ebel. New York: Macmillan Co.

KESTER, RALPH J., AND WILLIAM L. HULL. 1973. "Identification of Empirical Dimensions of the Diffusion Process: Interim Report." Center for Vocational and Technical Education, Ohio State University, Columbus (October).

KIESLER, CHARLES A., AND SARA B. KIESLER. 1970. *Conformity.* Reading, Mass.: Addison-Wesley.

KILMANN, RALPH, AND IAN MITROFF. 1976. *Defining Real World Problems: A Social Science Approach.* St. Paul, Minn.: West Publishing.

KINTZER, FREDERICK C., AND STANLEY M. CHASE. 1969. "The Consultant as a Change Agent." *Junior College Journal* 39, April.

KIRBY, D., R. T. HARRIS, AND R. L. CRAIN. 1973. *Political Strategies in Northern Desegregation.* Lexington, Mass: Lexington Books.

KLINGENBERG, A. J. 1966. "A Study of Selected Administrative Behavior among Administrators from Innovative and Non-Innovative Public School Districts." *Dissertation Abstract,* 27-9A.

KLONGLAN, G., AND W. COWARD. 1970. "The Concept of Symbolic Adoption: A Suggested Interpretation." *Rural Sociology* 35: 77–83.

KNIGHT, K. E., AND W. P. GORTH. 1975. *Toward an Understanding of Educational Change: An Investigation of Seventy-seven Changes in Twenty High Schools.* Austin: University of Texas.

KOTLER, PHILIP. 1973. "The Elements of Social Action." In *Processes and Phenomena of Social Change,* ed. G. Zaltman et al. New York: Wiley Interscience.

KOTLER, PHILIP, AND GERALD ZALTMAN. 1971. "Social Marketing: An Approach to Planned Social Change." *Journal of Marketing* (July).

LAVIDGE, R. J., AND G. A. STEINER. 1961. "A Model for Predictive Measurements of Advertising Effectiveness." *Journal of Marketing* 25.

LAZARSFELD, PAUL F., AND JEFFREY G. REITZ. 1975. *An Introduction to Applied Sociology*. New York: Elsevier.

LEHNER, ANDREAS PETER. 1973. "The Design of an Alternative Academic Program for a Suburban High School Using Directly Obtained Client Needs Data." Ph. D. dissertation, University of Massachusetts, Ann Arbor. University Microfilms, File No. 74-8611.

LEVIN, HENRY M. 1974. "Educational Reform and Social Change." *Journal of Applied Behavioral Science* 10, no. 3.

LEWIN, KURT. 1952. "Group Decision and Social Change." In *Readings in Social Psychology*, ed. G. E. Swanson et al. New York: Henry Holt.

LIN, NAN, et al. 1966. *The Diffusion of an Innovation in Three Michigan High Schools: Institution Building through Change*. East Lansing: Michigan State University.

LINDBLOOM, C. E. 1959. "The Science of Muddling Through." *Public Administration Review* 19, no. 2 (Spring).

LIPPITT, G. 1969. *Organizational Renewal*. New York: Appleton-Century-Crofts.

LIPPITT, RONALD O. 1974. *Identifying, Documenting, Evaluating and Sharing Innovative Classroom Practices*. Final Report to the Office of Education, HEW.

LIPPITT, R.: J. WATSON; AND B. WESTLEY. 1958. *The Dynamics of Planned Change*. New York: Harcourt, Brace and Co.

LORTIE, DAN C. 1969. "The Balance of Control and Autonomy in Elementary School Teaching." In *The Semi-Professions and Their Organizations,* ed. Amitai Etzioni. New York: Free Press.

MARCH, JAMES G. 1972. "Model Bias in Social Action." *Review of Educational Research* 42, no. 4 (Fall).

MARCH, JAMES G., AND HERBERT SIMON. 1958. *Organizations*. New York: Wiley.

MASLOW, A. H. 1954. *Motivation and Personality*. New York: Harper & Row.

MCCLELLAND, DAVID. 1961. *The Achieving Society*. New York: Van Nostrand.

MCCUNE, SHIRLEY. 1974. "What Does Research Say about Getting Innovations into Schools? " *What Do Research Findings Say about Getting Innovations into Schools: A Symposium,* . ed. Temkin and Brown. Philadelphia: RBS.

MCGREGOR, D. 1960. *The Human Side of Enterprise*. New York: McGraw Hill.

MCKEACHIE, W. J. 1973. "Resistances to Evaluation of Teaching." Occasional Paper Number Two. The Center for the Teaching Professions, Northwestern University, Evanston, Illinois.

MERTON, ROBERT K. 1957. *Social Theory and Social Structure*. New York: Free Press. (Rev. ed., 1968.)

MILES, MATHEW B. 1964. "Innovation in Education: Some Generalizations." In *Innovation in Education*, ed. M. Miles. New York: Teachers College Press, Columbia University.

———. 1965. "Planned Change and Organizational Health: Figure and Ground." In

Change Process in the Public Schools, ed. R. O. Carlson. Eugene, Ore.; Center for the Advanced Study of Educational Administration.

―――. 1967. "Some Properties of Schools as Social Systems." In *Change in School Systems,* ed. G. Watson. New York: Cooperative Project for Educational Development, National Training Laboratories.

―――. 1974. "A Matter of Linkage: How Can Innovation Research and Innovation Practice Influence Each Other?" In *What Do Research Findings Say about Getting Innovations into Schools: A Symposium,* ed. Temkin and Brown. Philadelphia: RBS.

MILES, M. B.; H. A. HORNSTEIN; P. H. CALDER; D. M. CALLAHAN; AND R. S. SCHIAVO. 1971. "Data Feedback: A Rationale." *Social Intervention: A Behavioral Science Approach,* ed. H. Hornstein et al. New York: Free Press.

MILL, RICHARD. 1974. "What We Can Learn about Change Processes From ESEA Title III." In *What Do Research Findings Say about Getting Innovations into Schools: A Symposium,* ed. Temkin and Brown. Philadelphia: RBS.

MOSHER, E. K. 1969. *What about the School Research Office? A Staff Report.* Berkeley: Far West Laboratory.

NAGI, SAAD Z. 1974. "Gatekeeping Decisions in Service Organizations: When Validity Fails." *Human Organization* 33, 1, Spring, pp. 47–58.

National Institute of Mental Health. 1973. "A Manual on Research Utilization." DHEW Publication No. (HSM) 71-9059.

NELSON, CARNOT. 1970. "Information Dissemination in Educational Research." Working paper, Center for the Study of Scientific Communication, The John Hopkins University, Baltimore, Md.

NIAZ, MOHAMMED ASLAM. 1963. "Strategies of Planned Organizational Change." Dissertation presented to the faculty of the School of Public Administration, University of Southern California (February).

NIEHOFF, ARTHUR H. ed. 1966. *A Casebook of Social Change.* Chicago: Aldine.

NIEHOFF, ARTHUR H., AND J. C. ANDERSON. 1966. "Peasant Fatalism and Socio-Economic Innovation." *Human Organization* 25: 273–83.

OWENS, ROBERT G. 1970. *Organizational Behavior in Schools.* Englewood Cliffs, N.J.: Prentice-Hall.

OWENS, T. R. 1973. "Educational Evaluation by Adversary Proceeding." Pp. 295–305 in *School Evaluation: The Politics and Process,* ed. E. R. House. Berkeley: McCutchan.

PELLEGRIN, ROLAND J. 1965. "The Place of Research in Planned Change." Pp. 65–75 in *Change Processes in the Public Schools,* ed. R. O. Carlson et al. University of Oregon: Center for the Advanced Study of Educational Administration.

PETERSON, PAUL E. 1974. "The Politics of American Education." *Review of Educational Research* Vol. 44.

PIERCE, WENDELL H. 1974. "Is Innovation a Dirty Word?" In *What Do Research Findings Say about Getting Innovations into Schools: A Symposium,* ed. Temkin and Brown. Philadelhpia: RBS.

PINCUS, JOHN. 1974. "Incentives for Innovation." *Review of Educational Research* 44, no. 1, (Winter).

Planning for Creative Change in Mental Health Services: A Manual on Research Utilization. DHEW Publication No. (HSM) 13-9147. Rockville, Md.: National Institute of Mental Health.

POPHAM, W. J. 1974. "Results Rather than Rhetoric." Pp. 57–60 In *Evaluation in Education,* ed. W. J. Popham. Berkeley: McCutchan.

PROVUS, M. 1971. *Discrepancy Evaluation.* Berkeley: McCutchan.

RICHARDS, M. D., AND P. S. GREENLAW. 1966. *Management Decision Making,* Homewood, Ill.: Richard D. Irwin, pp. 423–28.

RIECKEN, H. W. 1972. "Memorandum on Program Evaluation." Pp. 85–104 In *Evaluating Action Programs,* ed. C. H. Weiss. Boston: Allyn & Bacon.

RIPPEY, R. M., ed. 1973. *Studies in Transactional Evaluation.* Berkeley: McCutchan.

ROBERTSON, T. S. 1971. *Innovative Behavior and Communication.* New York: Holt Rinehart & Winston.

ROGERS, EVERETT M. 1962. *Diffusion of Innovations.* New York: Free Press.

——. 1973*a. Modernization among Peasants.* New York: Holt, Rinehart & Winston.

——. 1973*b.* "Social Structure and Social Change." In *Processes and Phenomena of Social Change,* ed. G. Zaltman et al. New York: Wiley Interscience.

——. 1973*c.* Unpublished paper presented at the East-West Center Communication Institute, University of Hawaii (December).

ROGERS, E. M.; N. LIN; AND G. ZALTMAN. 1973. "Design for a Research Utilization System for the Social and Rehabilitation Service." Report to the Social and Rehabilitation Service for the Center for Research on Utilization of Scientific Knowledge, University of Michigan, Ann Arbor (September).

ROGERS, E. M., AND F. F. SHOEMAKER. 1971. *Communication of Innovation: A Cross Cultural Approach.* New York: Free Press.

ROSENAU, FRED S. 1974. *Tactics for the Educational Change Agent: A Preliminary Analysis.* San Francisco: Far West Laboratory.

ROSENSHINE, B., AND N. FURST. 1971. "Research on Teacher Performance Criteria." Pp. 37–72 In *Research in Teacher Education: A Symposium,* ed. B. O. Smith. Englewood Cliffs, N.J.: Prentice-Hall.

ROSTOW, W. W., *The Stages of Economic Growth,* Cambridge, England: Cambridge University Press, 1960.

ROTHMAN, JACK. 1974. *Planning and Organizing for Social Change.* New York: Columbia University Press.

SARASON, SEYMOUR B. 1971. *The Culture of the School and the Problem of Change.* Boston: Allyn & Bacon.

SCANLON, ROBERT G. 1973. "Strategies for the Implementation of Innovations: Individualized Learning Programs." Paper presented at the annal meeting of the AERA, New Orleans (February).

SCHEIN, E. H., AND W. G. BENNIS. 1965. *Personal and Organizational Change through Group Methods.* New York: Wiley.

SCHMIDTLEIN, FRANK A. 1974. "Decision Process Paradigms in Education." *Educational Researcher* 3, no. 5 (May).

SCHMUCK, RICHARD A. 1974. "Bringing Parents and Students into School Management." *Education and Urban Society* 6, no. 2 (February).

SCHMUCK, RICHARD. 1968. "Social Psychological Factors in Knowledge Utilization." Eidell & Kitchell (eds.). *Production and Utilization in Educational Administration,* Eugene, Oregon: UCEA, CASEA.

SCHMUCK, R. A., AND M. B. MILES. 1971. *Organizational Development in Schools.* Palo Alto, Calif: National Press Books.

SCHMUCK R. A.; P. RUNKEL; AND D. LANGMEYER. 1969. "Improving Organizational Problem Solving in a School Faculty." *Journal of Applied Behavioral Science* 5, no. 4.

———. 1971. "Using Group Problem-Solving Procedures." In *Organization Development in Schools,* ed. Schmuck and Miles. Palo Alto: National Press Books.

SCHMUCK, R. A.; P. RUNKEL; et al. 1972. *Handbook of Organizational Development in Schools.* Palo Alto: National Press Books.

SCHMUCK, R. A., AND PATRICIA SCHMUCK. 1974*a*. *Humanistic Psychology of Education.* Palo Alto: National Press Books.

———. 1974*b*. *Humanizing the School.* San Francisco: Jossey-Bass.

SCHON, DONALD A. 1967. *Technology and Change.* New York: Delacorte Press.

———. 1971. *Beyond the Stable State.* New York: W. W. Norton.

SCRIVEN, M. 1967. "The Methodology of Evaluation." Pp. 39–83 In *Perspectives of Curriculum Evaluation,* ed. R. Tyler et al. *AERA Monograph Series on Curriculum Evaluation,* no. 1. Chicago: Rand McNally.

———. 1972. "Pros and Cons about Goal-free Evaluation." *Evaluation Comment* 2: 1–8.

———. 1973. "Goal-free Evaluation." Pp. 319–28 In *School Evaluation: The Politics and Process,* ed. E. R. House. Berkeley: McCutchan.

SEASHORE, STANLEY. 1967. "Communication." Paper for the Mid-Career Education Project.

SERGIOVANNI, THOMAS J. 1969. "Factors Which Affect Satisfaction and Dissatisfaction of Teachers." In *Organizations and Human Behavior: Focus on Schools,* ed. F. Carver and T. Sergiovanni. New York: McGraw-Hill.

SERGIOVANNI, THOMAS J., AND FRED B. CARVER. 1973. *The New School Executive: A Theory of Administration.* New York; Dodd, Mead.

SHORT, E. C. 1973. "Knowledge Production and Utilization in Curriculum: A Specific Case of the General Phenomena." *Review of Educational Research* 43, no. 3 (Summer).

SIEBER, SAM D. 1968. "Organizational Influence on Innovative Roles." In *Knowledge Production and Utilization in Educational Administration,* ed. T. L. Eidell and J. M. Kitchell. Eugene: University of Oregon, Center for Advanced Study of Educational Administration.

———. 1973. "The Dynamics and Outcomes of an Educational Extension System." Paper presented at the meetings of the American Educational Research Association, New Orleans (February 26).

SIEBER, SAM D., AND KAREN S. LOUIS. 1973. "The Educational Extension Agent: An Evaluation of a Pilot State Dissemination Project." Paper presented at the meetings of the AERA, New Orleans.

SIEBER, SAM D.; KAREN S. LOUIS; AND LOYA METZGER. 1972. *The Use of Educational*

Knowledge, vols. 1 and 2, final report to the Office of Education. Available from the Bureau of Applied Social Research, Columbia University.

SIKES, WALTER W.; LAWRENCE E. SCHLESINGER; AND CHARLES N. SEASHORE. 1974. *Renewing Higher Education from Within.* San Francisco: Jossey-Bass.

SIKORSKI, LINDA. 1971. *Main Field Test of the ALERT Information System.* Berkeley: Far West Laboratory.

SIKORSKI, LINDA, AND HUTCHINS, C. L. 1974. *The Study of the Feasibility of Marketing Programming for Educational Change.* San Francisco: Far West Laboratory.

SMITH, KENNETH E., AND HOWARD M. SANDLER. 1974. "Bases of Status in Four Elementary School Faculties." *American Educational Research Journal* 11, no. 4 (Fall).

STAKE, R. E. 1967. "The Countenance of Educational Evaluation." *Teacher's College Record* 68: 523–40.

———. 1972. "An Approach to the Evaluation of Instructional Programs." Paper presented at the annual meeting of the American Educational Research Association, Chicago.

———, ed. 1975. *Evaluating the Arts of Education: A Responsive Approach.* Columbus, Ohio: Charles E. Merrill.

STAKE, R. E., AND C. GJERDE. 1974. "An Evaluation of the TCITY, the Twin City Institute for Talented Youth." *AREA Monograph Series on Curriculum Evaluation,* vol. 7. Chicago: Rand McNally.

STILES, L. J., AND B. ROBINSON. 1973. "Change in Education." In *Processes and Phenomena of Social Change,* ed. G. Zaltman et al. New York: Wiley Interscience.

STUFFLEBEAM, D. L. 1967. "The Use and Abuse of Evaluation in Title III." *Theory into Practice* 6: 126–33.

———. 1974*a.* "Alternative Approaches to Educational Evaluation." Pp. 97–143 In *Evaluation in Education,* ed. W. J. Popham. Berkeley: McCutchan.

———. 1974*b.* "Should or Can Evaluation Be Goal-free?" Pp. 43–46 In *Evaluation in Education,* ed. W. J. Popham. Berkeley: McCutchan.

STUFFLEBEAM, D. L. et al. 1971. *Educational Evaluation and Decision-Making.* Bloomington, Ind.: Phi Delta Kappan National Study Committee on Education.

SUCHMAN, E. A. 1972. "Action for What? A Critique of Evaluative Research." Pp. 52–84 In *Evaluating Action Programs,* ed. C. H. Weiss. Boston: Allyn & Bacon.

TELFER, R. G. 1966. "Dynamics of Change." *The Clearing House* 41 (November).

TEMKIN, SANFORD. 1974. "A School District Strategy for Interfacing with Educational Research and Development." *What Do Research Findings Say about Getting Innovations into Schools: A Symposium,* ed. Temkin and Brown. Philadelphia: RBS.

TEMKIN, SANFORD, AND MARY V. BROWN, eds. 1974. *What Do Research Findings Say about Getting Innovations into Schools: A Symposium.* Philadelphia: Research for Better Schools, Inc. (January).

THOMAS, J. ALAN. 1971. *The Productive School: A Systems Analysis Approach to Educational Administration.* New York: Wiley.

THOMPSON, JAMES D. 1967. *Organizations in Action.* New York: McGraw-Hill.

THOMPSON, VICTOR. 1969. "The Innovative Organization." In *Organizations and Human*

Behavior: Focus on Schools, ed. F. Carver and T. Sergiovonni. New York: McGraw-Hill.

TURNBULL, B. J., et al. 1974. *Promoting Change in Schools: A Diffusion Casebook.* San Francisco: Far West Laboratory.

TYLER, R. W. 1942. "General Statement on Evaluation." *Journal of Educational Research* 35: 492–501.

———. 1950. *Basic Principles of Curriculum and Instruction.* Chicago: University of Chicago Press.

WALTON, RICHARD E. 1965. "Two Strategies of Social Change and Their Dilemmas." *Journal of Applied Behavioral Science* 1 (April–June).

WARWICK, DONALD P., AND HERBERT C. KELMAN. 1973. "Ethical Issues in Social Intervention." In *Processes and Phenomena of Social Change,* ed. G. Zaltman et al. New York: Wiley Interscience.

WATSON, BERNARD C. 1974. "Research and Innovation: Unanswered Questions," In *What Do Research Findings Say About Getting Innovations Into Schools: A Symposium,* ed. Temkin and Brown. Philadelphia: RBS.

WATSON, GOODWIN. 1966. "Resistance to Change. In *Concepts for Social Change,* ed. G. Watson. COPED Series, vol. 1. Washington, D.C.: NTL.

———. 1973. "Resistance to Change." In *Processes and Phenomena of Social Change,* ed. G. Zaltman et al. New York: Wiley Interscience.

WEBB, EUGENE J.; DONALD T. CAMPBELL; RICHARD D. SCHWARTZ; AND LEE SECHREST. 1966. *Unobtrusive Measures: Nonreactive Research in the Social Sciences.* Chicago: Rand McNally.

WEBER, MAX. 1956. *The Protestant Ethic and the Spirit of Capitalism.* New York: Charles Scribner's Sons.

WEINTHALER, JUDITH A. 1974. "Needs Identification Report on Needs of Parents of Pre-School Handicapped Children." New Haven: Department of Special Education, Southern Connecticut State College.

Westinghouse Learning Corporation and Ohio University. 1969. *The Impact of Head Start on Children's Cognitive and Affective Development.* Springfield, Va.: Clearinghouse for Federal Scientific and Technical Information, Sales Department, U.S. Department of Commerce.

WIDMER, JEANNE M. 1975. "What Makes Innovation Work in Massachusetts? Strategies for State and Local Systems." Paper presented at the annual meeting of the AERA, Washington, D.C. (March).

WORTMAN, PAUL M. 1975. "Evaluation Research: A Psychological Perspective." *American Psychologist* (May), Pp. 562–75.

YORK, L. J. 1968. "Arrangements and Training for Effective Use of Educational Research and Development Information." ERIC ED-0260746.

ZALTMAN, GERALD. 1973. "Strategies for Diffusing Innovations." In *Marketing Analysis for Societal Problems,* ed. J. N. Sheth and P. L. Wright. National Conference on Social Marketing Urbana, Ill. (December).

———. 1974. "Control and Innovation." Unpublished working paper, Northwestern University.

ZALTMAN, GERALD, AND G. BROOKER. 1971. "A New Look at the Adoption Process." Unpublished working paper, Northwestern University.

ZALTMAN, GERALD, AND PHILIP BURGER. 1975. *Marketing Research: Fundamentals and Dynamics*. Hinsdale, Ill.: Dryden Press.

ZALTMAN, GERALD, AND ROBERT DUNCAN. 1977. *Strategies for Planned Change*. New York: Wiley Interscience.

ZALTMAN, GERALD; ROBERT DUNCAN; AND JONNY HOLBEK. 1973. *Innovations and Organizations*. New York: Wiley.

ZALTMAN, GERALD; PHILIP KOTLER; AND IRA KAUFMAN. 1972. *Creating Social Change*. New York: Holt, Rinehart & Winston.

ZALTMAN, GERALD, AND NAN LIN. 1971. "On the Nature of Innovations." *American Behavioral Scientist* 14, no. 5 (May/June), Pp. 651–74.

ZALTMAN, GERALD, AND CHRISTIAN R. A. PINSON. 1974. "Perceptions of Innovations Over Time." Unpublished working paper, Northwestern University.

ZALTMAN, GERALD; CHRISTIAN R. A. PINSON; AND REINHART ANGELMAR. 1973. *Metatheory and Consumer Research*. New York: Holt, Rinehart & Winston.

ZALTMAN, GERALD, AND RONALD STIFF. 1973. "Theories of Diffusion." In *Consumer Behavior: Theoretical Sources,* ed. S. Ward and T. Robertson. Englewood Cliffs, N.J.: Prentice-Hall.

Index

A

A VICTORY model, 227–230
Acceptance processes, incomplete, 45
Action-implications dimension of change
  tactics, 100, 103–104
Action research, as change tactic, 81, 94
  dimensions of, 100–101
  situational considerations, 114–115
Activity dimension of change tactics, 100,
  103
Adaptation, in political process model,
  55–56
Administrator's perspective, 14
Adoption:
  in collective innovation decision model,
    60, 61
  in individual-oriented models, 65, 66
  in political process model, 55–56
  in research, development, and diffusion
    models, 67
Adversary model, 268, 270–272
Advertising, as change tactic, 81, 84
  dimensions of, 100–101
  situational considerations, 112
Affectee, identifying, 226
Alternative solutions, in planning process,
  169, 170
  adoption or rejection of, 172–174
  processes for generating, 169
  testing, 169–171
Altman, Tamara C., 85, 87
Anderson, J. C., 33
Angelmar, Reinhart, 234
Applicability, in evaluation, 258
Appraising, 251
Argyris, Chris, 136, 139, 294
Articles, as change tactic, 94
  dimensions of, 100–101
  situational considerations, 112–113

Attitude formation, in individual-oriented
  models, 65
Authoritative/participative models, 61–64
  authority versus collective innovative
    decision, 61–62
  collaborative versus noncollaborative
    approaches, 62–64
Authority patterns, 9–11
Authority strategy, 76–77, 81
Awareness:
  of change program, control and, 238
  in individual-oriented models, 64, 65
  in planning process, 148–153

B

Balbridge, J. Victor, 13, 71, 87, 93, 96
Barnett, Homer G., 42, 44
Beckhard, Richard, 153
Behavioral testing, 170–171
Belasco, James A., 22
Benedict, Larry G., 203, 208
Benne, Kenneth D., 77–78, 79, 81, 128,
  131, 139
Bennis, Warren G., 62–64, 131, 139, 302
Benzen, Mary M., 80, 83
Berman, Paul, 72
Bernstein, M., 177
Blake, R. R., 52, 53, 139
Blanzy, J. J., 95
Bloom, Benjamin, 68, 172, 177
Blum, Henrik L., 242
Blumberg, A., 131, 132, 133, 139
Books, as change tactic, 94
  dimensions of, 100–101
  situational considerations, 112–113
Brainstorming, 145, 151
Brooker, G., 64
Brown, Mary V., 97

Bureaucratic authority patterns, 9
Bushnell, David S., 62

C

Campbell, Donald T., 53, 261
Campbell, R. F., 52
Capacity to change, control and, 237
Carlisle, D. H., 96
Carlson, Richard O., 25, 53–54, 93, 96,
    301, 302
Carpenter–Huffman, P., 31, 34, 254
Carter, Faunor, 44
Carver, Fred B., 178
Cataldo, Everett F., 54
Causal analysis, 232, 234–240
Central office control, 9
Centralization:
    implementation and, 223–224
    in organizational change models, 58, 59
Change–planner systems perspective, 292
Chase, Stanley M., 303
Chesler, Mark, 302
Chin, Robert, 77–78, 79, 81, 128, 131
Chorness, M. H., 93, 95
Clark, David L., 67, 289, 291, 294
Class differences, as barrier to collabora-
    tion, 300–301
Client need assessment, 128–129, 141–
    142, 154–155, 182–220
    basic concepts, 184–188
    basic procedures, 188–220
    defining clients' needs, 189, 205–213
    evaluating utility of information,
        217–220
    focusing effort, 189, 192–197
    identifying clients, needs, and defin-
        ers, 189, 195, 198–204
    measuring status of need, 189, 213–
        217
    preparation, 189, 191
    reasons for, 182–184
Client validity, 187–188
Clients of schools:
    assessment of needs: see Client need as-
        sessment
    defined, 186
    as forces for change, 27
    influence of, 7–8

Coercive change, 63
Coercive strategies, 76, 78, 81
Coffing, Richard T., 182–220
Coleman, James S., 10, 53
Collective bargaining, 12, 13
Collective decision making, 36, 42
Collective innovation decision model,
    60–62
Commitment:
    as barrier to change, 41
    control and, 237
    strategy development and, 82–85
Communicability:
    in evaluation, 258
    resistance to change and, 37–38
Communication, as manipulative, 74–75
Communications network, 173
Comparative evaluation, 257
Compatibility of innovation, resistance to
    change and, 43
Complexity:
    implementation and, 223
    in organizational change models, 57, 59
    resistance to change and, 42
Comprehensive/prescriptive concept of
    change, 15
Compulsory attendance laws, 6
Computer-assisted instruction (CAI), 22
Coney, R., 95
Configurational perspective of knowledge
    utilization, 291
Conflict:
    as barrier to change, 35
    in organizational change models, 58, 59
Conflict reduction, 224
Conformity, as barrier to change, 41
Confrontation, as change tactic, 94
    dimensions of, 100–101
    situational considerations, 115
Constraints, in planning process, 162–169
Consultation, as change tactic, 97
    dimensions of, 100–101
    situational considerations, 119–120
Context evaluation, 265–268
Context feedback, 175, 245
Context-input-process-product (CIPP)
    evaluation model, 265–268
Control, 9, 174–176, 230–247
    defined, 231

environmental, 11–13
external governance structure of schools, 11–13
implementation and, 231–240
management and, 243–245
objectives and, 242–243
organizational information system (OIS), 245–247
plan and, 242
standards and, 240–241
Control beliefs, as barrier to change, 33–34
Cooke, Robert, 26, 36, 44, 60, 149, 150, 239, 280, 283n, 301
Cooperative Project for Educational Development (COPED), 292
Corwin, 5, 25, 29
Cost–benefit studies, 258
Cost-to-receiver dimension of change tactics, 101, 107
Cost-to-sender dimension of change tactics, 101, 107
Costs, evaluation and, 259
Coughlan, Robert J., 60–61, 149, 150, 261, 302
Countenance model, 264–265
Cox, Keith, 245–246
Crain, R. L., 54
Crandall, David P., 87, 93
Crisis, as aid to collaboration, 302
Criteria setting, in evaluation process, 250, 251
Cultural barriers to change, 31, 33–34, 300–301.
Culture of the School and the Problem of Change, The (Sarason), 31

D

Data processing, evaluation and, 258
Davis, Howard, 227
Deal, Terrence E., 71, 96
Decentralization of authority, 36
Decision group size, resistance to change and, 43
Decision-maker validity, 188
Decision makers, 183, 186
    defined, 186–187
    see also Client need assessment

Decision-making stage of planning process, 172–174
Definers:
    defined, 189n
    see also Client need assessment
Demb, A., 138
Demographic patterns, as forces for change, 28
Demonstrability, resistance to change and, 42–43
Demonstrations, as change tactic, 75, 94
    dimensions of, 100–101
    in planning process, 169–172
    situational considerations, 113
Denham, Carolyn, 72, 96
Derr, C. B., 138, 139
Description, in evaluation process, 253–254
Development, in political process model, 55–56
Dewar, Robert, 93
Diagnosis stage of planning process, 148–153
Didactic strategy, 76, 77, 81
Diffusion:
    in collective innovation decision model, 61
    in political process model, 55–56
Diplomacy, 224–225
Direct mail:
    as change tactic, 94
    dimensions of, 100–101
    situational considerations, 112
Discrepancy evaluation, 261–263
Dornbusch, Sanford M., 250, 251, 258
Downs, Anthony, 21
Dreeban, Robert, 9
Drucker, Peter F., 12–13
Duncan, Robert, 23, 25, 28, 30, 36, 51, 53, 56–59, 131, 148, 149, 170, 176, 221, 222, 236, 239, 280, 283n
Dysfunctional consequences, control and, 240

E

Ease-of-use dimension of change tactics, 101, 105
Eastabrook, Glenn, 73, 95

Eaton, J. W., 36
Economic strategy, 76–77, 81
Economist's perspective, 14
Education, as rational tactic, 75
Educational change:
  basic principles for, 311–315
  evaluation of programs: see Evaluation
  forces for, 21–29
    client groups, 27
    external, 28
    knowledge, 26
    new personnel, 25
    new treatments for existing personnel,
      25
    personal frustration, 28–29
    power relationships, 26
    reference groups, 27
    social value of output, 27
    technological change, 26
    unrealistic expectations, 23–24
    upward adjustment of expectations,
      24–25
  models of: see Models of educational
    change; Proactive/Interactive
    Change Model (P/ICM)
  nature of, 3–13
    conduct of education and, 4–7
    influence system and, 8–13
    publics and clients of schools and, 7–8
  perspectives on, 13–19
  resistance to, 29–47, 163
    control and, 239
    cultural, 31, 33–34
    defined, 30
    innovation attributes, 41–44
    organizational, 36–39
    personal incompatibility, 44–45
    personality factors, 44
    psychological, 39–41
    social, 34–36
    unavailability of resources, 44
  strategies of, 71–89, 163
    development of, 82–89
    types of, 73–82
Educational organization information sys-
    tem, 245–247
Educational policy maker, 14
Educational research, 86

Educationese, 299
Eibler, H. J., 93
Eichholz, Gerhard, 45, 46
Empirical–rational strategies, 77, 81
Employees of schools, influence of, 8
Emulative change, 63
Endorsements, as change tactic, 96
  dimensions of, 100–101
  situational considerations, 117
Enis, Ben M., 245–246
Enthusiasm, generation of, 224
Entry standards, teacher, 5, 7
Environmental control, 11–13
Environmental elements:
  involving in decision-making, 135–136
  relationships with, 17–18, 126
Environmental feedback, 245
Environmental models, 54–56
  Levin's polity model, 54–55
  Stiles and Robinson's political process
    model, 55–56
Estafen, Bernard D., 280
Ethnocentrism, as barrier to change, 34
Etzioni, Amitai, 302
Evaluation, 177–178, 249–273
  allocation, 250, 251
  applicability and, 258
  appraising, 251
  communicability and, 258
  comparative, 257
  criteria setting, 250, 251
  data processing and, 258
  description in, 253–254
  external, 254–255
  finances and, 258
  focused, 260–267
    context-input-process-product (CIPP)
      evaluation model, 265–268
    countenance model, 264–265
    discrepancy approach, 261–263
    experimental and quasi-experimental
      research, 260–261
    program–audit model, 263
  formative, 253
  frequency of, 259
  in individual-oriented models, 65, 66
  internal, 254–255
  judgment in, 253–254

nature of task and, 258–259
noncomparative, 257
number of evaluators and, 259–260
objectives of, 258
objectivity in, 257
organizational arrangements and, 259
organizational components and, 251,
    252
reactive effects of, 255–257
sampling decision, 250–251
summative, 253, 254
theoretical components and, 251–252
timeliness in, 258
unfocused, 266, 268–272
    adversary approach, 268, 270–272
    goal-free, 266, 268–269
    responsive, 268, 269–271
Expectations, as force for change, 23–24
Experimental evaluation research, 260–261
External change agents, potential need for,
    134–135
External evaluation, 254–255
External governance structure of school,
    11–13

F

Facilitative strategies, 78, 79, 81
Factionalism, as barrier to change, 35
Far West Laboratory, 89
Fatalism, as barrier to change, 33–34
Federal aid, 11
Feedback:
    context, 175, 245
    as control element, 175–176
    environmental, 245
    input, 175, 176, 245
    process, 175, 176, 245
    product, 175, 245
    survey: *see* Survey feedback
Feedback/interaction dimension of change
    tactics, 100, 102–103
Feedback system:
    as change tactic, 97
    dimensions of, 100–101
    situational considerations, 120
Festinger, Leon, 84

Field agents:
    as change tactic, 94
    dimensions of 100–101
    situational considerations, 114
Field-testing:
    as change tactic, 94
    dimensions of, 100–101
    situational considerations, 117
Finances, evaluation and, 258
Financial/material dimension of change
    tactics, 101, 107
Financial resources generation:
    as change tactic, 97
    dimensions of, 100–101
    situational considerations, 118
Fiscal resources, as force for change, 28
Florio, David H., 138, 156, 161
Focused evaluation, 260–267
    context-input-process-product (CIPP)
        evaluation model, 265–268
    countenance model, 264–265
    discrepancy approach, 261–263
    experimental and quasi-experimental re-
        search, 260–261
    program–audit model, 263
Follow-up dimension of change tactics,
    101, 106
Foot-in-door strategy, 239
Formalization:
    implementation and, 223
    in organizational change models, 58, 59
Formative evaluation, 253
Foster, George M., 33
Frey, N., 35
Friendship patterns, innovation adoption
    and, 93
Frustration, as force for change, 28–29
Fullan, Michael, 73, 95
Funding, as change tactic, 74

G

Gardner, John, 153
Gary, Lucius, 42
Gatekeepers, 38, 41–42, 225, 226
Gatlin, Douglas S., 54
Getzels, J. W., 52
Giaquinta, J. B., 174, 177

Gideonse, Hendrik D., 87
Giles, Michael W., 54
Glaser, 294
Goal displacement, 6
Goal-free evaluation, 266, 268–269
Goal-free evaluator (GFE), 268–269
Goal setting, as change tactic, 81
Goals, clarity of, 243–244, 258
Gorth, W. P., 96
Griffiths, Daniel E., 302
Grinstaff, L., 44
Gross, N., 37, 40, 174, 177, 236
Group insight, as barrier to change, 36
Group solidarity, as barrier to change, 34–35
Guba, Egon G., 67, 76–77, 80, 81, 156, 289, 291, 294

H

Hage, Gerald, 93
Hagen, Everett E., 31
Hall, Gene E., 95, 98
Hand, Herbert H., 280
Harris, R. T., 54
Hastings, J. T., 172, 177
Havelock, M. C., 45, 47, 136, 138, 139, 158, 289–291, 302
Havelock, R. G., 10, 15, 45, 47, 75, 96, 97, 112, 113, 114, 119, 120, 136, 138, 139, 148, 156, 158, 161, 289–291, 294, 299, 302
Hawkins, Wilbur D., 93
Hawley, Willis D., 37
Heider, Fritz, 44
Hierarchy, as change tactic, 74, 81
Hodson, William A., 200, 208, 215, 217
Holbek, Jonny, 23, 25, 36, 38, 53, 56–59, 131, 148, 175, 176
Homans, George C., 44
Homeostasis, resistance to change and, 41
Hood, Paul, 93
Hornstein, Harvey, 75
Hughes, Larry W., 93
Hutchins, C. L., 44, 73, 91, 96
Hutchinson, Thomas E., 184, 188, 200, 203, 208, 214, 215, 217

I

Imagery dimension of change tactics, 101, 107
Immediacy dimension of change tactics, 101, 106–107
Impersonal tactics, 103
Implementation, 174–176, 221–230
  A VICTORY model of, 227–230
  assessment of, 231–240
  barriers to, 174
  change–planner skills for, 224–226
  in collective innovation decision model, 60, 61
  nature of the change and, 226–227
  organizational characteristics and, 222–224
  see also Control
In-service classes:
  as change tactic, 81, 97, 303
  dimensions of, 100–101
  situational considerations, 119
Inactive relationships, 126
Incremental/remedial (I/R) concept of change, 15
Individual-oriented models, 64–66
Individuals, overemphasis on, 244
Indoctrination, 62–63
Inference trees, 234–240
Influence system, 8–13
Influencers, identifying, 225, 226
Information dissemination, as rational tactic, 75–76
Information/linkage tactics, 92, 93–95
  dimensions of, 100–101
  situational considerations, 112–116
Information systems:
  as change tactic, 94
  dimensions of, 100–101
  situational considerations, 115
Informative strategies, 76, 81
Innovation attributes:
  causing resistance to change, 41–44
  list of, 18–19
Input, barriers to, 299–301
Input evaluation, 265–268
Input feedback, 175, 176, 245

Insecurity, resistance to change and, 40
Institutionalization of change roles:
  as change tactic, 96
  dimensions of, 100–101
  situational considerations, 117
Integration strategies, 140
Interaction, need for, 126–127
Interactional change, 63
Interactive relationships, 126–127; *see also*
  Proactive/Interactive Change
  Model (P/ICM)
Internal evaluation, 254–255
Interpersonal relations:
  impact of change on, 44
  in organizational change models, 58, 59
Interpersonal tactics, 103

J

Janowitz, Morris, 9, 10
Johnson, David W., 44
Johnson, J. A., Jr., 27, 39
Jones, Garth N., 78, 81, 86
Judgment, in evaluation process, 253–254

K

Kahn, R., 15, 51, 80, 176, 304
Kahneman, D., 179
Kasulis, Jack, 43, 239
Katz, D., 15, 51, 80, 176, 304
Keller, Fred S., 68
Kelman, Herbert C., 76, 80, 83, 84, 86
Kester, Ralph J., 76, 81
Kiesler, Charles A., 41
Kiesler, Sara B., 41
Kilmann, Ralph, 294
Kintzer, Frederick C., 303
Kirby, D., 54
Klemt, Laura, 249*n*
Klinenberg, A. J., 93
Knight, K. E., 96
Knowledge:
  as force for change, 26
  in individual-oriented models, 64, 65
Knowledge–broker system, 292

Knowledge building, as rational tactic,
  75–76
Knowledge–resource organizations, 157
Knowledge utilization, 277–310
  communications gap and, 288–289
  concept of, 278–280
  defined, 278
  eclectic model of, 292–298
  organizational collaboration, aids and
    barriers to, 298–305
  perspectives on, 289–298
  principles for, 305–310
  survey feedback and problem solving
    example, 280–288
Kotler, Philip, 7

L

Langmeyer, D., 132, 173
Lazarsfeld, Paul F., 294
Leadership change, as aid to collaboration,
  302
Legal tactics, 74, 85–86, 92, 97–98
  dimensions of, 100–101
  situational considerations, 118
Legitimation:
  in collective innovation decision model,
    60, 61, 62
  in individual-oriented models, 65
  in political process model, 55–56
Lehner, Andreas Peter, 182–183, 190, 191,
  203, 211, 212, 218
Levin, Henry M., 4, 24, 53, 54–55
Lewin, Kurt, 69, 148
Lin, Nan, 18–19, 95, 240, 278
Lindbloom, C. E., 15
Linkage, 130, 134–135, 140–142, 151,
  155–162
  awareness of resources and constraints
    and, 167–169
  categories of forces, 156
  decision making and, 172–173
  defined, 140–141
  knowledge sources and, 157
  knowledge utilization and, 155–156,
    279, 289
  models, 158–162, 292–298

Linkage, *(Continued)*
  need for, 139, 155–156
  normative differences and, 156–157
  potential processes, 157–158
  see also Information/linkage tactics
Linkage process (LP) model, 159–162
Lipham, M., 52
Lippitt, Ronald O., 30–33, 34, 36, 41,
    69–71, 131, 298, 302
Longitudinal prediction, 234, 235
Lortie, Dan C., 5
Louis, Karen S., 292
Loyalty, as barrier to collaboration, 300

M

Madaus, G. F., 172, 177
Magnitude of change, control and, 238–
    239
Management, control and, 243–245
Management by objectives (MBO), 146
Manipulative strategies, 73, 74–75, 81–88
March, James G., 136, 146
Maslow, A. H., 184–185
May, J., 131
McClelland, David, 31
McCune, Shirley, 73, 96
McGregor, D., 52
McHenry, Emmet, 283*n*
McKeachie, W. J., 40
McLaughlin, Milbrey Wallin, 72
Meetings:
  as change tactic, 94
  dimensions of, 100–101
  situational considerations, 114
Microsystem building, 290
Miles, Matthew B., 80, 87, 96, 131, 136,
    138, 139, 149, 150, 153, 183, 302
Miller, Richard, 95, 96
Mission statement, in planning process,
    145–147
Models of educational change, 51–71
  authoritative/participative, 61–64
  authority versus collective innovative
    decision, 61–62
  collaborative versus noncollaborative
    approaches, 62–64

environmental, 54–56
  Levin's polity model, 54–55
  Stiles and Robinson's political process
    model, 55–56
individual-oriented, 64–66
internal versus external, 53–54
Lippitt, Watson, and Westley problem-
    solving model, 69–71
organizational, 56–61
  survey feedback-problem solving col-
    lective decision models, 60–61
  Zaltman, Duncan, and Holbek model,
    56–59
research, development, and diffusion,
    53, 66–69
see also Planning model; Proactive/
    Interactive Change Model (P/ICM)
Mohrman, Monty, 283*n*
Mohrman, Susan, 283*n*
Mosher, E. K., 95
Mouton, J. S., 52, 53, 139

N

Nagi, Saad Z., 38
Natural change, 63
Need fulfillment, defined, 185–186
Need processing, 289–290
Needs; *see also* Client need assessment de-
    fined, 184–185
Needs assessors, 186, 187
Negative performance/authority cycle,
    10–11
Nelson, Darnot, 25
Network building:
  as change tactic, 97
  dimensions of, 100–101
  situational considerations, 120
Niaz, Mohammed Aslam, 78, 81, 86
Niehoff, Arthur H., 34, 40
Noise dimension of change tactics, 100,
    104
Noncomparative evaluation, 257
Normative differences in educational or-
    ganizations, 156–157

Normative–reeducative strategies, 77–78, 81
Norms, as barrier to change, 35

O

Objectives:
  control and, 242–243
  of evaluation, 258
Objectives stage of planning process, 154–162
Objectivity, in evaluation, 257
Ombudsman organization, 292
Organization information system (OIS), 245–247
Organizational arrangements, evaluation and, 259
Organizational barriers to change, 36–39
Organizational change models, 56–61
  survey feedback–problem solving collective decision model, 60–61
  Zaltman, Duncan, and Holbek model, 56–59
Organizational climate, 16
Organizational collaborations, aids and barriers to, 298–305
Organizational development (OD), 131
  as manipulative tactic, 75
  as normative–reeducative strategy, 78
Organizational environment, 16–17
Organizational health inventory, 151–153
Organizational rigidity, as barrier to change, 37
Organizational structure, implementation and, 222–224
Owens, Robert G., 184–185
Owens, T. R., 270

P

Packaging:
  as change tactic, 94–95
  dimensions of, 100–101
  situational considerations, 115–116
Parents:
  as force for change, 27
  operational aspects of schools and, 8

Participative models, 62–64
Perceived relative advantage, resistance to change and, 42
Perception:
  in individual-oriented models, 64, 65
  selective, 39–40
Performance gaps: *see* Educational change, resistance to
Performance standards of teachers, 5–6, 13
Perry, R., 131
Personal contact dimension of change tactics, 100, 102
Personal frustration, as force for change, 28–29
Personal incompatibility, as barrier to change, 44–45
Personal tactics, 103
Personal threats, as barrier to collaboration, 300
Personnel:
  as forces for change, 25
  new treatments for, 25
  selection of, 9
  upgrading performance with, 22
Personnel strategies, 80
Persuasive strategies, 76, 78–79, 81
Peterson, Paul E., 72
P/ICM: *see* Proactive/Interactive Change Model (P/ICM)
Pierce, Wendell H., 88, 95
Pincus, John, 18, 25, 29
Pinson, Christian R. A., 30, 234
Planned change, 62
Planning:
  environmental elements:
    involving in decision making, 135–136
    relationships with, 126
  external change agents, potential need for, 134–135
  initiating process of, critical questions in, 130–131
  interaction, need for, 126–127
  issues for, 131–132
  model: *see* Proactive/Interactive Change Model (P/ICM)

Planning *(Continued)*
  organizational decision making/action
    authority, 132–134
    risk and, 136–137
    systematic planning, need for, 127
    temporary systems and, 137–139
Point-in-time analysis, 234–235
Policy maker's perspective, 14
Political finesse, 224–225
Political process model (Stiles and Robinson), 55–56
Political strategy, 76, 77, 80, 81
Polity model (Levin), 54–55
Potential-coverage dimension of change
    tactics, 101, 105
Power-coercive strategies, 78, 81
Power relationships:
  as barriers to change, 38–39
  changes in, as force for change, 26
Power strategies, 73–74, 78–88, 238
Preference survey, 145
Preservice classes, as change tactic, 97, 303
  dimensions of, 100–101
  situational considerations, 118–119
Pride, as barrier to collaboration, 300
Proactive/Interactive Change Model (P/
    ICM), 127–130, 139–142
  dangers in application of, 178–179
  deficient planning and, 179–180
  diversity in, 140
  flexibility in, 140, 141, 144, 146, 178–179
  implementation of, 144–181
    alternative solutions, 169, 170, 172–174
    control: *see* Control
    decision making, 172–174
    demonstration, 169–172
    evaluation: *see* Evaluation
    implementation stage: *see* Implementation
    mission statement, 145–147
    needs assessment: *see* Client need assessment
    problem identification, 148–153
    problem solving purposes, 154
    resources and constraints, 162–169

  linkage, 130, 134–135, 140–142, 151, 155–162
    awareness of resources and constraints
      and, 167–169
    categories of forces, 156
    decision making and, 172–173
    defined, 140–141
    knowledge sources and, 157
    knowledge utilization and, 155–156, 279, 289
    models, 158–162, 292–298
    need for, 139, 155–156
    normative differences and, 156–157
    potential processes, 157–158
  locus of planning, 129–130
  temporary system for, 138–139
  turnkey phase of, 140, 141, 171–173
  see also Planning
Proactive relationships, 126–127
Problem identification stage of planning
    process, 148–153
Problem recognition, in individual-oriented
    models, 64, 65
Problem-solving model (Lippitt, Watson,
    and Westley), 69–71
Problem-solving purposes stage of planning process, 154
Problem-solving strategy, 159, 160, 292
Problem-solving techniques, 36, 42, 280–288
Process evaluation, 266–268
Process feedback, 175, 176, 245
Product–development tactics, 72–74, 81–83, 92, 95, 110–111
  dimensions of, 100–101
  situational considerations, 116–117
Product evaluation, 266–268
Product feedback, 175, 245
Professionalism, as aid to collaboration, 304–305
Program–audit model, 263
Provus, M., 262
Psychological barriers to change, 39–41
Psychological strategy, 76–77, 81
Psychologist's perspective, 14
Public authorities, as force for change, 27

Publicity, as change tactic, 81
Publics of schools, 7–8

R

Radicalness of innovation, resistance to change and, 42
Rappaport, Donald, 62
Rational strategies, 73, 75–77, 81–86, 237–238
Rationalistic bias, 243
Reactivity, in evaluation, 255–257
Redundancy dimension of change tactics, 104
Reeducative strategies, 78–79, 81
Reference groups:
  as forces for change, 27
  resistance to change and, 34
Reitz, Jeffrey G., 294
Rejection:
  forms of, 46
  in individual-oriented models, 65, 66
Repeatability dimension of change tactics, 101, 104–105
Reports:
  as change tactic, 94
  dimensions of, 100–101
  situational considerations, 112–113
Research, development, and diffusion (RD&D) models, 53, 66–69, 158, 192
Research for Better Schools, Inc., 78, 79
Research utilization: *see* Knowledge utilization
Resources:
  in client need assessment
    allocation of, 194–197
    identification of, 193–194
  in planning process, 162–169
  unavailability of, as barrier to change, 44
Responsive evaluation, 268, 269–271
Reversibility of change, 227
Rewards and punishments, power strategies based on, 73–74, 81, 86
Risk, initiation of change and, 136–137
Robertson, T. S., 44–45, 148

Robinson, B., 14, 28, 53, 55–56, 69, 86, 87, 88, 93, 96
Rogers, Everett M., 25, 33, 39, 44, 45, 46, 61–62, 64, 67, 68, 102, 131, 148, 156, 278, 289, 290, 294, 304
Rosenau, Fred S., 80, 103, 108, 112, 113, 114
Rostow, W. W., 31
Rothman, Jack, 232
Routinization, 6
  in collective innovation decision model, 60, 61
  resistance to change and, 37
Runkel, P., 132, 173
Rutherford, William L., 95, 98

S

Sabotage, 88
Safer, L. Arthur, 60, 149, 150, 302
Salespeople:
  as change tactic, 94
  dimensions of, 100–101
  situational considerations, 113–114
Sampling decision, 250–251
Sandler, Howard M., 73*n*, 93
Sarason, Seymour B., 3, 30, 31, 34, 35, 38, 183
Scanlon, Robert G., 78
Schein, E. H., 131
Schild, E. O., 179
Schmidtlein, Frank A., 15
Schmuck, Patricia, 58
Schmuck, Richard A., 58, 95, 96, 131, 132, 136, 139, 148, 173
Schon, Donald A., 125, 136, 299, 302
School districts, structure of, 9–11
Scott, W. Richard, 250, 251, 258
Scriven, M., 255, 268, 269
Seashore, Stanley, 299
Segmentation of educational system, control and, 239
Selective perception and retention, 39
Self-renewing school, strategy development in, 88–89
Self-renewing social system, 139
Sergiovonni, Thomas J., 7, 178

Shoemaker, F. F., 25, 44, 61–62, 64, 67, 102, 131, 148, 156, 304
Short, E. C., 155, 294
Sieber, Sam D., 79, 81, 87–88, 292
Sikes, Walter W., 28–29, 44, 45
Sikorski, Linka, 44, 73, 85, 87, 91, 96
Silberman, Harry, 44
Simon, Herbert, 136
Sims, Henry P., Jr., 280
Skinner, B. F., 68
Smith, Kenneth E., 73n, 93
Social barriers to change, 34–36
Social interaction concept, 292
Social interaction model, 159
Social value of output, as force for change, 27
Socialization, as barrier to collaboration, 301
Socialization change, 63
Solution processing, 290
Stability dimension of change tactics, 99, 100
Stake, R. E., 253–254, 264, 269
Standardization, resistance to change and, 37
Standards:
  control and, 240–241
  defined, 240
Stanley, J. C., 261
State aid, 11, 12
Status differences, as barriers to collaboration, 300–301
Stiff, Ronald, 44–45
Stiles, L. J., 14, 26, 28, 53, 55–56, 69, 86, 87, 88, 93, 96
Strategies of change, 71–89, 163
  development of, 82–89
  types of, 73–82
Stress induction, as change tactic, 81
Students:
  as force for change, 27
  influence of, 7–8
Stufflebeam, D. L., 175, 177, 269
Subsidizing change tactic, 97
  dimensions of, 100–101
  situational considerations, 118
Subversion, 88

Suchman, E. A., 255
Summative evaluation, 253, 254
Survey feedback, 36, 42, 149–151, 280–288
Survey feedback–problem solving–collective decision model (SF–PS–CD), 60–61
Symbolic testing, 170–171
Systematic planning, need for, 127
Systems analysis, 15, 178

T

Tactics of change, 80–82, 91–121
  dimensions of, 98–107
    action implications, 100, 103–104
    activity, 100, 103
    cost to receiver, 101, 107
    cost to sender, 101, 107
    ease-of-use, 101, 105
    feedback/interaction, 100, 102–103
    follow-up, 101, 106
    imagery, 101, 107
    immediacy, 101, 106–107
    noise/redundancy, 100, 104
    personal contact, 99, 100, 102
    potential coverage, 101, 105
    repeatability, 101, 104–105
    stability, 99, 100
    time required for target, 101, 107
  information/linkage, 92, 93–95, 100–101, 112–116
  legal, 74, 85–86, 92, 97–98, 100–101, 118
  product-development, 72–74, 81–83, 92, 95, 100–101, 116–117
  situational considerations in, 108–120
  training/installation/support, 74, 75, 92, 96–97, 100–101, 118–120
  user-involvement, 92, 95–96, 100–101, 117
Teacher unions and associations, 8, 12
Teachers:
  collective bargaining by, 12, 13
  incentives of, 6–7
  isolation of, 4–5, 6
  negative authority cycle and, 10–11

performance standards, 5–6, 13
principals, relationship with, 37–38
routinization and, 6
salaries of, 13
Teaching, nature of, 4–7, 13
Teaching–evaluation plans, resistance to,
    40–41
Technocratic bias, 244–245
Technocratic change, 26, 63
Telephone use:
  as change tactic, 94
    dimensions of, 100–101
    situational considerations, 114
Telfer, R. G., 31
Tempkin, Sanford, 93, 96, 97
Temporary system:
  as change tactic, 97, 137–139, 239
    dimensions of, 100–101
    situational considerations, 120
Testimonial, as change tactic, 81
Testing stage of planning process, 169–172
Thomas, J. Alan, 14
Thompson, James D., 10, 136
Thompson, Victor, 153
Time requirements, control and, 237–238
Timeliness, in evaluation, 258
Trainees-become-trainers change tactic,
    96, 100–101, 117
Training/installation/support tactics, 74,
    75, 92, 96–97
    dimensions of, 100–101
    situational considerations, 118–120
Training manuals:
  as change tactic, 95
    dimensions of, 100–101
    situational considerations, 116
Traitability, 227
Trial stage:
  in research, development, and diffusion
    models, 67
  in individual-oriented models, 65
  in Proactive/Interactive Change Model,
    169–172
Trust, generation of, 224
Turnbull, B. J., 42, 43, 44, 72, 82, 95, 96,
    97, 108–109, 245

Turnkey phase of planning process, 140,
    141, 171–173
Tye, Kenneth A., 80, 83
Tyler, Ralph, 261–262

U

Unanticipated consequences, control and,
    240
Unfocused evaluation, 266, 268–272
  adversary approach, 268, 270–272
  goal-free, 266, 268–269
  responsive, 268, 269–271
Unintended consequences, control and,
    240
Unpredicted events, evaluation and, 258–
    259
User, identifying, 226
User-convenience dimension of change tac-
    tics, 101, 105
User-involvement tactics, 92, 95–96
  dimensions of, 100–101
  situational considerations, 117
Utilitarian strategy, 78, 81

V

Value strategy, 76, 77, 81
Value system, as aid to collaboration, 301

W

Walton, Richard E., 79, 81
Warwick, Donald P., 80, 83, 84, 86
Watson, Bernard C., 89
Watson, Goodwin, 34–35, 39, 136, 239
Watson, J., 69–71, 131
Webb, Eugene J., 255, 256
Weber, Max, 31
Weinthaler, Judith A., 203
Westley, B., 69–71, 131
Widmer, Jeanne M., 72, 95, 96
Work shops, as change tactic, 94
  dimensions of, 100–101
  situational considerations, 115
Wortman, Paul M., 251–253

Y

York, L. J., 96

Z

Zaltman, Gerald, 18–1., 23, 25, 30, 34,
    36, 38, 42, 44–45, 51, 53, 56–59,
64, 74, 78–79, 81, 86, 98, 131,
148, 149, 170, 175, 176, 221, 222,
234, 236, 239, 240, 278, 280,
283n, 301